A Companion to the Hanseatic League

Brill's Companions to European History

VOLUME 8

The titles published in this series are listed at *brill.com/bceh*

A Companion to the Hanseatic League

Edited by

Donald J. Harreld

BRILL

LEIDEN | BOSTON

Cover illustration: Town seal of Lübeck, 1280, as depicted in Ernst Wallis' *Illustrerad verldshistoria*, (Stockholm 1882, p. 333). http://commons.wikimedia.org/wiki/File:Stadssigill_foer_staden_Luebeck.png (accessed 4 September 2014)

Library of Congress Cataloging-in-Publication Data

A companion to the Hanseatic League / edited by Donald J. Harreld.
pages cm. — (Brill's companions to European history, ISSN 2212-7410; volume 8)
Includes bibliographical references and index.
ISBN 978-90-04-28288-9 (hardback : acid-free paper) — ISBN 978-90-04-28476-0 (e-book) 1. Hanseatic League—History. 2. Hansa towns—History. 3. Europe, Northern—Social conditions. 4. Europe, Northern—Economic conditions. 5. Europe, Northern—Commerce—History. I. Harreld, Donald J.

DD801.H22C66 2015
382.0943—dc23

2014044089

This publication has been typeset in the multilingual "Brill" typeface. With over 5,100 characters covering Latin, IPA, Greek, and Cyrillic, this typeface is especially suitable for use in the humanities. For more information, please see www.brill.com/brill-typeface.

ISSN 2212-7410
ISBN 978-90-04-28288-9 (hardback)
ISBN 978-90-04-28476-0 (e-book)

This book is printed on acid-free paper.

Contents

List of Maps and Figures

List of Contributors

Mike Burkhardt
is the author of *Der Bergenhandel im Spätmittelalter: Handel, Kaufleute, Netzwerke* (Colonge, 2009).

Ulf Christian Erwert
has taught medieval and economic history at Chemnitz University of Technology, Helmut-Schmidt-University Hamburg, Free University of Berlin and the universities of Munich, Regensburg, Halle and Münster. He is the author of numerous articles on the Hanse, the Portuguese overseas expansion, the political economy of pre-modern princely courts and early modern living standards.

Rolf Hammel-Kiesow
is the associate director of the Archives of Lübeck and an honorary professor at the University of Kiel. He is the author of many works on the history of the Hanse. Since 1994 he has been a member of the Executive Board, and since 2010, the Chairman of the Hansischer Geschichtsverein.

Donald J. Harreld
is Associate Professor and Chair of History at Brigham Young University. He is the author of *High Germans in the Low Countries: German Merchants and Commerce in Golden Age Antwerp* (Leiden, 2004).

Carsten Jahnke
is Associate Professor for Medieval History at the SAXO-Institute, University Copenhagen. He is the author of many works on the history of the Hanse and the history of the Baltic area.

Michael North
is Professor and Chair of Modern History at the University of Greifswald, Honorary Doctor of the University of Tartu and Director of the International Graduate Program "Baltic Borderlands". His recent books include *The Expansion of Europe, 1250–1500* (Manchester 2012) and *The Baltic: a History* (Cambridge, Mass. 2015).

Jürgen Sarnowsky
is Professor of Medieval History at Universitaet Hamburg. He is a board member for the Hansischer Geschichtsverein, and is the author of numerous articles on Hanse history and more general medieval history topics.

Stephan Selzer
is professor of medieval history at Helmut-Schmidt-Universität / Universität der Bundeswehr in Hamburg. Selzer is the author of many publications on social and economic history including *Die mittelalterliche Hanse*, (Darmstadt 2010).

Introduction

Donald J. Harreld

In Spring, 1870, the city of Stralsund celebrated the 500-year anniversary of the "Peace" that bears its name that ended the war between the Hanseatic League and the Kingdom of Denmark. The Peace of Stralsund is generally considered to mark the zenith of Hanse commercial power.[1] One result of this celebration was the founding of the Hansische Geschichtsverein, organized to promote Hanse history and to connect Hanseatic studies to the broader German historiography.[2] Thanks in part to the publication agenda of the Hansische Geschichtsverein, Hanse studies have flourished since the association's organization. The *Hansische Geschichtsblätter*, the *Hanserecesse*, the *Pfingstblätter*, to name only a few of the series published by the association have provided generations of scholars an outlet for serious scholarship on the Hanse.

The earliest scholars involved in the Hansische Geschichtsverein were, not surprisingly, local historians and archivists located in the principal hanseatic towns of northern Germany. In the early years, most of the works published in the *Hansische Geschichtsblätter* slanted heavily toward political and diplomatic history topics and were fitted into the emerging nationalist histories of a newly formed Germany. Of course his trend in historical scholarship was not unique to German history. Late nineteenth-century national histories included measurable doses of political propaganda in even the best cases.

By the early twentieth century, however, Hanse history had come into its own, and the focus of Hanse studies began to include social and economic history topics much more than they had in the preceding decades. One only need to review the list of the luminaries working in the field of Hanse history since the first part of the twentieth century to quickly realize that Hanse history had moved from the realm of political history and antiquarian studies to a field intensely interested in economic and social issues. Indeed, for a half century, the widely read work by Ernst Daenell set the bar in Hanse scholarship.[3] Daenell's massive two-volume work depicted the Hanse as a type of commercial republic founded on economic power. But more than that, his work was

1 Philippe Dollinger, The German Hansa (Stanford: Standford University Press, 1970), 71.

2 Wilhelm Mantels, "Der Hansische Geschichtsverein," *Hanische Geschichtsblätter* 1 (1871): 3.

3 Ernst Daenell, *Die Blütezeit der deutschen Hanse von der zweiten Hälfte des 14. Bis zum letzten Viertel des 15. Jahrhunderts* (Berlin: Reimer, 1905/1906).

 | DOI 10.1163/9789004284760_002

meticulously detailed to the point of serving as a reference manual for later scholars.

Several contemporaries, Rudolf Häpke, Fritz Rörig, and Walther Vogel, among others, formed what might be considered the next generation of Hanse historians. Rudolf Häpke's most well know contributions to Hanse history focused on the league's presence in the Low Countries, and particularly in Bruges, which was the topic of his dissertation.[4] Fritz Rörig, an expert on the history of Lübeck and the Hanse more broadly,[5] was particularly interested in the Hanse towns. His best know work in English, *The Medieval Town*, is a translation of the book *Die Europaïsche Stadt im Mittelalter*.[6] In it, Rörig examines the reasons for he saw as the decline of the Hanse towns' due to Dutch and English competition. While Rörig was most interested in the Hanse towns, his sometime collaborator, Walther Vogel focused on Hanse ships and shipping. Vogel's work, *Geschichte de deutschen Seeschiffahrt*, continued to be influential for researchers for decades after its publication.[7]

Following the Second World War, political overtones infused Hanse scholarship particularly as Marxist scholars attempted to fit Hanse history into their theoretical framework,[8] but scholars' understanding of the character of the Hanse began to undergo significant change in other ways as well. One of the best-known attempts at writing a general history of the Hanse in the decade or so following the war was Karl Pagel's *Die Hanse*, which perpetuated the notion that the Hanse acted as a homogenous body and a powerful arm of the Holy Roman Empire.[9] Pagel had missed the mark according to many of the scholars of the time, including Ahasver von Brandt who set out to refute Pagel's characterization of the Hanse cities as a medieval power bloc.[10] It was, in effect, von Brandt who soon set a new tone for Hanse scholarship with his characteriza-

4 Rudolf Häpke, *Brügges, Entwicklung zum mittelalterlichen Weltmarkt* (Berlin: Curtius, 1908). See also, Rudolf Häpke, ed., *Niederländische Akten und Urkunden zur Geschichte der Hanse und zur deutschen Seegeschichte* (Munich: Duncker & Humblot, 1913).

5 See for example, Fritz Rörig, Der Markt von Lübeck: Topographisch-statistische Untersuchengen zur deutschen Sozial- und Wirtschaftsgeschichte (Leipzig: Quelle & Meyer, 1922).

6 Fritz Rörig, *Die Europaïsche Stadt im Mittelalter* (Göttingen: Vandenhoek & Ruprecht, 1955).

7 Walther Vogel, *Geschichte der deutschen Seeschiffahrt* (Berlin: Reimer, 1915).

8 Andreas Dorpalen, *German History in Marxist Perspective: the East German approach* (London: Taurus, 1986), 97.

9 Karl Pagel, *Die Hanse* (Brunswick: Georg Westermann Verlag, 1952).

10 Ahasver von Brandt, *Die Hanse und die nordischen Mächte im Mittelalter* (Opladen: Westdeutscher Verlag, 1962).

tion of the Hanse as dynamic and pliable organization.[11] For time being, however, Hanse history remained largely the concern of German historians until the 1960s with the publication of Dollinger's survey.[12]

Philippe Dollinger was a student of both Marc Bloch and Lucien Febvre at the University of Strasbourg, where he spent almost his entire career. His book, *The German Hansa*, broke new ground when it was published over forty years ago. It was groundbreaking not because it presented anything particularly new about Hanse history—it was a survey after all, and had its share of errors—but because it freed the study of the Hanse from the fetters of regional and national histories and from the often politicized histories written since the Second World War. This is not to suggest that in the decades prior to Dollinger's book there was nothing particularly interesting happening in the field of Hanse history—quite the contrary, as I have pointed out—but it presented the first successful unified Hanse history accessible to a broad international readership by a non-German author.

The publication of Dollinger's book solidified the ongoing scholarly movement that placed Hanse history in an international context, and one that was no longer strictly dominated by German scholars. It still remains one of the most widely read books on Hanse history in English. Indeed, aside from Dollinger's, T.H. Lloyd's book, *England and the German Hanse*,[13] may be the best-known book on the Hanse available in the English language. But this is not to say that scholars writing in English have failed to engage with and contribute to Hanse scholarship. Quite the contrary; far more scholarship on the Hanse is being produced in English than ever before.[14]

A variety of scholars during the past twenty or so years have re-examined some of the older concerns of Hanse scholars and have refined previous conclusions and have opened up new avenues of research. For example, following the lead of von Brandt decades earlier, Ernst Pitz took up the constitutional issue again late in his career and reinforced the diffuse nature of Hanse

11 Ahasver von Brandt, "Die Hanse als mittelalterliche Wirtschaftsorganisation," in A. v. Brandt, et al., eds., *Die Hanse als mittelalterliche Wirtschaftsorganisation* (Cologne: VS Verlag für Sozialwissenschaften, 1963), 9–37.

12 Philippe Dollinger, *La Hanse* (*XIIe–XVIIe Siècles*) (Paris: Aubier, Éditions Montaigne, 1964). The book was subsequently published in German in 1966 and in English in 1970.

13 T.H. Lloyd, *England and the German Hanse, 1157–1611: A study of their trade and commercial diplomacy* (Cambridge: Cambridge University Press, 1991).

14 Most recently see, Justyna Wubs-Mrozewicz and Stuart Jenks, eds., The Hanse in Medieval and Early Modern Europe (Leiden: Brill, 2013).

governance.[15] Volker Henn's work on communications between and among the Hansards and his research on their regional interests has given Hanse scholars a new direction for research.[16] Indeed, many different methodological approaches have been applied to the history of the Hanse. For scholars of the new institutional economics, the Hanse has been extensively held up as an example of the process of organizational and institutional change.[17] Sheilagh Ogilvie, for example, has made extensive use of the explanatory power of the Hanse in her recent work on medieval institutions.[18] The principles of the new institutional economics has been applied directly to the case of Hanse town governance,[19] the development and function of transnational markets,[20] and in conflict resolution,[21] to name only some of the most recent examples.

Place theories and network theories have been an important influence on a variety of scholarly pursuits,[22] and have provided a fruitful direction for Hanse research, as the recent work of Ulrich Müller attests.[23] And recently, social

---

15 Ernst Pitz, *Bürgereinung und Städteeinung. Studien zur Verfassungsgeschichte der Hansestädte und der deutschen Hanse.* Quellen und Darstellungen zur hansischen Geschichte (Cologne: Böhlau, 2001).

16 Volker Henn, "Innerhansische Kommunikations- und Raumstrukturen: Umrisse einer neueren Forschungsaufgabe?" in Stuart Jenks and Michael North, eds., *Der hansische Sonderweg? Beiträge zur Sozial- und Wirtschaftsgeschichte der Hanse* (Cologne: Böhlau, 1993), 255–268 and also "Was war die Hanse?" in Jörgen Bracker, Volker Henn and Rainer Postel, eds., *Die Hanse. Lebenswirklichkeit und Mythos* (Lübeck: Schmidt-Römhild, 1998), 14–23.

17 Avner Greif, *Institutions and the Path to the Modern Economy: Lessons from Medieval Trade* (Cambridge: Cambridge University Press, 2006), 105.

18 Sheilagh Ogilvie, *Institutions and European Trade: Merchant Guilds, 1000–1800* (Cambridge: Cambridge University Press, 2011).

19 Kaire Põder, "Credible Commitment and Cartel: The Case of the Hansa Merchant in the Guild of Late Medieval Tallinn," *Baltic Journal of Economics* 10 (2010): 43–60.

20 Sigrid Quack, "Global Markets in Theory and History: Towards a Comparative Analysis," in Jens Beckert and Christoph Deutschmann, eds., *Wirtschaftssoziologie.* Kölner Zeitschrift für Soziologie und Sozialpsyshologie, Vol. 49 (Wiesbaden: VS Verlag für Sozialwissenschaften, 2009).

21 Albrecht Cordes, "Merchant's expectations regarding procedure before foreign courts according to Hanseatic priviledges (12th–16th Centuries)," LOEWE Research Focus "Extrajusdicial and Judicial Conflict Resolution" Working Paper, no. 4, 2013.

22 For example, Ulrich Müller, "Networks of Towns—Networks of Periphery? Some Relations between the North European Medieval Town and its Hinterland," in Sunhild Kleingärtner and Gabriel Zeilinger, eds., *Raumbildung durch Netzwerke?* (Bonn: Habelt, 2012).

23 Ulrich Müller, "Case Study 3: Trading centre—Hanseatic towns on the southern Baltic Coast: Structural continuity or a new start?" in Babette Ludowici, et al., eds., *Trade and Communication Networks of the First Millennium AD in the northern part of Central Europe:*

network analysis has become of particular interest for scholars of the Hanse because of its ambiguous structure and the increasingly clear importance of merchant relationships in its function.[24] Indeed, network analysis figures prominently in the works presented in this volume, particularly the contribution by Ewert and Selzer, who have been instrumental in defining the field of network analysis in Hanse studies.

This present work is an attempt to bring some of the more recent developments in Hanse history together for an international audience of scholars and students for whom the German language presents some difficulty. Rather than a critique of past scholarship, or a foray into the "cutting edge", this book is intended to represent the "state-of-the-field" in Hanse history. In addition to the essays, this volume contains a bibliography that includes the works cited in the text as well as important works of scholarship on Hanse history broadly conceived.

This volume is presented in two sections. The first section presents a narrative of Hanse history from earliest times (Hammel-Kiesow), through the Hanse's *Golden Age* (Sarnowsky), and ending with the late Hanse period (North). As with any attempts at periodization, the chronological dividing lines between these three chapters are somewhat arbitrary. As a general rule, the Peace of Stralsund in 1370 was marked as the beginning of the *Golden Age*, and the Peace of Utrecht in 1474 was the most useful date for the start of the later period. The three authors were not held strictly to this admittedly arbitrary division, but for the most part honored this periodization scheme. The contributions in the second section deal with topics of particular interest in recent scholarship: a separate chapter on the Baltic trade (Janke), one that explains the structures of kontors and outposts (Burkhardt), and finally, one on social networks (Ewert and Selzer). The goal for this volume is to present a solid treatment of current Hanse scholarship in English, rather than to attempt any kind of exhaustive survey.

In the first chapter, "The Early Hanses," Rolf Hammel-Kiesow examines the earliest evidences for German trade associations in the Baltic and North Sea. Building on a tradition of settlement archaeology methodologies,

---

Central Places, Beach Markets, Landing Places and Trading Centres (Stuttgart: Konrad Theiss Verlag, 2010).

24 Justyna Wubs-Mrozewicz, *Traders, Ties and Tensions: The Interaction of Lübeckers, Overijsslers and Hollanders in Late Medieval Bergen* (Hilversum: Verloren, 2008), 29; see also: Justyna Wubs-Mrozewicz, "Rules of Inclusion, Rules of Exculsion: The Hanseatic *Kontor* in Bergan in the Late Middle Ages and its Normative Boundaries," *German History* 29 (2011): 2–4.

Hammel-Kiesow also employs a version of the world system approach to explain shifts in trade flows. First, by examining coin hoard evidence, Hammel-Kiesow shows the development of trade routes that connected the two main regions that would become commercially important for Hanse merchants. Early German merchant communities operated in Schleswig from which west and central European and Baltic trades radiated. By the end of the eleventh century, merchants settled at Lübeck in the Baltic region and in the city of Cologne in the North Sea region. Second, Hammel-Kiesow situates German settlement in the Baltic along with the advance of conquest and conversion. Following these developments, German merchants began a process of settlement eastward into the Baltic region. Germans eventually became enmeshed in the commercial relations of Scandinavia, Prussia, and farther east.

Also of great importance for this earliest phase of Hanse development was the shift from traveling trade associations to the eventual development of Hanse *Kontor* between about the twelfth to the fourteenth century. The traveling associations had obvious commercial benefits for merchants, and they also facilitated social functions. Eventually, German merchants, influenced by contact with Italians, developed a system of fixed main office, freight carriers, and on-site factors. In spite of its more settled nature, this system was still transitory until the development of *kontors* (early in the fourteenth century) created a more permanent institutional arrangement.

In chapter 2, "The 'Golden Age' of the Hanseatic League," Jürgen Sarnowsky, traces the progress of united action on the part of Hanse towns that resulted in large part as a result of the problems that arose in Flanders in the mid-fourteenth century and most particularly following the Peace of Stralsund in 1370. Indeed, because of its success in presenting a unified front, the Hanse began to exert considerable economic and political influence in Northern Europe in the second half of the fourteenth century. Though its war with Denmark threatened to hamper commercial stability, the Hanse's success in the war put it in a particularly strong position following the Peace of Stralsund (1370).

Sarnowsky points out, however, that in the years following the Peace, upheaval within the Hanse towns, particularly in Lübeck, threatened the stability of the Hanse. Only after the constitutional crises were resolved in the Wendish towns could the Hanse solidify its strength and face the many outside threats. After about 1418, it was the various territorial lords that posed the greatest threat to Hanse autonomy and resulted in greater cooperation between the towns. So, in spite of the periods of unity that followed the Peace of Stralsund and again later around 1418, the Hanse experienced significant periods of crisis that forces Sarnowsky to call into question the characterization of this period as a "golden age" for the Hanseatic League in spite of the towns' commercial success. The towns continued to push for autonomy and instances of Hanse "unity" tended to be for limited periods of time.

The winds of trade were shifting following the Treaty of Utrecht in 1474, as Michael North highlights in his chapter on the Hanse in the early modern period (chapter 3). Dutch competition and the rise of the Southern German merchants from Nuremburg and Augsburg altered much of the trade in northern Europe as did the success of the Livonian towns in the East. By the early decades of the sixteenth century, political power in the Hanse towns was also shifting as the effects of the Reformation were increasingly felt, and Denmark began to exert greater power in the Baltic. The composition of the ruling groups in Hanse cities changed as Protestants gained power. And in spite of Lübeck's support in his succession conflict, Danish King Frederick I refused to expel the Dutch from the Baltic thwarting the Hanse's attempts at domination in the region.

The Hanseatic League became steadily less relevant during the Thirty Years War, and by the last Hanse Diet (1669) had contracted to the point that only Hamburg, Bremen and Lübeck were much interested in continuing to claim its privileges. It is surprising that the three cities were able to maintain their Hanseatic identity until the early years of the nineteenth century.

The second section of the book looks more closely at three important themes in Hanse history: *Kontors* and Outposts, Social Networks, and the Baltic Trade. There were any number of themes that could have been highlighted in this section; the choice of these three topics simply reflects the very good work being done recently by these scholars. Each of these topics is worthy of a book-length study in its own right, and they seemed particularly appropriate for a "state-of-the-field" treatment that this volume attempts to present.

In the chapter on "*Kontors* and Outposts," Burkhardt, very much influenced by network theory, looks in much greater detail at the institution that formed an important point of discussion in the earlier chapters. This chapter focuses on the important reasons that Hanse merchants grouped together while abroad and the benefits that accrued from fixed associations at the "junctions" of their trade networks. Indeed, in Burkhardt's view security was the single most important reason for the development of the Hanse's principle *kontors*. On the face of things, and from an organizational perspective, it was negotiating and maintaining privileges in foreign ports that were the core function of the *kontors*. But security for the merchant and his goods was likely what brought Hanse merchants together and kept the *kontors* functioning over the long haul.

Burkhardt situates the organization of the *kontors* within the context of a medieval corporate body. In this regard, *kontors* would have been familiar to both the Hanse merchants and the officials of the towns in which they were located. The *kontor* does not, therefore, represent a "completely new organizational structure," rather it was one that developed over a long period of time. One important aspect of long-term development for Hanse merchants was the many regulations instituted in the *kontors* that were intended to regulate trade within the *kontor* and between Hanse merchants.

Although the *kontors* were set up as enclaves where merchants could live and work with others from Hanse towns, Burkhardt describes life in the *kontor* as very hard for the residents who were not full-fledged merchants. According to Burkhardt, the male-dominated *kontors*, where merchants, assistants, and boys (placed with a merchant to obtain an education) created a community that was, indeed, different from home. The boys were subjected to often-violent rites of passage and were occupied with menial tasks. Assistants, in spite of their status that allowed them more freedom than the boys, were very much under the merchants' authority—though beatings were not allow once a boy became an assistant. Even most of the merchants living at the *kontors* were junior partners, which meant that they were beholden to the wishes of the "home office."

Nevertheless, virtually all of the daily work at the *kontors* was geared toward trade and the maintenance of regulations and relationships that continued to insure commercial security. As a result, the *kontors* also served a political function for the Hanse towns. The *kontors* were in a particularly good position to disrupt trade if necessary. Boycotts, embargoes, and blockades were especially successful during the height of Hanse commercial power in the thirteenth and fourteenth centuries. This was, however, a two-edged sword, as rulers could just as easily close down Hanse *kontors* when it suited them.

Outposts also served Hanse merchants in various parts of the North Sea and the Baltic on a temporary basis. Unlike the four *kontors*, outposts were much smaller and were usually open only seasonally. Burkardt suggests that there may have been as many as 50 Hanse outposts, including some on the Atlantic coast of France, and in Lisbon. The use of the outposts was tied to the trade in a specific commodity, for example salt along the Atlantic coast, or Herring in the North Sea.

Although the *kontors* and outposts served a variety of functions, they figured also in the construction of social networks, which is the topic Ulf Christian Ewert and Stephan Selzer take up in Chapter 5. After explaining the theory and methodology of social networks, Ewert and Selzer trace the population movements of the High Middle Ages that brought large numbers of Germans to the Baltic regions. The newly settled Germans maintained connections with their relatives in the west, which was the foundation for an extensive kin-network. Kin-networks were important not only for commercial dealings, but they also had a profound effect on the political relations between Hanse towns. Indeed, as Ewert and Selzer point out, these family ties and the affect they had on inter-city relations calls into question our understanding of the "hierarchical-bureaucratic" nature of the Hanse's political structure.

Kin networks, were only one kind of social network that could develop. Ewert and Selzer also show the way non-kin networks can be determined by using (for example) wills, fraternal association membership, real estate transactions, etc. Sources like these illustrate the difficulty of reconstructing social networks, but they also open a new window on our understanding of these networks. Indeed, because the majority of Hanse firms were very small and often family based, reconstructing social networks are crucial to understanding the character and structure of Hanseatic commerce. It should come as no surprise that it is due primarily to the work of Ewart and Selzer that the entire field of network analysis has taken exciting new directions as it is applied to the study of the Hanse.

In the chapter, "The Baltic Trade," Carsten Jahnke examines Hanseatic activities in the core region. Historical study of the Baltic came directly out of the nationalist history movements that were the focus of archivists, editors of source books, and even political propagandists at the end of the nineteenth century. Indeed, according to Jahnke, the political overtones in Hanse research intensified following the Second World War as regional political interests overshadowed a more unified understanding of the Baltic milieu. This situation changed with the fall of the Iron Curtain as a new generation of scholars initiated an international effort at rethinking the history of the Baltic.

For his part, Carsten Jahnke provides an excellent overview of the Hanse's Baltic trade routes, major commercial centers, and connections to the Baltic hinterland. There were two primary westbound routes from the Baltic. The first, by way of Lübeck and Hamburg was secure but costly. The second route, around Skaw and through the Sound, became important in the thirteenth century. This route was less costly, but more dangerous. Within the Baltic, a variety of overlapping regional trade routes served, on one hand, to combine smaller cargoes into larger ones for international trade, and on the other hand, to break up larger international cargoes into smaller units for regional and local trade. Tracing the trade routes is particularly important because few marketable goods were produced in the Baltic area, rather the Baltic trade centered on goods produced in the Baltic "economic zone" which included regions far inland from the Baltic.

The Hanse merchant trading in the Baltic was not simply a "monolithic wholesaler," rather he was a diversified enterpriser. This is made clear by Jahnke's presentation of the wide array of products that merchants traded in the Baltic. These included Baltic produced goods like amber, cereals, herring, and beer. But Hanse merchants also moved goods through the Baltic that originated in the hinterland, like wax, furs, timber, and metals, to name only the most important goods. So the Baltic traders that Jahnke describes were multifaceted entrepreneurs.

We might say that a consensus has been building in Hanse history over that past decades that suggests that all aspects of the Hanse were multifaceted without the kind of hierarchies so much of the earlier scholarship proposed. The genesis of this volume was the growing need for a jumping off point for an international audience of scholars interested in Hanse history that would bring readers "up to speed" on new research. The contributions to this volume, then, attempt to engage readers with both the historical narrative and the methodological and theoretical approaches to the study of the Hanse. The contributors represent the latest generation of Hanse scholars, and hopefully point the way for young scholars to engage in the subject. The work being done by younger scholars is not only promising, but will surely yield more volumes such as this one in the coming years as even more discoveries are made about the history of the Hanse.

Indeed, the entire field of Hanse history has been taken in new directions during the past twenty years as the hurdles scholars encountered during the Cold War have been removed. Archives are far more accessible than they were for a previous generation of Hanse scholars,[25] and the study of Hanse history has begun to attract a broader group of practitioners. It is now relatively common to find scholars of Hanse history not only in Germany, but also throughout Europe and North America. This expansion will enrich our knowledge of the Hanse.

25 Lennart Bes, Edda Frankot, and Hanno Brand, eds., *Baltic Connections. Archival Guide to the Maritime Relations of the Countries around the Baltic Sea (including the Netherlands)* 3 Vols. (Leiden: Brill, 2007).

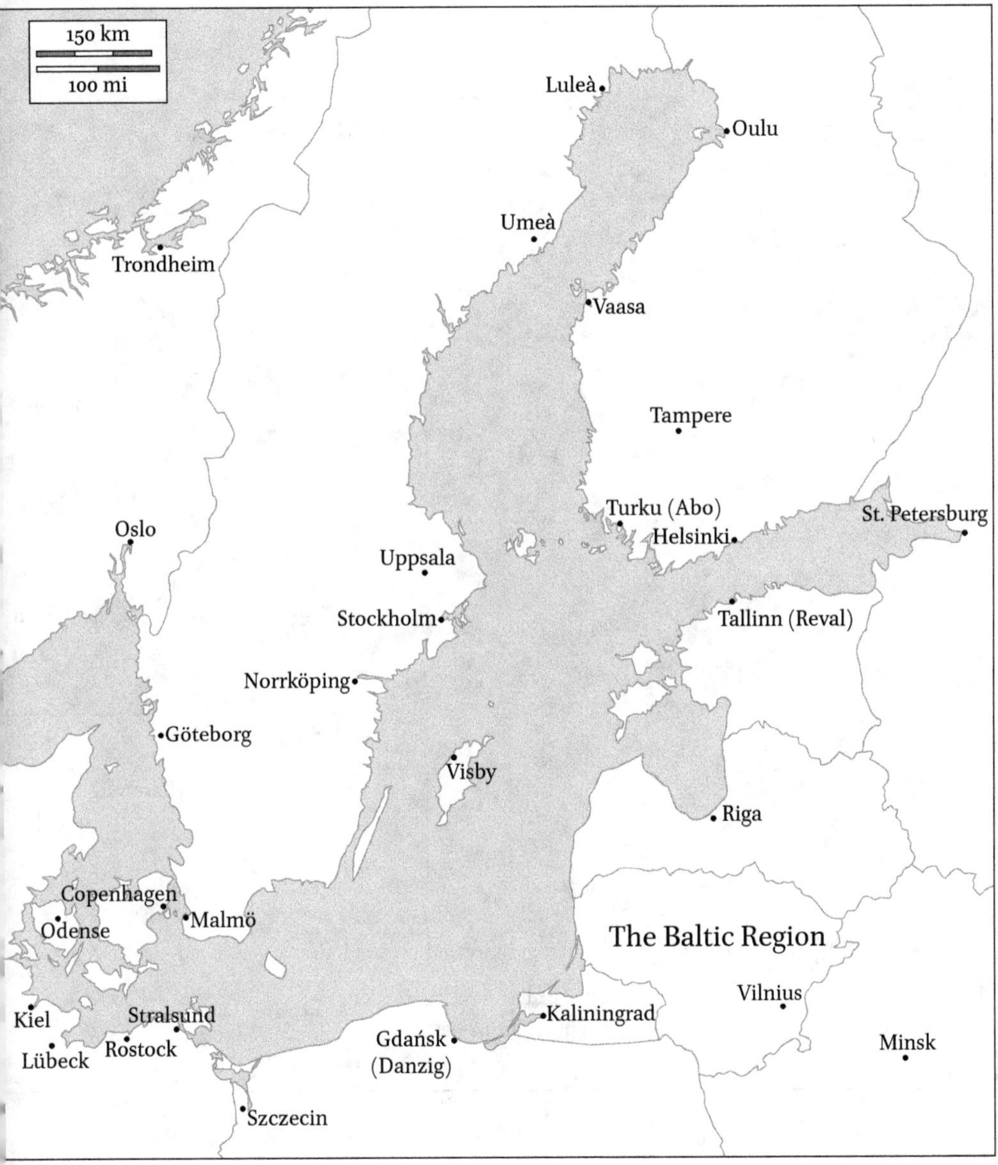

MAP 0.1 *The Baltic region.*

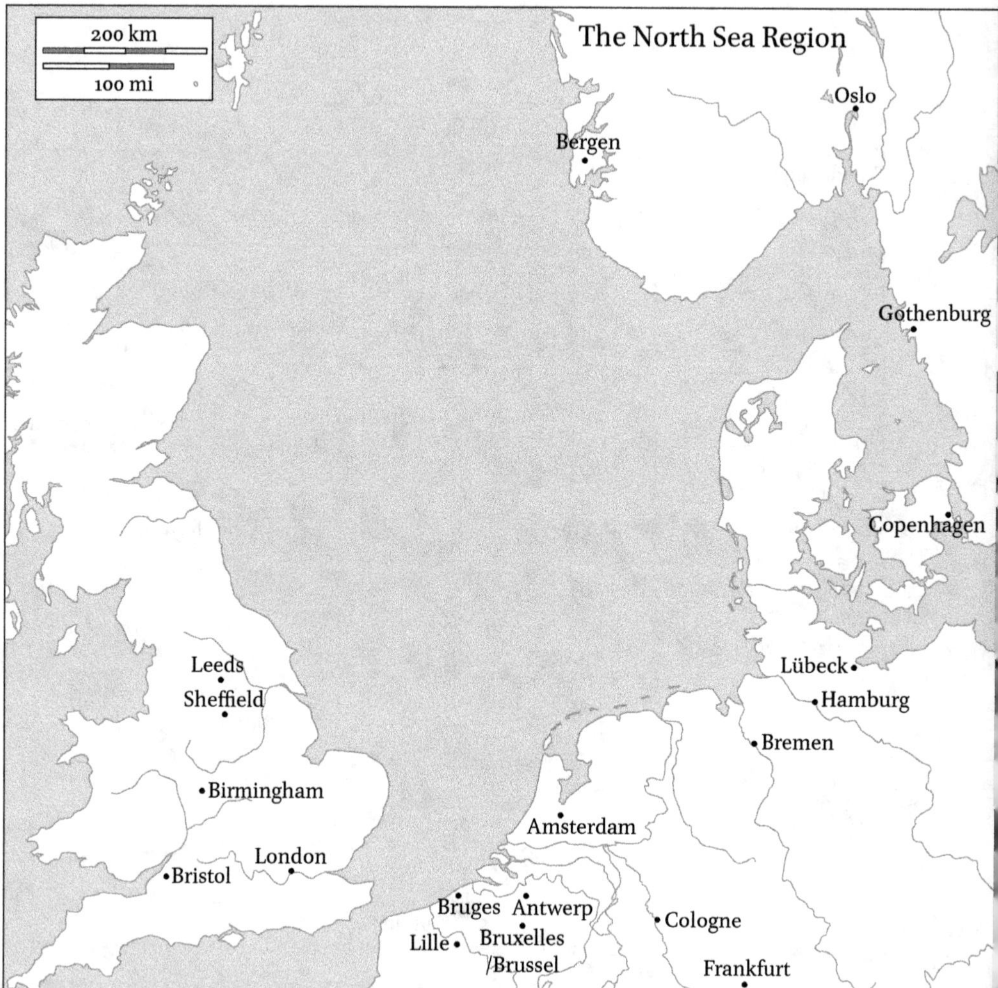

MAP 0.2 *The North Sea region.*

PART 1

General Hanse History

CHAPTER 1

The Early Hanses*

Rolf Hammel-Kiesow

Introduction

Over the last five decades, the scholarly picture of the Hanse's pre- and early history has changed considerably.[1] Not only is this true of the original homeland of these Lower German merchants, between the Lower Rhine and Elbe Rivers, where settlement archaeology has unearthed new time-depth dimensions of economic development,[2] but also of the Baltic Region, which has been the primary focus of this change. Sixty years ago, German historians who had been reluctant to acknowledge "older approaches regarding city life on the Baltic's south coast" before the arrival of Lower German merchants as 'culture bearers'[3] began for the first time to revise the existing historical construct of

---

* Translated by Lore Schultheiss.

1 An overview of the early Hanseatic history until the mid fourteenth century is found in: Philippe Dollinger, *Die Hanse*, with a contribution, "Zur hansischen Geschichtsforschung 1960–1997" by the same and Antjekathrin Graßmann (Stuttgart: Kröner 5. expanded edition, 1998), 17–88, 488–493; Johannes Schildhauer and Konrad Fritze and Walter Stark, *Die Hanse* (Berlin: VEB Deutscher Verlag der Wissenschaften, 1974), 11–111; Heinz Stoob, *Die Hanse* (Graz et al.: Styria, 1995), 18–165; the section "Von den 'Hansen' zur Hanse" (1150–1300/50) with contributions by Erich Hoffmann, Volker Henn and Derek Keene, in Jörgen Bracker, ed., *Die Hanse—Lebenswirklichkeit und Mythos*, vol. 1 (Hamburg: Museum für Hamburgische Geschichte, 1989), 29–49 (4. improved edition of the text volume ed. Jörgen Bracker and Volker Henn and Rainer Postel, Lübeck: Schmidt-Römhild, 2006); Rolf Hammel-Kiesow, Die Hanse [C.H. Beck Wissen 2131] (München: Beck 5. newly revised edition. 2014), 21–64; Rolf Hammel-Kiesow, Matthias Puhle and Siegfried Wittenburg, *Die Hanse* (Darmstadt: Primus-Verlag 2009), 8–52, 110–126; Gisela Graichen and Rolf Hammel-Kiesow, *Die deutsche Hanse. Eine heimliche Supermacht* (Reinbek bei Hamburg: Rowohlt 2011), 13–105; Stephan Selzer, *Die mittelalterliche Hanse* [Geschichte kompakt] (Darmstadt: Wissenschaftliche Buchgesellschaft 2010), 13–43; Carsten Jahnke, Die Hanse [Reclam Sachbuch; Reclams Universal-Bibliothek Nr. 19206] (Stuttgart: Philipp Reclam jun. 2014), 25–50, 132–161.

2 For example: Gabriele Isenberg, "Soest, ein frühes Wirtschaftszentrum (1.–12. Jahrhundert n. Chr.)", *Bericht der Römisch-Germanischen Kommission* 83 (2002), 265–281.

3 Fritz Rörig, "Das Meer und das europäische Mittelalter," in idem *Wirtschaftskräfte im Mittelalter. Abhandlungen zur Stadt- und Hansegeschichte*, ed. Paul Kaegbein (Cologne: Hermann Böhlaus Nachf, 1971; first published 1951), 647.

 | DOI 10.1163/9789004284760_003

the Baltic southern coast as "in large measure dead"[4] prior to the Germans' arrival. While some still held to this idea into the 1950s, more recent settlement archaeology and numismatic examination, as well as fresh interpretations of written sources based upon a new line of questioning, have created a new picture of the south Baltic coast as a multi-facetted cultural and economic landscape. Settlement archeology determines or specifies the location, origin, duration of settlement and habitation of early (sixth-tenth centuries) and medieval (eleventh-twelfth centuries) trading centers. The evaluation of discovered coinage provides hypotheses that help to plausibly reconstruct the dynamics of the economic relations in the region between Western Europe and Northwest Russia.[5]

The integration of the Baltic Region into Western and Central Europe beginning in the eleventh century is now the object of interdisciplinary and international research, in which the recent view of the 'discovered,' 'conquered,' and 'Christianized' people, namely the indigenous population of the areas surrounding the Baltic Sea, is presented from a different perspective under the term 'Europeanization'.[6] In Hanseatic research before World War II, long-range merchants from Lower Germany, and in their wake the nobility, farmers, and craftsmen, were the primary players in the incorporation of the Northeast Baltic region into Western and Central European culture. However, new approaches examine the entire Baltic Region, with one example being the investigation of power-politics in the Nordic Kingdoms of Denmark and Sweden and their role, as well as the Catholic Church's role, in the mission to the southern and eastern Baltic Regions.[7] Researchers classify the integration

4 Fritz Rörig, *Die Entstehung der Hanse und der Ostseeraum* (Cologne: Hermann Böhlaus Nachf., 1971; first published 1951/52), 564.

5 Christian Radtke, "Schleswig im vorlübischen Geld- und Warenverkehr zwischen westlichem Kontinent und Ostseeraum," in *Haithabu und die frühe Stadtentwicklung im nördlichen Europa*, ed. Klaus Brandt, Michael Müller-Wille and Christian Radtke, Schriften des Archäologischen Landesmuseums, vol. 8 (Neumünster: Wachholtz-Verlag, 2002), 379–429.

6 Nils Blomkvist, *The Discovery of the Baltic: The Reception of a Catholic World-System in the European North* (AD *1075–1225*), The Northern World, vol. 15 (Leiden and Boston: Brill, 2005).

7 Philip Line, *Kingship and State Formation in Sweden 1130–1290*, The Northern World, vol. 27 (Leiden and Boston: Brill, 2007); William Urban, *The Baltic Crusade* (Chicago: University of Chicago Press, ^{2}1994); Alan V. Murray, ed., *Crusade and Conversion on the Baltic Frontier 1150–1500* (Aldershot et al.: Ashgate, 2001); Iben Fonnesberg-Schmidt, *The Popes and the Baltic Crusades 1147–1254*, The Northern World, vol. 26 (Leiden and Boston: Brill, 2007); Thomas Lindkvist, "Crusades and Crusading Ideology in the Political History of Sweden, 1140–1500," in Alan V. Murray, ed., *Crusade and Conversion on the Baltic Frontier 1150–1500* (Aldershot et al.: Ashgate, 2001), 119–130.

of the Baltic Region into the Christian occidental world not as a singular process, but as part of a European expansion that included Central Eastern Europe, the Iberian Peninsula and the British Isles.[8] The most comprehensive approach of the last few years characterizes the process as the integration of the peripheral Baltic Region into a "Catholic world system," in the sense of Braudel and Wallerstein.[9]

The Baltic Region: From the Turn of the First Millennium to the Beginning of the Twelfth Century

As early as Roman times, both metals and slaves from the forests of northern and northeastern Europe were highly sought after in both southern and western Europe. As time went on, the demand for these goods grew steadily, both in the Frankish Empire and in the Muslim territories surrounding the Mediterranean. In the Carolingian period, an additional demand for northern furs developed as well. According to archeological sources, the direct trade routes of Baltic merchants shifted during the late ninth century, and began to pass through the Russian river system to Byzantium and from there into the Caliphate.

However, the Scandinavians (Vikings) did not initiate the shift; instead, the trade route's foundation had been laid by the Arabs and Khazars. Nevertheless, a Scandinavian slave trade directed towards the southeast, which lasted for about a century, facilitated the arrival of an estimated 50–100 million Dirhem (Arabic silver coins) in the Baltic Region.[10] These Dirhem served as the currency in a 'weight-money' economy that extended from Iceland and Ireland in the west to Scandinavia, the Baltic States, and well into Russia in the east. Furthermore, this economy, by virtue of the Dirhem, was at least temporarily tied to the currency relations of the Caliphate. With the Dirhem as a key

8 This approach was already basis for the Reichenau lectures 1970–1972; see Walter Schlesinger, ed., *Die deutsche Ostsiedlung des Mittelalters als Problem der europäischen Geschichte*, Vorträge und Forschungen, vol. 18 (Sigmaringen: Jan Thorbecke-Verlag, 1975); Charles Higounet, *Die Deutsche Ostsiedlung im Mittelalter* (Berlin: Siedler, 1986); French edition, *Les Allemands en Europe centrale et orientale au Moyen Âge* (Paris: Aubier, 1989).

9 Blomkvist, *Discovery*, 35–95.

10 Ralf Wiechmann, "Der Wandel des Währungssystems bei den Elb- und Ostseeslawen. Zur ältesten Münzprägung in Mecklenburg-Vorpommern," in *Geld und Kredit in der Geschichte Norddeutschlands*, ed. Klaus-Joachim Lorenzen-Schmidt, Studien zur Wirtschafts- und Sozialgeschichte Schleswig-Holsteins, Bd. 43 (Neumünster: Wachholtz-Verlag, 2006), 43–68, 44.

component, the weight-money system facilitated trade in this expansive economic area as a mode of standard currency.[11]

What has yet to be determined is why the influx of silver had already slowed by the 940's and then ended around 970. It seems more than certain that there were a number of reasons, among them the decreased production of silver from mines in western Asia and the collapse of Samanid rule (873–999) in Chorosan and Transoxania (south and southeast of the Aral Sea).[12] Furthermore, the success of a Christian Mission in Sweden and Norway may have significantly affected trade between the Baltic and the southeast due to the Catholic Church's prohibition of the slave trade. In response, merchants in the Baltic Region once again oriented themselves towards the west. Meanwhile, new silver deposits had been discovered in the Hartz Mountains, the Black Forest, and in the Vosges which now enabled the buyers of central and Western Europe to deliver the coveted precious metal.[13] Thus the initial development of the trading system into which the early Hanses[14] were integrated can be traced to about the turn of the first millennium A.D.

During the eleventh century, the transport routes along the Baltic coast were ruled by the traditional kingdoms of the north, namely Denmark and the Svear Empire, as well as by the princes of the Kievan Rus and by their tributary princes in Novgorod. In addition, the Polish Kingdom was actively engaged in

---

11 Wiechmann, "Wandel des Währungssystems," 50f.

12 Newest overview of research on money circulation in the Baltic region during the time of the Vikings until the end of the eleventh century Hendrik Mäkeler, "Wikingerzeitlicher Geldumlauf im Ostseeraum. Neue Perspektiven," *Quaestiones Medii Aevi Novae* X (2005), 121–149.

13 Heiko Steuer, "Münzprägung, Silberströme und Bergbau um das Jahr 1000 in Europa—wirtschaftlicher Aufbruch und technische Innovation," *Aufbruch ins zweite Jahrtausend. Innovation und Kontinuität in der Mitte des Mittelalters*, ed. Achim Hubel and Bernd Schneidmüller, Mittelalter-Forschungen, Bd. 16 (Ostfildern: Jan Thorbecke-Verlag, 2004), 117–149.

14 Strictly speaking, one should speak of the Hanse not before 1358, although the term is already used to refer to groups of Low German merchants previously. With regard to trade in Northeast, North and Northwest Europe, viewing Low German long-distance traders and the councils of the cities from which they derive with their common interests as developping the Hanse under the specific circumstances of the mid-14th century should be avoided. But to be short and concise, we use the term "early Hanse" to express that the more institutionalized form of "stede van der dudeschen hense" developed from these beginnings. The essential characteristics and especially their purpose and privileges based on foreign trade were already present in the 13th century. For joint actions of the early Hanseatic merchants and cities in the 13th century, I use as a collective term "*gemene kopman*" or "*gemene stede*" even if these terms were not used until the 14th century.

Baltic politics until the death of Boleslav III Schiefmund (died 1138).[15] The role played by the western Slavic areas as well as by the inhabitants of Courland on the Baltic south coast is unknown due to the cultural lack of a writing system. Western and central European merchants who wished to participate in the profitable eastern trade in this region were obliged to do so in accordance with the dictates of the rulers or functioning elites of these Baltic abutters.

The trade goods of the Baltic Region must have been profitable, as millions of western and central European coins reached the hands of merchants and rulers in this area starting at the beginning of the tenth century. Trade routes can be reconstructed by looking to the origin of these coins. Additionally, the manner in which they were handled provides clues regarding the various economic zones and their changes over time.

Based on such evidence, one can distinguish three distinct Baltic trade routes in use during the eleventh century:[16] the first targeted Danish and Swedish territories. In these areas, coins from Cologne and the Frankish realms arrived by boat via the Rhine River and North Sea. The second trading route led to the Baltic States and the land of Novgorod. In these areas, Frisian coins, which also arrived by sea, comprised the majority of the hoards. This second route, this sea route, may have been the northern route, the Route of Kings, which primarily connected the Malar region with Ladoga. It ran along the eastern Swedish coast, at the latitude of the Aland Islands, then along the northern coast of the Gulf of Finland to the Neva River and from there into Russia.[17] Thirdly, in the western Slavic region, comprising the southern coast of the Baltic Sea to the Vistula River, domestic coins circulated in company with Italian ones.[18] It was primarily the Lower Saxon merchants who went to the trading centers of the Baltic's southern coast by way of land. Yet this area could also be reached by sea via the route described by Adam of Bremen, which ran along the southern Baltic coast from either Schleswig or Oldenburg to Jumne

15 Blomkvist, *Discovery*, 328; regarding Poland's role in the process of 'Europeanization' of the Baltic region, see: Roman Czaja, Marian Dygo, Sławomir Gawlas, Grzegorz Myśliwski, Krzysztof Ożóg, *Ziemie polskie wobec Zachodu. Studia nad rozwojem średniowiecznej Europy* (Warszawa: Wydawnictwo-DiG, 2006) [engl. summary: The Polish Lands versus the West. Studies on the Development of Mediaeval Europe], 429–447.

16 Ralf Wiechmann, *Edelmetalldepots der Wikingerzeit in Schleswig-Holstein. Vom "Ringbrecher" zur Münzwirtschaft*, Offa-Bücher, vol. 77 (Neumünster: Wachholtz-Verlag, 1996), 81–83, 101f.

17 Blomkvist, *Discovery*, 290–295, with map 294.

18 Mäkeler, "Wikingerzeitlicher Geldumlauf," [bei Anm. 47].

(Wolin) and on to Novgorod.[19] The most westerly region of the western Slavic realm, Wagria, where Old Lübeck was situated, seems to have been the intermediate zone; attainable both by land and by sea.

The distribution of coins reveals two economic regions.[20] The first was a continuous area formed by southern Sweden and its south Baltic neighbors, but also comprising Denmark and Poland. This area supported an intensive trade and market exchange that required small 'coins' (below penny size) for local trade. This is indicated by the high fragmentation rate of discovered coins, as well as by the numerous probing marks created in order to verify silver content. The second economic area comprised Gotland, the Baltic States, and Russia. In Russia, a great number of discovered hoards have been dominated by Frisian coins that undoubtedly came there by direct exchange. It appears that this second area continued the traditions of Viking period trade. Eleventh century rune stones from the Malar area prove close trading relations with Novgorod. In the late eleventh century, St. Olaf's Church was erected in Novgorod, and the western trade seems certain to have taken place by means of the so-called Frisian Guild in Sigtuna (ca. 1070). This guild probably did not consist of Frisians, but rather Swedish merchants specializing in the trade with Friesland.[21] The western Baltic Region, including Poland, on the other hand, seems to have developed another, 'more modern', structure aimed at market exchange.

According to one highly plausible theory, the number of hoards in a region is directly proportional to the power of the ruler in a respective region to set exchange controls. On one end of the scale, a large number of hoards containing a supra-regional mix of coins would indicate missing coinage. At the other end of the scale, a near complete lack of hoards containing only regional coins of a single type indicates an area of strictly monitored coinage.[22] The origin of coinage in Denmark, Sweden and in the Principality of Novgorod around the turn of the millennium was the earliest indicator for the advance of a western/ central European coin-based economy. However, the princes of Svear and Novgorod abandoned coinage again approximately half a century later. In this

19 *Magistri Adam Bremensis Gesta Hammaburgensis ecclesiae Pontificum* ed. Werner Trillmich and Rudolf Buchner, Quellen des 9. und 11. Jahrhunderts zur Geschichte der Hamburger Kirche und des Reiches Ausgewählte Quellen zur deutschen Geschichte des Mittelalters, Bd. XI (Darmstadt: Wissenschaftliche Buchgesellschaft, [5]1978), II, c. 22.

20 Radtke, "Schleswig," 382–384.

21 Regarding Novgorod Blomkvist, *Discovery*, 396; regarding Sigtuna Radtke, "Schleswig," 391.

22 K. Johnsson, "Coin circulation and the pattern of hoarding in the Viking Age and Middle Ages," *XII. Internationaler Numismatischer Kongress Berlin 1997*, 911–916, 916.

new era of regionalized coinage in the Baltic, only Denmark continued to make its own coins by the turn of the twelfth century. However, western Slavic rulers also began to make their own coins around same time.[23] The many hoards from this time found in the northern and eastern regions point to a diminished control over money circulation. Meanwhile, the dearth of hoard findings from the same period, as well as the coinage of silver Agrippiner in Old Lübeck and the copper coins of Mecklenburg, indicate strong control by the rulers.[24] This constitutes a single piece in a mosaic depicting the development of strong western Slavic-Abotritish power in the period commencing with the culmination of the eleventh century; additional pieces will be discussed below.

The most important emporium for the trade between the Baltic and West/Central Europe was the City of Schleswig. It was here that the coins brought from the west were converted into the weight-money economy of the Baltic Region.[25] German merchants who were interested in Baltic trade, especially the Saxons, Westphalians, Frisians, and merchants from the Lower Rhine, also traveled to the fairs and market of this City on the River Schlei. Many of them even settled there. As early as 974, and following the conquest of Haithabu by Emperor Otto II, a *colonia Saxonum* complete with warriors, merchants and craftsmen was established, and by about 1080, the chronicler, Adam von Bremen, dubbed the city on the River Schlei *civitas Saxonum*.[26] Presumably the Frisians were the most important group of established merchants in the empire and must have had a powerful position in the city. This seems likely given the confidence King Niels of Denmark placed in them at the beginning of the twelfth century when he trusted his security to their exclusive protection (*Fresonum presidio*). Furthermore, the twelfth-century charter for the City of Schleswig granted merchants from Saxony and Friesland (*hospes de ducatu Saxoniae* or *hospes de Frisia*) significant advantages over other strangers.[27]

Throughout the twelfth century, the transit route from the North Sea to the Baltic Sea located between Hollingstedt and Schleswig was clearly most

---

23 Only mention in the written record for the year 1114 for the Zirzipanese in eastern Mecklenburg in the *Annales corbeienses*, MGH SS III, 8; regarding coin findings—partially even from the mid eleventh century—and their numismatic valuation Wiechmann, "Wandel des Währungssystems," 55–68.

24 Silver coating still sometimes found on some of the copper coins could also indicate counterfeiting; Wiechmann, "Der Wandel des Währungssystems," 65–68. Mäkeler, "Wikingerzeitlicher Geldumlauf," [near note 102].

25 Radtke, "Schleswig," 387f.

26 *Adam, Gesta Pontificum*, I, c. 57, 228/229; Schol. 81 (82), 392–393.

27 Schleswiger STR § 29; Erik Kroman and Peter Jørgensen, ed., *Danmarks gamle Købstadslovgivning, vol. 1 Sønderjylland* (Copenhagen: Rosenkilde og Bagger, 1951), 3–17.

important in accommodating traffic between west/central Europe and the Baltic.[28] The cathedrals in Ribe and Schleswig as well as numerous other churches in Jutland dating from 1120–1260, all of which were constructed using tuff (tufa) from the Rhine region, are proof of the very pronounced South-North trade. Written, architectural, and archeological sources demonstrate close trade relations between the Rhineland (especially Cologne) and Schleswig. These commercial relations reached as far as Southern France in the west and more than likely extended beyond Schleswig in the east. Beyond its geographically advantageous location in the center of trade, the metamorphosis of Schleswig into a clerical and royal center during the twelfth and thirteenth centuries further exemplifies the importance of the City on the River Schlei.[29]

On the southern coasts of the Baltic Sea, we have definitive proof that Saxons settled in the important Slavic trade centers of Wolin and Stettin in the time of Adam of Bremen (mid-eleventh century) and in the time of the missionary, Otto of Bamberg (early twelfth century). Indirectly, we can also demonstrate Saxon settlement in Old Lübeck.[30]

During the very lifetime of the chronicler from Bremen, Western Europeans began to become more and more interested in the Baltic; Adam's interest in the unknown countries of the North is the first proof of that. Since Adam reports that ships constantly left the port of Schleswig in order to sail to the lands of the Slavs, Sweden, Samland, and Greece (meaning Novgorod in Northwestern Russia), it is most probable that he received his information about the Slavic Regions from merchants.[31]

Beginning with the last quarter of the eleventh century, economic development in the Baltic Region appears to have accelerated; a trend that is consistent with what was happening in both western and central Europe. Indicators of this acceleration include the expansion of Schleswig (especially its port), and

---

28 Klaus Brandt, ed., *Hollingstedt an der Treene: Ein Flusshafen der Wikingerzeit und des Mittelalters für den Transitverkehr zwischen Nord- und Ostsee* (Neumünster: Wachholtz 2012).

29 A new valuation of the importance of Schleswig, also during most of the thirteenth century, is made by Carsten Jahnke, "… und er verwandelte die blühende Handelsstadt in ein unbedeutendes Dorf." "Die Rolle Schleswigs im internationalen Handel des 13. Jahrhunderts," in Gerhard Fouquet, Mareike Hansen, Carsten Jahnke and Jan Schlürmann, ed., *Von Menschen, Ländern, Meeren. Festschrift für Thomas Riis zum 65. Geburtstag* (Tönning et al.: Der andere Verlag, 2006), 225–268.

30 Lech Leciejewicz, "Sachsen in den slawischen Ostseestädten im 10.–12. Jahrhundert," *Zeitschrift für Archäologie* 21 (1987), 75–81.

31 Adam, Gesta Pontificum, IV, 1, p. 434. Regarding the Slavic areas ibid. II, 21, 22.

the establishment of a merchant settlement near Old Lübeck, which was, with the exception of Prague, the first castle-town in the Slavic Region permanently inhabited by long distance traders.[32] To the obvious detriment of nearby Wolin (Vineta/Jumne/Jomsburg), Stettin (on the Oder) developed into an important commercial center along the Oder River. Meanwhile, trade relationships on the Baltic Region grew stronger. From about the turn of the twelfth century, one notices a distinct Russian influence on the churches of Gotland, an island whose population had voluntarily converted to Christianity during the eleventh century when returning merchants brought along Christian priests.[33] Additionally, marriages between Swedish, Danish, Polish and Russian ruling families demonstrate close dynastic and more than likely commerce-related connections. For example, Prince Mistislaw Vladimirovich, or King Harald of Novgorod in Nordic sources, married the daughter of the Swedish King, Inge I and in turn their daughter, Ingeborg, was married to Knut Lavard, who reigned as both Jarl of Schleswig and, for a short time, King of the Abotrites (d. 1131). According to the Knytlinga Saga, which dates from the second half of the thirteenth century, their son, Waldemar I of Denmark (b. 1131; r. 1157, d. 1182), was supposedly born in Russia and spent his early childhood in Novgorod.[34]

Trade, Mission and Conquest: The Baltic Region in the Twelfth Century

During the twelfth and thirteenth centuries, it is impossible for the historian to distinguish between the missions and the commerce of the Baltic Region. However, it is possible to identify three distinct groups that inserted themselves into this complicated arrangement. These groups were the Roman Church, the merchants (primarily Lower German), and the nobility. Beginning in the early twelfth century, the attention of German princes was increasingly drawn to the Baltic Region. Lothar of Supplingenburg, who was proclaimed Duke of the Saxons in 1106, directed his political influence towards the northern Slavic lands, in particular, against the Ruganer and the continental Ranes. Lothar considered Denmark not only a country merely bordering the empire, but also an important political power worthy of consideration

32 Ernst Pitz, *Europäisches Städtewesen und Bürgertum. Von der Spätantike bis zum hohen Mittelalter* (Darmstadt: Wissenschaftliche Buchgesellschaft, 1991), 241.

33 Blomkvist, *Discovery*, 385–390.

34 Anti Selart, *Livland und die Rus im 13. Jahrhundert*, Quellen und Studien zur baltischen Geschichte, vol. 21 (Cologne: Böhlau, 2007), 34.

within the context of his own political initiatives, which, in their entirety, reached as far as the Baltic coast. Thus began an era of battles for dominion over the southwest Baltic coast and eventually over the entire Baltic Region. Descriptions of these events, which primarily emanated from the accounts of the German Chroniclers, including Otto of Bamberg,[35] Helmold of Bosau,[36] Arnold of Lübeck,[37] and Henry of Latvia,[38] as well as the account of the Dane Saxo Grammaticus,[39] seem to depict the actual processes and power struggles of this era in a distorted manner given the complete absence of a consideration for operations of power politics and for commercial issues within these accounts. For instance, an expansion of the western Slavs could be rendered plausible by the following archaeological evidence. The western Slavs erected the fortified trading post, Bulverket in Tingstaede Traesk (Sea), on Gotland in 1133, and then settled near Riga in the Duna-Delta. Blomkvist even speaks (in a slightly provocative fashion) of a "Slavic Hanse."[40] Furthermore, the proliferation of Slavic ceramics, ceramics dominant on the Danish Islands (Eastern Denmark including Southern Sweden, Oeland, and Gotland) between the first half of the eleventh century and about 1200, demonstrates a strong cultural influence that developed as a result of Slavic migrations through these areas.[41] Written sources attest to Slavic settlement in Danish towns; such settlement facilitated a permanent pipeline for the supply of goods originating from the Slavic homeland on the southern Baltic coast. These goods, in particular furs, wax, and honey, were in turn used by the Danes to satisfy the demands

---

35 *Die Heiligenleben des Bischofs Otto von Bamberg*, in Lorenz Weinrich, ed., *Vitae sanctorum episcoporum Adalberti Pragensis et Ottonis Babenbergensis Historiam Germanicam et Slavicam illustrantes*, Ausgewählte Quellen zur deutschen Geschichte des Mittelalters, vol. 25 (Darmstadt: Wissenschaftliche Buchgesellschaft, 2005), 120–493.

36 Helmold von Bosau, *Slawenchronik*, newly transcribed and explained by Heinz Stoob, Ausgewählte Quellen zur deutschen Geschichte des Mittelalters, vol. 19 (Darmstadt: Wissenschaftliche Buchgesellschaft, 1973).

37 Arnoldi Chronica Slavorum, ed. Georg Heinrich Pertz and Johann Martin Lappenberg, MGH SS rer. Germ. 14 (Hannover: Hahn, 1868, new edition 1978).

38 *Heinrici Chronicon Livoniae*, ed. Von L. Arbusow and A. Bauer (Heinrich von Lettland, Livländische Chronik, newly translated by Albert Bauer), Ausgewählte Quellen zur deutschen Geschichte des Mittelalters, vol. 24 (Darmstadt: Wissenschaftliche Buchgesellschaft, 1975).

39 *Saxo Grammaticus. Gesta Danorum. Danmarkshistorien*, eds. Karsten Friis-Jensen and Peter Zeeberg, vol. 1–2 (Copenhagen: Det Danske Sprog—og Litteraturselskap, 2005).

40 Blomkvist, *Discovery*, 322–324.

41 Mats Roslund, *Guests in the House. Cultural Transmission between Slavs and Scandinavians 900 to 1300 A.D.*, The Northern World, vol. 33 (Leiden et al.: Brill, 2007), 472–530.

of German merchants.[42] During the time of Henry of Old Lübeck (1095–1127), who had more than likely been crowned King of the Abotrites by Lothar III (though the traditional account is ambiguous), the western Slavs were probably a considerable factor in the power structure of the region. This suspicion is affirmed by the afore-mentioned coinage, produced during this time period, as well as by the sheer size of the Slavic fleets. According to Snorri Sturluson, Ratibor's fleet supposedly comprised 300 ships in the year 1136. By the assessment of additional sources, the fleet of Prince Boguslaw of Pomerania boasted as many as 500 ships in 1184.[43]

Following the death of Henry of Old Lübeck, Lothar III appointed Jarl Knut Lavard (the Dane) King of the Abotrites. Jarl Knut was, of course, married to the Novgorod Princess Ingeborg and as result of his elevation and by virtue of his marriage, became ruler of the southwest Baltic coastline, including the key trading centers of Schleswig and Old Lübeck, and more than likely controlled or at least had designs upon the domination of the east-west seaborne trading route to Novgorod. It is in this context that the Knytlinga Saga of the late thirteenth century provides another fascinating clue.

In the saga, Knut's marriage is attributed to his contact with a merchant from Sambia, who suggested to Knut the advantages offered by the trade with the Baltic States and Russia itself in such a manner that Knut is thought to have established additional contacts to these areas by means of his marriage to the Novgorod Princess. In the saga, the new seaborne trading route, the Austerwegr, may have been used as basis for the saga's poetic narration. It crossed the open waters of the Baltic Sea from Gotland and led on from Northern Courland either into the Gulf of Finland or into the mouth of the Duna River, taking the place of the "older route of the Kings."[44] Unfortunately, Knut Lavard was murdered in 1133. However, this murder was not exclusively the product of internecine quarrels and jealousy within the Danish Dynasty. It had much to do with Knut's involvement in disputes regarding the dominion of the Baltic Region.

These disputes involved two coalitions. One comprised Knut Lavard and Novgorod, and was opposed by the other, which included the Kings of Poland and Svear as well as the Prince of the Kievan Rus. In the wake of Knut's death, Lothar III himself took control of the coastal region. There he erected the

---

42 Radtke, "Schleswig," 409f.

43 Lech Leciejewicz, "Maritime activities of the Western Slavs in the Early Middle Ages," in Vytautas Kazakevičius and Vladas Žulkus, ed., *The Balts and their Neighbours in the Viking Age*, Archaelogia Baltica vol. 2 (Vilnius: Zara, 1997), 95–104, 101.

44 Blomkvist, *Discovery*, 401f.

Segeberg Castle and in 1134, presumably from his court in Halberstadt, awarded certain privileges to the Gotlanders residing within his sphere of influence. In this, the western Slavs did not fail to recognize the danger that threatened their political and cultural independence. In his chronicle, Helmold of Bosau meticulously and precisely analyzes the situation associated with the erection of Segeberg Castle from the perspective of a Slavic Prince.[45] What is more, the Slavs razed Old Lübeck almost immediately after the death of Lothar in 1138. Obviously, the Slavs had seen a center for German influence in the presence of this castle settlement. However, by destroying the old settlement, they had paved the way for the establishment of the Lower German city of Lübeck, which received its charter only a short time later in the year 1143.

We can place the origin of early Hanseatic history within this era while remaining fully aware that the era was actually a continuum comprising three distinct turning points: the first taking place around 970/1000, the second around 1075, and the third and final turning point between 1120 and 1150. However, the direct influence of Lothar on the southwestern Baltic was only one of several events through which the cards in the Baltic Region were dealt anew at that time. In the period between 1120 and 1140, Gotland (primarily) separated from the Empire of the Svear, opened its doors to foreign merchants from the West and South (previously, only Russian merchants seem to have played any role as guests), and developed into a central emporium for the trade between East and West that maintained its importance for the next 150 years. Meanwhile, Novgorod also split off from the Kievan Rus and became a Boyar Republic under an elected prince. However, Novgorod's separation from the Kievan Rus resulted in the loss of its trade relations with Byzantium. This development not only affected Novgorod itself, but also Birka/Sigtuna.[46] Ultimately, the three regions central to Baltic trade, including the southwestern coastal areas that had come under German influence, the Island of Gotland that had become a trans-shipment and trading center, and the 'Republic' of Novgorod, which was centrally located for trade with Russia, became conjoined during the 1130s. This development would come to shape the history of the Baltic Region for the next 150 years.

During this period, the Low German merchant settlement of Lübeck received a city charter, and for the first time introduced a model for the western European communal town into the Baltic coast. By adopting the name Liubice (Middle Low German Lubike), the new inhabitants of that settlement proclaimed the continuation of the ruined Slavic castle town's

45 Helmold, *Slawenchronik*, c. 53.

46 Blomkvist, *Discovery*, 392–400.

tradition of trade.[47] Greater legal security for Lower German merchants, a shorter route to the Baltic Sea in comparison with the route via Schleswig for western Westphalian and Lower Saxon merchants, and direct access to salt and herring served as the foundation for the rise of Lübeck. As for the land connection to Hamburg, which would later become so important to the Hanseatic trade, it seems only to have become economically significant during the first decades of the thirteenth century after both cities succeeded in securing increasingly bigger shares of the traffic that had previously taken place via Schleswig and the sea.[48]

As early as 1143, Lübeck had become a center for transshipment of herring and salt. In addition, Lübeck served as a hub for the sea to land and land to sea transport of Baltic trade goods headed to the south and southwest. Many of the merchants interested in the Baltic trade and the herring catch, who until then had been residents of Bardowiek, relocated to the better-situated city of Lübeck. Due to a decrease in his revenues from Bardowiek, Henry the Lion then intervened to take possession of Lübeck. In 1159, he had the recently burned city rebuilt. The rise of Lübeck only coincided with the rule of the Saxon duke, but its increasing importance made Henry the Lion interested in the new city in the first place. However, the city's ascent was very slow, primarily because the Low German merchants lacked ships! In response, the merchants of Lübeck reacted to this situation in 1159 when they requested that their new overlord, Henry the Lion, "send messengers into the main towns and kingdoms of the North, Denmark, Sweden, Norway and Russia, and [...] [offer] them peace [and] access to free trade in his city, Lübeck."[49] Among other things, this meant an exemption from duties for the Russians, Normans,

47 Rolf Hammel-Kiesow, "Neue Aspekte zur Geschichte Lübecks: von der Jahrtausendwende bis zum Ende der Hansezeit. Die Lübecker Stadtgeschichtsforschung der letzten zehn Jahre (1988–1997). Teil 1: bis zum Ende des 13. Jahrhunderts," *ZVLGA* 78 (1998), 47–114, 61–65; Rolf Hammel-Kiesow, "Die Anfänge Lübecks: Von der abotritischen Landnahme bis zur Eingliederung in die Grafschaft Holstein-Stormarn," in Antjekathrin Graßmann, ed., *Lübeckische Geschichte*, 4th ed., (Lübeck: Verlag Schmidt-Römhild, 2008), 38–45.

48 Carsten Jahnke, "Handelsstrukturen im Ostseeraum im 12. und beginnenden 13. Jahrhundert. Ansätze einer Neubewertung," *Hansische Geschichsblätter* 126 (2008), 167–168. Carsten Jahnke, "The City of Lübeck and the Internationality of Early Hanseatic Trade," in JustynaWubs-Mrozewicz and Stuart Jenks, eds., *The Hanse in Medieval and Early Modern Europe* (The Northern World. North Europe and the Baltic c. 400–1700 A.H. Peoples, Economies and Cultures, Vol. 60). (Leiden: Brill 2013), 37–58.—Single merchants from Lübecker, of course, appeared earlier already, like 1187 in Hamburg-Neustadt, *Arnoldi, Chronica, Slavorum* III, c. 20, 110.

49 Helmold, *Slawenchronik*, c. 86.

Swedes, Ölandians, Goths, Livs and all the peoples of the East. This exemption was still documented in the first charter of municipal law drawn up between 1226 and 1234.[50] By employing these free trade policies with regard to their Baltic neighbors, it is possible that they were already trying to compete with the more prominent center of transshipment in Schleswig to divert larger shares of goods to Lübeck than ever before. It was in this manner that they attempted to draw sufficient tonnage to the city on the Trave from the seafaring merchants of the Baltic region.[51] The common, or mutual, trading organization of the *gilda communis* comprised of Gutnish and Low German merchants presumably developed from this cooperation; this will be discussed later in more detail. The great town seal of Lübeck is reminiscent of this era of joint trade. There is an intensive discussion what type of ship the seal depicts. Most likely it is a hybrid type that combined elements of the early cogs as well as of Scandinavian ships.[52] The seal may depict the helmsman, or the *stýrimaðr* of Nordic sources. The helmsman was often the ship's owner and responsible for granting the merchant admission to the board community. In the seal, this is attested by the helmsman's outstretched right arm. Under the treaty, the merchant was granted protection and security through the *stýrimaðr*, ensuring that both could form a trading company.[53] Thus, the seal image presumably mirrors the state of trade in the city of Lübeck in the first centuries of its existence.

50 UBStL 1, no. 32.

51 These 'free trade politics' probably were less connected with a basically new kind of trade policy, which was not set on skimming off the trade any more, but which supposedly also considered the profitability of the detour of free trade, as Blomkvist, *Discovery*, 697f., states. Rather, the Lower German merchants and Henry the Lion simply obeyed the force of circumstances: Only people with ship space could participate in sea trade.

52 Ellmers, Detlev, "Kogge und Holk als Schiffe der Hanse," in Michael Hundt and Jan Lokers, eds., *Hanse und Stadt. Akteure, Strukturen und Entwicklungen im regionalen und europäischen Raum. Festschrift für Rolf Hammel-Kiesow zum 65. Geburtstag* (Lübeck: Schmidt-Römhild 2014), 53–67, 58–61; Reinhard Paulsen, "Die Koggendiskussion in der Forschung. Methodische Probleme und ideologische Verzerrungen" *HGbll.* 128 (2010): 19–112, 86–96; Detlev Ellmers, "Koggen kontrovers," *HGbll.* 128 (2010): 113–140; Carsten Jahnke, "Koggen und kein Ende. Anmerkungen zu den Thesen von Reinhard Paulsen und Detlev Ellmers," *ZVLGA* 91 (2011): 305–320.

53 Carsten Jahnke, "Zur Interpretation des ersten Lübecker Schiffssiegels," *ZVLGA* 88 (2008), 21–22.

The Advance of Low German Merchants in the Baltic Region

On the south Baltic coast, the advance of the merchants was closely linked to the conquest and settlement of the coastal lands by the nobility and the farmers acting in connection with the forceful proselytizing of the Slavic—and in the thirteenth century –Prussian populations. In the Baltic States, proselytizing took the form of crusades featuring active and decisive participation by the merchants. Danes, Germans and Swedes (the latter mainly operating in Finland) carried out these crusades. However, the expansion of trade by Low German merchants to the Scandinavian countries occurred by peaceful means.

Conquest, conversion, and the expansion of commercial relationships did not progress continuously from West to East. After the conquest of Wagria and Polabia and the founding of Lübeck in 1143, the progress of the conquerors was initially halted. Only in 1164, with the subjugation of those Slavic lands extending to the Peene River, did Low German merchants begin to settle in greater numbers in locations that were primarily established adjacent to previously existing seaports (for example, in 1189 Rostock is documented as comprising a market with a church). However, these settlements soon surpassed the neighboring seaports. Only in the thirteenth century (starting with Rostock in 1218) did these settlements receive their charters, which, for a long time, obscured the actual origin of these branches. The majority of the settlers arrived from Lübeck by sea. However, as early as 1180, the Slavic city of Stettin was eclipsed by a German settlement whose inhabitants had arrived by land from the middle lower German area around Magdeburg.

While rather tentative progress was being made on the south Baltic Coast, Low German merchants set their sights toward Gotland via Lübeck in order to advance from there on to Novgorod and on to the Baltic Coast. This particular goal was in accordance with the tradition of those merchants who had previously participated in the trade of Baltic goods via Old Lübeck. In consequence, the changes that resulted from the founding of the German city of Lübeck did not take the form of a break with tradition or a new beginning. Rather, they can be explained as a continuous development from an existing system. The groups of people who participated had already known each other for centuries by virtue of their contacts in Schleswig, Old Lübeck, Wolin, and other trading centers.

For decades now, scholars have discussed when exactly the Low German merchants might have been able to reach Gotland in significant numbers. However, scholarly interpretation of the Artlenburg Treaty of 1161, the treaty by which Henry the Lion negotiated peace between the Goths and the Germans after their bloody clashes at an unnamed location, has been a point of controversy. At present, archeological, numismatic, and written sources demonstrate that, beginning in the Carolingian era, one is least able to discern the activity of individual Low German merchants trading in the Baltic region; one of the earliest clues is a birch bark document from Novgorod in the 1020s written in the old Low German language, but employing the Latin alphabet.[54] On the other hand, in recent years, historic and archeological findings, especially findings from the archeology of seafaring, have shown that the superiority of the Low German merchant in the Baltic region did not start immediately upon the founding of Lübeck, but that it was earned through a long process that lasted approximately 100 years. The requisite ship space provided to the Low German merchants, primarily by the seafaring merchants of the Goths, has already been discussed. The Goths were extremely important to the aspiring city of Lübeck; thus a great deal of support exists for a thesis advocated by Scandinavian historians that the conflicts predating the Artlenburg Treaty took place in the Duchy of Saxony. According to the most recent and most thorough interpretation, Odelricus was probably not the guild master for the German merchants of Gotland, but an officer of Henry the Lion in the Duchy of Saxony who was given a mandate to punish crimes against Goths unconditionally and to avoid any delay in their affairs. One can only conclude that if the Goths had retreated from the Duchy of Saxony, the economic consequences would have probably been disastrous.[55]

Trade between Low German merchants and Russia in the second half of the twelfth century is clearly documented. On Gotland in the 1180s, these Low German merchants confiscated the trading goods of Russian merchants from Novotorzôk (Torzhok in northwest Russia) for unknown reasons.[56] The Russian-Gotlandish-German Treaty of 1191/92, in which an "old peace" is mentioned, was the result of the ensuing negotiations that took place in Novgorod through the Gutnish negotiator Arbud. Recently, Russian research attributes this negotiation to Henry the Lion and thus the 1160s. Among other things,

54 Valentin L Janin, "Mitteilungen auf ungewöhnlichem 'Papier'—Die Birkenrindendokumente von Novgorod," in Michael Müller-Wille, ed., *Novgorod. Das mittelalterliche Zentrum und sein Umland im Norden Russlands* (Neumünster; Wachholtz-Verlag, 2001), 109–120, 113.

55 Blomkvist, *Discovery*, 415–439; Thomas Riis, "Noch einmal das Artlenburg-Privileg—ein Werk Heinrichs des Löwen oder des Domherrn Marold?" in Hundt and Lokers, eds., *Hanse und Stadt*, 79–84; Detlev Ellmers, "Wie verlässlich ist das Artlenburg-Privileg überliefert?" *HGbll*, 132 (forthcoming).

56 Jon Lind situates the disagreements in Sweden and interprets Novitork as a mid Swedish city; Blomkvis, 462.

the treaty stipulates that merchants and emissaries had the right to sail to Novgorod, Germany, and Gotland unhindered.[57] Of course, this only makes sense if Low German merchants in the 1160s were already involved in trade with Novgorod.

Since the 1180s, German merchants had placed a secondary emphasis on the Russian trade as well as on the Duna trade in Livonia (which roughly corresponds with modern-day Estonia and Latvia). This practice began first in Gotland and here too, as in the case of Novgorod, they acted as companions to Gutnish merchants. Danish and Norwegian merchants were active there as well.[58] The Christianization of Livonia began a short time later. The first missionary, Meinhard, arrived in the mid 1180s "in the company of merchants" (*cum comitatu mercatorum*).[59] All the crusaders and their materials were shipped by way of Lübeck to Gotland and then on to Livonia. As a result, Lübeck and the transport capacity of the Low German merchants and skippers attracted the attention of papal policy makers in Europe.[60] In 1201, the city of Riga, seat of a bishopric and chapter of a cathedral, developed next to an older domestic settlement, like almost all cities in the Baltic region. In 1211, the settlement in Riga lured numerous merchants by granting them privileges. Riga was the second German city founded in the Baltic region; operating in the double function typical of this time and area, it served both as a support for the Christian mission as well as for the expansion of a trading sphere for the merchants.

Meanwhile, German merchants in Visby on Gotland settled and formed a German community (that in 1288 was to be united with a Gutnish community into a township). Long-distance traders from Lower Germany departed from Smolensk and made their way to the trading centers of Polozk and Witebsk on the Duna and there established a connection with Kiev and that part of Russia that until that time had been oriented toward Constantinople. In 1229 these merchants had forged a trade agreement with the prince in Riga. On their way through Novgorod and by means of their trade on the Duna, it is probable that the early Hansard merchants also brought Oriental luxury goods into the economic centers of northwestern Europe. This was in addition to local products

57 Anna Leonidovna Choroškevič, "Der Ostseehandel und der deutsch-russisch-gotländische Vertrag 1191/1192," in Stuart Jenks and Michael North, ed., *Der hansische Sonderweg? Beiträge zur Sozial- und Wirtschaftsgeschichte der Hanse*, Quellen und Darstellungen zur hansischen Geschichte, N.F., Bd. 39 (Cologne: Böhlau-Verlag, 1993), 1–12.

58 *Heinrici Chronicon Livoniae*, I, c. 11, 8f.

59 Ibid., I, c. 2, 4f.

60 Urban, *Crusade*; Fonnesberg-Schmidt, *Popes*; Murray, *Crusade and Conversion*.

that consisted of wax and furs.[61] As early as the 1170s or 1180s, a rotunda church was built in Smolensk by local contractors on the grounds of the "German Court" (named so later in the thirteenth century). It was built in a form common to northern Germany and Scandinavia. The clients were probably Gutnish merchants (possibly already in the company of German merchants). This is excellent proof for the cooperation that existed between the local population, or, more accurately, the local rulers and the foreign merchants.[62]

And yet during the twelfth century, trade relations with Denmark and Sweden grew stronger. Henry the Lion had supposedly already concluded a commercial treaty with the king of the Swedes,[63] possibly in a mutual gesture of "free trade," a privilege he had granted to the Swedes in Lübeck. By at least the thirteenth century, German merchants, craftsmen, and miners were immigrating to Sweden, which realized an economic boom by virtue of the copper mining in Falun. Low German merchants settled in Kalmar around 1220 and took part in the founding of Stockholm in 1251. All told, the country's primary export goods were copper and iron, but also included agricultural and animal products such as fish and furs. Fabrics and salt were imported.

At that time, the provinces of Halland, Schonen (Scania), and Blekinge—all present-day possessions of Sweden—were part and parcel of the dominion of the Danish King. Consequently, Denmark, in possession of both Sund and Belt, ruled the entry and exit into and out of the Baltic Sea. Beginning in the fourteenth century (until recently Denmark was often called the 'fateful power of the Hanse'), this would become of great political importance to the trade traffic of the Hanseatic Cities. From the late twelfth century on, the herring market of Schonen became extremely important to the economy of the Wendish Hanse cities. Schleswig lost its function as a supra-regional fair and market to the East-West international trade fair that had been developing in Schonen since the first half of the twelfth century. Low German merchants from Lübeck could sail directly to the fairs in Schonen, to which they brought salt from Luneburg

61 Hans Wilhelm Haussig, *Die Geschichte Zentralasiens und der Seidenstraße in islamischer Zeit* (Darmstadt: Wissenschaftliche Buchgesellschaft, 2. unveränderte Auflage 1994), 172f., 183ff.

62 Oleg Ioannisyan, "Between Byzantium and the Romanesque West: The Architecture of Old Rus in the tenth-thirteenth Centuries," in Michael Müller-Wille, ed., *Rom und Byzanz im Norden. Mission und Glaubenswechsel im Ostseeraum während des 8.–14. Jahrhunderts, vol. 2*, Akademie der Wissenschaften und der Literatur, Abhandlungen der geistes- und sozialwissenschaftlichen Klasse Jg. 1997, 3/2 (Stuttgart: Steiner, 1997), 297–323, 314f.

63 *Die Urkunden Heinrichs des Löwen, Herzogs von Sachsen und Bayern*, revised by Karl Jordan (Stuttgart: Anton Hiersemann 1957), no. * 115, 172 (in the following UHdL); Blomkvist, *Discovery*, 526.

and returned with freight herring that was coveted as Lenten fare. This trade in mass goods, unlike the Schleswig trade, which was apparently more focused on luxury goods, provided their operations with a second and very promising division. One can more fully appreciate the importance of the Fairs of Schonen to the City of Lübeck if one considers the fact that the powerful city on the Trave was obliged to submit to the Danish King, Knut VI, in order to free their merchants and ships that had been arrested at the fairs.

It is not known when merchants from the Baltic Region first arrived in Norway, but by the early thirteenth century Norwegian trade connections included England, Flanders, Holland, and the North German sea coast. By 1240, the export of grain, flour and malt to Bergen from Lübeck was already established. In Bergen, dried cod, produced in Northern Norway, was collected and made ready for export. Beginning in the mid-thirteenth century, the merchants of the Wendish Hanse Cities eventually succeeded in ousting the English and Flemish from the Norwegian market. This was accomplished with rye, which, due to agrarian development of lands pertaining to the Eastern settlements of Holstein, Lauenburg and Mecklenburg, was being produced in steadily increasing amounts. Furthermore, merchants primarily from the Wendish Hanse Cities began to make use of their position as 'winter seaters' in Bergen to take control of the market for dried cod as well.[64]

In 1231, the German Order initiated the conquest of Prussia, beginning their campaign in the heart of that country. That same year, Thorn (Torun) was founded and then Elbing in 1237 soon after the coast had been reached. However, Lübeck's participation in the foundation of this city is not supported by the sources as stated in earlier historical literature. With the issuance of the first, and second city charters to Koenigsberg in 1255 and 1286, the latter necessitated by the unfortunate destruction of the original city, all of the important (eventual) Hanse cities of the Baltic Region were established. Rural settlement began in the inland areas beyond the more established eastern communities of the Germans and intensified, reaching its furthest extent toward the end of the century in the most easterly portion of eastern Prussia. These rural settlements constituted a hinterland to the south Baltic coast from Mecklenburg to the Memel River and thus became the production area for the goods of the Hanseatic trade.

64 Arnved Nedkvitne, *The German Hansa and Bergen 1100–1600*. Quellen und Darstellungen zur hansischen Geschichte N.F. vol. 70 (Cologne: Böhlau 2014); Mike Burkhardt, *Der hansische Bergenhandel im Spätmittelalter. Handel—Kaufleute—Netzwerke*. Quellen und Darstellungen zur hansischen Geschichte, N.F., vol. 60 (Cologne: Böhlau 2009).

From the thirteenth to the nineteenth centuries, the agricultural and forestry products of this hinterland region, including grain, wood, ashes, pitch, and more, were precisely those provisions and raw materials needed by the densely populated 'industrial nations' of the Late Middle Ages and Early Modern Times. Such nations included Flanders, Brabant, the northern Netherlands, and England. Consequently, from the fourteenth century, the Dutch, Zealanders, and the English had all tried and eventually succeeded in eliminating the Hanseatic transit trade and purchasing these goods directly from their respective production areas.

The last chapter in the chronology for the expansion of Low German merchants throughout the Baltic Region was composed in the late thirteenth century when merchants from Lübeck received transit privileges within the Kingdom of Poland. In Poland, they followed the Vistula Route and established connections to Krakow and Hungary, the former well known for its rich copper deposits (Krakow was later called the copper house of the Hanse). In addition, connections to Silesia and Bohemia were also established. In Silesia, the merchants were drawn to the gold mines and in Bohemia, commercial relationships promised to deliver wax, tin, and silver. However, the extensive activity of individuals from Lübeck in the area was more than probably aimed at the exploitation of the Oriental Route created by the Vistula, Bug and RotreuBen, by which the merchants of Lübeck hoped to reach the Italian colonies of the Black Sea. After all, Kiev, which had until that point in time served as the hub for Oriental goods, had been conquered by the Mongols in 1240 and subsequently been removed from the trading system operating between the Orient and Eastern Central Europe.[65] With this penetration, the expansion of the Low German merchants within the Greater Baltic Region was complete.

Cologne, Flanders, and England

The second locus for the development of the Hanse lay to the West, where merchants from the City of Cologne played a role similar to that played by the merchants of Lübeck in the East. Thus, the Hanseatic region may be depicted as a great imaginary ellipse containing two foci in the cities of Lübeck and Cologne,[66] the latter vicariously representing the entire Lower Rhine with which the cities of the Ijssel and Zuijdersee were closely connected. Between

65 Roland Gehrke, *Die Hanse und Polen*, Hamburger Beiträge zur Geschichte der Deutschen im europäischen Osten, vol. 2 (Lüneburg: Nordostdeutsches Kulturwerk, 1996), 7–51, 19.

66 Stoob, *Hanse*, 88.

this region and the eastern Duchy of Saxony, a territory strongly connected to the Baltic Region, was Westphalia. Collectively, merchants from Westphalia played an important role as both turntable and bridge in the trade relations between the East and the West until the fifteenth century.

In Western Europe, Flanders developed into a region of production and trade[67] centered on the wool cloth industry, which took off considerably in the mid-eleventh century. As early as the beginning of the twelfth century, the Counts of Flanders in Ypres, Lille, Messen, and Torhout established the first fairs in Northern Europe. During the same century, a new trade route was opened leading from Cologne, through Brabant and on to Ghent and Bruges. The route increased the importance of Flanders as a transit country for goods from England and France, which were delivered to the markets in Brabant and Germany.

The trading system of the Flemish, especially that trade conducted by the merchants of Ghent, who were supported by Emperor Frederick I, prompted counter measures by the merchants of Cologne, the most densely populated and economically powerful city in the empire. The latter erected an emporium restraint on trade goods in 1169, which was primarily aimed at the purchase of wine by Flemish merchants to the south of Cologne. Then, by special request of Frederick I, the merchants of Ghent had their earlier privileges affirmed by the Archbishop of Cologne, allowing them to travel and conduct business up the Rhine River and past Cologne.[68]

The people of Cologne, on the other hand, found an ally in the King of England, who loathed to see the strong position of the Flemish merchants in the English wool trade (English wool had been imported to Flanders since the early twelfth century) strengthened by an additional take-over of the trade in Rhine wine. Should this have occurred, the Flemish would have completely dominated the trade of northwest Europe by exercising their ability to bring wine from the Rhine River to England, English wool to Flanders, and Flanders cloth to the Rhine. To prevent this, King Henry II of England, in 1175/76, granted to the merchants of Cologne the furthest-reaching privileges for trading abroad of any twelfth-century German city.[69] In the thirteenth century,

67 David Nicholas, *Medieval Flanders* (London et al.: Longman, 1992), 111–115.

68 Regesta Imperii IV 2, 3, revised by Friedrich Opll (Vienna: Böhlau, 2001) n. 1855; also see ebd. n. 2469.

69 Hugo Stehkämper, "Friedrich Barbarossa und die Stadt Köln. Ein Wirtschaftskrieg am Niederrhein," in Hanna Vollrath and Stefan Weinfurter, ed., *Köln. Stadt und Bistum in Kirche und Reich des Mittelalters. Festschrift für Odilo Engels zum 65. Geburtstag*, Kölner Historische Abhandlungen, vol. 39 (Cologne: Böhlau-Verlag, 1993), 367–413, 404–413;

these privileges became, in turn, the rock to which the privileges of Baltic cities were anchored and from which emerged the association of Low German merchants, or the *hansa Alemanie* (London, 1282).

In England, merchants from the Baltic cities encountered merchants from Westphalia and the Lower Rhine, who had already been trading there for some time.[70] The encounter did not go smoothly. The personal interests of individual groups within the city prevailed and as a result ensured that the branch of Lower Rhenish merchants from Cologne and the branch of merchants from the Baltic would remain distinct from one another. Until the early sixteenth century, merchants from the Baltic, including those from Hamburg, dominated trade with the eastern coast of England from Lynn to Newcastle. On the other hand, trade conducted by the merchants of Cologne and Westphalia was concentrated on the Stalhof in London as well as on Ipswich and Colchester. The Stalhof served as the *gildhalla* for the merchants of Cologne, as documented, from 1175/76 on. Only in the mid-thirteenth century did a joint venture between merchant groups of the Empire develop.

In the Empire, the trade in Flemish cloth was still in Flemish, especially Ghentish, hands throughout the first half of the thirteenth century. The presence of Flemish cloth is noted in the Baltic as early as the twelfth century as cloth from Ypres available at Novgorod in 1153. Whether or not Flemish merchants had personally gone as far a Novgorod in the twelfth century is uncertain, but their arrival was a documented occurrence in the late thirteenth century. In 1262, all Flemish merchants were granted an exemption from duty in the areas surrounding Brunswig and Magdeburg, and in 1268 Ghentish merchants received special privileges in Hamburg where they sold fabric and French wine and obtained grain from Holstein and Altmark for their return trip. In 1273 the Flemish are noted to have been present in the City of Kiel, and then a short time later in the Baltic cities of Wismar, Stralsund, and Greifswald.[71] Meanwhile, merchants from the Baltic cities had been active in Flanders since

---

Franz Irsigler, "Köln und die Staufer im letzten Drittel des 12. Jahrhunderts," in Wilfried Hartman, ed., *Europas Städte zwischen Zwang und Freiheit. Die europäische Stadt um die Mitte des 13. Jahrhunderts*. Schriftenreihe der Europa-Kolloquien im Alten Reichstag (Regensburg: 1995), 83–96; Terrence H. Lloyd, *England and the German Hanse, 1157–1611: A Study of their Trade and Commercial Diplomacy* (Cambridge: Cambridge University Press, 1991).

70 For a new interpretation of what happened see Carsten Jahnke, "'Homines imperii' und 'osterlinge'. Selbst- und Fremdbezeichnungen hansischer Kaufleute im Ausland am Beispiel Englands, Flanderns und des Ostseeraumes im 12. und 13. Jahrhundert" *HGbll.* 129 (2011): 8–24.

71 Nicholas, *Flanders*, 168f.

the mid-thirteenth century.[72] Supposedly, these Baltic merchants were successful in preventing the Flemish merchants from purchasing Baltic goods during the latter half of the century and subsequently forced the Flemish to return home without any freight. As a result, only the early Hanse merchants are supposed to have garnered the revenue available from the lucrative Eastern trade with Flanders. After 1270, Flemish merchants had also lost their hegemony over the trade with England.[73] And to make matters worse, Low German merchants now muscled their way into the business of exporting the English wool to Flanders as well. However, even their stake in the export of English wool was relatively small when compared to that of the Italian merchants. Finally, in 1294, the *mercatores Romani imperii* officially denied passage to Flemish ships attempting to sail in the Baltic Sea.[74] Therefore, from the fourteenth century on, Flemish merchants, and especially those from Bruges, concentrated on the intermediary functions of commerce, working as both brokers and hosteliers. However, this retreat from the active pursuit of trading abroad, turned out to be anything but a backward step into passivity. On the contrary, it eventually allowed Bruges to become the 'cradle of capitalism'.[75]

Thus it was that by approximately the middle of the thirteenth century, the early Hanseatic trading system had taken shape. Merchants from the cities between the Lower Rhine and the Elbe moved their long distance trading operations both to the East and to the West. In the East, this was especially true of trading ventures in Visby, in Novgorod and, by way of the Duna, in Smolensk. In the West, England and Flanders was the key. The merchants, in turn, sold the goods they purchased in these and other respective target countries in their hometowns or at trade fairs on the Lower Rhine. Merchants from the new Baltic cities moved directly into their Western target countries. Trade routes in the Baltic were primarily sea routes, however the land route that ran from Lübeck to the West via Westphalia was the most heavily traveled due to the strong domestic trade amongst the merchants from the Lower Rhine and Westphalia; nevertheless, from Hamburg on, the sea route was utilized as well. One must also be cautious not to underestimate the volume of traffic that arrived in the southern cities of Brandenburg, Altmark and Lower Saxony.

72 Carsten Jahnke, "Homines imperii," 24–29.

73 Nicholas, *Flanders*, 177f.

74 *Hansisches Urkundenbuch*, ed. Hansischer Geschichtsverein, vol. 1, revised by Konstantin Höhlbaum (Halle: Verlag der Buchhandlung des Waisenhauses, 1876) [abbreviated HUB 1], No. 1154, 1155.

75 James M. Murray, *Bruges, Cradle of Capitalism, 1280–1390* (Cambridge: Cambridge University Press, 2005), 189f.

These supplied important trading goods and were also consumers of goods that had originated from trading branches abroad.

However, it wasn't until the outset of the fourteenth century that the Flemish, English, Norwegian, Danish, Swedish, Slavic, Baltic and Russian merchants were almost completely driven from the primary routes of the early Hanseatic trading system. Virtually no information exists regarding the extent of trade conducted by these other groups.

The Traveling Associations of the Low German Merchants

During the middle Ages, merchants throughout Europe banded together in voluntary associations in order to safeguard their interests by means of joint trading. Aside from an obvious interest with regard to trade, these associations also performed social and religious functions. Usually, the organization of these associations was such that they could make decisions, decide on procedure, and punish rule breaking at their meetings. Such merchant associations were primarily organized into two larger conglomerations, including those formed by merchants in their respective hometowns and those formed at the travel destinations of merchants abroad.[76] The former can be further differentiated into associations comprising all the merchants within a town (for example those in St. Omer and Valenciennes), and into associations that united the merchants in their travel destinations (i.e., the association for the Schleswig travelers from Soest and the fraternities Danicum in Cologne). This was particularly true of the association formed in the bigger cities with far-reaching trade relations.

The *kore*, law of self-governance, allowed the merchants to manage their own affairs without the need for a judge. The *kore* was the crux of specific rights of merchants (ius mercatorum), the origin of which dated back to antiquity. This ability to self regulate was a feature of the (free) union, a basic form

76 Meir Kohn, "Merchant Associations in Pre-Industrial Europe," in idem, *The Origins of Western Economic Success: Commerce, Finance, and Government in Pre-Industrial* Europe (Hanover: Department of Economics, Dartmouth College, 2003), http://ssrn.com/abstract=427763 (accessed August 6, 2008); critical towards the positive image of merchant unions in research: Roberta Dessy and Sheilagh Ogilvie, *Social Capital and Collusion: The Case of Merchant Guilds*, CESifo Working Paper Series No. 1037, September 2003, http://ssrn.com/abstract=449263 (accessed August 6, 2008); Selzer, *Mittelalterliche Hanse*, 13–30. A new approach by Sheilagh C. Ogilvie, *Institutions and European Trade: merchant guilds, 1000–1800* (Cambridge: Cambridge University Press, 2011).

of organization of medieval society, which is demonstrated in the early Middle Ages in the rural community, thus was a commercial and urban phenomenon of the 11th century.

However, in the written tradition, the aristocratic and manorial view of the class society predominated. The *Einung* was not sufficiently noted in the written sources, and when it was, only in a devaluated manner. As a result, its actual importance to medieval society, and the role of the individual within it, remained unrecognized for far too long. The *Einung*, which often formed under circumstances of social and political disorganization, was a voluntary alliance of individuals created for mutual aid and based upon the principles of agreement and consensus. This meant that the members (associates) of an *Einung* promised to keep the regulations of their federation. In each case, these regulations had been decided upon by *Willkuer* (voluntary agreement).[77]

In the twelfth century, long distance trade to locations abroad was organized around caravans for land-bound trade and around convoys for sea-bourn trade. During the thirteenth century, this mode of organization continued in the context of regionally variable durations. The uncertainty of highways and roads, highlighted by a constant fear of robbery, compelled merchants—who since Carolingian times had possessed the right to carry a sword—to travel in groups. However, individual merchants still went on long journeys with only a few companions as well. In Northern Europe, such trips are documented in the late ninth century excursions of Ottar, and they are memorialized in the thirteenth century epos of 'Good Gerhard'.[78]

In early Hanse times, however, traveling associations seem to have been the standard. Both enroute and upon their arrival at destinations abroad, these merchant alliances were called *Hansen* throughout Western Europe. In the early middle Ages, the meaning of the term "Hanse" is documented as 'group/crowd' (lat. *cohors*). A second meaning referenced the fee that was collected for participation in joint trading (and which, originally, was most probably a manorial and possibly royal tribute). Finally, the third referred to the right to trade

77 Otto Gerhard Oexle, "Gilde und Kommune. Über die Entstehung von 'Einung' und 'Gemeinde' als Grundformen des Zusammenlebens in Europa," in Peter Blickle, ed., *Theorien kommunaler Ordnung in Europa* (München: Oldenbourg, 1996).

78 Janet Bately and Anton Englert, ed., *Othere's Voyages. A late ninth-century account of voyages along the coasts of Norway and Denmark and its cultural context*, Maritime Culture of the North, vol. 1 (Roskilde: Viking Ship Museum, 2007); Sonja Zöller, *Kaiser, Kaufmann und die Macht des Geldes. Gerhard Unmaze von Köln als Finanzier der Reichspolitik und der "Gute Gerhard" des Rudolf von Ems*, Forschungen zur Geschichte der älteren deutschen Literatur, vol. 16 (München: Fink, 1993).

jointly. Thus, as often is the case in the Middle Ages, personal, legal and occupational characteristics were covered by a single word.[79] In the mid-eleventh century, such a 'Hanse' is documented for the first time, albeit indirectly, within the statutes of the Valencienne merchant guild, whose members were forbidden to trade with a *hanseur* (a foreign and thus traveling merchant). Furthermore, the latter could under no circumstances become members of the guild.[80] This disposition exemplifies the mistrust that traveling foreign merchants faced—especially from their colleagues.

Since Carolingian times, merchants who applied were taken under the protection of kings and equipped with guarantees for safe conduct (protection privileges).[81] Consequently, these merchants answered directly to the king and continued to do so even when the sovereigns, in whose jurisdiction the guild operated, were the ones to obtain the royal safe-conduct. The individual merchant now needed only to apply for admission to the circle of merchants benefiting from the king's protection agreement with the particular guild operating within the respective jurisdiction.

In the twelfth and, especially, the thirteenth century, the *regnum Teutonicum* presided over a period in which, ever more royal rights were ceded to the territorial sovereigns. As a result, royal protection for merchants within the Empire lost importance, but continued to be vital to foreign excursions. Thus, each merchant guild within the Empire, regardless of its origins, which had sought the king's protection, became part of a larger association of the king's, or emperor's, merchants and in turn became known abroad as hominess, or *mercatores imperatoris* ("people" or "merchants of the emperor").[82] Irrespective of economic and/or regional competition, there existed a constitutionally defined union of all German merchants abroad, who were under the king's protection.

Before engaging in an excursion abroad, the members of a guild would have formed a Hanse and elected a *wik*/Hanse earl, who subsequently received a charge for ensuring the protection granted by the king—or in his name by the

79 Ruth Schmidt-Wiegand, "Hanse und Gilde. Genossenschaftliche Organisationsformen im Bereich der Hanse und ihre Bezeichnungen," *Hansische Geschichtsblätter* 100 (1982), 21–40.

80 Hans van Werveke, "Das Wesen der Flandrischen Hanse," *Hansische Geschichtsblätter* 75/76 (1957/58), 7–20, 8f.

81 Regarding the following Ernst Pitz, *Bürgereinung und Städteeinung. Studien zur Verfassungsgeschichte der Hansestädte und der deutschen Hanse*, Quellen und Darstellungen zur hansischen Geschichte; N.F., vol. 52 (Cologne: Böhlau-Verlag, 2001), 246–273.

82 Jahnke, "Homines imperii," 1–8, 53–57.

townleader of the guild. In other words, he was charged with holding the court of merchants, leading the traveling company on excursions abroad and levying fees owed to the king for their protection. No oaths have ever been documented in connection with the early merchant guilds and traveling groups—neither as pledge to the king or town ruler nor as fellowship oaths for members of the merchant guilds and traveling companies. The afore-mentioned *kore*, the right to decide, was also central to the specific rights of traveling merchants (ius mercatorum). In consequence, merchants on trade excursions were able to conduct their own affairs beginning in the early Middle Ages. This form of autonomy was, in turn, acknowledged by the various sovereigns.

The traditions of the twelfth and thirteenth centuries with regard to the constitution of traveling companies, the Hansen (sometimes they are also called 'guilds'), have not been conclusively demonstrated. While sources from the *regnum teutonicum* mention only the traveling companies of individual cities,[83] the Hansen of Flanders possessed the ability to admit outside merchants. However, this admission was sometimes possible only with the payment of exorbitant fees intended to ensure that outside access could be limited. In England, merchants, who met while actively engaged in trade, had been permitted, to organize a Hanse since the 1120's. This organization was, to some extent, based on the hometown guild, which enjoyed royal protection throughout the isles and sovereign territory of the English crown on the continent. The same right also applied to foreigners;[84] this is why merchants from Cologne, Kiel, Hamburg, and Lübeck made contracts with the English king in behalf of their Hanse in the first place.

Delimitation towards foreign merchants (merchants not from their town), even when they haled from a neighboring town within the same region, represented a key characteristic in the history of trade. Therefore, overcoming this competition abroad on a permanent basis became an important accomplishment for Low German Merchants who, perhaps in the late twelfth century and certainly by the thirteenth century, were thus enabled to face their respective treaty partners as a single unit. This alliance was accomplished in various branches (offices, *Kontore*) and countries at various times. For example, beginning at the end of the twelfth century in Novgorod where the alliance

83 Ernst Pitz, "Einstimmigkeit oder Mehrheitsbeschluß? Ein heimlicher Verfassungsstreit um die Vollmachten der Ratssendeboten auf den Hansetagen," in Wilfried Ehbrecht, ed., *Verwaltung und Politik in Städten Mitteleuropas. Beiträge zu Verfassungsnorm und Verfassungswirklichkeit in altständischer Zeit*, Städteforschung A, vol. 34 (Cologne: Böhlau-Verlag, 1994), 115–146, 138f.

84 Klaus Friedland, *Die Hanse* (Stuttgart: Kohlhammer, 1991), 102f.

was forged together with Gothic merchants. During the early thirteenth century, West European merchants also formed similar, although non-permanent alliances. These included the association of *mercatores de XVII villes* including members from Flanders and Northern France (first documented in 1230), which, at the time of their decline, was called the 'Hanse of 17 cities', and the nations of the Italian merchants, who, like the Flemish and French, had also formed a *universitas* at the fairs of Champagne. Sometime around 1200 (documented in 1241), Flemish merchants from 52 cities had formed an umbrella organization in London, the "Hanse of London". However, since the fourteenth century, these organizations were of no further importance.[85] Similar associations comprising fair attendees were supported by sovereigns in Flanders as well as in the regions of the Lower Rhine, and the Ijessel. This support was intended to add greater importance to the trading traffic of the twelfth- and thirteenth-century fairs, which represented advancing markets.[86]

In the Baltic, the traveling companies that sailed from Lübeck to Gotland, and later to Novgorod and Riga, seem to have formed, almost exclusively, abroad at their respective trade destinations on Gotland or in Riga. However, such organization could occur at an important milestone along their way as in the case of those forming during the journey to Novgorod at the mouth of the Neva River. These were the first associations of the early Hanse to consist of merchants gathered from a collection of various individual traveling companies. In response, these merchants and their companies discontinued their competition with each other and thus constituted *universitas mercatorum* in arrangements that differed from town to town though part of the comprehensive *universitas mercatorum*. This is very obvious in the trade treaties of the twelfth and first half of the thirteenth centuries as in the case of the 1229 treaty the Prince of Smolensk concluded with the long distance traders from Riga, Visby, Lübeck, Soest, Munster, Dortmund, and Bremen. This treaty was composed in Riga "in front of the many merchants of the Roman Empire" and confirmed "by the seal of all merchants".[87] The Novgorod Schra (Order of St. Peter's

85 Nicholas, *Flanders*, 166–168; van Werveke, "Flandrische Hanse," 15–17; Kohn, "Merchant Associations," 6–8.

86 Friedland, *Hanse*, 99; Franz Irsigler, "Jahrmärkte und Messesysteme im westlichen Reichsgebiet bis ca. 1250," in Peter Johanek and Heinz Stoob, ed., *Europäische Messen und Märktesysteme in Mittelalter und Neuzeit*, Städteforschung A, vol. 39 (Cologne: Böhlau-Verlag, 1996), 1–33.

87 HUB 1, no. 232.

Court) was composed in the mid-thirteenth century and cites "the wisest of all cities in the German realm" as its authors.[88]

The merchants themselves called the organization, which they formed on Gotland (and which is the best preserved of all) around the middle of the thirteenth century, *universitas mercatorum Romani imperii Gotlandiam frequentantium* (the association of merchants from the Roman Empire visiting Gotland).[89] In this way, they essentially declared that their members were connected, not through local or regional origin, but by virtue of belonging to the Empire and in consequence of their shared trading destination, Gotland, the central gather point for the Eastern trade. This *universitas* included the provision for self-governance and (most likely already in 1229, see above, or at the latest beginning in the mid-thirteenth century) a seal with the above-mentioned text as an inscription. In scientific literature, this federation is called the "Gotländische Genossenschaft" (Gotlandish Union), a term of the scientific art from the nineteenth century, which is undocumented in the sources.

Gutnish and German merchants on Gotland formed the *gilda communis*, which thus also became (or was part of) the *universitas mercatorum*. In 1191/92, this merchant association dispatched an emissary, the Goth Arbud (Herbord), to the Prince of Novgorod for the purpose of finalizing a trade treaty. Ultimately, the prince, as the English king would also eventually do, acknowledged this federation of merchants stemming from various ethnic origins as the recipient of the rights stipulated by the treaty. The formation of a *universitas* was the consistent and legal consequence of a certain trading practice in which Gutnish merchants initially transported their Low German trade partners from Lübeck to Gotland and probably, a bit later, from Gotland to Novgorod. At first, this transportation took place on Gutnish ships, but was later carried out on mixed fleets. Such cooperation was so successful for both parties that it was also extended to the trade with England. This community of Gutnish and Low German merchants lasted more than 100 years and was one of the few 'international' mainstays of early Hanseatic history.

The *gilda commnunis* thus seems to have been a federation of local Gutnish merchants and German guests in Visby enjoying an autonomous jurisdiction. The latter was probably the reason why Bishop Albert of Riga made the 1211 establishment of a *gilda communis* in Riga and in the Duna trade contingent

88 Wolfgang Schlüter, ed., *Die Novgoroder Schra in sieben Fassungen vom XIII. bis XVII. Jahrhundert.* (Lübeck: Lübcke und Nöhring, 1916).

89 Detlef Kattinger, *Die Gotländische Genossenschaft. Der frühhansisch-gotländische Handel in Nord- und Westeuropa*, Quellen und Darstellungen zur hansischen Geschichte, N.F., vol. 47 (Cologne: Böhlau-Verlag, 1999), *passim*; Jahnke, "Homines imperii," 29–47.

upon his personal approval.[90] Naturally, without autonomous control, the guild would not have been able to restrict his own rights as mayor and sovereign.

The manner in which trade dealings were performed in the early Hanseatic era is rarely documented. However, the Low German merchants seem to have been flexible and obviously did not attempt, as an earlier image of the German advance into the Baltic Region suggests, to enforce their own forms of law. Instead, as is documented in Estonia, they conformed to local trading habits.[91] Among other reasons, this was certainly a question of survival, and that probably not merely in the economic sense, so long as their own position was not strong enough to enable them to dictate conditions themselves. In accordance with a virtually document-free system of exchange, union trade conducted by the members of the city guilds is only recorded in some few individual cases. However, from these few cases, one may conclude that early Hanseatic traveling companies, or the individual town traveling companies from which they were comprised, also engaged in collective trading. From the efforts put forth by merchants and cities since the late twelfth century to attain freedom from the joint liability so closely associated with collective trade, one can deduce that this form of trading was common.[92]

Beginning in the mid-thirteenth century, company trading in the form of bilateral Hanse *wedderlegghinge* (refutation) is well documented; its origins more than likely stretching back to the tenth century. The term *wedderlegghinge* expresses the apparently archaic founding action for the company, or pooling of capital. One can just imagine two merchants standing across the table from one another and pushing two piles of money together to form the collective capital for the company. The essential characteristics of such a company were shaped during a mainly document-free time period as can witnessed in the simple proportions of 1:1 and 1:2 employed for the deposit of capital. This capital was managed only by one of the two partners involved and this partner was usually the one with the smaller deposit. This partner consequently conducted trade excursions, but likely did so without the obligation to follow special instructions, and this in spite of the tendency of sources to sometimes refer to this partner as a page or serf subservient to the other, who was called the lord. The profits were often shared, which may not be under-

90 HUB 1, No. 88.

91 Blomkvist, *Discovery*, 505, 519f.

92 Rolf Sprandel, "Die Interferenz von Gesellschaften und Genossenschaften im hansischen Handel," in Nils Jörn, Detlef Kattinger and Horst Wernicke, ed., *Genossenschaftliche Strukturen in der Hanse*, Quellen und Darstellungen zur hansischen Geschichte, N.F., vol. 48 (Cologne: Böhlau-Verlag, 1999), 79–100.

stood as a form of pay-off in those cases in which there were different deposits. Meanwhile, there was no uniform practice for the division of the losses. In the mid-twelfth century, merchants were already used to taking the goods or the money of a colleague on a trading excursion (the colleague did not take part in the excursion), but whether they took these as a form of company trade or in connection with a commission business cannot be conclusively demonstrated from the city charter of Medebach.[93]

Staring in 1230, trading companies of Lübeck citizens and foreign merchants are finally, although indirectly, mentioned in the oldest customs registry for the City of Lübeck.[94] A similar form of joint trading, in which one partner functioned exclusively as a 'silent partner' so to speak, is found in old Nordic sources dating from the tenth century. The pooling of goods, known as *felag*, was a very common institution and is documented in runic inscriptions as well as in the literature of thc sagas. In one type of *felag*, fellow traders embarked on trading excursions together, while in the other, only one of the partners traveled and then conducted the business alone. In Scandinavia, the intensive development of merchants' law in the twelfth and thirteenth centuries gives one reason to believe that these forms of trading and incorporation were the result of an independent development and were not adopted by the North from Mediterranean practices.[95]

The economic success of the early Hanse merchants was therefore achieved with decidedly and legally basic forms of trade as well as with the trade of unions, company trade in the form of refutation, and commission and private trade (proper trade). These forms were common in Northern Europe and, therefore, cannot have been the reason for the shear impact of early merchants from the (later) Hanse. The actual key to success probably had more to do with the exclusion of internal competition and unified action in the targeted areas located within their trading territory. The most important effects of this unified action were three. First, the merchants were able, jointly and without competition, to purchase sizable amounts of goods to meet large demands

93 Albrecht Cordes, *Spätmittelalterlicher Gesellschaftshandel im Hanseraum*, Quellen und Darstellungen zur hansischen Geschichte, N.F., vol. 45 (Cologne: Böhlau-Verlag, 1998), 58–64.

94 UBStL 1, No. 32, p. 38.

95 Carsten Müller-Boysen "félagi, mötunautr, háseti und gildbrothær. Die Spuren genossenschaftlicher Organisationsformen unter Kaufleuten im frühmittelalterlichen Skandinavien," in Nils Jörn, Detlef Kattinger and Horst Wernicke, ed., *Genossenschaftliche Strukturen in der Hanse*, Quellen und Darstellungen zur hansischen Geschichte, N.F., vol. 48 (Cologne.: Böhlau-Verlag, 1999), 13–26, 15–19.

within their vast hinterland. The merchant's biggest advantage was the connection between the land and sea-borne trades, which, for the domestic merchants of the early Hanse and for the seafaring merchants of the Baltic, directly linked both the purchasing and selling regions. Due to the amounts of trade goods exchanged, they soon became indispensable to the economy of the respective target countries and their rulers. During the thirteenth century, the merchants and cities of the early Hanse developed the connection between land and sea-borne trade into a superior logistical advantage, in which infra structure provided by the cities and merchant associations, including port facilities, shipping yards, storage locations, and displays for goods, played the pivotal role. In those times (as today), means and routes of transportation, as well as storage facilities, were deciding criteria in the expansion of markets. Quite important was the cog, which in earlier historiography had been considered to be the central innovation of the Hanse merchants. Aside from the first documented cogs of the Baltic, all of them coming from South Jutland, the cog was not an especially large, fast, or durable ship; Scandinavian ships were more efficient by far. And yet the cog was a completely economical form of transportation. It could be built with reasonable effort (for example, with sawn over hewn planks), it could be steered across the North and Baltic Seas with relative security, and it could be hard for pirates to grapple with because of its high sides.[96]

Despite these advantages, it was not the cog that aided the Hanse merchants in attaining their ultimate success, but their own economic superiority. Second, the strength of the position held by the merchants of the early Hanse enabled them to gain extensive privileges, which, above all, contained legal protections and custom discounts, or waivers and ensured a relatively autonomous position (which during the early thirteenth century applied initially only to Novgorod and in part to the Guildhall in London) for their branches (offices, *Kontore*). This relatively autonomous position was a key difference between this and other kinds of trade branches, such as the Fondaco dei Tedesci of

96 Ole Crumlin-Pedersen, "Die Bremer Kogge—ein Schlüssel zur Geschichte des Schiffbaus im Mittelalter," in Gabriele Hoffmann and Uwe Schnall, ed., *Die Kogge. Sternstunde der deutschen Schifffsarchäologie*, Schriften des Deutschen Schiffahrtsmuseums vol. 60, (Hamburg: Convent-Verlag, 2003), 256–270; Christian Radtke, "Die Kogge," in Heinrich Mehl, ed., *Historische Schiffe in Schleswig-Holstein. Vom Nydamboot zur Gorch Fock* (Heide: Westholsteinische Verlagsanstalt Boyens, 2002), 38–50. An intensive debate is taking place between Paulsen, "Koggendiskussion", Ellmers, "Koggen kontrovers", Jahnke, "Kein Ende", Ellmers, "Kogge und Holk."

Venice, which served as a control for foreign merchants.[97] Within their own jurisdiction, Low German merchants had the right to pronounce and enforce punishments. They were independent of the respective mayors, except for cases involving conflicts between (early) Hanse merchants and townspeople.

Third, an interest common to the cities from which the merchants came arose from the organizational form of legal unions in the *gemene kopman* of the foreign offices. This common interest facilitated the development of a union of Hanse cities, also from the communities of the *gemene kopman* of the foreign branches. After all, the merchant guilds of the individual towns were as much a part of the *gemene kopman* of the foreign branches as their comrades were members of the urban merchant guilds, which, in turn, were a part of the municipality of the respective hometowns. One can see how closely the merchants and cities were interwoven from the fact that trading treaties (privileges), originally negotiated by merchants in the branches abroad, formed the basis of trade for the entire alliance well into the sixteenth century.

'Commercial Revolution' and the Position of Long Distance Traders on the Council

The economic, social and urban pre-requisites for the increasingly closer connection between the merchants' traveling companies and the cities are depicted in this chapter. Their political history follows.

With regards to economic history, the thirteenth century bore 'commercial revolution' as a theme. The term 'commercial revolution' was coined to describe the fundamental changes to the trading organization of the Italian merchants that had taken place since the twelfth century. The long distance traders no longer traveled to the trade fairs; instead, they conducted their business from the offices in their hometowns. They sent out factors to the buying and selling places, which in turn settled there and conducted the business of their senior in situ on location. This system enabled the senior partner to be

97 Angelo Pichierri, *Die Hanse—Staat der Städte. Ein ökonomisches und politisches Modell der Städtevernetzung*, Stadt, Raum und Gesellschaft, vol. 10 (Opladen: Leske & Budrich 2000), 82; Anna Leonidovna Choroškevič, "Der deutsche Hof in Novgorod und die deutsche Herberge (Fondaco dei Tedeschi) in Venedig im 13. / 14. Jahrhundert. Eine vergleichende Vorstudie" in Ortwin Pelc and Gertrud Pickhan, eds., *Zwischen Lübeck und Novgorod. Wirtschaft, Politik und Kultur im Ostseeraum vom frühen Mittelalter bis ins 20. Jahrhundert. Norbert Angermann zum 60. Geburtstag* (Lüneburg: Nordostdeutsches Kulturwerk, 1996), 67–87.

simultaneously 'present' in several places at once, thus increasing his volume of trade. Because this kind of trade required more money than before (in Italy the trading of goods and money was combined), and as a result of the introduction of documents for credit, new dimensions of trade became possible. From the end of the thirteenth century, these new dimensions of trade were known and learned by the Low German merchants attending the fairs of Champagne. As a result, a division of labor occurred, which, in turn, divided the traditional career of the traveling merchant into three professional fields: (1) the settled merchant concerned with financing and the organization of his wholesale and long distance trade; (2) the carriers, land carters, and skippers who delivered the merchants' goods to the desired location, and (3) the factor, or associate of the trading company, who resided abroad.[98]

However, one did not operate through resident factors within the Hanse's region, rather one appointed a representative or junior (younger) trade partner for each individual trade excursion. This development in the Low German region seems to have occurred over an extended period of time, which began, at the latest, in the twelfth century. This is proved in the city charter for the tiny Westphalian town of Medebach (dated to the mid-twelfth century), which mentions the practice of entrusting another merchant with a trip 'to Denmark or to Russia' with one's own goods or buying money.

The transition from traveling merchant to resident merchant also had a social aspect rooted in the individual choice of lifestyle. Obviously, the succession of various trade forms had already taken the course that follows long before the thirteenth century: to begin with, a young traveling merchant would extend his business, eventually trading with areas where he could not be present himself, and then, later, would completely settle down and dispense with seafaring altogether. The life of a landowner possessing private means would have been the next logical step.[99] In this regard, it was probably not older merchants settling down, a practice which must already have existed in the eleventh and twelfth centuries, but rather the greater number of individuals choosing this profession in the thirteenth century and the correspondingly enormous economic potential of expansion for these individuals, which led to

98 Peter Spufford, *Power and Profit. The Merchant in Medieval Europe* (London. Thames & Hudson, 2002), 19. For a new approach on the political impacts which led to the commercial revolution which differs from Raymond de Roovers theory see Edwin Hunt and James Murray, *The History of Business in Medieval Europe 1200–1550* (Cambridge: Cambridge University Press, 1999), 55–57.

99 Gerhard Rösch, "Zur Bildung des Kaufmanns und Seefahrers in Nordeuropa. Zwei Texte des 13. Jahrhunderts," *Hansische Geschichtsblätter* 110 (1992), 17–41, 38f.

the increasing rank of councilmen, who were also long distance traders in the Hanse region.

Therefore, during the thirteenth century, apart from long distance traders, members of the urban elite came from families who, in part, had had, as members of the social group of *ministeriales* (Dienstleute des Stadtherrn im "gehobenen" Dienst), experience with territorial administration for two or more generations, but had also had experience in representing their own personal interests in the presence of their respective town lords. The financial possibilities that likely lay open to individual members of these elite groups were by far greater than what historians had assumed only a few decades ago.[100] Arnold Fitz Thetmar, operating in London, was known as the first chronicler of London. His strong hereditary roots to the German trading centers (his father had been from Bremen and his mother from Cologne) make it seem natural that from 1251 on, he served as alderman of the German merchants traveling to England. Presumably, it was he who provided substantial support to Richard of Cornwall in his campaign to capture the crown and title of King of the Romans. In gratitude of this support, Bremen and Cologne, the hometowns of his parents, received special and improved privileges for their dealings in England.[101]

Until the end of the fourteenth century, social origin and wealth were the decisive criteria for the social acceptance of urban elites into the nobility. After all, in the twelfth and thirteenth centuries, a number of those employed in the business of long distance trading had themselves originated from the very social groups responsible, during the same period, for the emergence of the lower nobility of the country. In fact, contemporary sources began to describe knighthood and urban citizenship as being dissimilar in rank only near the end of the fourteenth century.[102] The significant constitutional status, which Lübeck had held as a free town since 1226, may have been possible, in large part, due to the quality of rank maintained by its elites.

Returning to the subject of council membership for merchants, it is clear that their numbers on the council depended on the economic structure for

100 Wolfgang von Stromer summarizes: "Hochfinanz, Wirtschaft und Politik im Mittelalter," in Friedhelm Burgard, Alfred Haverkamp, Franz Irsigler and Winfried Reichert, eds., *Hochfinanz im Westen des Reiches 1150–1500*, Trierer Historische Forschungen, vol. 31 (Trier: Trierer Historische Forschungen, 1996), 1–16, 8–13.

101 Natalie Fryde, "Arnold Fitz Thedmar und die Entstehung der Großen Deutschen Hanse," *Hansische Geschichtsblätter* 107 (1989), 27–42.

102 Hammel-Kiesow, "Neue Aspekte," 67–73; Kurt Andermann and Peter Johanek, eds., *Zwischen Nicht-Adel und Adel*, Vorträge und Forschungen, vol. 53 (Stuttgart: Thorbecke 2001).

the respective city. As a roughly drawn rule, one can safely assume that the councils of cities located on a seaboard were dominated by the merchants of the long distance trade. Meanwhile, one can also assume that in inland cities, where trades in handicrafts possessed a greater economic importance, there would be a more pronounced participation on the councils by the craftsmen. However, in reality, a great many guildsmen (even when the sources could only list them as such) were of higher status than the merchants. During the constitutional wars of the late thirteenth century (e.g. Erfurt 1283, Braunschweig 1292/94), council participation by the tradesmen was a reality in many inland cities. Yet, in other cities, long distance traders were successful in excluding the representatives of elite groups with competing interests from the council: in Goslar the lower nobility, in Magdeburg the Episcopal ministerials, in Hamburg the land-owning families, and in Lübeck the landowners of similar rank.

From Princely to Municipal Protection of Merchants

As previously noted, major political powers in the Baltic Region continually attempted to control the most essential elements of the profitable East-West trade, namely the sea routes and the ports. So far, in tracing the succession of these powers within the region since the early twelfth century, one must note the following developments: First, the initial formation of western Slavic states, including indications for the formation of a 'Slavic Hanse'; second, the reign of Knut Lavard, who connected the western and eastern Baltic regions (facilitated by his marriage to a princess of Novgorod); third, the ascension of Lothar III, whose continued expansion in the region was likely only impeded by his death. About 20 years after Lothar's death, his grandson, Henry the Lion, became the protector of the Low German merchants. And while he did not found Lübeck or select the city's economically advantageous location, he did support the Low German merchants of his realm by means of both his power and his reputation. Beyond the aforementioned dispatch of an emissary to the northern lands for the purpose of negotiating the peace treaty of Artlenburg between the Goths and Germans (Artlenburg Treaty), Henry concluded treaties with Sweden, and possibly Novgorod. Under his protection, the merchants traded and expanded their trade areas while negotiating the treaties he as ruler had concluded. In short, it was a typical relationship for the era: the ruler utilizing his position of power and authority to provide protection to the long distance merchants of his realm.

After the deposition of Duke Henry in 1180/81, the position of Low German merchants in the Baltic was significantly weakened due to their extreme distance from the Emperor. Thus it seems rather paradoxical that the first truly spectacular progress in the Baltic advance of the Low German merchants should have been documented in written sources only after the dethronement of Henry the Lion. To demonstrate: Around 1180, they settled in Visby only to advance to the Duna Delta soon thereafter and by 1191, had finally obtained their own court in Novgorod.[103] With the annexation of North Elbia into his empire, Knut VI of Denmark had succeeded in building up a Danish superpower, which, under his brother and successor, Waldemar II, finally began to extend beyond Denmark (including Schleswig) beginning in 1219.

This expansion proceeded from Denmark, via Hamburg and Lübeck along the south Baltic coast from 1219 to Sambia and Estonia (including the islands of Dago and Oesel), and, on the opposite shore, included Oeland as well as the provinces of Blekinge, Skane, and Halland, which are now located in the southern portion of modern-day Sweden.[104] In the time of the *pax Waldemariana*, the Low German merchants of the southwest Baltic coast, and especially those of Lübeck whose city was under the direct governance of Waldemar II himself (Waldemar had confirmed all of Lübeck's privileges), were able to expand their trade connections in peace upon the now tranquil Baltic Sea.[105] Naturally, they also did so under a guarantee of royal protection. During this period, the eventual Hanse cities of the south Baltic coast, almost all of which lay within Waldemar's Baltic empire, each received their city charters. These included charters for cities such as Rostock and Wismar, whose charters were granted by the lords of Mecklenburg in the years 1218 and 1228 respectively, and Danzig and Stralsund, which received their charters in about 1224 and 1234. In addition, new offices/branches of German merchants were established or sprang up besides existing trading settlements, as, for example, were the case in Stettin.

This arrangement continued without conflict until 1220 when Waldemar attempted to force the submission of Livonia and in the process threatened the interests of the merchants and the Bishop of Riga. Ultimately, the era of

103 Blomkvist rightfully points to this, *Discovery*, 700.

104 N.G. Heine, "Valdemar II.s Udenrigspolitik. Kampen am Østersøvaeldet," in *Østersøproblemer omkring 1200*, Humanistiske Studier II. Instituts arbejder fra Aarhus Universitet (Aarhus: Universitetsforlaget Munksgaard, 1941), 9–85.

105 Additionally as members oft he Danish realm the Lübeck merchants benefited from the Danish privileges in England; see Jahnke, "Homines imperii," 13–18.

princely protection for the Low German merchants came to an end with the termination of Waldemar's rule of North Elbia (1223) and of the south Baltic coast (1227). As a result, Lübeck became a free Imperial City, and all of the cities had to handle the essential elements of the princely protectorate on their own. The development of the latter was inevitable, for none of the north German princes had sufficient power to administer the region and the Emperor was too far away to bear any significant influence upon the North (a condition which only deteriorated with the imperial struggle against the pontificate which intensified beginning in 1239). At that point, those Low German cities not within the dominion of the Danish Kings, which had constantly faced uncertain times ever since the dethronement of Henry the Lion in 1180/81, had now far more to administer, with what were, at the time, still largely insufficient municipal resources.[106]

However, the mission to Livonia had brought the merchants of the early Hanse, and especially the city of Lübeck, a powerful new ally: the Pope. In principle, the mission to Livonia was, at that time, in a state of tension between the archbishopric of Lund, which in the early 1170s had presented the Pope with the initial plans for the proselytizing of Estonia, and the archbishopric of Hamburg-Bremen, which had been active in Livonia since the 1180s when the missionary Meinhard had arrived at the Duna Delta aboard the ships of the Low German merchants (it was at the Duna Delta that the Bishopric of Riga was founded in 1201). For the crusaders who were to protect the Bishopric of Riga and then spread the Christian faith from it, Lübeck was the main port for the reception of supplies. Thus it was that the city attracted the political attention of papacy and subsequently became factored into their official policy for the Baltic region.[107] It was in this context that Pope Gregor IX forced King Waldemar II of Denmark to lift his blockade on the port of Lübeck in 1234. To accomplish this, Gregor threatened to grant the Livonian bound crusaders, who had already assembled in and, in turn, been prevented from leaving Lübeck by Waldemar's blockade, permission to forcefully end the blockade with military power, which meant war against a Christian king.[108] Good relations between the city council of Lübeck and the Curia, though at times fraught

---

106 Stuart Jenks, "Die Welfen, Lübeck und die werdende Hanse," in *Die Welfen und ihr Braunschweiger Hof im hohen Mittelalter*, ed. Bernd Schneidmüller (Wiesbaden: Harrassowitz-Verlag, 1995), 483–522, 491f.

107 Fonnesberg-Schmidt, *The Popes*; Rainer Herrmann, "Lübeck und die Päpste (1201–1267)," *ZVLGA* 75 (1995) 9–52.

108 *Diplomatarium Danicum*, ed. Niels Skyum-Nielsen et al., København, 1/6, No. 183; Carsten Selch Jensen, "Urban Life and the Crusades in North Germany and the Baltic Lands in the

with problems, eventually led to a situation beginning in 1254, in which Lübeck received regular papal guarantees of its imperial privileges following the termination of imperial protection.[109]

A New Era: The Beginning for the Cities

In the late 1220s a new era featuring the cities as the protectors of the merchants began. To some extent, this era also marked the beginning of the Hanse as an urban organization. However, it would be a few more years until this fact would be documented and thus, visible for posterity. This development had already begun in the time of the traveling merchant companies, which, at that point, succinctly demonstrated their capabilities with the Treaty of Smolensk in 1229. All in all, the municipal protection of merchants and the political actions of the merchant traveling companies occurred simultaneously and served to complement each other.

When the protection of the sovereign ceased, the merchants and the cities developed various strategies (depending on time and location) in order to obtain trading privileges (charters and privileges) abroad.[110] These trading privileges/charters can be divided into three groups. First, there were those privileges jointly obtained by representatives of the *gemene kopman*. Second, there were those that had come about through the initiative of Lübeck and which applied to all Low German merchants. And finally, there were those of individual towns, which, while possibly becoming a fourth group designation, often provided an incentive for other cities to obtain the same, or at least similar, privileges.

These 'foreign treaties' were complemented by the treaties concluded between cities within the Empire; these inter-city treaties served to create an environment of political cooperation, especially when it came to the security of highways and the realization of mutual legal claims. The conclusion of such treaties also makes apparent the close cooperation of the merchants and the urban councilmen; and one may assume that members of the urban elite filled leading positions with long distance traders. In fact, and in spite of the absence of definitive proof from the sources, the aldermen of the merchant unions may have been recruited from members of the urban elite as well.

Early Thirteenth Century," in Alan V. Murray, ed., *Crusade and Conversion on the Baltic Frontier 1150–1500* (Aldershot et al.: Ashgate, 2001), 75–94, 82f.

109 Herrmann, "Lübeck," 44–52.

110 For the following see Jenks, "Welfen," 507–522.

From the privileges jointly obtained by the merchants, one can conclude that the people of Lübeck were continually advancing into the foreground of privileged Hanse cities. In treaties concluded until the mid-thirteenth century, Lübeck and her citizens were only mentioned next to the representatives of the other cities, and never first (1229 Smolensk and 1237 England). Beginning in the second half of the century, Lübeck almost always appeared at the top of such lists (1252 Sweden, 1259/60 and 1269 Novgorod).[111]

When it came to the second category of charters, those that applied to all merchants and which had come about due to Lübeck's initiative, the city of Lübeck served as the acting institution. In contrast to the privileges of the first group of charters, these did not serve local trade traffic within the foreign branches, but primarily served to secure and pacify the routes bound for foreign trading places as well as to reduce or waive the customs on these routes. Such charters occur until the late thirteenth century, and were, for the most part concluded with persons of a clerical rank (Archbishop of Livonia, Estonia and Prussia, the Bishops of Courland and Oesel, the Livonian master of the order, Cardinal, priest and Legate Guido, and many others) and primarily served to secure the sea route to Riga and Novgorod.[112]

The possible fourth group, after the individual city charters, comprised the so-called 'privileges by union' or 'unified privileges.' Almost everywhere, Lübeck was the first of the future Hanseatic Cities to obtain certain privileges for their own merchants, and this when considering the entire trading region of the Hanse: a region that included Scandinavia and the area along the entire East-West route from Livonia via Pomerania and Mecklenburg to England, Holland and Brabant. The desire of other cities to obtain identical rights resulted in a new phenomenon: privileges by union. In fact, the (granted) privileges of this group began with King Erich IV's transference of rights from the merchants of Cologne to the merchants of Soest (in Denmark) in 1232, but it is interesting that, in 17 of 23 subsequent charters issued from that time until 1298, Lübeck was listed as the first transferee.[113]

The mid-thirteenth century privileges of Flanders present a special case. These privileges were negotiated by a town councilman of Lübeck named

111 Antjekathrin Graßmann, Rolf Hammel-Kiesow, "Lübeck," in *Lexikon des Mittelalters*, vol. 5 (München et al.: Artemis, 1991), 2146–2150.

112 HUB 1, No. 243 (1232) until *Urkundenbuch der Stadt Lübeck*, ed. Verein für Lübeckische Geschichte, vol. I (Osnabrück: H. Th. Wenner, 1976; New printing of the 1843 edition) [in the following: UBStL I], No. 637 (1295); Jenks, "Welfen," 515f.

113 Jenks, "Welfen," Appendix 1, 521f; in two cases, Lübeck, together with the *ceteri civitatis Sclavie et maritime*, the Wendish cities, acquired the first charter.

Hermann Hoyer, who was later joined by in the negotiations by Jordan Boizenburg of Hamburg. Both were *nuncii speciales* and endowed with charters from several cities (Cologne, Dortmund, Soest, Munster, Aachen [which did not become a member of the eventual Hanseatic League]) authorizing the use of full executive powers for the negotiations. However, they eventually obtained privileges, which applied to all merchants within the Empire (*mercatores imperii*). Therefore it was, about the middle of the thirteenth century, that the cities in the developed portions of Western Europe had taken the place of merchant unions with special emissaries, who were accredited by the city to negotiate contracts with the Princes of the East (i.e. Novgorod). These emissaries would operate for approximately another 100 years.

However, the privileges of Flanders were ultimately the result of a defeat in trade politics on the part of the early Hanse's town emissaries. Their original objective had been to found a Low German merchant town, which they would call New-Damme, near Bruges. This was planned in order to expand the policy of city founding, which was so successful in the Baltic Region and, simultaneously, so dependent upon the demands of long distance trade, to the West. New-Damme was to serve as an emporium in the West with the transit trade being forbidden to residents. In this way, its function would be similar to Lübeck (East-West transshipment) and Visby (transshipment to the east of the Baltic) and adhere to a similar agenda for the practice of transshipment.[114] But, the project failed about the same time that an additional attempt to jointly found a city in Sambia with the aid of the German Order had failed. That city was to have been established in accordance with the Law of Riga, which was, more or less, akin to being established in accordance with merchant law. Presumably, the elite of the early Hanse concluded from the two cases, that the foundation of cities in accordance with general merchant laws would not have been any more feasible particularly in territorially well-organized areas. Moreover, around the middle of the thirteenth century, all of the potential localities available for the development of new cities had already been taken: Konigsberg was founded in 1255 as the last of more significant (later) Hanse cities.

Simultaneous to the era of gaining shared privileges abroad by means of the above-mentioned initiators, the Low German cities concluded numerous treaties that primarily constituted agreements between cities. On the one hand, this was done in order to ensure the greatest possible safety for merchants engaged

114 Klaus Friedland, *Die Hanse*, Urban-Taschenbücher, vol. 409 (Stuttgart et al.: Kohlhammer, 1991), 123f.; Klaus Friedland, "Die Kaufmannsstadt," in Eckhard Müller-Mertens and Heidelore Böcker, ed., *Konzeptionelle Ansätze der Hanse-Historiographie*, Hansische Studien XIV (Trier: Porta Alba Verlag, 2003), 141–154.

in travels upon the land or the sea. Such treaties often included the noble sovereigns. On the other hand, they were intended to create common municipal laws in the spirit of a continuing development of the old merchant right. Originally, there were bilateral agreements, as, for example, those sealed between Lübeck and Hamburg in 1241 or between Munster and Osnabruck. These bilateral agreements were soon complemented or completely replaced by regional groups. For example, the agreements between Munter and Osnabruck were replaced in 1246 upon the conclusion of the Alliance of Ladbergen. This alliance included a regional group comprising the Westphalian cities of Munster, Osnabruck, Minden, Coesfeld and Herford. Another such group was created by the City Alliance of Werne in 1253 and included Dortmund, Soest, Munster and Lippstadt.[115] In Lower Saxony, Munden and Northeim also came together to form a treaty in 1246, which became, as it were, the first precursor of the Lower Saxon Alliance of Cities. This alliance would come to include up to 15 cities under the leadership of Braunschweig.[116] In these covenants and treaties, one can recognize for the first time, the particular regions, which constituted the Hanse. These regions included cities in the Zuijdersee, Westphalian, Lower Saxon, Wendish, Prussian and Livonian areas. However, throughout the Hanse, regional and individual municipal interests were far older than the Hanse itself and as a result often super-ceded certain specific interests of the Hanse. It was, therefore, often a difficult process, which initially led to joint trading within the individual regions and, eventually, supra-regionally.

Due to their competition with one another, the Wendish cities had a particularly difficult time coming together. The subsequent core group of the Hanse, including Lübeck and Hamburg, had worked closely together since 1241,[117] but only in 1259 did the Baltic cities of Lübeck, Wismar and Rostock conclude a treaty for the protection of seafaring, which in 1265 was extended to include, among other things, the decision to council together annually about common affairs. Stralsund, which was besieged and partially destroyed by Lübeck in

115 Eva-Marie Distler, *Städtebünde im deutschen Spätmittelalter. Eine rechtshistorische Untersuchung zu Begriff, Verfassung und Funktion* [Studien zur europäischen Rechtsgeschichte; vol. 207] (Frankfurt/Main: Vittorio Klostermann 2006).

116 Johannes Schildhauer and Konrad Fritze and Walter Stark, *Die Hanse* (Berlin: VEB Deutscher Verlag der Wissenschaften 1974), 76f; Matthias Puhle, "Der sächsische Städtebund und die Hanse im späten Mittelalter", in *Hansische Geschichtsblätter* 104 (1986), 21–34, 21f.

117 Not 1230! See further Klaus Wriedt, "Die ältesten Vereinbarungen zwischen Hamburg und Lübeck," in *Civitatum communitas. Studien zum europäischen Städtewesen. Festschrift Heinz Stoob zum 65. Geburtstag*, ed. Helmut Jäger et al., Städteforschung A/21 (Cologne: Böhlau, 1984), 756–764; Jenks, "Welfen," 507–513.

1249, most probably because of their competition for the herring grounds near Rugen, and Greifswald only joined this union of cities in 1281 and only after Greifswald had mediated in the dispute between Lübeck and Stralsund.[118]

Therefore, one may not overestimate the effectiveness of these treaties. They were agreements to bear both military and financial burdens jointly. And yet, the most concrete problems associated with cooperating in order to restore the order of peace remained unsolved. Each city had to personally ensure that the land and sea routes would be free of robbers and pirates.[119]

However, the aforementioned treaties do document the dynamics with which the cities had to contend in their struggle against "peaceless" conditions. These dynamics soon caused the cities to abandon the regional setting for their original treaties. In 1280, Lübeck and the German municipality of Visby sealed a treaty, which Riga also joined in 1282, for the protection of trade traffic "between the Oeresund and Novgorod, or across the entire Baltic and in all of its ports".[120] Thus, the sea routes most central to the Baltic Region, which had previously been controlled by the kings of Denmark and Sweden, as well as the rulers of the Russian principalities, were, for the first time, placed under municipal protection and control; and even though there would be another setback during the early fourteenth century, this development and the process associated with it was a promising prospect.

In some cases, strategies for securing land and sea routes were carried out in cooperation with princes and noblemen. In the year 1283, the Treaty of Rostock, which was concluded for the purpose of upholding the peace on land and sea, numbered, among others included in the treaty, the Dukes of Saxony and Pomerania, the Prince of Rugen, the Lords of Mecklenburg and eight named Wendish cities (low German cities situated on the southwestern Baltic coast where historically Wends—Slavonic people lived) that were also joined by Hamburg, Kiel and Stettin.[121] In one case, the leader of the alliance, the Duke of Saxony, intervened with the King of England on behalf of the seaside towns engaged in a dispute with the Norwegian king and attempted to include England itself in the trade blockade against Norway.[122] Meanwhile,

118 Rolf Hammel-Kiesow, "Wismar und die Hanse—Der Dreistädtevertrag von 1259," in Kathrin Orth and Eberhard Kliem, eds., *Jahrbuch 2011 der Deutschen Gesellschaft für Schiffahrts- und Marinegeschichte e. V.*, 14. Jg., 2011 (Wismar: Isensee-Verlag Oldenburg 2011), 24–36.

119 Mohrmann, *Landfriede*, 35–38.

120 HUB 1, No. 863, 906.

121 HUB 1, No. 917 and 954; Mohrmann, *Landfriede*, 50–84.

122 HUB 1, No. 967.

the seaside towns had already been able to obtain just such a pledge from the King of Denmark.[123] Thus, with the treaty of the Wendish cities (1280s), we are already encountering within the eastern region of the Hanse a treaty of peace and security, which included both princes and rulers and served as the basis for an active policy of blockade against Norway intended for the realization of their economic interests. These economic interests also drew Denmark into the alliance (and tried to do so with England).[124] The Treaty of Rostock concluded for peace on land and at sea, already exhibited structural characteristics similar to those common in the Confederation of Cologne during the period from 1367–1385. These structural characteristics included the (later) Hanse cities as central to the treaty, close connections and arrangements with both princes and noblemen, and joint sanctions carried out by the members to enforce their political trade goals.

More than a decade before, the cities and merchants in the Eastern Hanseatic trade region, as they had in the West, had begun to rally together for joint actions intended to enforce their various trade interests. In 1268 and 1277/78 they declared trade blockades against Novgorod,[125] and in the 1280's they, together with the Spaniards, realized their interests against the City of Bruges by removing the emporium to Aardenburg (1280–1282) until the privileges they desired had been affirmed.[126] In 1284, the aforementioned blockade of Norway occurred and in conjunction with it, the first case of 'Hansification' (Verhansung) when Bremen merchants were prohibited from further trade with the seaside towns.[127] Letters from Kampen and Zwolle delivered to Lübeck in the year 1294 attest to the fact that trade competitors, such as the Frisians and the Flemish, were prevented, presumably by force, from trading in the Baltic Region, while Gotlandish merchants were barred from trading in the Western Sea (i.e.—the North Sea).[128] Furthermore, in 1282, the individual town Hanses of merchants from Cologne, or the Rhineland, Lübeck and Hamburg, had formed a *Hanse Alman(ie)* in London. Presumably, this was more a response to the pressure from the London city government and the English king than an act of voluntary accord. However, the rivaling groups of

123 HUB 1, No. 956.
124 HUB 1, No. 954.
125 HUB 1, No. 655, 656, 816.
126 HR I, 1, No. 12–27, 8–15.
127 HR I, 1, 16f., no. 34, 20f.
128 HUB 1, no. 1154, 1155.

German merchants in London merely formed a union; a complete fusion only came about during the fifteenth century.[129]

A few years later, the resolution of the cities already features those characteristics so typical of the institutionalized federation of the *stede van der dudeschen hense*. A 1305 invitation from Lübeck to Osnabruck contained precisely those three statements, which, since the late fourteenth century, had always had to appear within a letter of invitation Hanseatic Diets (contemporarily called *tagfahrten*). This enabled *vulmechtig* [authorized] emissaries of the urban council to participate in the deliberations. These statements addressed: 1. the affair(s) to be decided on the *tagfahrte*, 2. the date for the *tagfahrte*, and 3. the call to send authorized emissaries to the rendezvous.[130] In other words, from the turn of the thirteenth to the fourteenth centuries, the Hanse cities had already achieved a degree of organization comparable to that achieved following the consolidation of the organizational structure into *steden van der dudeschen hense*.

In light of the successful joint trade conducted by the cities, Lübeck was victorious in the feud it had had with Visby regarding the predominance of the *gemenen stede* within the alliance during the last decade of the thirteenth century. Visby styled itself the representative for the *gemene kopman*, whose headquarters were in their city and whose rights the city defended (*ius illud quod* [...] *a mercatoribus in Godlandia observatur*; the law, which is applied by the merchants of Gotland). Lübeck, on the other hand, viewed itself as speaker for the town councils (city governments) of those Low German cities whose merchants participated in the joint foreign trade of the *gemenen kopmans*. In the 1290s, the city council of Lübeck tried to eliminate Visby from the competition for dominance over the union of the *gemenen stede* in the Baltic Region. They did so by trying move the high court (appellate court), designed for travelers journeying along the way from Visby to Novgorod, to Lübeck (1293–95) and by successfully abolishing the seal of the common merchants of Gotland (1299).

In one case, which already shows the typical characteristics of traditional decision-making, which were more heavily documented starting with the second half of the fourteenth century, cities interested in the trade with Novgorod, were asked by representatives of the Wendish cities to give their consent to the relocation of Novgorod's trade court jurisdiction from Visby to Lübeck.

---

129 Dollinger, *Hanse*, 61f; Nils Jörn, "With money and bloode," *Der Londoner Stalhof im Spannungsfeld der englisch-hansischen Beziehungen im 15. und 16. Jahrhundert*. Quellen und Darstellungen zur hansischen Geschichte, N.F., vol. 50 (Cologne: Böhlau 2000).

130 HR I, 1, no. 82, 43f.

Lübeck argued that this corresponded with the reinstitution of the old law. Only a few cities (Riga and Osnabruck are known) ever refused their consent to this action by the Wendish cities. Those that did, raised the issue that at the Court of Novgorod, those *libertates* had always been effective that had been kept by the 'common merchant' of Gotland for the longest time.[131] Lübeck did not succeed. In the 14th century the appellate court took place by annual turns in Visby and Lübeck, a classic compromise.

The prohibition on the further use of the common merchant's seal is even more revealing of the stance taken against Visby. The city is not addressed by name, but the decision clearly stated that the seal of the common merchants was never to be used again on Gotland. This prohibition was justified by the rational that other cities did not have this chance, and by the consideration that each city had its own seal with which to affix its stamp upon the affairs of its merchants.[132] This withdrawal of a centralized legal means for authentication within a particular city corresponds to the legal constitution for the alliance of those cities, which were unwilling to permit that something that they had not unanimously consented to, should receive a seal of approval in the name of them all.

Consequently, in the period from the turn of the thirteenth until the fourteenth century, the alliance of the *gemene stede* had developed the organizational criteria necessary to enable the alliance to create the institutionalized form of the *dudesche hense* about a half-century later. The economic and political turbulence in the first decade of the fourteenth century, which brought the majority of the Hanse's core members, the Wendish cities, under the sovereignty of the noble lords and in turn limited the foreign and economic political autonomy of these cities, was at fault for this delay. After all, throughout the first two decades of the fourteenth century, the Wendish federation of towns, which constituted the most active of the regional Low German federations involved in the affairs of the early Hanse, was thrown back and temporarily subjected by the renewed Danish aggression under King Erich Menved (1286–1319) and by a form of the princely politic of re-vindication employed by the sovereigns of the southwest Baltic coast. In 1306, Lübeck was forced to seek protection from the Danish King in its struggle against neighboring princes (no help came from the partners in the treaty that was extended in 1296 and included Wismar, Rostock, Stralsund and Griefswald). Furthermore, Lübeck was obliged to pledge its support to the transfer of the city, by any means

---

131 HR I, 1, no. 66–69; regarding Riga and Osnabrück no. 70–72; whether the transfer of jurisdiction to Lübeck ever took place is questionable; see also no. 80, 41f.

132 HR I, 1, no. 80, 41f.

necessary, to Erich Menved. This pledge stood in total contradiction to Lübeck's status as a free imperial city and the privileges of the Empire, which had been obtained in 1226. In 1311, Wismar was conquered by its sovereign; in 1313 Rostock fell to the Prince of Mecklenburg due to the treachery of certain urban elites; and in 1314, Stralsund, in a newly negotiated treaty with the Prince of Rugen, was forced to make heavy payments and to disclaim certain privileges and the unlimited right to form alliances. A turn around began in 1316 when Stralsund triumphantly survived a siege lasting several months and supposedly used the ransom obtained for the captured Duke Erik of Saxony, to erect the splendid display located on the wall of the town hall.[133] The financial resources held by the coalition of princes were exhausted; and when Erich Menved and his rival, the Margrave Waldemar of Brandenburg, died in 1319, the cities were once again able to pursue their own political agendas, which had been interrupted for about 15 years.

The Development of the *Kontor* Association

From the turn of the thirteenth and until the fourteenth century, there were numerous groups of Low German merchants located within the countries targeted by the Hanse trade; these were primarily in the form of individual town guilds. Permanent offices did not yet exist, with the exception of the *gildhalla* in London. This was either because the stay of the merchants in certain areas was still temporally limited, as in Novgorod where there were 'summer-seaters' and 'winter-seaters' using the facilities for about four to six months at a time, or because the Low German merchants still maintained no right to assemble, as was the case in Flanders and Norway. At times, the 'governments' of the host countries comprehensively designated the individual groups as an "entity of merchants from the Empire". On the one hand, this designation would have corresponded to their de *jure*, outdated status as royal merchants. On the other hand, the designation would have corresponded to their constitutional form of organization as a free union of numerous associations for individual towns and regions.

Joint privileges for all local Low German merchants only existed in Novgorod (where the Gutnish merchants were also included) and were subject

133 Rolf Hammel-Kiesow, "Hansestädte im Städtelob der frühen Neuzeit," in Roman Czaja, ed., *Das Bild und die Wahrnehmung der Stadt und der städtischen Gesellschaft im Hanseraum im Mittelalter und in der frühen Neuzeit* (Toruń: Wydawnictwo Uniwersytetu Mikołaja Kopernika, 2004), 19–55, 45.

to a single execution for all participants. These joint privileges were also available in Flanders, but were subject to multiple executions for various recipients. Until the end of the century, the oft-quoted "Hanseatic" privileges in England applied only to merchants of the *gildhalla* in London and co-existed alongside privileges for individual cities; privileges which continued to exist and were constantly renewed. Privileges for the individual cities were also the rule in the Scandinavian Empires and along the south Baltic coast.

One way in which Lübeck influenced Peter's Court in Novgorod, a city to which merchants were still sailing in traveling associations, was the great impact it had on the *schra*, the rules of Peter's Court, since the late 13th century. In Bergen, a fledgling community of German merchants was ruled by the Law of Lübeck: a great accomplishment for the people of Lübeck. The same situation applied to Schonen, where the Baltic cities were granted the Law of Lübeck as part of their privileges. However, while the Baltic of the early fourteenth century was, in this regard, dominated by Lübeck,[134] the branches in the West gained an ever-growing measure of independence. In Bruges and in Flanders, the Low German merchants obtained, among other provisions included within the First Common Privilege of 1309, the right to assemble, which right lent additional force to their joint appearance. But the considerably differentiated and firmly established legal system of the West had definitely hindered the development of a common merchant law similar to that, which had developed in the "Wild East". Accordingly, merchants also took to settling their disputes with reference to the laws of their respective hometown. For this reason alone, it is reasonable to assume that the influence of Lübeck could not have been as strong in the Baltic Region.

It is the sign of a progressive institutionalization, that, during the first half of the fourteenth century, permanent *kontor*-communities were established even in the foreign branches of Bruges and Bergen. It is also a sign that the term *dudesche hense* (1358), was employed by the common cities in order to describe themselves. Novgorod had already granted the merchants their right to assemble, if temporarily limited for respective individual traveling groups, between the turn of the twelfth and the beginning of the thirteenth centuries. The master of the guild in Novgorod was also authorized to exercise the high jurisdiction, which for other "hanseatic" branches was executed by a court in the host country. In Bergen, the Germans' right to assemble was ensured by an affirmation of privileges issued by the king in the year 1343. In Bruges, the

134 This Lübeck-centered interpretation in been increasingly discussed; see Wubs-Mrocewicz and Jenks, *Hanse, passim*; Jahnke, *Hanse, passim.*

Low German merchants had received a similar affirmation in 1309. The *kontor*, which, at first, was the only one of the big four not to have its own building (the merchants assembled in the refectory of the Carmelite monastery), set the rules in 1347. This, in turn, resulted in the 1356 intervention by emissaries of the council for the *gemene stede*. The preparatory meeting for the council emissaries in Lübeck is considered to mark the seminal event in the First Day (Founding Day) for the Hanseatic League.

Thus, one cannot draw a mono-casual portrait for the 'advance' of the merchants and cities of the Hanse. For each targeted area in the economic territory of the Hanse, individual factors determining economic and political actions must be identified on the basis of development within the individual Hanse regions and cities (which, however, did not make continuous progress in any one direction throughout the three discussed centuries). The result seems, most often, to indicate specific purposeful actions, which drove development. Ultimately, it was very much the exploitation of both bigger and smaller opportunities, interrupted by or connected to a number of failed ventures, that elevated the Low German merchants and their cities to a leading position, which, around the mid-fourteenth century, they defended by means of the "*hense van den dudeschen steden*."

CHAPTER 2

The 'Golden Age' of the Hanseatic League

Jürgen Sarnowsky

The 'Golden Age': General Introduction

When the Hanseatic League had won its first war against Denmark and concluded the peace treaty of Stralsund in 1370,[1] it reached without any doubt the height of its influence. It controlled the straits between Denmark and what today is Southern Sweden, its privileges in Scania (Skåne) and Gotland were renewed, while some years earlier it had maintained and extended its position in Flanders. The assemblies of the towns' representatives, the *Hansetage*, had become an effective means of organizing its defence and co-ordinating measures against threats for the towns' privileges, and the 'Confederation of Cologne', concluded at the assembly at Cologne in 1367, continued after the peace as an instrument of even closer co-operation. Its standing was confirmed when Emperor Charles IV came to Lübeck in 1375 and addressed the town council as 'lords'.[2] Not without overstatement, historians have called the Hanseatic League during this period a 'great Northern European power'.[3]

The period around 1370 has generally been recognized as the 'Golden Age' or the 'bloom period' of the Hanseatic League;[4] it may also be conceived of as the beginning of its history in a proper sense.[5] Nevertheless, its situation soon became increasingly difficult because of the formation of modern states and increasing competition. It only partly maintained its position in the wars with Denmark (1427–1435), Holland and Zeeland (1438–1441), and England (1468–

1 See e.g. the articles in *Hansische Geschichtsblätter* 88 (1970).

2 *Die Chroniken der niedersächsischen Städte: Lübeck*, vol. 1, Die Chroniken der deutschen Städte, vol. 19, ed. Karl Koppmann (Leipzig, 1884; repr. Göttingen: Vandenhoeck & Rupprecht, 1967), p. 553.

3 "Nordeuropäische Großmacht," chapter heading in Philippe Dollinger, *Die Hanse* (Stuttgart: Kröner, 1989), 89.

4 The latter e.g. as title of the classical study Erich Daenell, *Die Blütezeit der deutschen Hanse, Hansische Geschichte von der zweiten Hälfte des XIV. bis zum letzten Viertel des XV. Jahrhunderts*, 2 vols. (1905–06, repr. Berlin, New York: Duncker und Humblot, 1973).

5 As convincingly argued by Carsten Jahnke, "Die Hanse: Überlegungen zur Entwicklung des Hansebegriffes und der Hanse als Instutition resp. Organisation." *Hansische Geschichtsblätter* 131 (2013): 1–32.

 | DOI 10.1163/9789004284760_004

1474), its privileges were not automatically renewed, and the merchants from England and elsewhere demanded equal rights in the Baltic. Several times, the town councils' position was threatened by internal upheavals, while the princes of the Empire tried to increase their power by attempting to reduce the self-government of the towns. The towns reacted by forming closer confederations, the *tohopesaten*, in the middle of the fifteenth century, but were only partly successful. Thus the 'Golden Age' of the Hanseatic League soon developed into a period of dangers and partial decline, but the towns were at least able to continue their independent policies and their internal development. The institution of the *Hansetage* was strengthened by several regulations, the towns agreed on measures against rebels, the closer association of the 'Confederation of Cologne' (ended in 1385) was finally partly revived by the *tohopesaten*, and the trade was adapted to the new situation. Thus, a period of crisis only started after 1474 when the Hanseatic trading posts, *kontore*, in Novgorod, Bruges, and elsewhere faced increasing problems and many towns either decided to or were forced to end their co-operation within the League. Thus the 'Golden Age' of the Hanseatic League, starting in the 1350s and finally ending in 1474, was succeeded by decades of decline and efforts for renewal in the Early Modern Period.

The Conflict in Flanders: Strengthening Ties between the Hanseatic Towns

The later thirteenth and earlier fourteenth centuries were the formative period of what became the Hanseatic League.[6] By 1350, the trading posts, the *kontore*, had developed their internal organization, which is shown by the regulations for the Bruges *Kontor* of October 1347. The assemblies of the towns' representatives, the *Hansetage*, had not as far as we know begun to become regular, but there were at least assemblies with certain representatives from more than one region even before 1300. One example is an assembly at Lübeck in about 1299 that included messengers from Riga,[7] which is known from the report of Hinrich Kale from Dortmund who played only a secondary role. As secretary of the Dortmund town council Kale probably had no mandate to participate in decisions, and Riga was only represented because the town had been in conflict with the Teutonic Knights (since 1297) and was asking for the mediation of the Wendish towns. But at least the mechanisms for invitations had

6 Cf. Rolf Hammel-Kiesow, *Die Hanse* (Munich: Beck, 2000), 51–67.

7 HR I 1, 80.

developed as can be seen from a letter of Lübeck to Osnabrück from about the same time.[8] Faced with problems in Flanders, Lübeck invited Osnabrück (and other towns) to send authorized representatives to an assembly at Lübeck. While this did not continue into the 1330s or 1340s, it was again the situation in Flanders that finally led to the institution of the *Hansetage* as quite regular assemblies of representatives of towns discussing problems of overall importance, and coming from at least two regions that included Lübeck, or at least the Wendish towns.[9]

The Bruges statutes of 1347 not only fixed an equal representation of the three 'thirds' in Bruges formed by the Wendish and Saxon towns, by Westphalia and Prussia, by Gotland and Livonia, they were also intended to strengthen the *kontor's* standing towards Bruges.[10] Thus, in 1351, when a ship from Greifswald was robbed by an English pirate who was condemned in Sluys, and when this was followed by repressions against Hanseatic goods in England, the German merchants blamed Bruges, demanded more rights in the town, especially concerning the weigh scales, and suggested moving the *kontor* to Aardenburg or Antwerp in the case their demands were not met.[11] The Wendish and Saxon towns reacted by consultations and by letters to Bruges, Ypres, Ghent, and the count of Flanders asking for help concerning the complaints of the merchants. Though the scales were conceded, the tensions remained. As is known from a later letter asking for formal support for the envoys[12] in February 1356, there was an assembly in Lübeck discussing the situation in Flanders. This was probably the first *Hansetag*, though nothing is known about its participants. It commissioned a group of nine town councillors representing the three 'thirds' in the Bruges *Kontor*, three from Lübeck, Hamburg, and Stralsund, four from Dortmund, Soest, Thorn, and Elbing, and two from Gotland and Livonia.[13] They met in Bruges in June 1356, confirmed the statutes of 1347, and decreed

8 HR I 1, 79.

9 Thus the definition of Volker Henn, "Hansische Tagfahrten in der zweiten Hälfte des 14. Jahrhunderts" in *Die hansischen Tagfahrten zwischen Anspruch und Wirklichkeit*, ed. Volker Henn, Hansische Studien, vol. 11 (Trier: Porta Alba, 2001), 1–21, at 3.

10 Volker Henn, "Entfaltung im Westen: ‚Hansen' auf den niederländischen Märkten," in *Die Hanse. Lebenswirklichkeit und Mythos. 2. Aufl. des Textbands der Hanse-Ausstellung*, ed. Jörgen Bracker, Volker Henn, Rainer Postel (Lübeck: Schmidt-Römhild 1998), 50–57, at 56; for Bruges cf. James M. Murray, *Bruges: Cradle of Capitalism, 1280–1390* (Cambridge: Cambridge University Press, 2005).

11 HR I 1, 158–61; Dollinger, *Hanse*, 89–90.

12 HR I 1, 199 § 3.

13 HR I 1, 200.

additional regulations for the *Kontor* and its aldermen. This has been interpreted as the submission of the *Kontor* to the control by the towns' assemblies,[14] especially because there were similar developments for Novgorod, Bergen, and London. But the German merchants in Bruges had turned to the towns and received instructions several times before, so evidently the close relationship to the towns was not new,[15] and after 1356, the *Kontor* often had to react or even to negotiate immediately without being able to consult the towns' representatives. So, the confirmation of its statutes by the commission was probably intended to strengthen the regional division in the *Kontor*.

The events that followed were even more important for the development of the institutions of the Hanseatic League. The commission of 1356 achieved nothing to change the situation in Flanders. Rather, the Hundred Years War led to an increase of taxes and prices in Bruges which concerned all merchants, and an extension of the Bruges staple resulted in the prohibition of direct sales of salt and grain 'from ship to ship' between foreigners. In this situation, the towns' assemblies, the *Hansetage*, finally became the main instrument for the co-ordination of the towns' policies.[16] In January 1358, the representatives of the Wendish and Saxon towns (Lübeck, Hamburg, Rostock, Stralsund, Wismar, Braunschweig, and Goslar) met with envoys from Prussia (town councillors from Thorn and Elbing) in Lübeck.[17] Though the Westphalian towns with their strong relationship to Flanders were not present, the assembly decided on wide-ranging measures.

While before the trading post was only moved out of Bruges, this time the blockade concerned the whole of Flanders. The river Meuse was to be the Western border for all Hanseatic commercial activities. No goods from the Hanseatic region should be sold to Flanders or to dealers with relations to Flanders, and no one was allowed to buy products from Flanders, especially Flemish cloth. Even merchants from other regions of Europe should be hindered in their dealings with Flemish traders. Every merchant and every town was requested to follow the blockade by threat of being excluded from the Hanseatic League and its privileges. All negotiations, agreements, and compensations between Flanders and the German merchants should only

14 Cf. Ernst Pitz, *Bürgereinung und Städteeinung. Studien zur Verfassungsgeschichte der Hansestädte und der deutschen Hanse*, Quellen und Darstellungen zur hansischen Geschichte N.F. LII (Cologne, Vienna, Weimar: Böhlau, 2001), 233–34.

15 Volker Henn, "Über die Anfänge des Brügger Hanse*kontors*," *Hansische Geschichtsblätter* 107 (1989) 43–66, at 61–63.

16 Pitz, *Bürgereinung*, 365–417.

17 HR I 1, 212.

continue or get acceptance and ratification if they were agreed by all towns involved. The blockade was not only the instrument of an urban alliance introduced and decided on by the assembly of the towns' representatives, it was also to be brought to an end by this alliance. Also significant is the terminology used in the documents. Nearly every article of the records of the assembly refers to the Hanseatic League, and several times we find the phrase *steden van der dudeschen hense* ('towns of the German Hanse').[18]

Before 1358, the phrase *dudesche hense* is rare and mostly used by foreign authorities like the English or Norwegian kings, while the merchants termed themselves mostly as 'traders of the Empire' or 'common merchant'. It has been argued that the recurring use of *dudesche hense* in the documents of 1358 is related to this situation (the blockade of the whole and economically very powerful county of Flanders), which required a concentration of forces. Indeed, January 1358 marks the beginning of a new self-awareness of the towns though the loose urban corporation did not fit into Western constitutional patterns and was addressed as *Hanse* nearly only in written diplomatic correspondence.

The next step were negotiations with duke Albert of Bavaria who ruled over the counties Hainault, Holland, and Zeeland. He granted the Hanseatic towns wide-ranging privileges for his territories with the consequence that the *Kontor* moved to Dordrecht in May 1358. Despite his support, the blockade of Flanders was not complete because Hanseatic goods came to Flanders partly via Kampen, Utrecht, and Nijmegen, and partly by merchants who did not keep to the regulations. Nevertheless, the Flemish dependency on imported victuals was so great that shortages in their supply nearly resulted in a famine. Thus, once again the Hanseatic League's privileges could be secured and extended by a blockade.[19] Count Louis III and the Flemish towns granted the rights for the whole county that before only applied to Bruges and the Zwin. In cases of doubt, the decision should be in favour of the German merchants. They were allowed to trade also in small quantities and received compensations from the town of Bruges which also covered debts of their hosts. The new form of cooperation between the towns had passed its test. From now on, all common activities of the towns were discussed and co-ordinated by the assemblies of the towns' representatives, of which there were 68 between 1356

---

18 Cf. Thomas Behrmann, "Über Zeichen, Zeremoniell und Hansebegriff auf hansischen Tagfahrten," in *Die hansischen Tagfahrten*, 109–24, at 122; Hammel-Kiesow, *Hanse*, 64–65.

19 Survey in Peter Stützel, "Die Privilegien des Deutschen Kaufmanns in Brügge im 13. und 14. Jahrhundert," *Hansische Geschichtsblätter* 116 (1998), 23–63.

and 1407, mostly meeting in Lübeck.[20] The strategy agreed on by the assembly of January 1358 was completely successful.

The Hanseatic League at War with Denmark (1361–1370)

In the 1330s Denmark suffered from a period of weakness and was dominated by count Gerhard III of Holstein. Efforts of the Hanseatic towns and Northern German princes to restore internal peace were not successful,[21] and as a result the election of Waldemar IV 'Atterdag' as king after Gerhard's death in 1340 was widely welcomed. Waldemar concentrated on the restoration of royal power at first by renouncing parts of his kingdom. He resigned Scania to Sweden in 1343 and sold Northern Estonia to the Teutonic Knights in 1346. But this did not mean that he was satisfied with the situation. In 1350, he made clear that his final goal was the restoration of the Baltic empire of his predecessors.[22] In 1360, Waldemar finally decided to reverse his policies and start an expansion.[23] He used the weakness of the Swedish King Magnus to re-conquer the formerly lost territories in Southern Sweden, Scania, Halland, and Blekinge, though Magnus had paid him a compensation for his losses before. In July 1361, he turned to Gotland, defeated its peasant army and finally accepted the homage of Visby, which had been absent from the fighting and now submitted itself to the victorious king.[24] Though Waldemar allowed Visby to continue its co-operation within the Hanseatic League and renewed its privileges, the towns felt a threat by the change of power in the Northern European kingdoms, especially since the king had raised the taxes on Scania. Again the towns' assemblies were the institution to discuss and co-ordinate the towns' activities and measures.

---

20 Henn, *Tagfahrten*, 4.

21 See e.g. the treaty of 1338, HUB 2, 606.

22 See Niels Skyum-Nielsen, "König Waldemar von Atterdag von Dänemark: Persönlichkeit und Politik," *Hansische Geschichtsblätter* 102 (1984), 5–20, at 9; Anders Bøgh, *Sejren i kvindens hånd: kampen om magten i norden ca. 1365–1389* (Aarhus: Universitetsforl., 2003), 13.

23 In general cf. Bøgh, *Sejren*, 24–53, 292–93; Niels Bracke, *Die Regierung Waldemars IV. Eine Untersuchung zum Wandel von Herrschaftsstrukturen im spätmittelalterlichen Dänemark*, Kieler Werkstücke vol. 21 (Frankfurt am Main, 1999); Erich Hoffmann, "König Waldemar IV: als Politiker und Feldherr," in *Akteure und Gegner der Hanse. Zur Prosopographie der Hansezeit*, ed. Detlef Kattinger, Horst Wernicke (Weimar: Hermann Böhlaus Nf., 1998), 271–87.

24 Jochen Götze, "Von Greifswald nach Stralsund. Die Auseinandersetzungen der deutschen Seestädte und ihrer Verbündeten mit König Valdemar von Dänemark 1361–1360," *Hansische Geschichtsblätter* 88 (1970), 83–122, at 83.

It was probably the success of the blockade in Flanders that encouraged them to resist Waldemar, who had at this point considerably strengthened his position.[25]

Already in the beginning of August 1361, an unknown group of representatives of the town councils gathered in Greifswald and preliminarily decided to suspend all relations with Denmark and Scania. Anyone wanting to sail to Flanders through the Øresund had to be careful not to trade with its merchants; otherwise he would be severely punished.[26] The final decision was postponed to an assembly some weeks later when negotiations with Norway and Sweden had begun and more envoys of towns had arrived so that finally the Wendish, Pomeranian, and Prussian towns were represented.

The records, which are dated 7 September 1361, list Lübeck, Hamburg, Wismar, Rostock, Stralsund, Greifswald, Anklam, Stettin, Kolberg, Kulm, and Danzig. Any trade with Denmark and Scania was forbidden and an alliance was concluded with Kings Magnus of Sweden and Håkon of Norway. For the first time, it was decided to exact a special custom, the *Pfundzoll*, to finance the war. This was to be paid in all towns at the Sea and also in Prussia, from all ships and goods that were exported from their harbours and countries, and was fixed at 0.56 percent of the value of the ships and goods reckoned in Flemish pounds *groot* (four 'English pennies' or sterlings per pound).[27] Once paid, the merchants and skippers received documents to prove that they had paid the custom and were freed from any further exaction. The period for the levying of the duty was limited to 29 September 1362.[28] This was an important decision. At this point, there were only common duties in the trading posts, the *Kontore*, which only German merchants had to pay, while the right to exact customs generally was reserved to the territorial lords and princes. Now the towns claimed this right for themselves which could lead into conflict in territories with strong authorities like in Prussia, which was dominated by the Teutonic Knights, especially since the duty had to be paid by everyone. Nevertheless, the incoming money would help the towns to finance a war that would normally end up with debts. Though this first levy proved to be a failure—mainly

---

25 Erich Hoffmann, "Konflikte und Ausgleich mit den skandinavischen Reichen," in *Die Hanse. Lebenswirklichkeit und Mythos*, 66–77, at 71; but cf. Götze, "Stralsund," 86.

26 HR I 1, 258.

27 Four 'English pennies' or sterlings were 1⅓ *groot*; the Flemish pound *groot* was mostly reckoned in 20 shillings or 240 *groot* or 720 'English pennies' or 5760 mytes, cf. Peter Spufford, *Handbook of Medieval Exchange*, Royal Historical Society Guides and Handbooks, vol. 13 (London: Royal Historical Society, 1986), 215 and 255.

28 HR I, 1, 259 § 2.

because the money was to be collected and then distributed centrally, not, as later, by the towns themselves—, the *Pfundzoll* became an important instrument of the Hanseatic League's policies, to be revived again in 1367.

The whole campaign was determined by bad luck and wrong decisions.[29] Though the agreements with the counts of Holstein, the Teutonic Knights, and the kings of Sweden and Norway were clear, there was only one attack of Holstein against Jutland, while the Wendish towns had to carry the burden of the war nearly all alone. The fleet, under the command of the mayor of Lübeck, Johann Wittenborg, in April 1362, first turned to the fortresses at the Øresund to secure free passage from the Baltic to the North Sea. When help from Sweden failed to materialize, Wittenborg decided to employ the men from the ships in the siege of Helsingborg. At this point, Waldemar attacked the Hanseatic fleet and was able to destroy or capture the greater part of the ships so that Wittenborg was forced to conclude a disadvantageous truce. Though he succeeded in bringing back the weakened fleet to Lübeck, he soon ran into difficulties because of earlier personal misbehaviour and died, perhaps by execution.[30]

Waldemar flanked this success by a diplomatic offensive. He persuaded Magnus of Sweden and Håkon of Norway to change sides, gaining Håkon's support through marriage with his younger daughter Margaret. He also travelled to the rulers of Christian Europe, visiting the Emperor Charles IV in Prague, Pope Urban V in Avignon, and others. He won over King Kazimierz III of Poland who kept the Teutonic Knights and the towns in Prussia and Livonia from interfering in the conflict. Meanwhile, the truce had been prolonged several times. Finally, in September 1365, because acts of piracy had no effect and the situation had deteriorated, the towns were forced to conclude the peace of Vordingborg. By this, their privileges in Scania were only partly renewed.

But this did not mean a full Danish success. In Sweden, in 1363, the Council of the Realm had expelled King Magnus and his son, King Håkon of Norway, who had been co-ruler of Sweden. Magnus's successor was his nephew, Albert III of Mecklenburg who did not support Waldemar's policies. When Waldemar did not keep to the promises made in the treaty of Vordingborg and raised taxes and customs on Scania and for the passage through the Øresund, he not only roused resistance by the Wendish, but also by the Prussian and Dutch towns which had not participated in the last war. Again the assemblies of the towns' representatives played a key role in bringing the towns from different regions together.

---

29 Götze, Greifswald, 88.

30 See the article of Gerald Stefke, "Der Lübecker Bürgermeister Johan Wittenborch, hingerichtet 1363," *Hansische Geschichtsblätter* 126 (2008), 1–144.

The Prussian towns were the first to ask for common measures against Denmark and Norway and tried to win over the Wendish towns which had gathered in Rostock in December 1366.[31] But the mission failed. The Wendish towns that were obviously still under the influence of their defeat by Waldemar rather decided to send the secretary of the Stralsund town council, Alardus, to Prussia with a letter to the grand master of the Teutonic Knights and the towns refusing any help. Nevertheless, the Prussians soon found support by Dutch cities, namely by Kampen and the towns at the Zuiderzee (today IJsselmeer).[32] In June 1367, when the Wendish and Pomeranian towns gathered at Stralsund, the Prussian towns Kulm, Thorn, and Elbing and Ludeke van Essen, commander of the Teutonic Knights at Danzig, already reported that they wanted to react against the threat by King Waldemar and to form an alliance with Kampen and the towns at the Zuiderzee.[33] The Wendish towns still hesitated, especially because Danish envoys had invited them to an earlier meeting in Denmark. Thus only the Prussian towns and those at the Zuiderzee united against Denmark and Norway at an assembly in Elbing in July 1367,[34] also supported by English and Flemish merchants who later declared that would also keep out of Denmark and Norway, not sending any weapons, victuals, and other goods.[35]

Only then, the Wendish towns decided in favour of a co-operation with the other towns. In November 1367, the town councils' representatives met in Cologne, which was the only *Hansetag* there, notably without the official participation of Cologne at the most important decisions. These included the formation of the 'Confederation of Cologne' by the Wendish and Prussian towns together with those from Holland and Zeeland and at the Zuiderzee, represented by Lübeck, Rostock, Stralsund, Wismar, Kulm, Thorn, Elbing, Kampen, Harderwijk, Elborg, Amsterdam, and Briel.[36] Though the alliances concluded with the North German princes and Sweden played an important role,[37] the 'Confederation' also meant a new quality in the relation between the towns. The firm alliance was not only intended for the time of the war but

31 HR I, 1, 388 § 13.

32 Cf. Job Westrate, "Abgrenzung durch Aufnahme. Zur Eingliederung der süderseeischen Städte in die Hanse, ca. 1360–1450," *Hansische Geschichtsblätter* 121 (2003), 13–40, at 17.

33 HR I 1, 402 § 1.

34 HR I 1, 403.

35 HR I 1, 421 § 16.

36 HR I 1, 413; cf. Erich Daenell, *Die Kölner Konföderation vom Jahre 1367 und die schonischen Pfandschaften*, Leipziger Studien aus dem Gebiet der Geschichte, vol. 1 (Leipzig, 1894), 1.

37 Götze, "Greifswald," 109.

was to be continued at least for three years after the peace. The detailed arrangements included the numbers of ships to be equipped by the different town regions: ten cogs (*Koggen*) from the Wendish and Livonian towns, five from Prussia, and four cogs and other ships from the Dutch cities, each cog with 100 men in armour and together with two smaller ships. A common route for the approach was agreed, and the goal was to conquer the Danish fortresses along the Øresund. While any trade with Denmark and Norway was prohibited, the *Pfundzoll* was renewed, this time to be kept in the towns were it was levied and to put in account later. Towns like Bremen or Hamburg and many cities in the North German hinterland kept apart or only contributed some money,[38] but their merchants at least participated by paying the *Pfundzoll*. Thus the 'Confederation of Cologne' turned the Hanseatic League into a town union, for 18 years, until it dissolved in 1385. The new self-image of the towns is reflected in a letter for the first time signed by the 'town councillors sent out to represent the towns of the German Hanse' (*consules nuncii civitatum de hanza Theotonica*).[39]

This was backed by a strong co-operation with the princes, especially with duke Albert II of Mecklenburg and his son, King Albert of Sweden, and also with the counts of Holstein. They allied with the Wendish towns and thus added themselves to the network around the 'Confederation of Cologne' in which the partners agreed not to conclude peace separately. When the military operations began, the contingents were greater than originally planned so that they reached their successes quite quickly. While the counts of Holstein operated in Jutland, the Mecklenburg forces turned to Scania and the Danish isles, and, between April and June 1368, the Hanseatic fleet conquered the fortresses along the Øresund, with the exception of Helsingborg which only surrendered after a long siege in September 1369. Waldemar was taken by surprise by the success of his enemies. As in the years after 1362, he had decided for a diplomatic offensive and was not present when the negotiations began. Håkon of Norway had already concluded a truce, and thus Denmark was in danger of being divided between the North German princes, as in the years before 1340, which was also not in the interest of the towns. The talks between the Danish Council of the Realm and the towns led to a preliminary peace in November

38 Volker Henn, "Zur Haltung der binnenländischen Hansestädte in der hansisch-dänischen Auseinandersetzung 1367/1370," in *Der Stralsunder Frieden von 1370: Prosopographische Studien*, ed. Nils Jörn, Ralf-Gunnar Werlich, and Horst Wernicke, Quellen und Darstellungen zur hansischen Geschichte, N.F. 46 (Cologne, Weimar, Vienna: Böhlau 1998), 271–87.

39 HR I 1, 116.

1369 and finally to the peace treaty of Stralsund on 24 May 1370 which marks the zenith of the towns' power. But this was less dramatic than it has been termed by earlier researchers: the Hanseatic League did not really become a 'great Northern European power' though it gained considerable influence on Baltic policies.

Denmark and the Hanseatic League after the Peace of Stralsund

The conditions for the restoration of peace were negotiated and the peace treaty prepared on another assembly of the towns' representatives at Stralsund in February 1370 at which the Wendish towns, representatives from Pomerania, Livonia, Prussia, the Zuiderzee area, Holland, and Zeeland, and members of the Danish Council of the Realm under Henning Putbus were present.[40] The towns' demands were moderate—contrary to that of the princes who had lost their influence on the developments. King Waldemar had to renew the towns' privileges in Denmark and Scania as they had been before the first war, only that they now applied to the whole group of cities united in the 'Confederation of Cologne' and to the other cities that participated in the German law of unions.[41] As a compensation for their expenses and losses, the towns should receive two thirds of the incomes from the Øresund fortresses of Skanör, Falsterbo, Helsingborg, and Malmø for the next 15 years, and they were allowed to administrate the fortresses themselves for security.

Waldemar, who was not present, was required to confirm the treaties with his great or majestic seal within one and a half years (29 September 1371) to ensure their validity even under his successors.[42] This was closely related to the regulation that in case of Waldemar's resignation or death his successor had to be appointed only by consent of the towns (*des ghelikes scole wy nenen heren untfaen, yd en sy by rade der stede*) and had to seal the treaties also with his great seal.[43] This did not mean that the Hanseatic League wanted to control the election of the Danish kings; it rather tried to ensure the continuous validity of its privileges in Denmark.[44] The importance of these conditions soon became obvious when Waldemar succeeded in postponing his confirmation of the peace until October 1371 and even then only used his small or secret seal.

40 Bøgh, *Sejren*, 29–33.

41 Hammel-Kiesow, *Hanse*, 109.

42 HR I 1, 530.

43 HR I 1, 524, S. 487.

44 Hoffmann, "Konflikte," 75.

But at least the peace had also been confirmed by several leading members of the Danish Council of the Realm.

Waldemar used the peace with the towns to re-establish his position.[45] The Mecklenburg dukes and the Swedish king were annoyed by the separate peace of the towns and thus made their own arrangements with Waldemar who in turn inspired Mecklenburg hopes for their dynastic succession in Denmark. Waldemar's son had died early, but he had two grandsons by his daughters, Olav, by Margaret and Håkon of Norway, and Albert IV, by Ingeborg and Henry III of Mecklenburg, brother to the Swedish king. Though Waldemar never clearly favoured Albert IV—he seems also to have promised the succession to Håkon—this was sufficient to pacify the dukes, and in consequence, the counts of Holstein were not able to continue their resistance. When Waldemar died in 1375, after long discussions, in May 1376, the Council of the Realm finally decided for Olav; but in fact, his mother Margaret reigned and continued the policies of her father with even more prudence and awareness.[46] After Håkon's death in 1380, Olav was also elected Norwegian King while Margaret took over government in Norway, too. This started the long-term personal union between Denmark and Norway.

Nothing is known about the consent of the towns in favour of the election of Olav in 1376, but this decision was clearly in their interest, because the possible union of Mecklenburg, Sweden, and Denmark (even under different members of the family) would have threatened the main Hanseatic trading routes. Thus, the towns retained their influence, especially because Margaret extended her authority only very carefully. As a consequence, though still the financial demands of the peace of Stralsund were not met, the towns gave back the Øresund fortresses to Margaret in May 1385. Nevertheless, before this was decided upon there were discussions at several assemblies of the towns' representatives, especially because the Prussian towns were not willing to concede this and demanded the prolongation of the 'Confederation of Cologne'.[47] Indeed, the *Hansetag* at Stralsund in June 1385 asked the town councils to

45 Bøgh, *Sejren*, 35–41.

46 Bøgh, *Sejren*, 75 et sq.; Vivian Etting, *Queen Margrete (1353–1412) and the founding of the Nordic Union*, The Northern World: North Europe and the Baltic c. 400–1700 AD, peoples, economies and cultures, vol. 9 (Leiden: Brill, 2004); ead., "Margrete—Mistress and Master of the North," in *Margrete I. Regent of the North. The Kalmar Union 600 Years. Essays and Catalogue*, ed. Poul Grinder-Hansen (Copenhagen: Danmarks Nationalmuseum, 1997), 18–23, 434.

47 See e.g. HR I 2, 297 §§ 2–3; events in detail: Bøgh, *Sejren*, 187–200.

discuss about the prolongation,[48] but it seems that nothing came out of it. The 'Confederation of Cologne' ended in 1385, probably because it was not needed anymore—which clearly demonstrates the pragmatic character of the urban co-operation.

After the dynastic succession in Denmark and also after the informal dissolution of the 'Confederation of Cologne', this became increasingly difficult. In 1387, Olav V died, and Margaret succeeded to take over the rule in Denmark and Norway by consent of both councils of the realm, though she soon presented another heir, her grand nephew Eric of Pomerania.[49] Before 1387, the dukes of Mecklenburg had not accepted Olav's succession, and they had held on to their claims and sent out pirates to attack Danish ships.[50] Margaret secured her southern borders by surrendering Schleswig to the counts of Holstein in 1386, and sent out ships in defense. After Olav's death, Albert of Sweden claimed Denmark and Norway for himself, but soon faced a rebellion by the majority of the Swedish nobility which invited Margaret. In February 1389, in the battle of Falköping, Margaret won the upper hand and succeeded in taking Albert as prisoner. The dukes of Mecklenburg reacted again by employing pirates to fight the Danish contingents and opened up their harbours in Rostock and Wismar for all enemies of Denmark. Lübeck and Stralsund tried in vain to restrain their activities, though meanwhile many trade ships had been attacked.

The pirates named themselves 'victual brothers' (*Vitalienbrüder*),[51] perhaps alluding to pirates in the Hundred Years' War or because they successfully brought victuals to Stockholm. The city was besieged by Margaret but held out for Albert because many of its citizens were German. The activities of the victual brothers proved overall successful. In 1391, Bornholm and Visby were conquered in the name of Albert, attacks concerned many places in the Baltic, and the trade between the Hanseatic towns and Scania was interrupted. Lübeck was occupied by other problems, but finally in 1395 mediated the treaty of Lindholm by which Albert III was freed for a nominal ransom of 60,000 marks while Stockholm was handed over to seven Wendish, Prussian, and

---

48 HR I 2, 306 § 22.

49 Sven Rosborn, "Erik of Pomerania: Union King and Pirate," in *Margrete I. Regent of the North*, 87–90, 436; Heinz Barüske, *Erich von Pommern, Ein nordischer König aus dem Greifengeschlecht* (Rostock: Hinstorff, 1997).

50 David K. Bjork, "Piracy in the Baltic," *Speculum* 18 (1943), 39–68.

51 Matthias Puhle, *Die Vitalienbrüder. Klaus Störtebeker und die Seeräuber der Hansezeit*, 2nd Ed. (Frankfurt a. M.: Campus, 1994); Gregor Rohmann, "Der Kaperfahrer Johann Stortebeker aus Danzig. Beobachtungen zur Geschichte der Vitalienbrüder," *Hansische Geschichtsblätter* 125 (2007), 77–119.

Livonian towns and to be administrated by them. If the ransom was not paid within three years, Stockholm was to be delivered to Margaret.[52]

The dukes of Mecklenburg never had enough money for their activities, and so Stockholm finally fell to Margaret in 1398. This completed (or nearly completed) the union of the three Northern kingdoms in her hand and in those of Eric of Pomerania which had been negotiated at Kalmar in 1397. Though the documents of the Kalmar Union were never formally ratified,[53] it became a reality until 1523—though with longer intervals of Swedish independency—with which the Hanseatic League was confronted. The towns reacted pragmatically and arranged themselves with the new situation, especially since Margaret continued her reserved policies and confirmed the Hanseatic privileges in her kingdoms. One great problem remained: the victual brothers continued their activities from Gotland, only partly controlled by members of the Mecklenburg ducal family. At this point, in 1398, the Teutonic Knights and the Prussian towns decided to act.[54] They gathered 84 ships with 4000 men, 50 knights of the Teutonic Order and 400 horses in the harbour of Danzig, the ships mainly chartered by or from the towns. When the troops had started the siege of Visby, an agreement was reached at the beginning of April. The pirates and Duke John of Mecklenburg had to move out of Gotland within two days and to promise that they would not any more disturb the merchants and the trade. Some pirates who resisted were killed, and the privileges of Visby were renewed.

While the Teutonic Knights kept Gotland until 1408—they even defended it against a Danish attack in 1403/04—two Prussian citizens, Arnold Hecht and Arnold Herferten, became admirals of a small fleet to deter the victual brothers from further attacks on trade ships. Since this was supported by the other Hanseatic towns, some of the victual brothers ended their activities in the Baltic and turned to Eastern Frisia where they found support by local rulers. Two campaigns by Hamburg, Lübeck, and the neighbouring towns in 1400 and 1401 helped to reduce their activities, and some of their leaders were executed, events which became very famous in later legends.[55] In fact, the victual

52 Bøgh, *Sejren*, 285–86.

53 Poul Enemark, "Denmark and the Union," in *Margrete I. Regent of the North*, 47–50, 435, at 47.

54 Friedrich Benninghoven, "Die Gotlandfeldzüge des Deutschen Ordens 1398–1408," *Zeitschrift für Ostforschung* 13 (1964), 421–77; Raymond H. Schmandt, "The Gotland Campaign of the Teutonic Knights," *Journal of Baltic Studies* 6 (1975), 247–58.

55 Rohmann, "Kaperfahrer"; Nicolai Clarus, *Bartholomäus Voet und die Freibeuter der Hansezeit. Untersuchungen zum Kaperwesen im Nordeuropa des frühen 15. Jahrhunderts*,

brothers soon renewed their attacks on Hanseatic ships, partly also backed by the counts of Oldenburg, and remained influential at least during the first third of the fifteenth century while Hamburg tried in vain to control them by building up its own territory in Eastern Frisia. Piracy was a threat to trade everywhere, especially when it was used as an instrument of naval warfare. In the aftermath of the peace of Stralsund, the Hanseatic League remained an important factor in Northern politics, but it was far from controlling the events. Rather, the kings and princes were able to consolidate their power, not only in the North but also in the West and even in the East of Europe.

New Conflicts in East and West

Soon after the Hanseatic League had given back the fortresses at the Øresund to Margaret of Denmark, in 1385, new conflicts arose in the most important trading centers in East and West, in the relations with Novgorod, Flanders, and England. Contrary to the time before 1350, the Hanseatic League now had a well-established system to discuss and put through effective measures against potential threats for its privileges, even including military operations. Nevertheless, the forms of co-operation depended always from the actual situation, as there was no clear leading role. Though Lübeck was the place of many *Hansetage* and issued letters on behalf of the towns even in between the assemblies, its role as a 'capital' was sometimes contended by Cologne, as the grand master of the Teutonic Knights played an important role for the negotiations with the Western European rulers which made him appear—not only in English sources of the fourteenth century—the actual 'head of the Hanse' (*caput Hansae*).[56]

This had also some relevance for the relations with the trading post in Novgorod, which were increasingly dominated by the Livonian towns.[57]

PhD diss. (Hamburg, 2012); more traditionally: *Störtebeker 600 Jahre nach seinem Tod*, ed. Wilfried Ehbrecht, Hansische Studien, vol. 15 (Trier: Porta Alba, 2005); *Gottes Freund—aller Welt Feind: von Seeraub und Konvoifahrt. Störtebeker und die Folgen*, ed. Jörgen Bracker (Hamburg: Zertani, 2001).

56 Hammel-Kiesow, *Hanse*, 78; Pitz, *Bürgereinung*, 343–65; Stuart Jenks, "A Capital without a State: Lübeck caput tocius hanze (to 1474)," *Historical Research* 65 (1992), 134–149; Heinz Stoob, "Lübeck als 'Caput Omnium' in der Hanse." *Blätter für deutsche Landesgeschichte* 121 (1985), 157–68.

57 For the *Kontor* in general see *Novgorod. Markt und Kontor der Hanse*, ed. Norbert Angermann, Klaus Friedland, Quellen und Darstellungen zur hansischen Geschichte N.F. 53 (Cologne, Weimar, Vienna, 2002).

If there were conflicts between their most important territorial lord, the Livonian branch of the Teutonic Knights, and the Russian principalities, in most cases this would have threatened the Hanseatic trade. Thus, when the Teutonic Knights attacked the principality of Pskov in 1367, North German merchants were arrested in Novgorod. The Order and the towns reacted by prohibiting the export of salt and herring to Russia, especially by Russian merchants in Livonia. In 1371, the trading relations were renewed, and in 1373 envoys from Lübeck and Visby came to Novgorod to secure the peace which had been established, but in the 1380s the situation became more difficult. The Knights wanted to extend their own trade into the *Kontor*, while the Prussian towns tried to increase their influence.[58] The Order's demands were explicitly rejected by the other towns who decided at the assembly in Lübeck in May 1388 that the Prussian merchants were allowed to go to Novgorod only when they did not deal with money from their spiritual or secular lords who could not claim the privileges of the German merchants for themselves.[59] But at the same assembly, a more far reaching decision was taken: to blockade the town of Novgorod because of the continuous troubles. Town councillors of Lübeck, Visby, and the Livonian towns were sent out to win over the master of the Teutonic Knights in Livonia and the Livonian bishops to support this measure, interrupting not only the trade over sea, but also on the Daugava. Also the king of Sweden, his Finnish officials, Stockholm, and the Prussian towns were asked to join the blockade. At the same time, there was a blockade in the West, in Flanders, which was an important market for the goods from Russia, which made the measures against Novgorod easier.

When the situation changed in the West, in the autumn of 1391, Lübeck sent out two experienced town councillors, Johann Niebur and Godeke Travelmann, to Livonia and Russia.[60] Since the Prussian towns did not succeed in joining the envoys,[61] Niebur and Travelmann were accompanied to Novgorod only by town councillors from Riga, Reval, and Dorpat. In August 1392, they reached an agreement which was soon termed 'Niebur's kiss of the cross' (*Kreuzküssung Nieburs*)—according to its specific Russian form of confirmation—and which would regulate the relations between the German merchants and the Russians for more than 100 years. It contained the mutual renewal of all privileges concerning the trade of the Germans in Novgorod and of the Russians in Livonia

58 Cf. Daenell, *Blütezeit*, 2, 103.

59 HR I 3, 380 §§ 11, 14.

60 For Niebur cf. Birte Schubert, "Der Lübecker Bürgermeister Johann Niebur," in *Akteure und Gegner der Hanse*, 53–65.

61 HR I 4, 26 § 2.

and on Gotland. These privileges would now remain valid even in times of war between Novgorod on the one side and Sweden, the Teutonic Knights, or the Livonian bishops on the other side.

Even some years earlier, new problems in Flanders had arisen. While the agreement of 1360 included the liability of Bruges for the hosts of the German merchants, the town did not keep to its promises, and some time later, also customs were extended and raised. When the merchants in the *Kontor* reacted by an effort to secretly move the trading post out of Bruges again in the winter of 1377/78, they failed. This time, the town was supported by Count Louis III who limited the rights of the German merchants and especially the jurisdiction of the aldermen. The Hundred Years' War and civil war in Flanders contributed in worsening the situation. When the French army of Charles VI and Louis III defeated the civic contingents at Rosebeeke near Courtrai in November 1382, most of the merchants had left Bruges.

After the death of Louis and the succession of the Duke of Burgundy, Philip the Bold, as count of Flanders early in 1384, the towns decided for negotiations which finally took place in Dordrecht and Antwerp in May and June 1387. Duke Philip offered compensations, but the towns' representatives presented too far reaching demands also including a 'moral compensation' so that the consultation ended without a result.[62] Therefore, the towns followed the invitation of Duke Albert of Bavaria then regent of Holland and Hainault to move the trading post to Dordrecht, again, under the same conditions as 30 years earlier. Thus, when the representatives of the councils of the Wendish, Saxon, Prussian, Livonian towns and of Visby met in Lübeck in May 1388, they opted for a blockade of Flanders under the same conditions as in 1358. Any trade west of the Meuse River was prohibited; no goods were to be sold to or from Flanders. There was one exception in 1389: the trade of the Teutonic Knights with amber who used their incomes to buy white cloth for their habits in Mechelen.

In May 1389, Duke Albert extended the rights of the North German merchants in Holland at least temporarily, obviously at request of the merchants in the *Kontor*, since the Wendish and the Prussian towns could not agree on a mission to the Netherlands and also hoped for more concessions from Flanders. This was critically received by the Prussian towns whose merchants increasingly neglected the blockade, as did the merchants of Kampen. Meanwhile the duke of Burgundy tried to influence the towns by winning over the grand master of the Teutonic Knights in Prussia. In May 1390, Konrad Zöllner von Rotenstein reacted by a letter to Lübeck, Stralsund, Rostock, and Wismar

62 HUB 4, 904.

asking to find ways for an agreement and peace with Flanders since the trade had been interrupted for a long time, while at the same time he made clear to the duke that he could not force the towns to end the conflict.[63] When envoys from Flanders turned to the merchants in the *Kontor* in Dordrecht, it was by Prussian intervention that negotiations took place in Hamburg in November 1391 at which participated not only representatives of the Flemish towns but also of the duke. This finally ended with a further success of the Hanseatic League, led by Heinrich Westhof and Jordan Pleskow from Lübeck. Its privileges were renewed, the position of the aldermen in the trading post in Bruges were strengthened. Under clear conditions the German merchants were to receive 11,100 pound *groot*, and there were to be public celebrations at the re-entry of the merchants into Bruges, with 100 men from Bruges apologizing for the injustice suffered by their guests. The Bruges merchants also had to finance pilgrimages to Rome, Jerusalem, and Santiago de Compostela.

While this was finally another victory, the relations with England became increasingly difficult. While the Hanseatic merchants drove out their English rivals from Scania after the peace of Stralsund by arresting goods and persons and by force, the English succeeded in establishing themselves in the Baltic and especially in Prussia where they demanded rights equal to that of the German merchants in England—which linked the Anglo-Hanseatic relations to those of England and Prussia at least until the peace of Utrecht in 1474. Additionally, in 1371/72, new duties on imports were imposed in England, tonnage and poundage, which applied to the Hanseatic goods and which the towns regarded as a violation of their privileges.[64]

Tensions increased when an English fleet captured several Hanseatic ships in the Zwin, before Bruges, in 1385. Since these included six ships from Prussia, Grand Master Konrad Zöllner von Rotenstein reacted by the confiscation of English goods in Prussia worth 20.000 pounds. When the English merchants returned home, Richard II granted them compensation by the arrest of Prussian goods in England.[65] Richard offered negotiations which took place in London in June 1386, but ended without any result. Therefore, in September 1386, the grand master prohibited the import of cloth and other goods from England and the export of ashes, pitch, tar and other products from the

---

63 HR I, 3, 470–71.

64 Stuart Jenks, *England, die Hanse und Preußen: Handel und Diplomatie 1377–1474*, 3 vols. (Cologne, Weimar, Vienna: Böhlau, 1992), Quellen und Darstellungen zur Hansischen Geschichte, NF. XXXVIII, at 2, 481–85.

65 HUB 4, 849–50.

forests.[66] In February 1388, this was followed by protests of the merchants in the *Kontor* in London who sided with the Prussians and again rejected the payment of tonnage and poundage. But when Richard sent envoys to Prussia in June 1388, soon a compromise was reached. In August 1388, the grand master and the English representatives concluded the treaty of Marienburg which ended the arrests, fixed rules for respective compensations, and allowed all merchants to move and trade freely in both countries so that the English could now also deal with Poles and Russians.

Though the problem was set aside, and the English merchants soon gained prominence in Prussian cloth trade,[67] the basic problems remained unsolved. The regulations for compensation proved to be too complicated, the levy of tonnage and poundage continued, as did assaults on Hanseatic ships, while the English trading post in Danzig and its governor had no clear standing in its relations to the towns and the Teutonic Knights.[68] Though Lübeck warned the Prussians not to risk a drawback, grand master Konrad von Jungingen cancelled the treaty of Marienburg in February 1398 because of the towns' complaints. Only because Richard II was succeeded by Henry IV who had been in Prussia himself and retained friendly relations with the Teutonic Knights, at first, no dramatic consequences followed. Henry instead confirmed the Hanseatic privileges in October 1399. Nevertheless, the internal tensions between the towns concerning their relation to England led to new problems. While in 1403, England and Prussia reached a preliminary peace, Lübeck was afraid of separate Anglo-Prussian agreements.

In October and December 1405, the English delegation succeeded in concluding a second treaty of Marienburg and an Anglo-Hanseatic treaty in Dordrecht in which it promised stronger measures against pirates and negotiations about compensation. In case of new complaints, the Prussians could turn to the royal officials.[69] Finally, negotiations began in Den Haag in August 1407, soon agreements were reached, and a treaty regulating the compensations was ratified in 1408. This was flanked by a new Anglo-Prussian treaty in London in December 1409 which should secure protection for the merchants

66 HUB 4, 876.

67 Jenks, *England*, 485.

68 Stuart Jenks, "Die Ordnung für die englische Handelskolonie in Danzig (23. Mai 1405)," in *Danzig in acht Jahrhunderten*, ed. Bernhart Jähnig, Peter Letkemann, Quellen und Darstellungen zur Geschichte Westpreußens 23 (Münster: Nicolaus Copernicus, 1985), 105–20.

69 Jenks, *England*, 534–35.

while abroad.[70] Nevertheless, the main problems remained: the levy of tonnage and poundage in England, the demands for equal rights by the English merchants in the Baltic, and the English government had considerable problems to secure the payments included in the treaties. Different from Flanders or even Novgorod, the Hanseatic League was far from being successful in their relationship to England, but at least, the treaties formed a basis for continuous trade and for further negotiations.

The Constitutional Crisis in Lübeck (1408–1416) and Its Consequences

Already during the negotiations with England, a crisis had started that threatened the core of the Hanseatic League. Neither the aspirations of Cologne nor the representation of the Hanseatic towns in the West by the grand masters of the Teutonic Knights could really challenge Lübeck's leading position; rather, it was its internal problems that led to a period of weakness. Since the fourteenth century internal unrest in any of the towns had been regarded with anxiety and alarm by the other towns—according to their point of view it reduced the liberties of the towns by limiting the power of the town council and disturbing the town's unity necessary to reach decisions—and they often reacted with defensive measures to avoid the spread to other towns.

This was based on experience. In April 1374 the craftsmen of Braunschweig, striving after more influence in political affairs, rose against their town council in the so-called *Grosse Schicht* ('great riot') of 1375–1376. Soon unrest in other towns followed: in Lübeck, Nordhausen, Stade, Hamburg, and in 1378 in Danzig, though always under different circumstances. In Braunschweig several mayors and town councillors were killed, and others fled. In consequence, the town was excluded from the Hanseatic League (by *Verhansung*), but this was revoked in 1380, though the old town council and the leading group of citizens had not been re-installed into their former position. More than likely, it was sufficient that the harmony and unity in the town had been restored, even by the success of the new town council.[71] Nevertheless, the exclusion remained an important instrument to influence the internal developments of towns. When Kersten Sarnow, who had just been elected to the town council, succeeded in driving the influential family of the Wulflams out of Stralsund in

70 Ibid., 544–46.

71 Stuart Jenks, "Die Einstellung der Hanse zu den Stadtaufständen im Mittelalter," in *Die hansischen Tagfahrten*, 75–108; Hammel-Kiesow, *Hanse*, 85–86, 109.

1389, the threat of exclusion alone led to a change. Sarnow was overthrown and finally executed early in 1393, and the Wulflams returned.[72]

In Lübeck other riots followed.[73] In 1380 and again in 1384, the butchers (*Knochenhauer*) rose against the town council's control of the market which linked the number of masters to that of the stalls. Though the town council offered some compromises, in September 1384, a leading group of butchers planned an overthrow by force. This was betrayed in time, and the butchers involved were executed. In consequence, from 1386 on, the guilds of craftsmen had to swear obedience to the town council, but this did nothing to reduce social tensions.

When Lübeck ran into financial difficulties with the campaigns against the pirates and other military operations around 1400, social unrest increased again. In 1403, the town council needed the consent of the municipality for new taxes; it was therefore forced to declare its critical financial situation publicly. Nevertheless, the brewers and other craftsmen denied new duties until the town council renounced the oath of obedience introduced in 1386. But the greater dues did not help to improve the town's finances, especially since Lübeck started a campaign into Mecklenburg led by Jordan Pleskow in 1404. When the town council introduced a new duty of one penny per barrel beer in October 1405, the municipality enforced the formation of a supervising committee of 60 members elected by the citizens, as had happened in other towns, to discuss measures for levying of dues. Soon, the committee of 60 occupied itself with different tasks. It collected complaints of the municipality against taxes, the restrictions on craftsmen, the heavy costs of diplomatic missions and the towns' assemblies, and against urban policies in general, and it presented them to the town council. Since early 1407, the committee of 60 had intervened in the town's administration by adding one of its members to each town council. Open conflict arose when the committee demanded a change in the rules for the election of the town council. For a long time, the town council had decided about its new members (by *Kooptation*) itself, but now the committee of 60 demanded their elections by the municipality. This led to the exile of 15 out of 23 town councillors including all four mayors and their families to Lüneburg and Hamburg in spring 1408. When an effort for mediation failed, in May 1408, a new town council of 24 was elected according to the new rules,

---

72 Ralf-Gunnar Werlich, "Wulf Wulflam—ein hansischer Diplomat aus Stralsund," in *Akteure und Gegner der Hanse*, 67–92, at 76.

73 Cf. the survey of events in Erich Hoffmann, "Lübeck im Hoch- und Spätmittelalter. Die große Zeit Lübecks," in *Lübeckische Geschichte*, ed. Antjekathrin Graßmann (Lübeck: Schmid-Römhildt, 1988), 79–340.

while the members of the old town council claimed to be the legitimate representation of the town. The conflict between old and new town council did not only threaten Lübeck's standing in the Hanseatic League but also the strength of the whole community.

Since Lübeck was an imperial city, soon royal authority was involved. In 1400, King Wenzel had been deposed by the electors at the Rhine, and in his place they elected Ruprecht, the Count Palatine of the Rhine. This was not accepted by Wenzel, and some princes and the old town council of Lübeck had supported him. Now the new town council did homage to Ruprecht and paid its taxes to him, while the king accepted the right of the municipality to elect the town council. Meanwhile the exiled mayor Jordan Pleskow and other town councillors in exile succeeded in getting a judgement by the royal court in Heidelberg that Lübeck should call back the exiles into the town. Since the new town council reacted by confiscating the property of the exiles and decided not to answer to further summons of royal courts, in January 1410, King Ruprecht declared the imperial ban (*Reichsacht*) against Lübeck. Only his early death in the same year and the following double elections prevented further measures.

Nevertheless, the consequences of the events were severe. A *Hansetag* in Lübeck scheduled for May 1408 was cancelled; instead there were assemblies of the towns in Hamburg in 1408 and again in 1410, and in April 1412 a common assembly of the town's representatives took place in Lüneburg. Lübeck had lost its leading role, but it was not clear which city would step into its place. The merchants in Bruges complained that they did not know whom to address.[74] This was strengthened by the fact that the new town council in Lübeck succeeded in 'exporting' its constitutional ideas to other Wendish towns. In spring 1410, there were upheavals and new town councils in Rostock and Wismar; and in Hamburg new regulations increased the influence of the municipality on the town's policies,[75] while the members of the old Lübeck town council left the town in direction to Lüneburg. The assembly there in April 1412 decreed that Hamburg or—if Hamburg's town council was restricted by its municipality—Stralsund had to care for the problems of the merchants abroad,[76] but in fact it was Lüneburg which took over central functions because it now hosted nearly the entirety of the old Lübeck town council.

The imperial ban against Lübeck concerned every merchant who had trade relations with the town, so the *Kontor* in Bruges had already warned the

---

74 Dollinger, *Hanse*, 369.

75 Pitz, *Bürgereinung*, 118–25.

76 HR I 6, 68 § 18.

Livonian towns and Braunschweig in June 1410 about possible consequences. The Western European princes, especially the dukes of Burgundy and Brabant, were ready to enforce the ban, and the *Kontor* would not be able to protect those merchants co-operating with traders from Lübeck.[77] In fact, Duke John of Burgundy wrote to the new town council in Lübeck in April 1411 that members of the old town council, namely Jordan Pleskow, had asked for the arrest of Lübeck goods worth up to 4,000 marks pure gold (256,000 guilders) as compensation for their losses. He did not follow their request but demanded to solve the conflict.[78] With his mission to Bruges, Jordan Pleskow at least succeeded in preventing the *Kontor* from a clear decision in favour of the new town council, but his other diplomatic missions, to Prussia and to the by then generally accepted Roman King, Sigismund, were even less successful. Sigismund confirmed the old town council because the new one failed to appear at the royal court, but he did not renew the imperial ban against Lübeck. In consequence, the assembly at Lüneburg in 1412 at which neither the new town council of Lübeck nor those of Rostock and Wismar were present, could not agree on excluding Lübeck from the Hanseatic League.

Both sides did not give up. The new town council tried to win over Sigismund, who was notorious for his financial problems, by promising great sums of money. In July 1415, for the promise of 24,000 Rhenish guilders, the King renewed the town's privileges, made a decision about regulations concerning the compensation for the old town council, and lifted the ban against Lübeck. Though Sigismund also made his decision known to the Danish King, Eric of Pomerania,[79] in September 1415 Eric took measures against merchants from Lübeck on Scania, in Bergen, and elsewhere in the Scandinavian Kingdoms. When the new town council was not able to pay the 24,000 guilders in Bruges in November 1415, Sigismund revoked his earlier decision and in spring 1416 again opted for the old town council.

This situation finally led to a compromise which ended the conflict, and the parties agreed on a meeting of the old and new town councils and royal envoys, mediated by the other Wendish and Pomeranian towns.[80] Jordan Pleskow and the other nine members of the old council in exile still alive returned to Lübeck and were joined by five members of the old council who had remained in Lübeck, five members of the new council, and seven other merchants, two of them being members of the famous *Zirkelgesellschaft* ('Society of Dividers')

---

77 HR I 5, 685–86.
78 HUB 5, 998.
79 HR I 6, 203.
80 Cf. Pitz, *Bürgereinung*, 128–38.

of the urban patriciate.[81] Though the oath of obedience by the craftsmen was renewed and the citizens had to pay new dues for the reduced contribution of 13,000 guilders to King Sigismund, the atmosphere in Lübeck calmed down. At the same time, the old town councils in Rostock and Wismar were re-installed, and in Hamburg the regulations of 1410 limiting the power of the town council were revoked in 1417 while its committee of 60 was dissolved. The constitutional crisis in Lübeck and the other Wendish towns was over; the Hanseatic League regained its former strength.

In this situation, the *Hansetage*, the assemblies of the towns' representatives, once again gained importance for common legislation, as it had in the summer of 1366. Still in the aftermath of the first war against Denmark, an assembly at Lübeck had decided that only citizens of the Hanseatic towns were allowed to participate in the Hanseatic privileges and to become aldermen in the *Kontore*—which was resisted by the merchants in the trading posts but repeated several times—, that condemnations in one town should be valid also in all other towns, and that no one should be received as citizen who in times of crisis had resigned his citizenship.[82] After the end of the constitutional crisis, there was obviously the wide-spread perception that more concrete regulations were needed. Therefore, the assembly in May, June, and July 1417, which started in Rostock but ended in Lübeck because of negotiations with Duke Henry of Schleswig, 16 Wendish, Saxon, Prussian, and Livonian towns discussed the first draft for a 'Statute of the Hanseatic Towns'.

This also was discussed at the outstanding, impressive assembly in Lübeck between June and August 1418 by representatives from 35 towns from all regions of the Hanseatic League, even including the towns at the Zuiderzee. It demonstrated the regained political importance of the towns that the Dukes of Schleswig and Mecklenburg were present, in addition to envoys from the Roman king, the grand master of the Teutonic Knights, and the archbishop of Bremen. Its main topic was the conflict about the duchy of Schleswig, but also relations with Frisia, Holland, England, Flanders, Scotland, and Norway were on the agenda.

On June 24, 1418, the 'Statute of the Hanseatic Towns' was finally passed.[83] It starts—not accidentally—with regulations in case of civic riots. Whoever made a conspiracy against his town council would not be tolerated anywhere,

---

81 Sonja Dünnebeil, *Die Lübecker Zirkelgesellschaft. Formen der Selbstdarstellung einer städtischen Oberschicht*, Veröffentlichungen zur Geschichte der Hansestadt Lübeck, B 27 (Lübeck: Schmid-Römhild 1996).

82 HR I 1, 376.

83 HR I 6, 557; vgl. Jenks, "Einstellung," 86–90.

but would be caught and executed. If any town council was weakened in its autonomy or even deposed by civic unrest, the town had to be excluded from the common privileges of the Hanseatic towns (*Verhansung*); no one should further more trade with its citizens or help and host them in his own town or region. Anyone resisting the restoration of the town council's power was himself to be excluded from the privileges. The other thirty-two paragraphs of the statute repeat the regulation of 1366 concerning the use of the privileges in the *Kontore*, deal with the dissolution of trading societies, purchases on loan, the winter break in maritime navigation, coinage, measures against pirates, and other aspects of trade and crafts. Though this was partly only a summary of earlier legislation and by no means systematic, it demonstrated the common interests of the towns.

This holds true also for the regular record of this assembly. It stresses the importance of the *vryheit und herlicheid* ('liberty and authority') of the town council,[84] and it regulates that only town councillors are allowed to represent the towns at the assemblies, not the scribes or notaries. Most important is the decision about the representation of the towns in between the *Hansetage*. Lübeck and the Wendish towns confirmed, after having been asked, that they would continue to deal with the many affairs after and before common assemblies in the best interests of the towns and the merchants, as they had done before.[85] The assembly of 1418 thus marks another climax in the development of the structures of the Hanseatic League. The regulations against civic unrest were confirmed and extended, the authorities of the town councils strengthened, the leading role of the Wendish towns was defined, and many other issues were decided upon. Though plans for a closer military co-operation did come into fruition before the middle of the fifteenth century, at least from the internal point of view, the Hanseatic League was in a new period of bloom. But at this point, the dangers were coming from outside.

The Wars with Denmark and Holland-Zeeland and Other Regional Conflicts

By around 1400, the Hanseatic League had finished most conflicts with its trading partners successfully or at least had maintained the status quo. In Flanders and Novgorod, privileges had been confirmed or even extended. The treaties of Den Haag (1408) and London (1409) had contributed to stabilize

84 HR I 6, 556 § 62.

85 Ibid., §§ 17, 87.

Anglo-Hanseatic relations, and when Denmark regained Gotland from the Teutonic Knights in 1408, another possible cause for conflict had been removed. Nevertheless, basic problems remained unsolved, like the status of the English merchants in Prussia, and the kings and princes tried to strengthen and intensify their rule by controlling their countries' trade and by also reducing the privileges of foreign merchants or favouring their rivals. In consequence, conflicts intensified, and the influence of the Hanseatic towns suffered many drawbacks.

These events also concerned the southwest of Europe. In the fifteenth century, ships from the Hanseatic towns reached the Atlantic and the Western Mediterranean.[86] In 1419, there was a Prussian ship in Sevilla loading oil and wine. When John II of Castile decided to attack the Flemish-Hanseatic salt fleet near La Rochelle in the same year, accusing the Hanseatic merchants of supporting the English in Southern France, this led to a seemingly endless commercial conflict. When the Flemish concluded a peace ten years later, the Castilian-Hanseatic conflict remained unsolved; and in 1433, the towns decided to prohibit the import of Spanish wool. This finally led to a truce under Flemish mediation in 1443 which was prolonged later. The German merchants were allowed to move freely and securely in Castile but promised to prefer Castilian ships for the transport of their goods, if possible, and not to rival the Castilians in the Bay of Biscay.[87]

This was far from being a success, but the events in the Baltic proved to be more important for the future of the Hanseatic League. Margaret of Denmark had already started efforts to regain the Duchy of Schleswig after the death of Duke Gerhard VI in 1404. In 1411, in the five years' truce of Kolding, she secured the Northern part of the duchy. When she died in 1412, her heir Eric of Pomerania continued her policies with even greater force. He aimed at restoring the Baltic empire of the earlier Danish kings, which meant that he wanted to eliminate the towns' privileges. The Schauenburg counts of Holstein claimed the Duchy of Schleswig based on the grant by Margaret in 1386, but in 1413 Eric accused them of treason and reclaimed the duchy. He used the constitutional

86 Examples in Werner Paravicini, "Jenseits von Brügge. Norddeutsche Schiffer und Kaufleute an der Atlantikküste und im Mittelmeer in Mittelalter und Früher Neuzeit," in *Konzeptionelle Ansätze der Hanse-Historiographie*, ed. Eckhard Müller-Mertens, Heidelore Böcker, Hansische Studien, vol. 14 (Trier: Porta Alba, 2003), 69–114; Simone Abraham-Tisse, "Les relations hispano-hanséates au bas Moyen Âge," *En la España medieval* 14 (1991) 131–61, and 15 (1992), 249–95.

87 Dollinger, *Hanse*, 337–38; Theodor Hirsch, *Danzigs Handels- und Gewerbsgeschichte* (Danzig, 1858, repr. Schaan, Liechtenstein: Sändig, 1968), 272–74.

crisis of Lübeck to keep the town out of the conflict, and when the old town council returned to Lübeck, the mayor Jordan Pleskow followed a policy of appeasement towards Eric, perhaps also because the counts of Holstein meanwhile had employed pirates who not only attacked Danish but also Hanseatic ships. After the end of the truce in 1416, war broke out again, only interrupted by further truces in 1418 and 1420. In 1423, Lübeck under Pleskow and other Wendish towns allied with Eric though they claimed that there should be intensive mediation before starting military activities. But at this point, the Hanseatic League was divided. The Prussian cities did not follow the demand of the grand master to form an alliance with Denmark,[88] while Hamburg sided with the Schauenburg counts.

Only when Pleskow died in 1426 did the situation change. Meanwhile, Eric had erected a new fortress at the Øresund and started the exaction of a new custom for ships passing the Øresund, which was to continue until 1857.[89] The towns at first tried to mediate between Denmark and the counts of Holstein, but this failed because they demanded Eric's renunciation of Schleswig. In October 1426, the Wendish towns allied with the counts of Holstein and declared war on Denmark, followed by the Saxon towns in March 1427. While count Adolf VIII finally regained most of Schleswig after the conquest of Flensburg in 1431, the Wendish towns were less successful. When Hamburg and Lübeck supported the first Schauenburg attack on Flensburg in 1427, it ended in failure, and the Hamburg town councillor Johann Kletze was made responsible for the defeat—though it had been caused by internal quarrels—and executed. Also, the fleet led by the mayor of Lübeck, Tidemann Steen, suffered heavy losses on sea, and one fleet with salt from Southern France was captured by the Danish. Then the Wendish towns which only had received some support from the Saxon towns resorted to piracy and employed the 'victual brothers' under Bartholomäus Voet.[90] Their operations, the conquest of Flensburg, and internal problems of Eric, especially in Sweden, finally averted a complete failure. In 1435, the towns and Eric concluded the peace of Vordingborg which brought a confirmation of the towns' privileges, though Eric continued the exaction of the Øresund customs.

Though Vordingborg had been a partial success, Eric soon lost the support of his subjects. In 1438/39, the three councils of the realm of Denmark, Norway, and Sweden deposed him, and he withdrew first to Gotland, later to Pomerania.

---

88 HUB 6, 521.

89 Dietrich Schäfer, "Zur Frage nach der Einführung des Sundzolls," *Hansische Geschichtsblätter* Jg. 1875 (1876), 33–43.

90 Clarus, *Bartholomäus*.

His successor was Christopher III of Bavaria, Eric's nephew, who renewed the towns' privileges, though his relations to the Hanseatic League were ambivalent, since he supported the efforts of the Northern German princes to subject their towns to their authority. When his position in Denmark had been stabilized, he also gave privileges to the Dutch rivals of the Hanseatic towns. After his death in 1448, this continued under his successor Christian I of Oldenburg who at first only reigned in Denmark and Norway. In March 1460, after the death of Adolf VIII of Schleswig and Holstein, Christian was also elected count of Holstein and duke of Schleswig to be confirmed in the treaty of Ripen of May 1460. At that point, the towns had to take into account the increased power of the Danish kings who continued to interfere in Northern Germany.

After King Eric had been deposed, Lübeck occupied the fortress of Helsingborg at the Øresund for some time. This became important during the second great conflict in the 1430s with the duchies of Holland and Zeeland.[91] During the war with Denmark, the pirates employed by the towns had also taken Dutch ships, in 1429, and since there was no compensation, the Dutch retaliated with an attack on 12 salt ships of the Hanse near Brest in May 1438. In consequence, the Wendish town closed the Øresund for Dutch ships and started a war dominated by acts of piracy. Though the Wendish towns tried in vain to get further support, especially from the grand master of the Teutonic Knights, Paul von Rusdorf, and though the other towns at the Baltic were concerned, the duchies of Holland and Zeeland suffered more from the lack of grain from the Baltic. When King Christopher III invited both parties to negotiations in Copenhagen, they agreed on a ten years' truce, in August 1441. Soon regulations for compensations were found, and though there were some quarrels about the payments and smaller conflicts, relations remained mostly peaceful.[92] This was based on the mutual understanding that the trade between the Hanseatic towns and Holland-Zeeland was important for both since it had caused severe problems to blockade the Dutch trade in the Baltic. The Dutch were not only rivals, but also important partners in trading and shipping.

The situation also changed in the Western trading posts. The *Kontor* at Bergen was increasingly controlled by the Wendish towns who claimed the

---

91 Louis Sicking, "Die offensive Lösung. Militärische Aspekte des holländischen Ostseehandels im 15. und 16. Jahrhundert," *Hansische Geschichtsblätter* 117 (1999), 39–51, esp. 42–44.

92 Dieter Seifert, *Kompagnons und Konkurrenten. Holland und die Hanse im späten Mittelalter*, Quellen und Darstellungen zur hansischen Geschichte, NF. XLIII (Cologne, Weimar, Vienna: Böhlau, 1997), 321–418.

staple for stockfish from Bergen for Lübeck, Wismar, and Rostock in 1446.[93] This led to tensions between the towns—and later favoured the increasing importance of the Iceland trade—while in 1455 there was also a violent attack by Hanseatic merchants, killing the bishop of Bergen, the Danish king's official at Bergen (who had before expanded his jurisdiction on the German craftsmen at Bergen and otherwise restricted the rights of the *Kontor*), and 60 of his supporters.

In Bruges new conflicts arose as well. When Burgundy changed sides in the Hundred Years' War, 80 Germans were killed at Sluis in June 1436, accused of supporting the English. In consequence, the trading post was moved to Antwerp. The Hanseatic blockade resulted again in a famine in Bruges, while Duke Philip of Burgundy favoured the demands of the German merchants. Finally, their privileges were renewed. The *Kontor* returned to Bruges but soon complained again about breaches of the privileges, attacks against Hanseatic ships, and Flemish efforts to form a monopoly for spices and rare materials. Therefore, the assembly of the representatives of 39 towns at Lübeck in May 1447 discussed measures to strengthen the standing of the *Kontor*. They subjected more goods to the Bruges staple and extended the exaction of the *Kontor's* dues also to Brabant, Holland, and Zeeland. When negotiations only led to mutual accusations, in 1451, the towns discussed moving the trading post again, first to Deventer, but this was not accepted by most of the merchants, and then to Utrecht. When Duke Philip occupied Utrecht in 1455, negotiations started. The return to Bruges was celebrated by an entry of 200 merchants on horses led by the mayors of Lübeck, Hamburg, Bremen, and Cologne, in August 1457. But in fact not much had been reached. The blockade had lost its importance as a means of securing the towns' privileges, because many merchants were not willing to follow the common decisions and because Bruges had lost its commercial role to other trading centers like Antwerp. The Hanseatic League was very slow in reacting to the changes in the West, perhaps also because now it was also threatened in its core region, by the policies of the Northern German princes.

93 Cf. Mike Burkhardt, "Das Hanse*kontor* in Bergen im Spätmittelalter—Organisation und Struktur," *Hansische Geschichtsblätter* 124 (2006), 21–70; Thomas Brück, "Die Korporationen der Bergenfahrer in den wendischen Städten unter besonderer Berücksichtigung Stralsunds," in *Genossenschaftliche Strukturen in der Hanse*, ed. Nils Jörn, Detlef Kattinger, and Horst Wernicke, Quellen und Darstellungen zur hansischen Geschichte, N.F. 48 (Cologne, Weimar, Vienna: Böhlau, 1999),135–63, at 147.

The Threat by the Princes of the Empire and the Formation of the *Tohopesaten*

At the great assembly of the towns' representatives in summer 1418, Lübeck proposed a close alliance, a *tohopesate*, of the towns for 12 years under its leadership. In the case of war, the contingents from the Wendish, Pomeranian, Westphalian, Prussian, and Livonian towns were fixed; they should be engaged if there were threats to single towns, even if the enemies were their own territorial lords.[94] The plans for an alliance failed, but were not forgotten when the Northern German princes intensified their policies to strengthen the control over their territories and towns. At first, forms of closer co-operation between the regional groups were discussed at an assembly of Saxon and Wendish towns in Braunschweig in March 1427 when the Wendish towns joined the Saxon confederation concluded in 1426. Then, in January 1430, at the assembly in Lübeck where representatives of 31 towns came together—the Wendish group, cities in Saxony, Pomerania, Prussia, Westphalia, and at the Zuiderzee, even Breslau—they not only agreed on mutual support against the Hussites but also against other attacks, even by their princes and lords.[95]

Again, contingents of the towns or regional groups were fixed, reckoned in basic fighting units of three to four men on horses (knight, archer, squire), the *Glevenien*. Lübeck had to provide 16 *Glevenien*, Hamburg 12, the Prussian towns 40, the Livonians 20, Cologne 20, Braunschweig 20, etc., together about 400 *Glevenien* from 51 towns and the two groups from the East, including 25 towns not present who were threatened by exclusion from the Hanseatic privileges. The whole force would have numbered 1200–1600 men, which was not without strategic importance, but it would have proved difficult to muster the contingents in time. Thus, it was also decided that the neighbouring towns should sent support immediately with full force. Additionally, the aggressors should not be supported by materials and money or by granting safe-passage. But because important questions like the problem of costs and payments to the mercenaries were postponed to the next assembly, the regulations had only preliminary character and were never put into force.[96] Nevertheless, similar plans recurred in the following years, thus at a common assembly of the towns' representatives in March 1441 and at a meeting of the Saxon towns in

94 HUB 6, 170.

95 HR I 8, 712 §§ 1, 18, 20–21, 27.

96 Matthias Puhle, *Die Politik Braunschweigs innerhalb des sächsischen Städtebundes und der Hanse im späten Mittelalter*, Braunschweiger Werkstücke, vol. 63 (Braunschweig: Waisenhaus-Buchdr. und Verl., 1985), 80.

the summer of the same year.[97] This *tohopesate* was in fact to be not much more than an extension of the earlier Saxon-Wendish alliance, but joined by the towns from Pomerania and the margravate of Brandenburg. It was limited to six years, dedicated to the protection of trade and merchants and to the co-operation against princes and lords.

But these plans only came into fruition when the threat by the princes had become more concrete. When, during internal trouble, the municipality and the most import crafts of the double town of Berlin-Cölln turned to the Margrave of Brandenburg and Elector Frederick II in 1442, the town council gave the keys of the town to its lord and resigned its office. Frederick separated the towns which had been united ten years ago, decreed regulations for the election of the town councils in favour of the craftsmen and the old town council's enemies, demanded the confirmation of the new town councillors by their territorial lord, and prohibited any agreements without his consent. The citizens resisted and had to be forced to comply by a contingent of 600 horsemen. The Elector took over high jurisdiction and placed his judge into the new town hall on a bridge between the two towns, and in July 1443, he also started to build his new residence in Cölln. Early in 1448, these policies led to civic unrest and to attacks on the elector's officials, but Berlin did not regain its autonomy. When it was invited to an assembly in 1452, it declared that it had been left alone in its conflict with the prince and left the Hanseatic League, though the formal resignation only followed in 1516/18. The subjection of Berlin-Cölln was the signal for other princes and lords also to restrict the rights of their towns. In February 1443, Elector Frederick met with Christopher III of Denmark and the dukes of Mecklenburg, Pomerania, Braunschweig, and Saxony in the pilgrimage place of Wilsnack. Only the absence of Adolf VIII of Schleswig and Holstein prevented common decisions—he had a different approach to the towns. Though Christopher of Denmark in the aftermath in March came to Lübeck to discuss Lübeck's offer of a meditation with the former King Eric of Pomerania, the towns knew about the princes' intentions.

Early in March 1443, the Saxon towns had already discussed measures to protect the towns, and this recurred on two assemblies together with representatives of the Wendish towns later in March and in June. They finally agreed on a defensive alliance, i.e. not to support those who attacked the towns,[98] and they again discussed the draft for a *tohopesate* from 1441 and planned to put it into force. When the Saxon towns met in August 1443 in Halberstadt, they decided on supplementary regulations: to turn also against any other attack,

97 HR II 2, 238.

98 HR II 3, 38.

even against merchants or peasants; to suppress internal unrest by force, if necessary; and to prefer the *tohopesate* in case of conflicting agreements. Rather indirectly it becomes clear that the partners in the alliance had been divided in three, with Lübeck, Hamburg, and Magdeburg being the heads of the thirds. They were allowed to admit other towns interested in cooperation.[99] When the *tohopesate* of 38 Wendish, Saxon, Brandenburg, and Pomeranian towns was concluded for three years on 30 August 1443 in Lübeck,[100] it was only the three heads that signed the contract. For the first time after the dissolution of the 'Confederation of Cologne' in 1385, there was a closer alliance of the towns, though limited to Northern Germany.

In 1444 Kolberg came into conflict with Duke Bogislaw IX of Pomerania, and Soest renounced fealty to Archbishop Dietrich of Cologne, while Braunschweig suffered from another internal riot in 1445. Though the *tohopesate* did not intervene in all these conflicts, it was clear that the towns needed mutual support. Thus it was Braunschweig and the other Saxon towns that pressed the other towns to renew the alliance. In May 1447, the three thirds of 1443 were joined by a fourth group formed by the towns of Westphalia and at the Zuiderzee, led by Münster, Nijmegen, Deventer, Wesel, and Paderborn. The older thirds became fourths, and the now 62 towns allied themselves for ten years—though it is not clear if the contract was in fact ratified. But the situation remained critical, especially since in August 1449, Mecklenburg and Pomerania allied against their towns, and Frederick of Brandenburg co-operated with them. The towns reacted with the renewal of the *tohopesate* of 1447. After some discussions, finally, in September 1450 at an assembly in Lübeck, the towns' representatives agreed on a new *tohopesate* without the Brandenburg towns and thus only with three thirds, the Hamburg third which had included the cities of the margravate united with that of Lübeck. In case of an attack by the princes, all towns had to send their troops; otherwise they were threatened by exclusion from the *tohopesate* and the Hanseatic League. The alliance was put into force for six years in Lübeck in April 1451.

This was the peak of the urban alliances. In fact, all *tohopesaten* concluded later were much more limited. Their real impact is uncertain. The alliances were only agreed upon temporarily and were never intended to become part of the overall structures of the Hanseatic League. Thus it seems anachronistic to ask if a chance was missed for further development and intensification of the

99 HR II 3, 60.

100 Cf. the map in Horst Wernicke, "Die sächsischen Städte in der Hanse," in Matthias Puhle, ed., *Hanse-Städte-Bünde. Die sächsischen Städte zwischen Elbe und Weser um 1500*, Bd. 1 (Magdeburg: Stadt Magdeburg Museen 1996), 29–35, at 33.

towns' co-operation. Rather, the *tohopesaten* fit into the usual pattern of loose and changing agreements typical in the history of the Hanseatic League. They could not prevent Berlin-Cölln drifting away, enforced by the electors; while it did not contribute to the success of Soest (1449) and of most of the Prussian towns (1454/66) which choose a new sovereign. But it may be that the alliances deterred some princes from more far reaching measures, as Stralsund could resist an attempt of the Pomeranian dukes to extend their authority in 1458 with the help of the other towns and the Danish king. It is thus no accident that the *tohopesaten* continued on a regional basis, especially between Lübeck and its neighbouring towns.[101]

Anglo-Hanseatic Relations until the Peace of Utrecht (1474)

Though many of the former demands had been renewed after 1409, Anglo-Hanseatic trade relations remained relatively undisturbed until the 1430s. In March 1431, the English Parliament decided to raise the poundage for foreign merchants by 50 percent. This led to a growing crisis until June 1434, when the *Hansetag* at Lübeck opted for a double strategy of negotiations and blockade and won the support of the grand master.[102] When England suffered a setback in the Hundred Years' War with the change of sides of Duke Philip of Burgundy in 1435, the negotiations led to the conclusion of the Second Treaty of London in March 1437. This met all demands of the Hanseatic League: its privileges were renewed, all new dues were abolished, and its representatives were allowed to start legal proceedings against any of the English officials if they violated the rights of the merchants.[103]

In consequence, the trade of the merchants from the Wendish towns at the East coast of England flourished, while the Prussians were confronted by the free trade of English merchants in Prussia. Though Danzig convinced the grand master not to ratify the treaty, the English side kept to the agreement, nevertheless enforced by its difficult political situation. Several times, Henry VI demanded equal conditions for English merchants in Hanseatic towns, in 1442 and 1446, but new problems in the Anglo-Hanseatic relations only arose after the English attack on Wendish-Prussian salt ships in May 1449. While the

101 Hans Sauer, *Hansestädte und Landesfürsten*, Quellen und Darstellungen zur hansischen Geschichte NF. XVI (Cologne, Vienna: Böhlau, 1971), 180, 185.

102 Jenks, *England*, 2, 585–86.

103 Cf. also Terry H. Lloyd, "A re-consideration of two Anglo-Hanseatic treaties of the fifteenth century," *English Historical Review* 102 (1987), 916–30.

Prussians decided for new negotiations, in June 1450 Lübeck requested that the German merchants in London should leave England. When the Lübeck merchants sailing to Bergen captured English envoys in July 1450, they were brought to Lübeck. In April 1452, Lübeck concluded an agreement with Christian I of Denmark to stop any English goods coming through the Øresund. Lübeck added an ordinance to completely stop all trade with English cloth. The English reaction was weak, owing to the defeats in the Hundred Years' War. The privileges were revoked only temporarily, as tonnage and poundage were soon introduced again, both later limited to Lübeck and the Prussians (until 1453). Negotiations scheduled for May 1454 did not take place because of the Thirteen Years' War between the towns and the Teutonic Knights in Prussia (1454–1466). The unstable balance in the Anglo-Hanseatic relations continued because of ongoing incidents, such as when the English took a salt fleet from Lübeck in July 1458.

This ongoing crisis only ended in war, when Danish contingents assaulted English ships in the Øresund, Pentecost 1468, and when the Hanseatic League was made responsible for the attack. In July 1468, the German merchants in London were arrested and their goods confiscated. Diplomatic efforts were in vain. The merchants were judged guilty before the crown council in November, with the exception of the traders from Cologne who came to separate arrangements with the English, who in consequence later were excluded from the Hanseatic privileges in April 1471.[104] An assembly of the towns' representatives in September 1468 had offered negotiations, as Edward IV was open to diplomatic initiatives and waited with the distribution of the confiscated goods until April 1469. At the same time, the towns prohibited the trade with England and called back the German merchants. When Duke Charles of Burgundy tried to mediate,[105] the Lübeck canon and syndic Dr. Johann Osthusen formulated a statement rejecting any common liability of the Hanseatic towns. Negotiations in Bruges failed, while the trade with England was interrupted, and the import of English cloth was prohibited from November 1470. The situation was complicated by the conflict between Edward IV and Richard Earl of Warwick, who in 1470 re-installed Henry VI.

---

104 Jenks, *England*, 2, 713–16.

105 Petra Ehm-Schmock, "Handelspartner, Reichsfeind, Städtefeind: Karl der Kühne und die Hanse 1465–1477," in *Les Relations entre la France et les villes hanséatiques de Hambourg, Brême et Lübeck. Moyen Age—XIXe siècle / Die Beziehungen zwischen Frankreich und den Hansestädten Hamburg, Bremen und Lübeck. Mittelalter—19. Jahrhundert*, ed. Isabelle Richefort, Burghart Schmidt, Diplomatie et Histoire (Brussels: Peter Lang, 2006), 149–76.

Edward regained the throne in May 1471. Before that, he had crossed the Channel with the help of 14 hanseatic ships, so that the towns were hoping for a favourable solution of the conflict. But Edward renewed the privileges of Cologne in July, at least temporarily, while the towns could not agree on the prohibition of trading with English cloth. Especially Danzig complained about Deventer, Wesel, and other cities that sold English cloth to Southern Germany. Its town council demanded to cancel the earlier decisions, and Danzig merchants in Bruges started to bring English cloth into the Baltic themselves. At that point, the ships from Danzig contributed mostly to the war of piracy directed against English, but also against French and Flemish ships. One of its captains, Paul Beneke, later became famous for his assaults (exploited by 20th c. nationalistic propaganda), one of which being directed against a galley from Florence with freight said to be worth 60,000 pounds *groot*, sailing under a Burgundian flag. Though Charles of Burgundy declared that he would demand compensation for losses of his subjects and prohibited any help for the Hanseatic ships like trade with booty and supply with victuals, he continued his efforts for negotiations.

In May 1472, English envoys proposed talks in Utrecht, and after some delays, in May 1473, Lübeck declared its consent to the preliminary conditions, also in the name of the other towns involved. When negotiations started in July, the English diplomats were struck by the wide ranging demands of the Hanseatic League, including compensation for the loss of the salt fleets in 1449 and 1458 as for the events in 1468.[106] Edward IV did not concede the transfer of the trading posts in London, Boston, and Lynn into the towns' property and the explicit exclusion of the merchants from Cologne, but wanted to conclude peace at nearly any price. Thus he confirmed nearly all regulations for the Hanseatic merchants according to the second treaty of London (1437), reduced some extra duties and guaranteed the quality of English cloth, while he completely gave up the demand for reciprocity for the English merchants in the Baltic which had been raised several times before. But this diplomatic success has to be assessed against the background of the fact that the trade of the Hanseatic League in England had lost its earlier importance already by 1420.[107]

---

106 Jenks, *England*, 2, 733–36.

107 Ibid., 745; cf. Stuart Jenks, "Der Frieden von Utrecht," in *Der hansische Sonderweg? Beiträge zur Sozial- und Wirtschaftsgeschichte der Hanse*, ed. Stuart Jenks, Michael North, Quellen und Darstellungen zur hansischen Geschichte, N.F. 39 (Cologne, Weimar, Vienna: Böhlau, 1993), 59–76; Lloyd, *Reconsideration*; Kenneth A. Fowler, "English diplomacy and the peace of Utrecht," in *Frühformen Englisch-Deutscher Handelspartnerschaft*, ed. Klaus Friedland, Quellen und Darstellungen zur Hansischen Geschichte, N.F. 23 (Cologne, Vienna, 1976), 9–26.

Conclusion

The so-called 'Golden Age of the Hanseatic League', which started in the middle of the fourteenth century and somehow lasted until the peace of Utrecht (1474), was no unity. Relative peak periods like the peace of Stralsund in 1370 and the assembly of the towns' representatives in Lübeck in summer 1418 alternate with periods of crisis in internal and external affairs, like the constitutional crisis in Lübeck from 1408–1416 or the relations with Denmark in the 1420s. The basic conditions and the parties involved always changed, as did the political aims of the participants. Thus it is not only difficult but perhaps also dangerous to generalize the events, especially since the characteristic as a bloom period has been disputed. Nevertheless, there are some tendencies and elements which are notable for the years between 1350 and 1474 when compared to the other periods.

After 1358, the assemblies of the towns' representatives, the *Hansetage*, became the most-important instrument for the co-ordination of the towns' policies and measures. This first proved successful during the blockade of Flanders after 1358, and continued during the wars with Denmark between 1361 and 1370. Even the peace treaty was negotiated at an assembly in Stralsund. Time and again, the towns agreed on measures to strengthen their decisions, also at the assembly in Lübeck in summer 1418. In the time of the great *tohopesaten*, the *Hansetage* were flanked by several meetings of the Wendish and Saxon towns while the number of common assemblies decreased. This seems to be a general tendency of the fifteenth century, leading to the period of reorganization in the 1550s. Nevertheless, the *Hansetage* of the fifteenth century left a growing corpus of legislation which regulated many aspects of civic life.

At least in two periods, the Hanseatic towns reached a higher degree of co-operation and organization, with the 'Confederation of Cologne' (1367–1385) and the *tohopesaten* of 1443/51. It is obvious that in both cases the alliances were only intended for limited periods and goals and that no permanent intensification of the Hanseatic League or even the formation of an urban union was intended, at least by most of the leading representatives involved. It has been pointed out that the imperial legislation only allowed urban alliances for the restoration of regional peace.[108] Maybe this influenced the towns' policies, but the restrictions are in line with the general tendencies of the town councils' policies, which aimed at defending their self-government and relative

108 See the Goldene Bulle of 1355/56. In: *Monumenta Germaniae Historica, Legum sect. IV.: Constitutiones et acta publica imperatorum et regum*, vol. 11: *Dokumente zur Geschichte des Deutschen Reiches und seiner Verfassung. 1354–1356*, ed. Wolfgang D. Fritz (Weimar: Hermann Böhlau 1978–1992), 535–633, § 15, at 600.

autonomy. Thus, the regulations against urban riots passed during the 'Golden Age of the Hanseatic League' are closely related to their reservations in taking over general and long-lasting obligations.

After 1350, the Hanseatic League was without any doubt mostly successful in maintaining and even extending the privileges which it had received earlier. This was achieved by its new institutions, the *Hansetage* and the closer alliances, while the old instrument of blockade lost much of its importance as becomes finally clear from the events in Bruges before 1458. Sometimes the towns were favoured by the circumstances like in the peace of Vordingborg (1435) or in that of Utrecht (1474), but in other contexts they proved at least equal to their opponents. Nevertheless, it goes too far to call the Hanseatic League a 'great Northern European power', even after 1370. Its potential was limited. The towns were able to control fortresses like that of the Øresund or other towns like Stockholm (1395–1398) only for some time, and their successes often depended on intensive diplomacy or support by territorial powers. In this perspective, e.g., the 'decline' from the peace of Stralsund to that of Vordingborg is not as sharp as it may seem.

In general, the years from 1350 to 1474 were a formative period in the history of the Hanseatic League. While the *Kontore* had developed before, the *Hansetage* and general alliances of the towns followed after 1350. And it was the 'Golden Age' which in fact shaped the public perception of the Hanseatic League that is most prevalent today.

CHAPTER 3

The Hanseatic League in the Early Modern Period*

Michael North

Introduction

The decline and dissolution of the Hanseatic League was a gradual process. While the collective alliance as an institution was increasingly less able to monopolize the trade of the North and Baltic Sea realms, or rather to direct and dictate the conditions of trade policy,[1] individual Hanseatic cities, like Hamburg and Danzig, rose up during the sixteenth and seventeenth centuries to become important centers of trade. The conflicts with England preceding the Peace of Utrecht in 1474—during which Cologne remained expelled from the League—had already shown that the cities' interests could no longer remain unified. While Lübeck continually hearkened back to old privileges and practiced an aggressive policy against Holland, as well as against Denmark, Hamburg and Danzig acted with significantly more flexibility.

Rivalry on All Fronts

The confrontations with Dutch shipping are a good first example of rivalry. As the grain export from Prussian Hanseatic Cities increased, the demand for space in Dutch and Zeeland ship holds also grew.[2] In Danzig, it was imperative to enlist the freight service of the Dutch and hence necessary to avoid being pulled into a war-like opposition to Holland as Lübeck had been (1511–1514). And while Lübeck's commerce declined in the first decade of the sixteenth century, Dutch shippers increased their share of Danzig's sea commerce from one quarter (1475–76) to fifty percent (1583).

---

* Translated by Christian Kemp.

1 For an overview of late Medieval trade see Michael North, *The Expansion of Europe, 1250–1500* (Manchester, 2012), 365–382.

2 Dieter Seifert, *Kompagnons und Konkurrenten: Holland und die Hanse im späten Mittelalter*, (Cologne: Böhlau, 1997).

DOI 10.1163/9789004284760_005

TABLE 3.1 *Danzig Sea Commerce 1460–1583 (Number of ships that called at or departed from Danzig)*

Ports of Departure or Origin	1460	1475/76	1530	1583
Niederlande	11	160	235	1015
Lübeck	59	168	24	66
Rostock	10	45	21	27
Stralsund	20	18	13	27
Wismar	5	18	3	3
Kolberg	2	1	10	50
Stolp	2	5	2	22
Warp	–	–	–	20
Rügenwalde	–	5	1	18
Stettin	1	7	6	15
Greifswald	3	3	2	11
Treptow	3	–	1	11
Köslin	–	–	–	10
Anklam	1	1	8	1

Source: Johannes Schildhauer, "Zur Verlagerung des See- und Handelsverkehrs im nordeuropäischen Raum während des 15. und 16. Jahrhunderts," in *Jahrbuch für Wirtschaftsgeschichte* vol. 4 (1968), 192–206.

Both the trade of Lübeck and that of the Wendish Hanseatic League cities grew with the Baltic Sea trade. However, the Dutch profited disproportionately from the trade and would fully control these cities economically at the close of the sixteenth century. Additionally, Bruges, the traditional destination of the Hanseatic merchants in Flanders, had been in decline since 1460, because the merchants had primarily frequented the Brabant trade fairs in Bergen op Zoom and in Antwerp. By the time the Hanseatic merchants finally completed a counting house in Antwerp in 1563, Antwerp's commerce had already passed its zenith.

Upper German rivals of the Hanseatic cities had on the other hand greatly profited from the Brabant trade fairs. As rivals to the people of Cologne, merchants of Nuremberg purchased English cloth at the Brabant trade fairs that they had dyed and finished on the spot in order to expand trade to the South and Southeast. Demand for silver in the Burgundian Netherlands in the last third of the fifteenth century drew the expanding trade of the Upper Germans with their silver, copper, fustian, and Venetian spices to Brabant, and especially to Antwerp. The widespread control of the middle European mining production by the Upper German capitol and the extension of Upper German commerce into Italy were prerequisites to this. Through an Italian trading branch, the citizens of Nuremberg achieved a key position in the continental spice trade that they focused on the Brabant and Frankfurt trade fairs. At the beginning of the sixteenth century, the Fuggers controlled the Portuguese spice trade in Antwerp because Portugal was dependent on Nuremberg metal-wares (primarily brass) as well as copper and silver for its exchanges with Africa and India. In addition, the Portuguese used the growing buying power of African gold in Flanders and Brabant, to purchase their spices in India with silver.[3]

The Upper German trade with the Baltic Sea area experienced a significant revitalization in the second half of the fifteenth century as a result of the growing importance of the Frankfurt trade fairs and the establishment of Nuremberg's merchants. In Frankfurt, the Hanseatic merchants, or their business contacts, met with the citizens of Nuremberg and Augsburg as well as Italians, and sold them herring, stockfish (dried cod), furs, leather, and wax. In exchange, the Hanseatic merchants obtained spices, Italian damask and brocade, metal, and samples from the Nuremberg arms industry. Aside from Frankfurt being the most important precious metals market of the empire, it also served as a center of accounting and payment balancing for transactions between the Hanseatic League and the Upper Germans. Upper German "Merchant Bankers" processed not only the money transfers for the Baltic Sea area, but they also took over a portion of the precious metals concern. Thus, the mint in Lübeck was supplied with the silver necessary for minting by Nuremberg merchants. At the close of fifteenth century and in the early sixteenth century, they entrusted the firm of Mathias Mulich with this task; the firm also served as a creditor for the city as well as for the Danish kings and the Duke of Holstein.[4]

---

3 Herman Van der Wee, *The Growth of the Antwerp Market and the European Economy, Fourteenth–Sixteenth Centuries* (The Hague, 1963).

4 Claus Nordmann, *Nürnberger Großhändler im spätmittelalterlichen Lübeck* (Nürnberg, 1933); Michael North, "Banking and Credit in Northern Germany in the Fifteenth and Sixteenth Centuries," in idem., *From the North Sea to the Baltic. Essays in Commercial, Monetary and Agrarian History, 1500–1800* (Aldershot, 1996), 811–826; W. von Stromer, *Oberdeutsche Hochfinanz 1350–1450*, vol. 1–3 (Wiesbaden, 1970). Gerhard Fouquet, "Geschäft und Politik, Ehe und Verwandtschaft—Briefe an den Nürnberg-Lübecker Kaufmann Matthias Mulich vom Winter 1522/23", in Helmut Bräuer, and Elke Schlenkrich, eds., *Die Stadt als Kommunikationsraum. Beiträge zur Stadtgeschichte vom Mittelalter bis ins 20. Jahrhundert. Festschrift für Karl Czok zum 75. Geburtstag* (Leipzig, 2001), 311–346.

The Upper Germans made themselves increasingly independent from the Hanseatic League's commercial mediations with Livonia and Prussia, in that they took up the direct exchange of goods with these markets. Therefore, the North-South trade lost considerable importance along the route between Frankfurt and Lübeck in the sixteenth century because the spice and copper trade was concentrated in Antwerp and the fur trade was concentrated in Leipzig. For the most part, the Fuggers and their successors shipped the upper Hungarian copper on the Vistula or down the Oder through Danzig, or Stettin to Antwerp. Only small quantities went through Hamburg and Lübeck in the west. Likewise, the trade exchanges of Upper Germany with the East proceeded more commonly along the overland routes through Breslau and Leipzig than along the longer route via Lübeck. Only seldom did Nuremberg's merchants still buy fish and Eastern wares from Lübeck or deliver plate and brass wares to Livonia. The commerce of the Upper German intermediary monopoly in money exchange was influenced little by these geographic extensions of trade. Furthermore, citizens of Nuremberg and Augsburg also conducted transactions for Hamburg and Lübeck, cities which at first gradually adopted the financial techniques of Upper Germany or the West.

In the Eastern Baltic region, the closure of the Hanseatic branch office in Novgorad, St. Peter's House (Peterhofes), also brought an apparent retreat of trade. After the loss of the Novgorad branch office, Hanseatic commerce had to seek new routes. The Livonian Hanseatic cities, Riga and more importantly Reval, whose trade with Lübeck developed dynamically over the course of the fifteenth and sixteenth centuries, profited from this. Still, political disagreements between Russia and Sweden could also endanger this trade, and the merchants were forced to reorient themselves multiple times. As a result of the conquest of Narva by the Russians, Reval was cut off from its Russian hinterland. In the short term, the merchants relocated their Russian trade from Reval to Viborg, and from 1559 on, concentrated on Narva, as this was the official Russian location for foreign trade. At the same time, the exports of Riga took an upswing, in which Lübeck, from ware to ware and to various extents, took part. While Riga's exports of flax, hemp, ash, and tar went overwhelmingly through the Øresund to Western Europe, and especially the Netherlands, Lübeck took over exports of leather, skins, and tallow almost exclusively. The merchant Wolter von Holstein, for example, drew leather, skins, and flax as well as tallow and wax from Riga, while he shipped primarily cloth and herring back.[5] Through the expansion of its hinterland into Lithuania and Russia at the

5 Marie-Louise Pelus, *Wolter von Holsten marchand Lubeckois dans la seconde moitié du seizième siècle. Contribution à l'étude des relations commerciales entre Lübeck et les villes*

end of the sixteenth century, Riga developed into the most important trading center of Livonia; however, in the period following, it was generally ignored by Lübeck, and frequented most by Dutch ships.

In the west, exchange shifted to England due to the interests of Hamburg. However, Iceland also became increasingly important as a result among other things of the decline of the Hanseatic Bergen-Norwegian trade.[6] In particular, criticism from the Upper German buyers over the quality of Lübeck's dried cod deliveries became more and more frequent. At the same time, the market share of dried cod decreased further because Lübeck did not adapt to competition from cheaper fish from the Netherlands and Iceland. While Lübeck firmly retained a trade office in Bergen in the sixteenth century, Hamburg had already co-opted the disputed route to Iceland from Lübeck by the close of the fifteenth century. Primary import articles from Iceland were fish and salt dried cod. These were traded by way of Hamburg to Middle and Eastern Germany, and a considerable portion was shipped directly to England and Amsterdam from Iceland. In exchange, Hamburg's merchants exported grain, flour, and particularly beer to Iceland.[7]

In the first decades of the sixteenth century, Hamburg's trade with England was based on the export of Icelandic dried cod (stock fish) as well as northern and middle German fabric to England, and in return English Indian ink was obtained and brought to the Dutch markets. A portion of the wares earmarked for England, like fabric from Salzwedel and Osnabrück, as well as wax and tar, were obtained and shipped by merchants in Antwerp. In this manner, profits obtained in the Netherlands were immediately converted into export wares, making payment easier.[8] With this system in place, Hamburg took Lübeck's place in the Hanseatic trade with England, which, as in the fifteenth century, was still dominated by Cologne and Danzig. As a rule, Lübeck carried out its English trade, and the simultaneously occurring distribution of its eastern wares, through Hamburg. Through privilege and settlement,

---

lioniennes, Quellen und Darstellungen zur hansischen Geschichte N.F. 25 (Cologne/Vienna, 1981), 207, 220. For general information see also Norbert Angermann, Die Hanse und Rußland in den Jahren 1584–1603," *Hansische Geschichsblätter* 102 (1984), 79–90.

6 Mike Burkhardt, "Die Geschichte des Bergenhandels im Spätmittelalter. Handel, Kaufleute, Netzwerke" (Doctoral Dissertation, University of Copenhagen, 2006).

7 Ernst Baasch, *Die Islandfahrt der Deutschen, namentlich der Hamburger von 15. bis 17. Jahrhundert* (Hamburg, 1889), 15, 76–77, 172.

8 Klaus Friedland, "Hamburger Englandfahrer 1512–1557," *Zeitschrift des Vereins für Hamburgische Geschichte* 46 (1960), 1–44, hier 8–14; Michael North, *Geldumlauf und Wirtschaftskonjunktur im südlichen Ostseeraum an der Wende zur Neuzeit (1440–1570)* (Sigmaringen, 1990), 159ff.

Hamburg's merchants drew back from active trade with England. This is taken from the account of the English merchant Matthias Hoep, who worked in London as a contact for Hamburg's merchants until 1570, and who for short time after his return to Hamburg received cloth from London and purchased it from the "Merchant Adventurers" in Hamburg from 1572 on. In the years to come the trade with England took place almost exclusively in Hamburg, whereby the Hamburg Clothiers Guild was involved in the marketing of the "Merchant Adventurers" imported cloth.[9]

However, the settlement of the "Merchant Adventurers" in Hamburg led to great conflicts between Lübeck and Hamburg, as well as between the Hanseatic Cities and England, which, in light of the background for the conflict between England and Spain, became a great explosive force in foreign policy.

The Lengthy Negotiations with England, the Emperor, and the Empire Concerning the Settlement of the "Merchant Adventurers"

In 1567, Hamburg had opened a residence for the English merchants (Merchant Adventurers) for ten years, which benefited both parties. Due to the loss of the Dutch market as a result of the Dutch Revolt, this trading post was critical for the "Merchant Adventurers". With this in mind, the Hanseatic League smelled an opportunity to regain the most preferable trade privileges on the British Isles, which were at that time disputed by England. Therefore, the Hanseatic Diet (*Hansetag*) called upon Hamburg to close the trading post of the "Merchant Adventurers" after the expiration of the ten year agreement, which England responded to with countermeasures such as the lockout of Hanseatic merchants from the cloth trading center in Blackwell Hall, London.

In this situation the counts of East Friesia and Emden as well as the city of Elbing offered the "Merchant Adventurers" a new domicile where they would be protected from the repressions of the Hanseatic League. Because protests against East Friesia bore no fruit, the Emperor and the Imperial Diet (*Reichstag*) were the only ones who could settle the situation; therefore they ordered an expulsion of the English. The Electoral Council (*Kurfürstenrat*) was already concerned with the affair at the outset of the year 1580,[10] and in

9 Richard Ehrenberg, *Hamburg und England im Zeitalter der Königin Elisabeth* (Jena, 1896), 76–101, 125.

10 *Danziger Inventar 1531–1591*, ed. Paul Simson, Nr. 8088 (Munich/Leipzig, 1913), 636. For the following see Michael North, "Reich und Reichstag im 16. Jahrhundert—der Blick aus der angeblichen Reichsferne", in Maximilian Lanzinner, and Arno Strohmeyer, eds., *Der*

December briefed a legation to the Emperor, which was supposed to use the monopolistic endeavors of the English company as an argument in the Imperial proceedings against Count Edzard of East Frisia. Peradventure an English delegation should appear before the Emperor at the same time, the envoys were to approach the Emperor with a memorandum composed by the Hanseatic legal counsel, Heinrich Sudermann, in which the contradiction between the monopolistic trade of the English and the simultaneous loss of privileges of the Hanseatic League in England was made apparent. In addition, the position of Count Edzard, who correctly pointed out that the loss of Hanseatic privilege in England lay thirty years in the past and that the Hanseatic League sought to achieve "under the appearance of monopolistic action [...] that the Holy Roman Empire should take up the cause and help the Hanseatic cities regain their privileges," had to be refuted.[11]

In order to influence the Emperor, the content of the Sudermann Memorandum, from January 1581, was compiled one more time in the same month for the Imperial Chamberlain, Hans Trautson. In the Memorandum, the important role of the Hanseatic League for defense and its privileges as well as the important role of its land and waterways against enemy powers was emphasized:

> The ancient Holy Roman Hanseatic League, a commendable body, or commune seen from many advantages, and furthermore the unifier of the cities of the Holy Roman Empire, has for more than three hundred years been a beneficial curtain-wall against all potential enemy potentates, for the maintenance of free country roads and access to water and land, to the bettering and growth of honest commerce and the renunciation of unbearable tolls, exactions, and burdens, whereby the German nation, by foreign un-Germans, to unbearable burdens and hardships may become [subject].[12]

In addition to this, Sudermann put together a variety of questions for the council of Frankfurt (*Frankfurter Rat*), which, through an interrogation of English merchants at the Frankfurt trade fair (*Frankfurter Messe*), was supposed to have provided the information about monopolistic practices.

Reichstag 1486–1613: Kommunikation—Wahrnehmung—Öffentlichkeit (Göttingen 2006), 221–236.

11 *Kölner Inventarband, Zweiter Band: 1572–1591*, ed. Konstantin Höhlbaum, Nr. 146 (Leipzig, 1903), 644.

12 Ibid., Nr. 147, 667.

At the Imperial Diet of Augsburg in 1582, Emperor Rudolph II made his position known on the trade obstructions of neighboring states and also commented on the complaints of the Hanseatic cities in a proposition that was given to the Imperial estates in a documentary supplement which included the petitions, memorandums, instructions and documentations of the past negotiations of the Imperial Hanseatic cities. With this the Imperial cities expressed themselves primarily only in the sense of the demands of the Hanseatic City.[13] At the same time, they bombarded the English ambassador, George Gilpin, and the representatives of the Hanseatic Cities with complaints and defensive writings. The Hanseatic cities came out of the memorandum war as victors, because the electoral and princely councils (*Kurfürstrat* and *Fürstenrat* respectively) took up deliberations on this problem. In case it did not come to a compromise between England and the Hanseatic cities with regard to the privileges, they recommended that:

> [...] all English and Merchant Adventurers, together with their companies, their shipping, and their destinations, to approach also the buying and selling and all stock trade to Emden and otherwise contained within the Holy Empire with special earnest. By official Imperial mandate this is forbidden to the Counts of East Frisia, as well as all other estates and subjects of the Holy Empire; moreover, to keep this mandate with obedience, they shall be liable by loss of title, fifes and other rights, which they have received, from their majesty and Holy Empire, imposed and offered.[14]

The Imperial cities commented on these considerations in a resolution conceived by Lübeck's legal counsel, Calixt Schein, and noted that the Hanseatic privileges and the monopoly problem were two different things, however the monopolistic practices of the "Merchant Adventurers"[15] in the Empire were independent from the influence of the English Queen. The Hanseatic Cities made a similar argument. Thereupon the Electoral (*Kurfürstenrat*) and Princely (*Fürstenrat*) Councils took the discussion up again, and both bodies dismissed the resolution; the dismissal served as a basis for a mandate in favor of the Hanseatic Cities. This banned the English, "monopolistic trade",

13 I am indebted to Dr. Josef Leeb for providing additional sources of the Holy Roman Empire.

14 *Kölner Inventarband, Zweiter Band: 1572–1591*, ed. Konstantin Höhlbaum, Nr. 170 (Leipzig, 1903), 734.

15 Ibid., Nr. 171, 734.

and threatened noncompliance with expulsion.[16] The joy of accomplishment remained but briefly. Although electoral Mainz, Cologne, Trier, Saxony, and Brandenburg, the Imperial Cities and numerous princes urged the publication of the decree—the Hanseatic Cities had heretofore written to Trier, Mainz, Saxony, and Brandenburg—the Emperor hesitated to draw it up, let alone put it into practice. Instead, he admonished the Counts of East Friesia, conveyed to the English envoys in a decree the contents of the decision of the Imperial Estates, and asked Queen Elizabeth to resolve the problems at the core of the Hanseatic grievances. Thus, on the one hand, the Emperor sought a compromise with England, and on the other hand, he had discovered the tactic of the Hanseatic Cities.

> [The Cities have] given no little cause to this widespread enfifement and reduction of their freedoms, in that they themselves initially opposed the Queen and also whose commands and charges, which in the crown at least must be, opposed, finally also the English have been driven from Hamburg and other ports against the request and warning of the Queen, from this has all of this refuse emanated.[17]

Only two options remained to the Hanseatic Cities, the first, seven additional and unsuccessful legations to England, which cost 150,000 *Tollar*, and concerning which a supplication to the Imperial Deputations Council (*Reichsdeputationstag*) of Worms was judged in 1586, and the second, the summoning of the Aulic Council (*Reichshofrates*).[18] After the English Queen had—in a 1589 letter to the Emperor concerning this—offered the Electors and the Hanseatic Cities a trade agreement, which should have ensured identical conditions in both kingdoms for the English and Hanseatic merchants but was rejected by the Hanseatic League, it appeared advisable to the Emperor and his consultant Electors to wait for further developments. Although the "Merchant Adventurers" had relocated their trading post from Emden to Stade in 1587, the Regensburg Diet of 1594 at first still feared open conflict and remained ready for compromise. Indeed, the envoys of Lübeck and Cologne managed

16 Haus-, Hof- und Staatsarchiv Vienna, Acta Antiqua 27, fol. 136–139 (spätere Kopie).

17 Quotation from Ludwig Beutin, *Das Reich, die Hansestädte und England (1590–1618)* (Berlin, 1929), note 4, p. 4 (Marcus, S. 55, Anm. 20, K. I. Nr 2179).

18 Nr. 24: Supplikation der Hansestädte an den DT mit Bericht über die 1585 erfolgte, Gesandtschaft zur Kgn. von England; von Dr. Heinrich Sudermann, Syndikus in Lübeck, mit vier Beilagen (in: Thomas Fröschl, ed. *Der Reichsdeputationstag zu Worms 1586* (Göttingen, 1994), 793.

to get the English question on the agenda, however, the Electoral Council hindered a publication of the decided upon decree of 1582. With this, new political situations arose, because Electoral Pfalz, for instance, as an alliance partner of England, was therefore dedicated to stall a judgment on the "Merchant Adventurers".

Only the Emperor's petition to the Wendish Hanseatic Cities to take part in the defense against the Turks (*Türkenhilfe*) and their response that they were by reason of the impairment of their commerce not in a position to do so brought a reversal in 1595. Now Rudolf II demanded the restoration of Hanseatic privileges in England and the abolition of the monopoly of the "Merchant Adventurers". Because England responded to this demand evasively, the Hanseatic Cities once again requested a ban from the Emperor on English trade in the Empire. After the Spanish envoy to the Empire and Archduke Albert, the Governor of the Spanish Netherlands, put pressure on the Emperor, the Aulic Council decreed the expulsion of the "Adventurers" from the Empire in 1597. The reclamation of Hanseatic privileges in England was also intended with the mandate released on August 1. The "Merchant Adventurers" protested sharply, and the Queen was also surprised by the mandate. She applied not only in writing to the Protestant Imperial Princes, rather also sent envoys to the Imperial Diet (*Reichstag*) and Regensburg, who were intended to prevent the execution of the mandate. The Hanseatic Cities were banned from all trade in England and the occupants of the Stahlhof ordered to leave London. The Hanseatic Cities, with the Emperor, still worked their way towards the execution of the mandate. Thus the people of Lübeck asked permission for the seizure of English goods, which was denied by Archduke Matthias, who attended his imperial brother at the Imperial Diet of Regensburg:

> [...] How evil really are several in the Empire, inconsiderate initial testers of the Hanseatic issued mandate, which was largely advised and settled in general diets and deputation councils, who still to this day would effect in the execution and operation of the same, also how unwilling to burden themselves with war in Germany's need to oppose the Turks, of this your Imperial Majesty is well aware [...][19]

To be sure, the Imperial Estates which like Elector Pfalz called for a lifting of the mandate, could still not push it through the Imperial Diet; the Aulic Council also encouraged the Imperial Circle (*Reichskreise*) anew to the enactment of

19 Beutin, *Das Reich*, 23 (Vienna, 26, 610–613).

the mandate, however with time this was avoided more and more, even by the Hanseatic Cities.

The "Merchant Adventurers" who had relocated from Stade to Middelburg, shipped their cloth into the Empire through middlemen from Bremen, Hamburg, and the Netherlands. The return of many English merchants to Stade—with the implication, they did not belong to the company of the "Merchant Adventurers"—threw Lübeck into a renewed state of alertness.[20] It began a new diplomatic and publicized offensive, which was directed at the Emperor and the Aulic Council (*Reichshofrat*). Hereby Lübeck stylized itself as a "Frontier City" of the Empire, which was established upon Imperial aid for the defense of the honor of the empire. Above all, injuries "to the Holy Imperial Sovereignty" committed by the English with the support of the Queen were branded, a brand whereby the humiliation of the Emperor was emphasized before the world:

> Now is nonetheless to pity, and not the Hanseatic Cities alone, rather the entire Roman Empire, that this highly onerous, highly invested affair, whereafter to whose execution *per publicatione mandatorum* was made a beginning, in such a way that it remains ignominious, harmful, and heated, and that the banned monopolistic English Company of the Adventurers, [...], the commendable Hanseatic City, and yes, the entire Roman Empire, with their self-serving, forbidden actions and practices should in such a way mislead, suck dry, cause damages and respect little, and that they everything, [...], as dissolute elude and with outward ignominy and irretrievable injury of the Empire can take to the waters unpunished.[21]

In these views, however, Lübeck stood increasingly alone in the Empire. Other cities, which, like Augsburg, had recently still supported a mandate against the monopolistic trade of the "Merchant Adventurers," suggested to the Hanseatic cities that they force a monopolistic position for themselves in English trade. They pleaded indeed to forbid the monopolistic practices, however under no

20 Ludwig Beutin, *Hanse und Reich im handelspolitischen Endkampf gegen England* (Berlin, 1929), 25–30.

21 Haus-, Hof- und Staatsarchiv Vienna, Acta Antiqua 27: 1599 Kurtzer Auszug der gantzen Englischen Mandatssachen, fol. 100–106. Quotation according to Nils Jörn, "Die Auseinandersetzungen zwischen Hanse und Merchant Adventurers vor den obersten Reichsgerichten im 16. und 17. Jahrhundert," *Zeitschrift des Vereins für Lübeckische Geschichte und Altertumskunde* 78 (1998), 337.

conditions did they wish to hinder the English trade in its entirety, because a ban would have harmful consequences for the cities' weavers.

Nevertheless, Lübeck obtained an investigation of Stade's dealings through the Aulic Council in 1601. Ehrenfried von Minkwitz was, on one hand, supposed to take account of the trade practices of the English and, on the other hand, to move the Hanseatic cities to financial contribution toward the war with the Turks. Because Lübeck and Hamburg had proved unfriendly towards the latest affair, Minkwitz could confirm no blatant violations against Imperial mandate in Stade. Moreover, Stade contributed four thousand florins to the war against the Turks. [22] Beginning in 1610, the Hanseatic cities were infused with new hope, as they wrested a mandate against the English trade in Northern Germany from the Emperor during the Julich-Kleveberg succession controversy, which was, however, not executed. As a result, Hamburg took a logical step and in the same year invited the English to return to the Elbe. After the arrival of the English cloth fleet in June of 1611, the English trading post was favored by the council, which, by way of a Hamburg legation and the Diet, was also favored by the Emperor. A renewed counter-initiative by Lübeck and Cologne at the Imperial Diet had no impact.[23]

The English historian Richard Grassby explains this by means of the masterful propaganda of the English, which propaganda the Hanseatic lawyers could have only opposed with academically composed, dispassionate memorandums.[24] The medium of the arguments (pamphlet vs. tract) would have thus decided success or failure. This view is correct when we include public opinion in the discussion. In keeping company with public opinion, the Merchant Adventurers and their publicists were altogether superior to the Hanseatic League, and the "crocodile" did immediate damage to the Hanseatic League in the eyes of observers. According to a contemporary text on the

22 Beutin, *Hanse und Reich*, 32–35. Nils Jörn, "Die Versuche von Kaiser und Reich zur Einbeziehung der Hanse in die Anstrengungen zur Abwehr der Türken im 16. und 17. Jahrhundert," in Nils Jörn, and Michael North, eds., *Die Integration des südlichen Ostseeraumes in das Alte Reich* (Cologne/Weimar/Vienna, 2000), 393–423.

23 Beutin, *Hanse und Reich*, 68–70.

24 Richard Grassby, "die letzten Verhandlungen zwischen England und der Hanse (1603–1604)," *Hansische Geschichsblätter*. 76 (1958), 73–120, hier 106, 114. See also/recently Nils Jörn, "The crocodile creature merchant: the Dutch Hanse. Die Widerspiegelung der englisch-hansischen Auseinandersetzungen in den Denkschriften englischer Kaufleute und Politiker in der zweiten Hälfte des 16. Jahrhunderts," in Antjekathrin Grassmann, *Niedergang oder Übergang? Zur Spätzeit der Hanse im 16. und 17. Jahrhundert* (Cologne, 1998), 63–91.

"monstrous creature," many of its teeth were missing and the rest were loose.[25] However, when we look at the memorandums that were delivered in the Latin language by the Hanseatic cities and the English envoys to the Imperial Diet, they appear similar in character. What differentiated the English, and the Hanseatic League, had more to do with the fact that the "Merchant Adventurers" could mobilize the England's public opinion and had backing from the English Queen through financial support while it was possible for the Hanseatic cities to mobilize only a part of the public at most.

The Strengthening of the Baltic Powers: Denmark and Sweden

Changes in the Baltic Region, especially the strengthening of Denmark and Sweden, also placed new challenges before the Hanseatic cities.[26] This political change partially collapsed with the spread of Lutheran teachings into the Baltic region and Scandinavia.[27] All Reformation movements in the Hanseatic cities had as much a religious-ecclesiastical purpose as a political-social concern. Above all, citizen committees were set up as monitoring bodies of the councils. In the course of the Reformation, new people came to power over these committees, such as Jurgen Wullenwever, who as spokesman for Lübeck's sixty-fourth committee put the Reformation into effect in Lübeck. In 1531, the Catholic mayor (*Bürgermeister*) fled and by 1533, Wullenwever advanced to become first a councilman and then the mayor. In this capacity, he intervened in the battles of power politics in the Baltic region. Indeed, Lübeck had brought the Swedish king, Gustav Wasa, and the Danish king, Frederick I, to the throne in 1522/23. Thereafter, both had pursued their own policy and no longer supported the Hanseatic monopoly against Dutch trade.

25 "A Monstruous creature, but most of their teeth are out and the rest are loose". John Wheller, *A Treatise of Commerce, wherin are shewed the commodities arising from a wellordered, and ruled trade, such as that of the Societies of Merchantes Adventurers is proved to bee, written principallie for the better information of those who doubt of the Necessarienes of the said Societie in the State of the Realme of Englande* (Middelburgh, 1601), 162, Quotation according to Jörn, "Crocodile creature," 83.

26 For an overview see: Michael North, *Geschichte der Ostsee: Handel und Kulturen* (Munich, 2011), 103–114.

27 See also Rainer Postel, "Der Niedergang der Hanse," in Jörgen Bracker, Volker Henn and Rainer Postel, eds., *Die Hanse: Lebenswirklichkeit und Mythos* (Lübeck, 1998), 165–193, here 177–180.

When Frederick I of Denmark asked Lübeck to support him in the conflict with his nephew, Christian II in 1531, Lübeck made support conditional upon the expulsion of the Dutch from the Baltic. This went too far for Frederick as well as for those Prussian Hanseatic cities dependent upon Dutch shipping. Because Frederick joined with the Dutch and lured his nephew to Denmark in order to imprison him there for the rest of his life, Lübeck stood alone in its conflict with Amsterdam and began a hijacking war against Dutch ships. After the Hanseatic cities entered into ceasefire negotiations in 1534, Wullenwever sought to stir up war again. Yet from his point of view he was unsuccessful in influencing the Danish succession: Frederick I died in 1533. In an overestimation of his own powers, Wullenwever took on the Danish crown as well as the Catholic Duke Albert of Mecklenburg, the Saxon electors, and Henry VIII. When the new Danish king Christian III successfully besieged Lübeck and even Gustav Wasa no longer supported it, the attempt at Lübeck's Baltic overlordship collapsed in 1534/35. At the peace negotiations of 1536, the council of Hamburg stepped into the foreground as mediator, and even Wullenwever had to accept the return of the old council members. Dutch supremacy in the Baltic was, in any case, not to be stalled in the long run by military means from the Hanseatic camp, especially after 1544 when Christian III finally agreed with Charles V upon free passage into the Baltic through the strait.

Even though the successor of Christian III, Frederick II, confirmed the Hanseatic trade privileges, tensions between Denmark and Hamburg increased. Moreover Denmark, which regarded Hamburg merely as a country town in Holstein, hindered the trade of the Elbe metropolis. In the meantime, although the Imperial Chamber Court (*Reichskammergericht*) agreed with the Imperial immediacy of Hamburg over the course of a long process (1548–1618), this immediacy was not recognized by Denmark-Holstein. Relations with Sweden were also strained, because Gustav Wasa considered Lübeck's attempts at the restoration of their Hanseatic monopoly an unfriendly act. In 1548, Gustav Wasa banned Lübeck's shipping and the trade with Sweden and confiscated ships and wares. His successor, Erich XIV, impeded trade with Narva, which was viewed as a rival to the Livonian cities. In the fight against Sweden, Lübeck allied itself with its old rival, Denmark, without, however, being able to motivate other Hanseatic cities for the war. In the Peace of Stettin in 1570, Lübeck obtained an unimpeded access to Narva and to Swedish ports, although this was soon disputed again by King Johann III of Sweden. Lübeck was also dealt a bad hand in the conflict between Sweden and Poland that would follow (1602–1605), and even the new Danish king Christian IV limited the trade of Lübeck and Hamburg as much as he could. The foundation of Glücksstadt in 1616 as a competitor to Hamburg and the establishment of a toll on the Elbe, as well as the occupation of Stade in 1619 were also part of this trade limiting policy.

Reorganization Attempts and the Thirty Years War

The conflicts surrounding the establishment of the merchant adventurers and the restoration of the trade privileges in England demonstrated that the Hanseatic League, as an organization, was only still partially capable of action in the sixteenth century. Even to receive the support of the Imperial Diet and the Emperor, a unified front would be a necessity. Correspondingly, it is unsurprising that leading protagonists like Cologne native Heinrich Suderman, the "legal counsel of the Hanseatic League," who also played an important role in the negotiations with the emperor and with England, attempted to reorganize the Hanseatic League as a body for the last time. This occurred in a time when the Hanseatic cities, in the wake of their financially depressing experiences during the Schmalkaldic War, attempted to become relevant again. From 1553 on, Hanseatic Diets were again held regularly, however, after 1568, they met only irregularly. To be sure, the Hanseatic Diet (*Hansetag*) of 1557 had adopted a "resolution of confederation" with initial enthusiasm, which resolution contained the representation of the Hanseatic Diet as well as a court of arbitration for disputes between cities and a collective proceeding against disturbers of the peace. However, the presence of cities in the Hanseatic Diet remained small, especially the Dutch cities, though even those of the Eastern Baltic were hardly seen anymore.

A "Hanseatic treasury" (*Hansekasse*), which was to be used for the financing of the alliance of cities, was not executed and even the establishment of one such in 1612 did not improve the collective financial maneuverability of the Hanseatic League. Only the designated legal counsel of the Hanseatic League, Heinrich Suderman, embodied and articulated the Hanseatic interests over an extended period. For thirty-five years he took part in all Hanseatic Diets and negotiations and led almost fifty diplomatic missions in the Netherlands and to England, and also to the Imperial Diet and the Emperor's Court. Even the reorganization of the Hanseatic branch office in Antwerp constituted one of his journeys, although this reorganization was only intended to develop economic relevance for a short time. That the office of legal counsel remained vacant for more than ten years after the death of Suderman accounts for the decline of its associated duties. In 1605, however, the Stralsund legal counsel Johann Doman succeeded to Suderman's position. Doman compiled a

Hanseatic maritime law, which was adopted by the Hanseatic Diet in 1614, yet his maneuverability was increasingly reduced. This was evident in the opening phase of the Thirty Years War.[28]

To start with, the Hanseatic cities had to fend off the reprisals of Christian IV; they could breathe easily again when the army of the Catholic League defeated him in 1626 and in 1629 forced him into peace. Yet the Hanseatic cities hesitated—in 1628 Braunschweig, Bremen, Danzig, Hamburg, Hildesheim, Cologne, Lübeck, Lüneburg, Magdeburg, Rostock, and Stralsund gathered at the Hanseatic Diet of Lübeck—to veer into the Imperial camp, because Imperial expansion was demonstrated clearly in the occupation of Mecklenburg by Wallenstein and the imperial attacks on Stralsund. However, nothing more than a cautious maneuver appeared possible to the cities. In the end, Lübeck, Hamburg and Bremen decided on a defensive alliance in 1630, which took over the leadership of the Hanseatic League. It was, however, less the defensive alliance than the economically meaningful position of Hamburg which kept the foreign powers at bay, while the alliance was strengthened by the Hanseatic cities. It appeared more lucrative to make use of Hamburg as a finance and communication center as well as the handling point of the weapons trade for their own defensive efforts. In 1636, negotiations between the warring parties took place several times, which by 1641 ended in the preliminary Peace of Hamburg.

For the Hanseatic cities, the successes of Sweden meant additional maneuverability in trade politics. Thus the Hanseatic League was included in the 1645 Peace of Brömsebro and subsequently, Hamburg and Denmark agreed upon the lifting the Glückstädter Elbe toll in the "Copenhagen Conception". However, Sweden claimed the mouths of the Elbe, Weser, and the Oder, and so eventually a toll on the Elbe was raised in Stade. Even at the Westphalian Peace Congress, the Hanseatic cities were present and were received into the Peace of Westphalia.[29]

The Hanseatic Cities were also included in the treaty between the Spanish and the Dutch and could thus restore their 1607 trade pact with Spain. Above

28 K. Friedland, "Der Plan des Dr. Heinrich Suderman zur Wiederherstellung der Hanse," *Jahrbuch des Kölnischen Geschichtsvereins* 31/32 (1956/57), 184–244.

29 Rainer Postel, "Hamburg zur Zeit des Westfälischen Friedens," in Klaus Bußmann and Heinz Schilling, eds., *1648: Krieg und Frieden in Europa* (Münster, 1999), 337–343; Rainer Postel, "Zur 'erhaltung dern commercien und darüber habende privilegia:' Hansische Politik auf dem Westfälischen Friedenskongreß," in Heinz Duchhardt, ed., *Der Westfälische Friede. Diplomatie, politische Zäsur, kulturelles Umfeld, Rezeptionsgeschichte* (Munich, 1998), 522–539.

all, the trade between Hamburg and Spain, which, in the 1670s, was more or less as important as the trade with England and according to the strong statement of the toll data from 1678 easily surpassed the trade with the Dutch, profited from this. With France, the Hanseatic Cities were likewise able to launch a trade treaty in 1655 that above all opened the doors for an intensified trade with France in the eighteenth century. However, interest waned at the Hanseatic Diet convoked by Lübeck. Also, in 1666, the Hanseatic branch office of Stahlhof burned in the course of the Great London Fire, and the catastrophe was discussed at the Hanseatic Diet. Most cities did not react to the warning expressed in the invitation to Lübeck—that the failure to send representatives meant the expulsion of the offending city from the Hanseatic League. Lübeck, Hamburg, Bremen, Danzig, Braunschweig and Cologne appeared all the same, while the Swedish-dominated cities of Wismar, Stralsund, and Greifswald stated their inability to continue an active participation in the Hanseatic Alliance. Accordingly, at the last Hanseatic Diet of 1669, the renewal of a smaller Hanseatic League was much discussed, without committing anyone to any collective political action. With this, a collective Hanseatic Policy gradually slipped away. The three cities of Lübeck, Bremen and Hamburg continued to exercise the foreign privileges of the Hanseatic League, as they were represented by it even in peace negotiations, for example, at Nimwegen in 1679. However, more and more, the economic advantage went to Hamburg, which, however, collaborated thoroughly with Bremen and Lübeck as a political equal.

The Rise of Hamburg and the Intensification of the Cooperation of the Hanseatic Cities at the Close of the Eighteenth and Beginning of the Nineteenth Centuries

The fact that Hamburg surpassed its Hanseatic neighbors economically had multiple explanations. Aside from readily declared neutrality during the Thirty Years War, the city on the Elbe had an unusually favorable location which, together with the Oder, connected Hamburg to a hinterland that extended to Silesia and further to Bohemia. The Hamburg trade was closely connected to the Leipzig trade fair (*Leipziger Messe*), which adjoined Eastern Central Europe to western European trade.[30] Connections to linen production in Silesia,

30 Yuta Kikuchi, "Hamburgs Handel mit dem Ostseeraum und dem mitteleuropäischen Binnenland vom 17. bis zum Beginn des 19. Jahrhunderts. Warendistribution und Hinterlandnetzwerke auf See-, Fluss- und Landwegen" (Doctoral Dissertation, University

Bohemia, Saxony, and Lausitz opened up a continuous supply of textiles, which in the eighteenth century were traded primarily in the American colonies, namely the Caribbean, by way of England. At the same time, Hamburg profited from the intensification of the French plantation economy in the West Indian islands, which delivered sugar, coffee, and cocoa to Hamburg by way of France. In Hamburg, the raw products were processed and further distributed in the North and Baltic Sea regions. In comparison to Hamburg, Bremen and Lübeck were at a disadvantage because the Weser network offered Bremen only a small hinterland. Lübeck, by virtue of its position on the Baltic Sea, was cut off from the intermediary trade with the North Sea and the Atlantic because all goods had to be transported either through the strait or overland by way of Hamburg. Contemporary assessments from the second half of the eighteenth century allow speculation that the disadvantages in the French trade in particular, which were noticeable for Lübeck as well as for Bremen, resulted in a low turnover in trade in comparison with Hamburg. Thereafter, the trade with Lübeck would amount to only a tenth of Hamburg's total trading volume; Bremen approached nearly one half of Hamburg's sales.[31]

In the 1770's and 1780's, trade with France had contributed to the upswing of Hamburg's commerce; and even after the outbreak of the revolution, this relationship was not initially diminished. On the contrary, Hamburg's merchants could purchase cheap luxury wares in France, and the French aristocratic emigration also brought cheap cultural assets to the Elbe. Northern Germany profited from the French-inspired foundation of the Batavian Republic in the Netherlands in 1795, especially Hamburg, which profited above all from an extension of commerce. Besides this, Hamburg took over a portion of the financial center functions from Amsterdam. The Hanseatic cities were made acutely aware of the vulnerability of international commerce by the short term occupation of Bremen as well as Ritzebüttel, a post belonging to Hamburg, by Hanoverian and British troops. This would repeat itself many times in the early years of the eighteenth century.

In light of the mounting dangers, the representatives at Hamburg, Bremen and Lübeck gathered again in May of 1795 for the first time since the Hanseatic Diet of 1669, and in the period following, began work on the "Hanseatic desiderata" for a collective declaration of neutrality. It was argued that unrestricted

---

of Greifswald, 2013). Michael North, "Hamburg: The Continent's Most English City," in idem, *From the North Sea to the Baltic: Essays in Commercial, Monetary and Agricultural History, 1500–1800* (Aldershot, 1996), 1–13.

31 Pierre Jeannin, "Die Hansestädte im europäischen Handel des 18. Jahrhunderts," *Hansische Geschichsblätter* 89 (1971), 41–73, here 58–60; Michael North, "Hamburg" 2–4.

Hanseatic commerce lay in the interest of all peoples and it swore to, as it says in the memorandum of the same name by Johann Georg Büsch, "the political importance of the freedom of Hamburg and her sister cities, Lübeck and Bremen, to the commerce of all Europe." Accordingly, it was believed for a long time that France would not be closed to these arguments.

The Peace of Amiens, in the year 1802, appeared to provide such hopes and also new energy. First of all, it briefly ended the disagreements between France and Great Britain and led to a new upswing phase for commerce.[32] The acts of war, including hijackings, ended and international trade and ship traffic came to life again and the high wartime assurance premiums fell away. France and Great Britain negotiated concerning the trade agreement of 1786, now in force again. At the same time, military armament at sea continued, and on May 16, 1803, Great Britain declared war on France after previously declaring an embargo on Dutch and French ships. The French army occupied Hanover and then Cuxhaven on the left bank of the Elbe, whereupon (the left bank) Great Britain imposed a blockade of the Elbe's mouth. Through this blockade, Hamburg, which until now—on grounds of its neutrality—had been only somewhat adversely affected by English-French conflicts, was cut off from international commerce and shipping. The commerce of the Elbe dwindled, against which backdrop Bremen (until the impending Weser blockade), Stettin, Lübeck, Copenhagen, and above all Emden profited. English merchants dispatched a portion of their wares to Copenhagen, Stettin and especially Lübeck, whose trade strongly increased. Emden in particular profited from the blockade of Hamburg because English, French, and American tradehouses set up shop on the Jade. English wares were shipped to France under the Prussian flag by way of Emden. Even English trade with Amsterdam went through Emden because the direct exchange was still forbidden. Otherwise, the city of Papenburg and the leadership of Kniphausen (which was overseen by the French) offered protection from hijacking with their neutral sea passes.

The trade in English wares proceeded from Emden into the hinterland as far as the Frankfurt trade fairs (*Frankfurter Messen*). However the merchants of Hamburg were also resourceful, in that besides Lübeck and Kiel, they used Tönning at the mouth of the Eider as a port, in which merchants, brokers, shippers, and assurance agents set up shop. Although half of the wares had to be transported over land, a great portion of the English wares journeyed

32 For the following see Michael North, "Die Auswirkungen der Kontinentalsperre auf das nördliche Deutschland und den Ostseeraum," in Andreas Klinger, Hans-Werner Hahn, and Georg Schmidt, eds., Das Jahr 1806 im europäischen Kontext. Balance, Hegemonie und politische Kulturen (Cologne/Weimar/Vienna 2008), 101–122.

to Hamburg by way of Tönning and the Elbe which, however, delayed subsequent shipment to the interior.[33] The total number of Hamburg bound ships declined from 2,108 (1802) to 1,947 (1803).

Losses were primarily in bulk goods, as recorded in relation to the hard coal imports, which burdened industry more than anything else. On the other hand, Hamburg's time as financial center and banking headquarters remained unbroken, because mail boats from Husum established a bi-weekly connection to London (with regular information on the exchange rates). The sea insurance industry also grew during the blockade period. This blockade was, with the exception of a few relaxations such as in the allowance of the cotton wool shipment between Tönning and Hamburg, officially lifted for the first time in October of 1805 as the French Army moved off to battle with Austria. The re-stimulation of Hamburg's shipping in all directions in November of 1806 effectively impaired the imposition of the so-called Continental Blockade.

As a result of the resignation of the Holy Roman Imperial Crown by Franz II and the dissolution of the Holy Roman Empire, the Hanseatic Cities also reorganized themselves anew. In order to avoid political reorganization (*Mediatisierung*) under the auspices of Prussia or Denmark, Bremen, Hamburg and Lübeck immediately took up negotiations concerning a Hanseatic Alliance, which was intended to fill the resultant vacuum left behind after the downfall of the Empire.[34] However the Prussian defeat near Jena and Auerstedt and the following French expansion burst into the discussion. The French victory over the Prussian Army near Jena and Auerstedt had given the French economic policy against Great Britain a new foundation. In the course of the pursuit of fleeing Prussian troops, the French took over Lübeck (the location to which the Prussian Field Marshall Blücher had withdrawn) on the sixth of November, Hamburg on the nineteenth of November, and Bremen on the twentieth of November. Because France now ruled great portions of the North and Baltic Sea coasts, an end to the trade with England appeared to lie near at hand. However, protectionist measures could only be enacted in cooperation with other states.

---

33 Walther Vogel, *Die Hansestädte und die Kontinentalsperre* (Munich, o.a., 1913), 13f.

34 Antjekatrin Graßmann, "Vom reichsfreyen Bürger zum vogelfreyen Republikaner'—Tradition und Chancen der drei Hansestädte 1806," in Michael North, and Robert Riemer, eds., *Das Ende des Alten Reiches im Ostseeraum. Wahrnehmung und Transformation* (Cologne/Weimar/Vienna, 2008), 126–142. Hans-Dieter Loose, "Der Verfall der Reichsordnung in der Wahrnehmung der Bürger der Reichsstädte Lübeck, Hamburg und Bremen 1801–1806," in Michael North, and Robert Riemer, eds., *Das Ende des Alten Reiches im Ostseeraum. Wahrnehmung und Transformation* (Cologne/Weimar/Vienna, 2008), 144–155.

Accordingly, the demands of the so called Berlin Decree (*Berliner Dekret*) of November twenty-first were also enacted with difficulty. Nevertheless, the regulations appeared suited to lastingly block the trade with England. This decree included a ban on trade and correspondence, a confiscation of English books and the arrest of British subjects as well as the stoppage of ship traffic between England, its colonies and the continent. While the British blockade of the Elbe had merely impaired the commerce of Hamburg, the measures of the Continental Blockade also had an effect on the exchange trade and, to a greater extent, on the insurance business because these measures also concerned correspondence with Great Britain.

Above all, the move to neutral (Danish) Altona offered one alternative. Otherwise, the representation of the "honorable businessmen", the so called Commerce Deputation, attempted to prevent the worst. First of all, an assessment of the English wares in the magazines of Hamburg's merchants and then of English property in Hamburg was obtained. This was acquired by civic means in order to forestall confiscation and also in order to avoid the eventual seizure of Hamburg's property in Great Britain.[35] The interruption of the transactions trade constituted an additional concern in that debt moratoria were declined, as these had led to chain reactions with regard to the debtors. The main problem was created by the English wares in the possession of Hamburg, which wares, according to the Berlin Decree, were declared "goodly prizes" and the confiscation of them would have meant a considerable loss of Hamburg's own properties. Political means were then attempted (the delegation to Posen for an audience with Napoleon on the fourteenth of December) to raise awareness of the fact that the retroactive application of the decree would ruin the Hamburg Community, while a ban on correspondence only benefited the English debtors at the expense of Hamburg's lenders. With regards to Napoleon, the people of Hamburg were met by deaf ears and only the French envoy to Hamburg, Louis Antoine Fauvelet de Bourrienne, could dodge Napoleon's demands to ship many of the wares located in the Hanseatic city to France. Hamburg was therefore drawn into informal contacts via Altona, through which correspondence between England and Hamburg traveled. As a result, the smuggling between Hamburg and Altona could hardly be controlled.

Furthermore, Tönning was also an important distribution center of wares bound for Hamburg, which then made their way to the Leipzig trade fairs. From there they reached Poland and Russia by land, while the English wares depot in Helgoland (since 1807) was connected with Northern Germany by smugglers.[36] This was important, as Denmark had joined the Continental Blockade in 1808

35 Vogel, *Die Hansestädte*, 19f.

36 Heckscher, *The Continental System*, 178f.

and Tönning lost importance as a smuggling port. Moreover, Hamburg's ships frequently sailed from 1807 until 1810, from Great Britain to Russia, but also to Sweden and to other Baltic seaports as well as sporadically overseas.

On the other hand, Lübeck had profited from the Elbe blockade for a long time, which was reflected in growing ship traffic until the year 1805/1806. In the year 1807, the ship traffic of Lübeck's port collapsed for the first time and in the years to follow was hardly able to recover. Unlike Hamburg or the Prussian ports, Lübeck had only a slight share in smuggling, especially because it was under the strict customs examinations of the French and at the same time was developed as a station for the French navy. Yet here also we must consider smuggling and illicit trade by way of Denmark, even though we do not have specific data at our disposal. Travemünde was, above all, a destination port for smuggling from Mecklenburg that, like Mecklenburg, was also afflicted by English hijackings.[37] An unbroken monitoring of the Continental Blockade in the North and Baltic Seas was not possible.

Two results were the Degrees of Trianon and Fontainebleu (August 5 and October 18, 1810), which attempted to root out smuggling with new measures. These included trade authorizations instead of expensive licenses, the levy of high customs fees on colonial wares, and also the burning of English industrial products. For better control over the planned measures, the three Hanseatic cities, as well as their affiliated districts were also—after the Netherlands had already been annexed in the summer of 1810 and become a department of the French crown—annexed and formed into the "three Hanseatic departments: Bouches de l'Elbe, Bouches du Weser, and Ems Supérior with capital cities in Hamburg, Bremen, and Osnabrück."[38]

The organization of the new departments was supposed to take over a committee, while the General Governor Davout represented the highest authority. Besides this, the district was supposed to become economically united through the design of a great canal building project (Canal de la Seine-Baltique). This canal was intended to lead from Lübeck by way of the old Stecknitzkanal to Hamburg and from there through Stade, Oldenburg, and Leer to the Züderzee. From there, a water connection to Antwerp and Paris already existed. This project, however, remained in the planning stages, just as a fortification of the sea route from Hamburg through the mud flats alongside the East Fresian islands to Holland.

---

37 Friedrich Voeltzer, "Lübecks Wirtschaftslage unter dem Druck der Kontinentalsperre" (Hamburg, 1925), 37–41.

38 Vogel, *Die Hansestädte*, 41. Burghart Schmidt, *Hamburg im Zeitalter der Französischen Revolution und Napoleons (1789–1813)* (Hamburg 1998).

Because Russia was not ready to join the Continental Blockade, the priorities of France changed one more time as the licenses proved to be especially profitable. These were intended—in that they relaxed the blockade for a short period—to absorb buying power in England as well as also bring money into the French state treasury. Besides, with respect to Northern Germany, grain exports had been considered on the occasion of a grain shortage in the British Isles. Yet of the ninety-one licenses issued by the end of 1810, only thirty-three ships from Hamburg, Bremen, and Lübeck made use of a license by the end 1810, which brought in approximately 445,000 francs from licensing fees. The licenses were distributed between nineteen ships from Hamburg, ten from Bremen, and ten from Lübeck. Although the council of Lübeck had recommended the use of the licenses, even in the sense of a trade policy of give and take, the exact declaration of their cargoes in advance of ordering a license from Paris seemed too complicated to the majority of Lübeck's citizens. By comparison, Danzig shippers alone used more than forty French licenses in the year 1810.[39]

On the whole, the Continental Blockade strengthened England's supremacy on the high seas over the long term. Therefore, it comes as no surprise that the Continental Blockade, especially for Hamburg, had promoted English trade rather than permanently impeding it. Thus, Great Britain became the premier trade partner of Hamburg, which was correctly described as "the most English city on the continent." At the end of the eighteenth century, the French colonial trade had, by comparison, clearly dominated Hamburg's commerce. Accordingly, after the re-stimulation of Hamburg's ocean shipping in the years following 1814, twenty to thirty ships from Hamburg sailed to London yearly, while in France, only the old connections to Bordeaux remained intact, and were serviced on a lower level.[40]

As a consequence of the Continental Blockade, Lübeck had completely lost its function as a middleman in the exchange between East and West and in the nineteenth century was forced to gradually grope its way back into Western Europe from a regional base in the Baltic Sea realm. Still, the experience of the Continental Blockade and the Napoleonic occupation appear important for the political collaboration of the Hanseatic cities. The so-called "Hanseatic Legion" also took part in the "liberation" from the French occupation, which then helped the Hanseatic cities to present a collective voice at the Parisian Peace Negotiations of 1814. The Bremen senator Johann Smidt, who after the liberation of Bremen in November of 1813 had already represented the

39 Voeltzer, "Lübecks Wirtschaftslage," 63f.

40 Kresse, *Hamburger Handelsflotte*, 72–75, 90–95.

Hanseatic cities at allied headquarters in Frankfurt, was able to block attempts at a Prussian expansion in the north of Germany. The great powers recognized the sovereignty of the three Hanseatic cities, who maintained this position as independent and neutral commerce republics at the Vienna Congress and during the negotiations concerning the constitution of the German Federation. This was to stimulate the further political cooperation of the Hanseatic cities as well as the formation of a regional Hanseatic "post-Napoleonic identity."[41]

41 Katherine Aaslestad, "Paying for War: Experiences of Napoleonic Rule in the Hanseatic Cities," *Central European History* 39 (2006), 641–675, here 672.

PART 2

Themes in Hanse History

CHAPTER 4

Kontors and Outposts

Mike Burkhardt

Introduction

Discussions concerning economic activities of the Hansards often immediately turn to *kontors* and outposts. Once a merchant had left his home waters, he found himself to be a stranger in areas with a different jurisdiction, and thus more vulnerable than at home. This was especially true for long distance traders. Many Hanseatic merchants traded with outside areas controlled by their hometowns or lords. They felt a special need for protection, assistance, and cooperation. Following both human nature and the directives of their hometown councils, they gathered and organized themselves into the group, "the merchants of the Hanseatic towns," later known as the *kontors* and outposts of the Hanseatic League.

Most of these outposts were situated at the edge of the region, usually known as the core area of Hanseatic trade. London in the Kingdom of England, Bruges in the County of Flanders, Bergen in the Kingdom of Norway, and Novgorod in the Russian principality of Novgorod were the largest of these outposts. At these junctions in the European trade network, the economic sphere, partly dominated by the Hansards, connected various trade regions with different economic and social cultures, goods, and customs. These connections provided Hanseatic trade with a huge influx of goods, ideas, and techniques. Traditionally the *Stalhof* in London, the *kontor* in Bruges, *Bryggen* in Bergen, and *Peterhof* in Novgorod are known as the *kontors* of the Hanse. Similar, but smaller Hanseatic trading posts in other towns were referred to as outposts or *Faktoreien*.

Since the *kontors* in London, Bruges, Bergen, and Novgorod are widely known, and most research about the Hanseatic outposts has been done on these four, we will concentrate on them in the first part of this chapter. However, the focus on these four *kontors* must not deter us from looking at smaller outposts and traders who went far beyond the "borders" of Hanseatic trade. Especially intriguing is the question of where to place the Hanseatic stronghold at Scania, a problem that will be discussed in the first section of the chapter.

© KONINKLIJKE BRILL NV, LEIDEN, 2015 | DOI 10.1163/9789004284760_006

The Four *Kontors*

Let's first take a closer look at the *Hansekontors* in London, Bruges, Bergen, and Novgorod. I will try to point out similarities and differences between the four *kontors* and their organization. We will look closely at the geographical conditions of the four towns, the internal organization of the *kontors*, trade and life in the different towns, and the place of the four *kontors* in a general Hanseatic economic and political perspective.

However, there is one important question to discuss first: Why did Hanseatic merchants organize their trading activities abroad in *kontors?*

Kontors and Privileges

The literature provides many different answers to the question: why did Hanseatic merchants establish *kontors* in London, Bruges, Bergen, and Novgorod? Since discussions on these theories could fill a whole book, I will concentrate on one particular motive that, like a golden thread, penetrates all of these answers—Security.

Security is most likely the main reason for establishing Hanseatic *kontors*. In a general organizational view, Hanseatic towns saw the *kontors* as institutions guaranteeing the trade privileges that Hanseatic trade in the Middle Ages was based upon. The privileges, or freedoms as they often were called in contemporary sources, mainly included certified rights regarding taxes and duties and toll payments to the respective towns, lords, or kings. Simultaneously, the privileges gave merchants a certain amount of self-jurisdiction. In some cases, merchants were given certain freedoms in their trade, which gave the Hansards an economic advantage over their competitors. However, these privileges did not provide eternal security. They could be changed, withdrawn, or extended at any given time, as many examples from each of the four *kontors* illustrate. When a new ruler ascended the throne, the privileges had to be renewed. This process often led to renegotiations and intriguing political activity among all participants, including the Hansards' competitors. To effectively represent all Hanseatic merchants with interests in a specific market, large organizations of Hansards banded together. As larger organizations, they could negotiate much stronger points than single merchants or smaller groups had the ability to. To make use of Niklas Luhman's system theory, the *kontors* enabled the Hanseatic towns to participate in a political system of the respective reigns. However, it is important to note that they did not want to appear as one political corpus.

To maintain the impression of uniformity within an organization, it was important to ensure that all Hanseatic merchants acted in accordance with the privileges. Violations of the rules, even by a few merchants, could result in decreased trust by the authorities and possibly the cancellation of important privileges. One main purposes of establishing *kontors* was to control the economic and social activities of the merchants as effectively as possible. The more control a merchant was exposed to, the lower the risk of him violating the rules. This is why most *kontors* were geographically closed entities, so that there was little chance that one of the merchants could do business without the knowledge of at least one other Hansard. Even in the case of Bruges, where the Hanseatic *kontor* did not have a geographical area under its jurisdiction, measures were taken to ensure mutual control.

The internal control, unity, and strength of the hanseatic towns satisfied two important reasons to establish and support *kontors* abroad. However, there were other advantages connected to them as well. One of these points is the security of the merchants' goods and life. As mentioned, being a stranger in a medieval town involved certain risks, and being a wealthy stranger might not always have reduced these risks. As a result, the merchants might have felt a need for mutual protection. Thus, an organized group of some hundred Hanseatic merchants, represented by spokesmen and clearly possessing economic strength and power, probably did reduce the urge of local denizens or other rivals to attack the merchants or take their goods by force. It also gave much more weight to complaints and demands on the rulers or the local authorities.

The *kontors* also reduced intra-Hanseatic competition. Since the hometowns relied on a wealthy and successful merchant class, and that merchant class made up the backbone of the town councils, the townspeople were interested in the economic success of as many of their merchants as possible. In all *kontor* regulations, we find measures with the objective to guarantee at least a certain level of equal competition conditions. For example, within the statutes of the *kontors*, one could find prohibitions to handle other Hansards' denizen trading partners or paragraphs regarding the maximum amount of goods a single merchant was allowed to sell. These regulations were to prevent heavy losses caused by internal intrigues or an artificial over-supply of special goods in a certain market. Thus, trade at the *kontors* ensured that most of the merchants made at least a modest profit. However, the rules were flexible enough not to set upper limits on the merchants' profits.

Last, but not least, I want to mention the social security that was provided by the *kontor*. In all four trading posts, the Hanseatic merchants were far from home. They stayed in a social environment with codes and unwritten rules different from what they were used to. Although medieval English, Norwegian, and Low German were by far not as different as their respective descendants are today, the languages spoken in the towns often were hard to understand for the Hanseatic merchants. The *kontors* provided a place where they could feel at home, especially for newcomers. Merchants could start their businesses right away without having to adjust to foreign customs first. Economics aside, the *kontors* provided merchants with other benefits. They provided a place for the merchants' questions to be answered in their mother tongue. Also, being able to conduct small talk without difficulty must have meant a lot to the merchants' sense of well-being. Finally, having an organized community of fellow countrymen was important in case of any problems. The *kontor* as an organization along with fellow merchants provided aid in legal matters, cases of illness, material losses to tricksters, robbers, or officials, economic negotiations, and death. The *kontor* provided Hanseatic merchants with potential business partners and social contacts. In many cases, we find merchants who served as assistants at one of the Hanseatic *kontors* and still remained connected in a business or social network years after they had left the outposts. The time spent together in a potentially hostile environment and the joint memories from the days at the *kontor* provided a strong base for maintaining social relations and served as a solid foundation for mutual trust in business matters.

Security can be seen as the overarching reason for the existence of Hanseatic *kontors*. From the towns's point of view, the *kontors* provided possibilities for internal control and thus secured the privileges and the towns's credibility. Local authorities might have taken advantage of the *kontors'* security system. They saw that the Hansards took care of most dangers concerning inner security and social peace for hundreds or even thousands of foreign young men populating the town. The merchants themselves found regulations that would guarantee them a certain minimum income without restricting them from making high profits. Furthermore, living at the *kontors* provided reliable security for goods and lives, and offered social security, mutual aid, and a huge variety of potential business partners and social relations.

The *kontors* were as much socio-political entities as they were economic ones. As social and political conditions underwent major changes during the late Middle Ages, the merchants' organizational environments had to adjust. Thus, we can see a permanent differentiation in the organizational level of Hanseatic merchants abroad. The *kontors* were not set up by Hanseatic towns, rather they developed from loosely connected merchant associations to more systematically structured entities representing the will of all Hanseatic merchants. This development fits well with Norbert Elias's observations in

"Civilizing Process,"[1] which shows that rather unplanned proceedings starting in the twelfth century led to a more centralized structure of power with more determined players in the political process. Before we look at the development of the *kontors*' organization and the background of this theory, we need to look at the different geographical conditions that the Hanseatic merchants found at the four main *kontors* in London, Bruges, Bergen, and Novgorod.

Geographical Observations

London, Bruges, Bergen, and Novgorod were situated at the edges of the maritime trade zone that covered the Baltic and the North Seas. Between London and Bruges at the western and southern shores of the North Sea, Bergen in the far north, Novgorod east of the Finnish Inlet, and the Hanseatic ports at the southern shores of the Baltic and North Seas, the Hansards controlled much of the trade between the interregional trade in the High and late Middle Ages. Within this area, the Hansards were still a big player in early Modern times. These two facts—the Hanseatic dominance in trade and the emergence of the four *kontors* at the edges of the North and Baltic seas trade zone—are the main reason the Hanseatic League is seen as an organization with its main focus on Baltic and North Seas trade and politics, despite most member towns being situated far away from any port or harbor.

The four *kontors* were situated in very different climates as well as cultural and geostrategic places. In all four towns, the *kontors* and their merchants were part of the town and the daily life. However, the intensity of contact and social and architectonical integration differed considerably.

In London, the *kontor* was situated in the middle of the town, at the banks of the Thames River. The *kontor* could be reached by sea-going vessels, but these large ships had to travel against the current to reach the town, which made blocking the harbor and *kontor* entrance fairly easy.

Bryggen in Bergen was placed at the northern banks of a bay that cuts eastward into the west Norwegian coast. Right beside the *kontor* on the northern banks was the royal castle, which controlled the entry to the bay, *Vågen*. The Norwegian town was situated at the southern shore. Most of the Hansard rivals in the dried cod trade had their warehouses there, namely English, Dutch, and Scottish merchants. Norwegian towns and *kontors* were connected by the settling of craftsmen, mostly of Germanic origin, at the eastern edge of *Vågen*.

1 Elias (1994).

In Novgorod, the *kontor* consisted of two parts: a "beachyard" located at the shores of the river Volchow, and the *Peterhof*, situated uphill.[2] The whole town of Novgorod consisted of yards spread over an area of 120 hectares, of which only 20 percent were actually built on.[3] The Peterhof might have looked like one of these, somewhat bigger, but not necessarily different, and thus could be seen as an integral part of the architectonic ensemble that made up the town of Novgorod. Novgorod's most important difference from the other *kontors* was its lack of a maritime connection to the open sea. Sea-going vessels could not travel all the way to the town. Therefore, the merchants had to reload their goods and transport them to the *kontor* in smaller boats or sleighs.[4] From a strategic point of view, Novgorod was the most vulnerable *kontor* for any kind of offense or blockade against the Hanseatic merchants.

Even Bruges could not directly be reached by ship. However, its harbor Damme was very close. Bruges owed its success as a trading center to a storm that opened up the inlet Zwin between the town and the North Sea in 1134. This made Bruges the only cloth town in Flandres with access to the sea.[5] Merchants could travel to Damme, which connected with Bruges by the river Reie and several other artificial channels, making it possible to reach the town's market place by water transport.[6] Unfortunately for Bruges and the merchants, the sea eventually took back what it had granted. During the thirteenth, fourteenth, and fifteenth centuries, the Zwin increasingly silted up. By the fourteenth century, it was reported that larger sea-going ships could not call at Damme anymore. The town of Bruges invested large sums of money to keep the lane open, but ultimately it was in vain.[7] Still, the town remained one of the most important trading centers in north-western Europe during the late Middle Ages.

In London, Bergen, and Novgorod, the Hanseatic *kontors* were architecturally closed entities with wooden palisades. Inside were wooden living houses, warehouses and assembly houses, gates and fences, and in the case of Novgorod, a church. However, in all three towns the merchants used public infrastructure, markets, churches, and night-life districts outside the marked *kontor* area. When the *kontor*'s houses were rented out, merchants had to find other places to live. In London, merchants rented rooms in the English neighborhood;[8] in

2 Angermann (1989), 172.
3 Mühle (1997), 163.
4 Angermann (1997), 284.
5 Henn (1989), 43.
6 Ryckaert (1990), 6f.
7 Schubert (2000), 19.
8 Jörn (2000), 417ff.

Novgorod, German boys lived with farmers to learn the Russian language; and in Bergen, accounts of prostitution and ritual processions are legend. When seen in this light, the three *kontors* were not as different from Bruges as it first seems, even though Bruges did not have a fenced area like the other three. In Bruges, the Hansards spread over the whole town. They rented rooms and houses, and mingled with Flamish, Dutchmen, Englishmen, Italians, and many other nationalities. Thus, it was much more difficult for the *kontors* to control business and social activities of the Hanseatic merchants. However, despite the claims of an older literature, there were many occasions for intercourse with local and rival merchants in the other three towns.

When Hanseatic merchants arrived at the *kontors*, they faced very different environments. In London and Bruges, they entered urban centers with their special flair; a mixture of people, languages, and cultures; and business ideas and practices. To manage their business successfully, they had to adopt a man-of-the-world attitude. In most cases, the stone houses, crowded streets, palaces, and heavy fortification were much more than what the merchants were used to from their hometowns, with the exception of Cologne and probably Lübeck. The climate of these two towns was comparably friendly. It was probably a little warmer than in the Baltic Sea towns and a little wetter than in the towns of the Rhine area, but this did not bother the merchants much.

Bergen and Novgorod, on the other hand, seem to have been the complete antipodes of the former two *kontors*. The climate was harsh and challenging for many merchants, especially during the winter. The ice and snow made it comparably easy to access the Novgorod hinterland during the winter months, though areas that were swampy and impenetrable in summer time, low temperatures, icy winds, and the very short period of daylight made living conditions extremely difficult. Snow was not a major problem in Bergen, but the constant rainfall made living conditions extremely difficult. The short winter days restricted the activities of the merchants and staff that stayed in these towns. Though Bergen and Novgorod were large towns in the high times of Hanseatic trade, their urban feeling must have been completely different from Bruges or London.

Bergen was by far the largest town in Scandinavia and for a long time the political and economic center of the Norwegian kingdom. Novgorod covered an area of 120 hectares and was the place where rich and important aristocrats had their houses and where they displayed their wealth.[9] But compared to London and Bruges, and even to towns like Cologne, Lübeck, or Bremen, Bergen and Novgorod must have appeared rather provincial, small, and restrictive,

9 Stoob (1995), 77.

or in other words "unfancy." One didn't travel there for culture, parading, or amusement, reasons that made London and Bruges attractive. The only reason to travel to these places was business.

With reference to the remarks above, we can conclude that it is impossible to define a Hanseatic *kontor* geographically. Each of the four *kontors* had its unique characteristics, both in terms of geography, climate, strategic position, and cultural environment. One of the few commonalities between the four was that the merchants did not feel at home there. They had to deal with other political authorities, jurisdiction, and business rules. To overcome possible emerging obstacles, they needed to be united, a task that demanded a strong organization.

Organization

The organization of the *kontors* in London, Bruges, Bergen, and Novgorod didn't differ substantially. Even though there were special tasks and functions to be carried out according to local conditions and expectations of the authorities, the main organizational framework was alike for the four *kontors*. The structure of the different *kontors* was not unique. They followed the organization of Hanseatic hometowns, using guilds, brotherhoods, and other social corporations as a blueprint. There was no need to create a completely new organizational structure, as most of the corporations in the merchants' hometowns worked well. To the merchants, a *kontor* was just another of these corporations.

A *kontor* was a private corporation. Theoretically all Hanseatic merchants who wanted to trade in the respective town had to be members of the *kontor*. They were the community that decided upon rules and agreements, discussed problems, and held hearings. Naturally, the merchants tried to reduce their administrative burden as much as possible. They were interested in a well functioning organization, but the main purpose of their stay was business. Therefore, they delegated many duties to a board. In all four *kontors*, the board was run by chairmen called aldermen. Their number varied from one to six, but their duties were the same—inner jurisdiction, outer representation, and communication and negotiation with the hometowns and foreign powers. The board of aldermen was assisted by a board of deputies. The board of deputies was responsible for special tasks, such as controlling the official weights, overseeing wood and food supplies, and taking care of guard control. Aldermen and deputies were elected annually. To be elected, one had to be a merchant from a Hanseatic town and stay at the *kontor* throughout the election period. Thus, being elected as an alderman or deputy meant more than being appointed to an honorable position, it meant that the individual merchant would deal with the huge burden of spending time for administrative purposes instead of business ones. Special regulations were imposed, like the rule that no merchant was to be elected twice in a row, to reduce this burden and spread the duty of running the *kontor* on as many shoulders as possible.

When written notes, documents, and official letters started to play an important role in interregional business and politics in the fourteenth and fifteenth centuries, the aldermen found it increasingly difficult to fulfill their tasks. To ease the burdens of the aldermen, a new position was established at the *kontors*: the clerk. In London, Bruges, and Bergen, a clerck was appointed in the middle of the fifteenth century. Only in Novgorod was there no official clerk. Instead, the priests of the Hansards' church at the Peterhof took over most administrative duties.

A clerk's main function was to assist the aldermen with juridical advice and maintain the *kontor*'s official written correspondence. Soon the clerk became a very important position at the *kontors*. They had several advantages on their hands. Since most of them had studied the law at a German university, they were familiar with the interpretation of law codes, privileges, and the *kontors*' statutes. They understood words and writing better than the aldermen, and they had no difficulties with Latin, which was the most important language for official correspondence in the Late Middle Ages. Additionally the clercks served at the *kontors* for several years. They knew the *kontor*'s statutes, the history of certain problems, and the inner structure of the community much better than the aldermen, who served for only a year.

Clerks assisted both merchants and hometowns. The clerks sent reports to the town council or merchant guilds in the towns, reporting important activities, developments, problems, and difficulties within the *kontor*. They even pointed out certain merchant offences against the rules and regulations. This information was especially important to the merchants's headmasters or partners, who were not at the *kontor* and had to rely on second hand information in cases of embezzlement or fraud. The clerks' close connection to the merchants and the hometowns secured them very attractive positions after working at the *kontor*. Many clerks can be traced to positions such as secretaries of the town councils or as priests at altars or churches in Hanseatic towns.

These descriptions make Hanseatic *kontors* appear to be well-functioning organizations that started from scratch by a merchant elite with a determined plan to run a trade base. However, this is not true, as the *kontors'* organization and legislation developed over a long time, beginning in the twelfth and thirteenth centuries. This process did not end until the *kontors* closed. The best remaining example of such a development are the seven versions of the

Novgorod Schra. The Schra was the name of the statutes aof the *kontor* in Novgorod. All four *kontors* had their statutes, which defined the rules and regulations of business and life at the *kontors*. Together with privileges, agreements with the local rulers, and ordinances from the hometowns, the statutes were the juridical base on which the merchants acted in their respective towns. This applied both to trade, when they had to cope with differences among each other, and when they had contact with the locals. Just as in modern law books, some of the paragraphs in the statutes had ancient roots. They derived from common merchant rules, unwritten regulations at the respective town or trading place, or from no longer preserved older versions of ordinances. In the case of the Novgorod Schra, we can follow the changes and extension of the legal regulations of the *kontor* very clearly. New articles were added when the merchants or the hometowns found them necessary to be written down; other older regulations were abandoned or changed, or when they were no more practicable or contrary to new rules. The permanent extension of the statutes can also be traced in the statutes of the *kontor* in Bergen, where a version that was written down in the middle of the sixteenth century contained regulations that were dated to 1489, 1492, 1522, and 1545.[10]

The statutes' development shows a much stronger influence of the hometowns in the fifteenth and sixteenth centuries compared to the time before 1450. In London and Bruges, particularly during the fourteenth and early fifteenth centuries, most articles were added to the statutes by initiative of the *kontors*' merchants. After the Peace of Utrecht in 1474, the hometowns took control of the legislation in the *kontors*.[11] Only in Bergen was there a reverse development. The *kontor* appeared much more independent in the late fifteenth and sixteenth centuries. One probable explanation is that the Hanseatic towns had to concentrate on their conflict with England and Flanders and deal with the rising Dutch competitors in the North and Baltic Seas. This made the *kontor* in Bergen seem less important in overall ranking, which reduced the amount of attention they received from the hometowns.

As noted, a Hanseatic *kontor* was run by a board of aldermen and a board of deputies, both of which were elected by merchants who were members of the *kontor*. The will of the merchant community had the most weight. It was collected and written down in the *kontors'* statutes, which served as guidelines for the board members' decisions and actions. All merchants at the *kontors* had to follow the statutes and other regulations. Violations against the statutes could

---

10 Burkhardt (2005b), 64.

11 Jörn (1999), 108–110; Henn (1987), 61.

be punished with fines, or, in very serious cases, with the exclusion from the *kontor* and its privileges.

When taking a deeper look into the *kontors*' statutes, there are remarkable differences between them.[12] This is partly caused by the differences in geography, climate, culture, and strategic terms presented above. Another reason for these differences is the different business customs and demands by the local rulers or authorities. For a comparative study of the statutes, I have to refer the reader to the edited or original versions of the statutes.[13] Still, I want to mention some important features from each *kontor* to show the differences in organization and structure that a merchant traveling between all four could have found in the Late Middle Ages.

According to their origin, merchants in London were organized into thirds. The first third consisted of merchants from Cologne, the towns in the county of Geldern, and the areas at the river Rhine's left banks. The second third of merchants were from Westphalia, Saxony, the Wendish towns (like Lübeck, Wismar, and Rostock), and the areas at the river Rhine's right banks. The third group of merchants was from Prussia, Livland and Gotland. These divisions were important in the annual elections of an alderman and his deputies. The regulations determined that merchants had to elect an alderman from one third that was not their own. Once an alderman was elected, two deputies were elected out of the other two thirds. Thus, the merchants tried to ensure that all regional merchant groups found their interests represented in the decision-making processes of the board. Different ideas of how to run the *kontor* and how to react to or interact with the local authorities according to the merchants' original and favored goods and routes can be traced in the sources left from all of the four *kontors*. However, in the case of London trading, and England as a whole, this diversity gets the most evidence. The first time we hear of a group of German merchants in London is in 1282, when the *aula hanse Almanie* is mentioned.[14] This particular building was the meeting point for merchants from the city of Cologne. By 1300, we have evidence of two German guild halls in London. In

12 Burkhardt, (2005b).

13 London: Rolf Sprandel, ed., *Quellen zur Hanse-Geschichte* (Darmstadt, 1982), 350–382; Bergen: Mike Burkhardt, "Das Hanse*kontor* in Bergen im Spätmittelalter," (unpublished master-thesis, Kongelige Bibliotek Copenhagen and Archiv der Hansestadt Lübeck, Kiel 2006), appendix 1; and, as an older version: Oscar Albert Johnsen, Oluf Kolsrud, Absalon Talanger, eds., *Norges Gamle Love, Anden Række 1388–1604, Andet Bind 1448–1482* (Oslo, 1934), no. 416, 674–690; Novgorod: Wolfgang Schlüter, ed., *Die Nowgoroder Schra in sieben Fassungen vom XIII. bis XVII. Jahrhundert* (Lübeck, 1916); Bruges: Archiv der Hansestadt Lübeck, Altes Senatsarchiv, Externa, Batavica, Kopiar IX.

14 Schubert (2000), 37.

the same building resided a hall of Cologne merchants and a hall of Germans,[15] who were probably merchants from other towns in the northern part of the German countries. The organizational separation of these two merchant groups shows different interests and ideas of how to look after a *kontor*. They also would later become the core of the Hanseatic *kontor* in London. Although there was a *gildhalda mercatorum Colonie et Alamanie* in 1323,[16] which is likely still the building named above, this duality between Cologne merchants and the rest of the Hansards becomes very obvious when following the history of the *kontor* in London. The famous name Stalhof, derived from the Hansards' most important export good from England, wool, does not occur in sources until 1320.[17] But it is not the only name for the *kontor*. In 1340 for example it was called the *Esterlinghall*, or hall of the merchants from the East. This name is not simply an accidental curiosity when compared to the near monopoly-like position of merchants from Cologne in the trade between London and Lower Germany. Rather, it indicates the growing importance of merchants from other parts of the Hanseatic area, most notably those from Prussia and the Wendish towns at the *kontor* in London.

As with London, the Hanseatic merchants were divided into thirds in Bruges. However, the regions that made up one third were completely different.[18] The first quarter consisted of merchants from Livland and Gothland; the second one of merchants from the Wendish and Saxon towns; and the third one of merchants from Westphalia and Prussia. For a moment this third subdivision seems to be a curiosity. The discussion about the reasons for this rather unusual division is not finished yet. However, beyond historical family bonds between the two regions, which resulted from the important role of families from Westphalia in the German colonization of the Baltics, there must have been enough common interests between these two groups of Hanseatic towns in the trade and politics with Bruges and Flanders to justify assembling both merchant groups in one third.

As far as we know, the organizational independence of the thirds went much further than in London. Each one, for example, had its own till for taxes and fines. Also, the administrative apparatus was much bigger in Bruges than in London. Each year six aldermen were elected, two out of each third.[19] Also the number of deputies, eighteen in all, was equally shared between the three

15 Weinbaum (1928), 46.
16 Keene (1989), 48.
17 Lappenberg (1851), 24.
18 Henn (1989), 45.
19 Sprandel (1982), 347ff.

groups. This structure survived until 1486, when the number of aldermen was reduced to three and the deputies to nine.[20] The development of the *kontor* of Bruges shows the same active players as in London. Of course, these were mainly the largest towns, which supplied the market with many more merchants than the smaller towns could. In 1252 and 1253, Countess Margaret II of Flanders issued documents to define and improve the rights of the *Mercatores Romani imperii*, merchants of the Roman Empire.[21] Other towns were interested in these privileges, namely Lübeck and Hamburg, both of which led negotiations. Both towns strengthened their positions with proxies issued by the towns of Cologne, Dortmund, Soest, Münster, and Aachen. Here again, Wendish and Westphalish towns were the first to negotiate privileges for their merchants. It was not until 1347[22] and 1356[23] that there were written statutes for the *kontor* in Bruges. However, that does not mean that nothing happened to the organization of the Hanseatic merchants in the town. On the contrary, in the statutes from 1356 we find they mirror a very complex organized group of merchants with the already named handicap of not having their own fenced area in the town. The statutes consisted of no less than ninty-five articles, most of which were concerned with trade regulations, but 16 concerning financing and organizing the *kontor*.[24]

As they lacked a natural meeting point as provided by the other three *kontors*, the Hansards in Bruges often used the monastery of the Carmelite order for meetings. Here they also had their archive and their own chapel,[25] and the first known statutes of the *kontor* were issued here as well. Although we have information to assume that the *kontor* had a building at its disposal already in the first half of the fifteenth century,[26] we do not have evidence of such a building before the Hansards rented the *Oosterlingenhuis* as a representative building in 1442.[27] Finally, in 1478, the construction of the *kontors* representative building at the *Oosterlingenplein* in the center of the town was finished.[28] Still, the monastery of the Carmelite order did not lose its importance, especially as it also was the most important religious center for the memorial of the

20 Sosson (1984), 181.
21 Sprandel (1990), 72f.; (1982), 182ff.
22 Hanserezesse I, 1, Nr. 143; Sprandel (1982), 347–349.
23 Archiv der Hansestadt Lübeck, Altes Senatsarchiv, Externa, Batavica, Kopiar IX.
24 Burkhardt (2005b), 71.
25 Asmussen (1999), 76f.
26 Burkhardt (2005b), 74.
27 Ryckaert (1990), 12.
28 Sosson (1984), 174–181; Asmussen (1999), 77.

Hanseatic merchants in Bruges. The golden age of Bruges as the trading center in Flanders was already history in the late fifteenth century, and the *kontor* as a whole moved to Antwerp in 1520.[29] Thus, we can say that the monastery served as the central building of the social, religious and political activities of the Hanseatic *kontor* in Bruges for the most of its time.

In Bergen the merchants were not divided into groups according to their origin. Here the merchants from the Wendish towns outnumbered all other Hansards by a huge margin. Lübeck was the most important hometown until the early sixteenth century, when merchants from Bremen started to take leading positions at the *kontor*. Wismar, Stralsund, and to some extent Rostock, Greifswald, and Hamburg also showed a lot of interest in the internal matters of *Bryggen*, the *kontor* in Bergen. At Bryggen the merchants elected three aldermen and probably eighteen deputies, the *Achteinen*. In the older literature we find that six aldermen were elected, which was supposed to be adopted from the *kontor* in Bruges, but this assumption was based on the wrong interpretation of a single source.[30] There is evidence for aldermen in Bergen by the late 1360s. Also, in Bergen, the number of merchants who were burdened with administrative tasks was reduced in the late fifteenth century. In 1476 the number of aldermen was reduced to one and the deputies to eight. One reason for this reduction might lie in the successful role of the secretary of the *kontor*, a position that was introduced in the 1450's.

A specialty of Bryggen was its inner structure. Like the *kontors* in London and Novgorod, it was situated on a fenced area. But as the Hansards took over this place, they adopted their own way of organizing it.[31] At Bryggen, one or two rows of houses bordered on an alley that led down to a landing place at the harbor. All the buildings connected to the alley made up a yard or, in the case of two rows of houses, a double yard. Each yard had its own name and council, which consisted of all merchants living in it. Some administrative functions of the *kontors* in London and Novgorod were delegated to the yards. Thus, for example, a yard's merchants were responsible for their own wood and beer; they collected taxes and fines, and had to take care for the fire protection and stability of the buildings in their yards.[32] This shared burden of administration might be another reason for the comparably small number of aldermen necessary to run the *kontor* in Bergen.

29 Blanckenburg (2001), 235.
30 Burkhardt (2006), 47–52.
31 Burkhardt (2005b), 61.
32 Burkhardt (2006), 36–41.

The *kontor* of Novgorod was run by a council of aldermen and deputies as well. Here, however, the alderman was not elected by the merchants, but appointed by envoys of Lübeck or Visby. These two towns competed for influence at the *kontor*. Visby was the front-runner in the early years of the *kontor*, but lost ground to Lübeck and Reval during the thirteenth, fourteenth, and fifteenth centuries. A specialty of the trade in Novgorod made it necessary to have more than one alderman annually. The Hansards came to Novgorod in two groups, one staying at the *kontor* in summer, the other one in winter. Thus, an alderman served for only one season before leaving the *kontor* in fall or spring with the remaining merchants of his group. The alderman appointed four deputies, or "wise men", to assist him in running the *kontor*. As was the case at the other *kontors*, the most important decisions were made by the assembly of all merchants, who decided general questions regarding trade and life at the *kontor*. The decisions were collected in the statutes of the *kontor*, the so-called *Schra*. For Novgorod we have the best evidence of the organic nature of the *kontor*'s statutes. The first known version of the *Schra* dates back to 1268. Several versions were edited by Schlüter,[33] and covered several centuries, which shows how remarkable the changes in the regulations were regarding trade and life in Nowogord in the Late Middle Ages.

Although different in their architectonical structure and importance of merchants from different hometowns, all four Hanseatic *kontors* were organized in a similar way. They all had one or more aldermen at the top of the administrative hierarchy. These were assisted by several deputies. The most important decisions had to be made by the assembly of all merchants present at the *kontor*. Election dates and, in the case of Novgorod, length of duty may have varied, but in general, the Hanseatic merchants chose to organize their most important trading outposts similar to the system they knew from home. The Hanse towns themselves were organized with an assembly and a council led by majors, and nearly all corporations, brotherhoods, and guilds were structured in the same way. Thus, it is possible to see a common base structure of organization at the four *kontors*. However, as this is the base structure of all interpersonal unions in the Hanseatic area in the Late Middle Ages, it is not useful to define a *kontor* with administrative terms alone.

33 Schlüter (1916).

Trade at the *Kontors*

All four Hanseatic *kontors* were situated at the edges of what was the core area of Hanseatic merchants' business activities. Therefore, they were very important for inputting foreign goods into the Hanseatic trade system. Hansards could buy luxury goods, special foodstuff, and raw materials with considerable security. The large trading places were protected by the local lords and provided safety from robbery. Prices and quality were more or less controlled by the local authorities. And, important for the merchants' business plans, there was a reliable quantity of certain goods on hand at these larger markets due to the trading centers' attractiveness to potential sellers or simply to royal privileges.

The Hansards themselves put further regulations and rules on the trade at their four *kontors*. Most of these regulations were written down in the *kontors*' statutes. They were read aloud to the community of merchants once a year to ensure that everybody at the *kontor* knew which actions were legal and which actions would cause trouble. Most regulations were enforced to prevent non-Hansards from participating in the merchants' privileges or to guarantee a certain amount of security for the Hanseatic merchants. Thus, some general rules at all *kontors* were as follows: No Hansard was allowed to run a company with a non-Hansard, all business transactions had to be carried out in public space, and no merchant should entice away other merchants' staff. Also, regulations regarding quality and quantity of traded goods were in the statutes. The regulations also show that the Hanseatic merchants not only feared their competitors of other origin, they also feared each other. In most cases, the most dangerous competitors for a Hanseatic merchant were other Hansards. One purpose of the many rules regarding trade and business was to take the edge off intra-Hanseatic competition. In a certain way it was the attempt to ensure as many Hanseatic merchants as possible a reliable profit. Another reason was to guarantee that all of the merchants observed the privileges, but we must not forget that these privileges themselves only were a means to make trade and thus profit more predictable to the Hanseatic merchants.

Goods and customs varied from *kontor* to *kontor*. I am not going to go into detail regarding trade routes and quantities of goods, as these topics are covered elsewhere. However, a description of the *kontors* would be incomplete without a short overall view of the main business activities in the respective trade ports. In London and Bruges, Hanseatic merchants met businessmen from all over western and southern Europe. They not only purchased exotic goods, they also became acquainted with new business ideas and techniques and learned about different cultural customs and latest fashions.

Bruges offered by far the most exotic and varied selection of trade goods in the region. The Hansards bought large amounts of spices, fine fabrics, and other luxury goods, which found their way to the local markets in the Hanseatic towns. Cloth was a very important commodity, but after the shift in the cloth production of Flanders, which occurred after large-scale unrest in the 1370s, Hanseatic merchants' interest decreased as they found alternative markets, mainly in England. In contrast to other *kontors*, the Hanseatic merchants did not often contact local producers of raw materials or semi-produced goods. In Bruges, most trade was carried out between merchants. Even the famous cloth from Flanders, which was largely sold in Bruges, had already arrived through intermediary merchants. Apart from exotic luxury goods, Bruges was one of the most important book suppliers to the merchant class.[34]

England mainly exported wool and, from the late fourteenth century onwards, cloth. Hansards had a good share in the wool and cloth trade, although they had to compete with Englishmen, Dutchmen, and Italians. During the thirteenth and fourteenth centuries, wool trade was decentralized. Hanseatic merchants exported large quantities of wool from London and the East English towns of Boston, Lynn, Hull, and Yarmouth.[35] Along with the shift from wool to cloth production, the trading routes changed, and London became the superior export harbor of the kingdom. Hansards still had their share in the market, but others, especially denizen merchants, controlled much of the export trade. In the English cloth production, there is an interesting example of market-oriented cooperation between English producers and Hanseatic merchants.[36] Several production areas in the English midlands focused a part of their production on the special needs of a Hanseatic town and its hinterland. According to the different fashions in Hamburg, Lübeck, and Danzig, the designs of cloth sold in Yarmouth, Boston, and Hull could differ significantly. Producers and merchants had constant contact, making production areas able to react quickly to changes in demand. This cooperation guaranteed a constant purchase of produced cloth, but it involved a certain danger of economic dependence.

While English cloth producers managed maintain some independence by orientating their production to different customer areas, the Norwegian suppliers of stockfish were entirely dependent on their Hanseatic partners. Stockfish, dried cod, was the most important export good in Norway. In the thirteenth century, stockfish became the royal staple for trade in the west Norwegian

34 Schubert (2000), 24.

35 Burkhardt (2007); Jenks (1992); Lloyd (1991).

36 Jenks, vol. 1 (1992), 452; Lloyd (1991), 84–92.

town, Bergen. The fish was caught in the northern Norwegian areas, primarily at the islands Vesterålen and Lofoten in February and March. They were then hung up in large wooden stands to dry in the cold fresh air. When the cod dried, the fishermen sold it to an intermediary, the so-called *Norderfahrer*, who then brought the goods in smaller vessels down to Bergen. Here the German merchants waited for their partners. The busiest months in Bergen were July and August, when thousands of *Norderfahrer* entered the small bay with their vessels packed with stockfish. Usually the *Norderfahrer* were not free to choose with whom they wanted to do business. Most of them had already taken loans from a Hanseatic merchant to buy flour, malt, beer, and other goods. Most of next summer's purchase would be used to pay back this loan. Thus, the *Norderfahrer* had to take new loans to buy new goods from the merchant. Thus each Hanseatic merchant had its fixed group of suppliers. Often these dependencies lasted for generations. Still, this system had also advantage for the Norwegians. Many farmers gave up work on the fields and concentrated on fishing and drying as a full-time occupation. They could earn more money and increase their families' living standard, as long as the system worked well.[37] However, this development also led large parts of northern Norway to depend greatly on grain imports. Only Hanseatic merchants were able to cover this demand, as their Dutch, English, and Scottish competitors did not have access to the large grain resources that the Hanseatic towns had in their hinterlands.

As in Bergen, Hanseatic merchants did not look for produced goods in Novgorod either. When the steady stream of Arabic luxury goods and silver died down in the eleventh century, the Russian town developed into the main supplier of wax, furs, and honey for the Baltic and North Sea markets.[38] The Hansards imported mainly salt, herring, and metal in exchange.[39] To guarantee a steady supply with the raw materials, the Russian sellers had their own cooperation. Still, there seem to have been some difficulties to ensure each merchant a large enough pile of export goods to make the journey profitable. Therefore the *kontor* had some very clear restrictions on trade in Novgorod. Merchants were only allowed to travel to the town once a year, in summer or in winter.[40] Summer travels lasted from April to October. In the winter season, which lasted from October to March, the merchants traveled with sleighs over land from Dorpat via Pskow to Novgorod. The advantage of winter travels was that it was much easier to reach large parts of the swampy hinterlands of the

37 Nielssen (1994).

38 Mühle (1997), 159.

39 Angermann (1997), 283f.

40 Angermann (1989), 174, Kattinger (1999), 220ff.

town when the water was frozen. Furthermore it was forbidden to import goods that valued at more than 1000 mark lübsch.[41] This regulation was likely implemented to reduce the risk of oversupply and the outcompeting of Hanseatic merchants by large and possibly cheap offers from a rich business man.

Of course, trade at the *kontors* was much more diverse than can be explained here. Many more goods were traded in all of the four *kontors*, every merchant tried to reach the best conditions, sometimes acting at or beyond legal borders. Large fines were imposed for those caught in the act, but since our sources only tell us about the uncovered offences against the statutes, we can only guess how many merchants defied them in secret. Given the fact that the Hanseatic towns managed to secure their privileges for several centuries, the large mass of the merchants still seems to have acted within the framework of legal regulations.

Trade and its control were the main purposes for the existence of the Hanseatic *kontors*. But in the view of the merchants and their staff, social life and cooperation might have been equally important when they came to one of the four towns and settled down in the *kontors*.

Life at the *Kontors*

Living abroad has never been easy. Even today with information available in advance, it entails practical and social difficulties to stay abroad for any period of time. How much more difficult must it have been for a medieval merchant who entered another cultural sphere with different legislation, customs, and languages? In most cases, he did not travel there with the purpose of getting acquainted with the region's culture. He simply wanted to do business with as little hindrance as possible. For this purpose, the *kontors* were the ideal place to go to. Here the Hanseatic merchant met an organization that was similar to the one he knew from his hometown. He met people of fellow origin, who knew his background and expectations and could give him guidance and information about local customs and the latest news. Everybody spoke a Low German dialect, ate the same foods, sang traditional songs, and followed other customs from the hometowns. In other words, a newcomer could feel at home, leaving him free to concentrate on business. Since all Hanseatic merchants in London, Bruges, Bergen, and Novgorod had to report to the *kontor*, it became the most important and reliable source of information to the Hansards. Prices, qualities, political actions, and local incidents were discussed here soon after they got to

41 Burkhardt (2005b), 72.

a merchant's knowledge. All Hansards profited from this exchange, following the old wisdom that only a well-informed merchant can be a successful one. But life at the *kontors* was much more than pure business.

Besides monasteries, the *kontors* might have been the most male-dominated, flat-sharing communities in the Middle Ages. Nearly all involved in the Hanseatic trade were men. At the *kontors* in London, Bergen, and Novgorod, women were not allowed to live permanently inside the fenced area. Thus, merchants, assistants, and boys had to organize life at the *kontor* themselves. They had to carry out all duties, even those that were usually considered part of the women's work sphere. Most of these tasks were taken on by boys, who lived at the *kontor* as helping hands and were to get a basic education in reading, writing, calculation, and business matters. They usually left their homes in one of the Hanse towns or in the rural areas of the Low German provinces by the age of 11 or 12 to accompany an older relative who was a merchant in a Hanse town. Before they entered their master's house, boys in Novgorod had to live with a Russian farmer family for half a year to learn Russian.[42] This was not necessary in Bruges, Bergen, and London, as the Germanic languages spoken there did not differ as much from Low German as they do today. Furthermore Low German was the business lingua franca in the Baltic and North Sea towns, so merchants could communicate with suppliers without any problem.

After they left their families, the boys entered a new union of tradesmen. Their loyalty was no longer with the family at home, but with their houselord and the other merchants at the *kontor*. From the *kontor* in Bergen, we are well informed of the way the boys were introduced into their new home.[43] In the famous "Bergen plays," the newcomers had to undergo several rituals of physical violence and psychological humiliation. These procedures varied slightly from yard to yard, but general characteristics were dunking into the harbor and waste holes, beating and kicking by the assistants and older boys, and hanging up in the chimney. After they were finally beaten up, in a covered corner in the meeting room they had to take an oath to follow the yard's rules, serve the other members of the household, and entertain with jokes and songs. Usually the boys recovered quickly. Most of them were used to physical privations and this *rite de passage* was the usual way to get admitted to an interpersonal union in the Middle Ages. We know such examples among others from boys participating in the hay harvest for the first time, introduction rites at universities and monasteries, and the consecration of new craftsmen, many of which survived in some form until modern times. Consequently, we are only informed

42 Angermann (1997), 284.

43 Hartung (1877).

of one case of death caused by the plays during the Late Middle Ages. There is a lot of speculation about the reason for these violent rites. However, it is likely that there are several ideas in them. First, the boys had to shift their private environment and loyalties. Second, participating in the brutalities made all members of the household part of a violation of normal life's rules. Since this violation was sanctioned through the organized form of the rites, it still made them accomplices in a semi-criminal act that only they shared with each other. Thus, the ritual beating up of newcomers also strengthened ties of already established members of the household, yard, and *kontor*. Third, the rule that every newcomer had to undergo the plays would have made sure that no one could drop out of the social hierarchy by virtue of birth, wealth, or age. No matter how things developed in reality, the fictional equalization of all members during the plays was an important mental pillar of the loyalty of all boys, assistants, and merchants to the legal and social rules at the *kontor* and to each other.

Once at the *kontor*, the boys had to take on cleaning, cooking, and good transports. Their cooking and cleaning, however, left much to be desired. The merchants in London saw themselves forced to issue a paragraph in the *kontor's* statutes regulating that waste had to be disposed and not to be thrown away in front of a neighbor's door or under a crane.[44] Also in the Novgorod *Schra*, we find regulations that ask to leave the brewery behind in a clean condition and not to cover roads and alleys with rubbish.[45] From a testament of Israhel Ruschman, a merchant who used to visit Bergen in the 1450s, we know that he let a Norwegian women wash his clothes against payment,[46] normally one of the boys' duties. Boys didn't have much privacy at the *kontor*. Their labor days were long and once finished, they had to share a small room with up to five or more other boys. In Bergen, fire was forbidden in all the wooden living houses at the *kontor*, and windows wouldn't be opened often because of the cold and moist climate. This led to uninviting conditions. As all the other inhabitants of the yard, the boys spent most of their free time in the common hall. The boys were under the absolute sovereignty of the houselord, whether it was the merchant himself or his partner or assistant, running the business at the *kontor*. The houselord was responsible for their offences and had the right and duty to punish them. But the boys did most of the hard physical work at the *kontor*, and they also received a basic education, something that many of them

44 Statutes of the *kontor* in Bergen (1572), §§ 48, 49.

45 Statutes of the *kontor* in Novgorod (4th version, 1355–1361), §§ 3–9, 42.

46 Bruns (1900), 94f.

would never have received in their home villages.[47] They were taught reading, writing, calculating, and business knowledge for pricing, weighing, and quality control. They also learned the merchant class social codes and received cultural, religious, and social stimuli, which broadened their minds and enabled them to start their own business career after their time at one of the *kontors*.

Once the boys had spent some time at the *kontor* and passed an examination, they could continue their presence at the *kontor* as a merchant's assistant.[48] These young men got even tighter involved in the daily business. They controlled the packing, weighing, and transport of goods in and out of the warehouse; they helped with bookkeeping and sometimes were allowed to make minor business decisions. They were slowly introduced to all aspects of a merchant's activities. Many of them entered the mesh of Hanse trade with their own small business, often as a junior partner of their tutor merchant. Assistants had a special standing at the *kontors*. Although still under the authority of their houselord, they had much more freedom than other boys did. From the *kontor* of Bergen, we know that assistants had their own sleeping room. This provided them with a better living environment, as well as privacy when, for example, they wanted to bring a prostitute to their room. In one of the yards' regulations from Bergen, we find even a rule stating that, while the assistants had to follow the houselord's orders, the merchants were not allowed to beat them.[49] No such rule is to be found regarding the boys. Also, in free time activities, the assistants had much in common with the merchants. Common forms of entertainment consisted of cards or skill games. Cheating and arguments were very common. However, the yard rules in Bergen prohibiting playing for money. From London and Bergen, we are also informed about ball games. The statutes in London ordered that there shouldn't be ball games in the guild hall, where goods were stored and business was done. In Bergen, regulations prohibited merchants and assistants from playing ball with the boys, most likely because of the violent aspects of these games putting the small boys' health in danger.

The merchants were the heads of their respective household,[50] and were responsible for the good behavior of the members of their household. They had to control them, punish them in case of minor offences, or report them to the aldermen in cases of bigger issues. Only the merchants were full-right members of the *kontor*. They gathered in the merchants' assembly that made the most important decisions in legal cases and issued new regulations to be

47 Burkhardt (2006), 60–64.
48 Burkhardt (2006), 64–66.
49 Bendixen (1895), 30.
50 Burkhardt (2006), 66–67.

obtained in the statutes. Though there were many merchants at the *kontors* in the thirteenth and fourteenth centuries, by the fifteenth century, the number of traveling merchants decreased. While merchants in earlier centuries seemed to have traveled regularly to the *kontors* and spent a lot of time away from their hometowns, it looks like they became more resident in one Hanse town towards the end of the Middle Ages. The merchants living at the *kontor* were mostly junior partners trying to establish themselves in a market segment and to get enough business rolling to settle down in a Hanse town themselves. This might also be a reason for employing secretaries at the London, Bruges, and Bergen *kontors*. As junior partners ran business abroad independently, the larger merchants who didn't visit the *kontor* in person might have felt the need to check and control to ensure trade still was done according to the rules.

Since some merchants didn't trade at the *kontors* regularly, they didn't own houses or rooms there. They had to find a merchant with a house at the *kontor* and live with him as a guest.[51] Although they had all rights in trade according to the privileges valid for all Hanseatic merchants, they didn't enjoy the rights of political and legal participation. On the other hand, they also didn't have to perform some of the duties, such as leading the night watch or paying full residential taxes. The permanent residents of the *kontor* didn't always have friendly feelings towards these intruders. In 1556, an older merchant, Tommies Eschink, traveled to Bergen's *kontor* for the first time in his life. The aldermen freed him from participating in the Bergen plays, but some assistants still beat him up without getting punished.[52]

For all groups, boys, assistants, and merchants alike, work set the tone of the life at the *kontors*. Agreements had to be made between suppliers and customers; goods had to be transported, sorted, weighed, checked, packed, and stored; books had to be kept; and decisions to be made. Most of the day was occupied by such activities. Still, community spirit was very important to the *kontor's* members. In the evenings, they gathered in common rooms to eat and talk together.[53] In Bergen, these houses were the only stone buildings at the *kontor* and the only ones to be heated. They provided a very natural meeting room for everybody. But also from Novgorod we know that the boys were taught basic knowledge, and the chess figures at the site of the *kontor* indicate that this was one of several pastimes of the *kontor*'s inhabitants.[54] Of course, life at the *kontor* meant much more than merchants' business. All activities of daily life

51 Burkhardt (2006), 68.

52 Koren Wiberg (1932), 96.

53 Jörn (2000), 433ff.; Burkhardt (2006), 42–44.

54 Mühle (1997), 163.

had to be done. Sometimes these led to disturbances and had to be regulated in the statutes. In Novgorod fistfights were on the agenda,[55] and the statutes at the Bergen *kontor* implied some major problems with internal violence at Bryggen.[56] Another regulation in Novgorod asked the inhabitants not to disturb other people when they were chopping wood or singing,[57] a rule that must have been difficult to fulfill given the very tense architectural structure of the *kontor*. Disturbing the peace was also a problem in London. Here the statutes dictated that no one should shout or knock on doors when he came back from a trip after the night guard had closed the gate.[58] Night watch was another important part of the statutes in the London, Bergen, and Novgorod *kontors*.

Of course, there are many examples of cooperation between merchants and denizen inhabitants of the host towns.[59] In Novgorod, merchants had to transport goods on Russian boats from the Baltic Sea along the Russian rivers,[60] and when the *kontor* was overcrowded, Russians made living and storing room available in their houses.[61] In London, many Hanseatic merchants had to rent houses in the town because the *kontor* didn't have enough capacity to house all of them.[62] In Bergen, the town's public wine cellar was run by the *kontor*.[63] Still, all three *kontors* were barricaded with strong palisades because public opinion could change quickly and if things became hostile, the Hanseatic merchants stood alone. Therefore, participation in night watch was one of the most important duties of all inhabitants of the *kontor*.[64] Permanent patrols with men and dogs were important to ensure security of lives and goods of those living at the *kontor*. But there was an internal reason for night watch, too. One of its purposes was to prevent illegal business in the dark hours. This becomes explicitely clear in the statutes of the *kontor* in Novgorod. Here it was demanded that night guards in the *kontor*'s church, the most important store for the Hanseatic merchants, had to be carried out by the assistants of two different merchants, in order to prevent clandestine arrangements and larceny.[65]

55 Friedland (1991), 46.
56 Burkhardt (2006), 31–41.
57 Statutes of the *kontor* in Novgorod (4th version, 1355–1361), § 48.
58 Statutes of the *kontor* in London (1460), § 52.
59 Burkhardt (2005a).
60 Angermann (1989), 174.
61 Friedland (1991), 47.
62 Lappenberg, 166f.
63 Burkhardt (2006), 46.
64 Burkhardt (2006), 33f., 64; Burkhardt (2005), 67, 69f.; Lappenberg (1851), 32.
65 Statutes of the *kontor* in Novgorod (4th version, 1355–1361), § 2.

Fire protection was another big issue. At the *kontor* in Bergen, all houses were built of timber. The only exceptions were the so-called firehouse (*ildstue*), the kitchen of each yard, and the adjacent meeting room. Since these were the only two rooms of each yard where open fire and heating were permitted, they became the natural meeting places in the cold and moist Norwegian climate. Further actions were taken to prevent the *kontor* from burning down. Several yards were pulled down in the fifteenth century, leaving fire protection lanes between the islands of yards left at the *kontor*. Furthermore, it was forbidden to tar the roofs of the houses, a regulation that did not directly lead to improving living conditions in the rainy town. Still, Bergen was struck by devastating fires, destroying parts or the whole *kontor* and the town several times during the Late Middle Ages. In these times, Hansards and Norwegians, Englishmen and Dutchmen worked hand in hand to protect the houses because in the wooden medieval towns, the spreading of the fire to a neighbor's house, even if he was a competitor, meant immediate danger to one's own property.

The Hansards didn't only contact the townspeople for official and business affairs. Many had friendly relations with denizens. English merchants regularly stood surety for Hanseatic merchants, and the merchants in Novgorod had close relations with Russian peasant families who regularly welcomed new boys to their household for some months.[66] From testaments of merchants who did business in Bergen, we know of friendships with Norwegians,[67] and in Bruges, close contact with townspeople was already shown by the fact that merchants had to rent rooms from local hosts.[68] A special problem at the *kontors* was women contact and sexuality. When discussing the *kontors* in London, Bergen, and Novgorod, we are talking about a large number of young men gathered in a small fenced area. In Novgorod, up to 800 men lived at the *kontor*;[69] in Bergen, up to 2000;[70] and in London, estimations get to even higher numbers. In other words, there was a large overdose of testosterone that needed an outlet to prevent violent clashes. Prostitution was one solution to this problem. Most famous is the red-light district in Bergen, which directly bordered on Bryggen,[71] but there is information about prostitution in the other *kontors* as well. The *kontor* in Novgorod had its own bathhouse where, according to a note

66 Angermann (1997), 284.
67 Bruns (1900), p. 1ff.
68 Greve (1994).
69 Angermann (1997), 282.
70 Bowitz Andersson (1982), 20.
71 Burkhardt (2005a), 139, 148f.

from 1416, the Hanseatic merchants "played" with Russian women.[72] In 1449, the merchants in London issued an article in the statues prohibiting prostitution at the rooms of the Stalhof.[73] Still, three years later a brawl was reported following a dispute of some merchants about who should take which women to his room.[74]

Usually internal disputes were settled peacefully with the help of other merchants or friends.[75] Only when this was not possible did the aldermen or deputies have to pass a sentence. As long as two Hanseatic merchants were involved, the *kontor* had the absolute jurisdiction. If the dispute was between a Hansard and a denizen, the local authorities had to be notified. This made supervising the merchants' activities difficult. To make sure offenses were reported to the aldermen, two merchants in each hostel were appointed to report all offenses. Because these spies didn't know the other informants' identities, the system ensured that only the aldermen knew all of them, making everybody feel like they were constantly being watched.

Life at the Hanseatic *kontors* was as manifold as anywhere. Due to lack of female influence, the tone might have been a bit rougher than in the merchants' hometowns, but altogether the *kontors* were a reflection of the north European medieval town society with its household hierarchies, interpersonal networks and activities, and internal organization. The Hanseatic merchants had very different lives at the four *kontors* according to local conditions, climate, customs, and culture. Especially in the *kontors* in London, Bergen, and Novgorod, the close life together in a potentially hostile environment strengthened interpersonal bonds. We can detect partnerships and social contacts of merchants who were together as boys at the same *kontor* years after they went home and settled as merchants in one of the Hanse towns. The *kontors* provided a platform for successful business and gave young men and merchants the opportunity to become acquainted with different cultures and customs. They also allowed for strong interpersonal bonds that sometimes lasted an entire lifetime and could build the base for successful economic and social networking.

---

72 Angermann (1989), 175.

73 Jörn (2000), 449.

74 Schubert (2000), 41.

75 Statutes of the *kontor* in Bergen (1572), § 11.

The Role of the *Kontors* in the Organization of Hanseatic Trade

Hanseatic trade was much more than trading activities of Hanseatic merchants within the *kontors*. The most important trade in terms of quantity of goods transported was inner-Hanseatic trade. Many more goods were shipped from Wismar to Rostock and from Lübeck to Danzig than were traded in the four *kontors*. And one part of the Hanseatic trade that is notoriously underrepresented in Hanse research is domestic trade in the interior. Merchants from towns like Melle, Havelberg, Krakow, Naumburg or Werben, all at one point recognized as Hanse merchants, might never have been seen at any of the *kontors*. Their trade was much more concentrated on the local scale and the interregional inland fairs at for example Frankfurt, Nuremberg, or Leipzig. South German merchants participated in the trade in Hanse towns as well. One of the most famous examples is the Mulich family from Nuremberg with strong business connections to the town of Lübeck. We often forget this part of Hanseatic trade when we concentrate on the trade of Lübeck and Danzig or the English and Falmish connections of merchants from Cologne.

Still, the *kontors* were important to the Hanseatic trade system. They provided many merchants and Hanseatic towns with goods that otherwise would have been hard or nearly impossible to access. This is especially true for the northernmost Hanseatic towns situated at the shores of the Baltic Sea. As sea transport was much cheaper and much more efficient that road transport the advantage of trade at the *kontors* was their access to the open sea. Even if goods had to be transported from the *kontor* to the Baltic Sea by boat on rivers, as in the case of Novgorod, this was still much cheaper than carrying the same quantity of goods by wagon from somewhere in Russia to the Hanseatic region. As trading centers for goods that were not available in the Hanseatic region in the same quantity or quality London, Bruges, Bergen, and Novgorod supplied many people in this region with much demanded and needed commodities. In Novgorod, besides furs, much of the wax needed in medieval churches, guild halls, and households was purchased. Bruges and London supplied the region with fine cloth, spices, literature, and a lot of luxury goods. From Bergen, stockfish, a durable fish needed as food during several of the 140 fasting days prescribed by the medieval church calendar, reached the markets at the continent and the British Isles. Many other goods were also transported in Hanseatic ships from the *kontors* to the towns, but the merchandise listed above comprised the most important commodities and attracted thousands of Hanseatic merchants' interest every year.

In exchange, the *kontors* provided a welcome customer market for products overproduced in the Hanseatic region. Here the Hansards could sell their cereals, flour, malt, beer, salt, metal, fabric, and other products which were not sellable in their home regions. Thus, the *kontors* fulfilled an important function within the interregional system of trade, which covered all of Europe and reached out to northern Africa and western Asia in the late Middle Ages. This function was also one reason for the decline of the *kontors'* importance in the sixteenth century. Bruges especially lost its dominant position in the interregional trading system when the Americas were discovered and used as an economic playground and the transatlantic trade became concentrated on other ports. Although London was still a major trading place in this new economic system, the conditions of trade and goods offered and requested changed. But most importantly, the way business was done changed and the Hanseatic model of privileged trade for their own merchants on behalf of other regions' business men was a business theory of a past age. Rulers, local authorities, and Hanseatic merchants alike no longer had interest in this kind of semi-monopolistic guaranteed trade.

We can see this change in business mentality in the change of interconnection between Hanseatic merchants that occurred during the second half of the fifteenth century. In the early decades of the fifteenth century, long lasting trade partnerships were the dominant way of organizing business for Hanseatic merchants. With their interpersonal connections, they were able to do business at many places and *kontors* thanks to a well-functioning network of partnership relations. By the end of the century, however, business networks were completely different. Merchants preferred short-term business contacts. There were far fewer long-term partnerships, which bound resources for several years, and networks among these corporations dimished as well.

This change in mentality made it increasingly difficult to convince Hanseatic merchants of the advantage of trade under the protection but also in following the restrictions of the *kontors*. Thus, it became much harder to force merchants to follow regulations and privileges. This, in return, lead to a lack of trust by the local authorities and rulers, who cut down on the exclusive rights for Hanseatic merchants. This led to even more offenses by the merchants. Of course there are also political and protectionistic reasons for the decline of the *kontors*. But it no coincidence that the closure of the *kontors* in Novgorod in 1479, Bruges in 1520, and the suspension of the privileges in London in 1552 happened in the same time as the change of business mentality in the Hanse region and an adjustment of the interregional trade system in Europe. The *kontors* were important centers of trade during the late Middle Ages, but they could not compete with other forms of trade organization in the system of the sixteenth century. Only the *kontor* in Bergen existed much longer, not being closed until 1776, but by then it was a mere shadow of its former importance and activity.

Another function of the *kontors* was more cultural. The exchange of ideas and thoughts was one part of trade that should be mentioned as well. At all four *kontors*, the Hanseatic merchants became acquainted with different business techniques and philosophies. It is very likely that they learned about new methods like double bookkeeping, used in Italy for centuries, bills of exchange, or the Dutch idea of free trade in London and Bruges for the first time. Even new fashions, lifestyles, political theories, and religious ideas were presented and exchanged at these junctions of interregional trade.[76] New ideas traveled faster from Venice, Paris, or London to towns like Kyritz, Osterrode, Kokenhusen, or Hörde. Although Hanseatic merchants weren't transforming their hometowns into modern centers of thought and culture since many were not willing to adopt many of the new ideas that hovered through the streets of London, Bruges, or Frankfurt, their experiences and reports must have left their traces in the common memory of the Hanseatic towns and thus influenced decisions and the development of society and political organization in the Hanseatic region.

The *Kontors* as Political Outposts

First and foremost Hanseatic merchants were businessmen, interested in profit and smooth trading. However, they were also well aware of political dangers to their business. Each war threatened trade; each lack of power made roads and waterways more vulnerable to robbery and piracy; each conflict could lead to seizure of goods or arresting of merchants. Thus, although the *kontors* were mainly of economic interest, the Hanseatic towns, and especially the towns at the Baltic Sea coast, had a vital interest in the political affairs of England, Flanders, Russia, and the Danish-Norwegian kingdom. The concentration of trade in the *kontors* provided the towns with the possibility to exert political power by force of economic means. Threats of trade boycotts were one important political weapon of the towns. Boycotts were especially successful in the fourteenth century when the towns could get their demands through with the blockade of Bruges in 1358 and of Bergen in 1368. The first known privileges for Lübeck's trade in Norway were issued after the town stopped all grain transports into the kingdom in 1248[77] and the staple of Bruges was transferred to Aardenburg, Dordrecht, Antwerp, Deventer, and Utrecht seven times between

76 On the case of religious movements see the interesting case of Hinrik van Hasselt: Wubs-Mrozevicz (2006).

77 Codex Diplomatarium Lubicensis, 1. Theil, nr. CLIII, CLIV.

1280 and 1457.[78] Also, in Novgorod, local conflicts led to boycott, unrest, and violence.[79] In the fifteenth century, the towns still used this weapon in political conflicts, but as the examples of the Hanseatic embargo against England of 1435 and of the Baltic Sea towns' blockade of trade with England between 1469 and 1474 show,[80] the lack of unity among the Hanse towns was already so huge that the action didn't have the same success as the blockades of the thirteenth and fourteenth centuries.

Still, most of the solutions of political differences between Hanse towns and local rulers were reached by diplomatic means.[81] Negotiations were difficult and expensive, so the towns would often send envoys from one or only a few towns, backing them with letters of support. Lübeck mostly was entrusted with such diplomatic missions. The council of Lübeck had gained a lot of experience with diplomatic missions since the thirteenth century and the economic power of this town gave their delegations much weight on the north European political scene. However, sometimes the political ambitions of the town councils went far beyond economic need or even contradicted the merchants' interests. In such cases, the *kontors* showed a remarkable independence in their decisions. In 1522 for example, on the brink of war between Denmark-Norway on the one side and the Hanse towns on the other, the *kontor* in Bergen and the towns' bishop and the royal governor signed a treaty that would prevent mutual impairment in case of armed conflict.[82]

But the Hanse towns were not the only towns that used the importance of the *kontors* as a political weapon. In 1479, the Russian tsar closed the *Peterhof* in Novgorod down in order to prevent the Hansards from cooperating with the Swedes in their war with Russia.[83] In 1467, the king of England confiscated all Hanseatic commodities in London and took the Hanseatic merchants prisoner. The Hansards were accused of cooperating with Denmark in its conflict with England and had to pay for English merchants' losses in the war.[84] We see that the *kontors* were of real economic importance to both sides and could be used as weapons in political conflict.

---

78 Asmussen (1999), 58ff.

79 Rybina (1998), 327f.; Angermann (1989), 175.

80 Burkhardt (2007), 82f.

81 Wubs-Mrozewicz (2007).

82 Archiv der Hansestadt Lübeck, Archiv der Bergenfahrerkompanie zu Lübeck und des Hansischen *Kontors* zu Bergen in Norwegen (1278) bzw. 1314 bis 1853, Nr. 1420.

83 Angermann (1989), 175.

84 Burkhardt (2007), 82f.

One More *Kontor*?

When we talk about Hanseatic *kontors* and outposts, we usually have four *kontors* in mind. However, there is one trading place that needs special attention—Scania of Denmark. Trade in Scania was far greater than the other outposts (*Faktoreien*) and its character and organization was much closer a *kontor* than the others. Scania was best known for its herring fairs.[85] In the Baltic Sea at Scania, the southernmost part of the Scandinavian Peninsula, huge schools of herring gathered every year. From the early thirteenth century, Hanseatic merchants came in large numbers to buy the fish and sell it in continental Europe. Led by those from Lübeck, merchants came with salt and traveled to Scania, where the herring was caught and preserved with the salt. The herring fishery was a huge industry in Scania in the thirteenth and fourteenth centuries. Thousands of Danish fishers and packers, men and women alike, found a livelihood in the fishery season lasting from late July to early November. But trade at Scania was much more than an exchange of salt and fish. Half of Europe met at the Scania fairs. Hansards, Hollanders, Englishmen, Scandinavians, Scotsmen, and Frenchmen came to Scania to trade with all kinds of merchandise. Everything from grain to fish, metals to timber, and cloth to luxury goods was sold at this interregional trading place.

Scania was especially attractive to the merchants from the Wendish towns at the southern shores of the Western Baltic Sea as it only was a short sea travel away from their hometowns and very cheap to access. In Scania, merchants from a certain origin lived together at special areas, the so-called *Vitten*. Each of the around thirty *Vitten* was autonomous in jurisdiction, administration, and trade. The most important and best situated of them were those of the merchants from Lübeck, Wismar, Rostock, and Stralsund. In 1400, there were about 900 merchants from Lübeck active in herring export from Scania. This number shows the attractiveness of the Scanian fairs to the Wendish merchants. But the Hanseatic merchants didn't just play an important part in the maintenance of this lively junction of interregional trade; the Hanse towns also laid the cause for its rapid decline in the early fifteenth century. In 1426, the Danish king, Eric of Pommern, raised a toll for all ships passing the Sound between Seeland and Scania. This measure was taken as a reaction to a Danish-Wendish conflict. The Wendish towns supported Duke Adolf of Schleswig against the Danish king. This dispute resulted in an armed conflict. Both the war and the sound toll caused a tremendous decline in the number of ships coming to Scania. As the councilors of Lübeck tried to keep Dutchmen and Englishmen out of the Baltic

85 About the herring trade and the fairs in Scania, see: Jahnke (2000).

Sea, they cut off a large area that asked for goods from the Scania fairs. This forced others, especially Hollanders, to find other ways to supply their home market with herring (mainly by introducing their own herring fishery). This also caused Wendish merchants to lose a large number of possible customers.

This early decline might be one reason why Scania is not seen as one of the main *kontors*. It was never named a *kontor* in the sources and it did not develop into a strong *kontor* community with an administration, written statutes, a clerk, and all the other institutional features we have seen at the other four *kontors*. But in 1400, Scania was like the other four *kontors* as they were to each other and much less like the smaller outpost.

The Outposts (Kaunas, Åbo, Boston, Hull, Lynn, Ravenser, Tönsberg) Geographical Situation

Besides the four *kontors* and the *Vitten* at Scania there was a large number of smaller outposts available to Hanseatic merchants who wanted to trade in the area between Smolensk in the east, Oslo in the north, Edinburgh in the west, and Lisbon in the south. We don't have a final definition of an outpost, however, according to the criteria found in enumerations specifying up to 50 Hanseatic outposts, a common feature of the outposts was that they were not permanently manned. Most of the year, the buildings were empty, only to be used during a short period of time every year. Outposts could be found in nearly every large town at the shores of the Baltic and North Seas, in the interior Baltic region, in the Low Countries, at the Bay de Bourgneuf, and in Lisbon. Some of them were not very important for the Hanseatic merchants. Trade in places like Rasborg in Finland or Lödöse in Sweden can't be traced in large quantities and is hardly named in the sources. Other outposts, however, are more well-known. Very important for Baltic trade in the fourteenth and fifteenth centuries were Hanseatic outposts in the East English ports of Newcastle, Scarborough, Hull, Boston, King's Lynn, Norwich, Yarmouth, and Ipswich. After the English cloth industry started large-scale production in the late fourteenth century, merchants from Hanseatic towns concentrated on one of the ports and its cloth producing hinterland as suppliers for their regional market. Cooperation went so far that different styles and designs were exported from the different ports fitting local demand in the towns. Formally, the outposts in England were under the sovereignty of the aldermen in London, but the merchants using the Stalhof in Boston felt much more bound to the *kontor* in Bergen. Most of the merchants went to Bergen on an annual summer business trip, than to the Stalhof in London.

The outposts in Lisbon and the French towns La Rochelle, Bourgneuf, Bordeaux, and Nantes were used as export ports for the Bay salt, a cheaper alternative to the expensive salt from Lüneburg. Here large convoys of Hanseatic ships gathered in early summer. The ships sailed back to the Hanseatic ports in the salt fleet, because on their own, they would have been an easy target for Dutch or English pirates. However, even traveling in a fleet did not guarantee a safe journey, which became clear in 1449 when the English captured the whole Hanseatic salt fleet. This action caused major political and economic disturbances between England and the Hanse towns.

Although Bruges was the central market for cloth trade in Western Europe, other towns in Flanders were also regularly visited by Hanse merchants. Among these we find Sluis, Gent, Bergen op zoom, Hoeke, and Dortrecht.

Also in the kingdoms of Denmark and Norway, there were additional outposts besides the *kontor* of Bergen and the Scania fairs. Oslo and Tönsberg, the trading centers of southern Norway, were important knots in the trade mesh of merchants from Rostock, Wismar, and Stralsund.[86] The most important commodity trade was herring from Bohuslen, the region southeast of Oslo at the shores of Kattegatt. The outposts were run by two aldermen, but they were much more restricted in their liberties than the *kontor* in Bergen. Hanseatic merchants were only allowed to stay in the towns for a maximum of six weeks and until 1447, they did not have the right to trade with each other or with the local peasants.[87]

Further south, Copenhagen, Landskrona, Kalundberg, Naestved, Ystad, Rønne, and Åhus, all situated at the Danish Isles or in Scania, hosted Hanseatic outposts. Here a small quantity of trade was carried out, comparable to the trade between Hanseatic towns and short-distance trade in all other coastal areas. Even in these towns, it was not necessary to have a permanent occupation.

In the eastern European outposts in the Baltic interior, the merchants found a completely different situation. Places like Kaunas, Vilnius, Witebsk, Polotsk, and Smolensk were far away from their hometowns and could only be reached by a special effort. These outposts needed to be more organized in the way the *kontors* or the outposts in France were. One of these trading places was Pleskau (Pskov), in modern Russia. Situated south of the mouth of the river Welikaja into the lake system leading to the Baltic Sea, the site was already used as a trading place in the early Middle Ages.[88] As in many other places of Hanseatic trade area, low German merchants started to visit Pleskau regularly

86 Thierfelder (1958).

87 Schubert (2000), 36.

88 Sedov (1992), 143ff.

in the twelfth century. They used to come during the winter with sledges from the mouth of the river Düna,[89] which was the place where German merchants eventually founded the town of Riga. In the thirteenth and fourteenth centuries, trade in Pleskau intensified, mainly due to the increasing importance of the *kontor* in Novgorod. Pleskau was situated on the travel road of the winter traders who came from Riga or Dorpat. The latter town showed vital interest in the affairs of the outpost of Dorpat and by this could gain some influence on the *kontor* in Novgorod as well.[90] But Pleskau was not only a stopover on the Hanseatic merchants' travels from the Baltic Sea to Novgorod. A lot of merchants stayed in the town for their own trading activities. Some of them never traveled as far as Novgorod, but stayed in Pleskau for business or continued to Polotosk of Smolensk. Those who stayed in the town for a longer time rented rooms in houses at the "German banks."[91] This term only suggests that the number of Hanseatic merchants who regularly visited Pleskau for economic affairs was large enough to make an impact in local perception.

Eastern Europe to as far as Smolensk was not the only region regularly penetrated by Hanse merchants and not considered within the range of Hanseatic trade. There are many other trading centers which for a longer time saw a steady stream of Hanseatic merchants and goods coming in. If we think of trade in upper German towns—like Frankfurt and Nuremberg; Lemberg and Krakow in nowadays Poland; Notow, Stockholm, and Iceland in Northern Europe; or Venice in Italy—Hanseatic merchants are hardly those who come to mind first. But our records show that they had a vital interest in these regions. Sometimes they were important for economic and social development of the town and its hinterland. For example, in Stockholm,[92] sometimes only risk-taking merchants would try to get a share in the local market, as was the case of the quite famous Venetian company of the Veckinghusen-brothers.[93] These examples show how diversified Hanseatic trade was, how different Hanseatic merchants acted and how difficult it is to define Hanseatic trade on the background of this diversity.

89 Hoffmann (1989), 37.
90 Angermann (1988), 273–276.
91 Angermann (1973), 277.
92 Wubs-Morzevicz (2007).
93 See: Stieda (1921).

Conclusion

Kontors and outposts were one important piece in the Hanseatic trading system. A huge part of Hanseatic merchants' trade was carried out here. Although in quantitative respect, trade between Hanseatic towns was the most important business in the region, *kontors* and outposts fulfilled an essential role in the trade mesh of the Baltic and North Sea regions. Only at these places could Hanseatic merchants get rid of the surpluses produced in their region. Only here they could acquire all the supplies, luxury, and exotic goods over which the burghers of the Hanse towns competed for better economic conditions.

The human desire to feel unique, to exhibit wealth and success, and to have a more comfortable life than their forefathers did was always an essential driving force for economic growth. In this respect the *kontors* and outposts with their supply of goods that otherwise never would have reached the Hanseatic markets were vital to developing a market-oriented business mentality in the Hanseatic region. As they had a demand for certain goods that only the Hanseatic merchants were able to supply, as in the case of Norwegian flour and cereals import, the Hansards had the unique chance to obtain monopolies such as trade conditions and privileges in the *kontors*. This was especially true in Bergen and Novgorod, and to a lesser extent even in London and Bruges. Thus, even the Hanseatic merchants had a vital role in the existence and growth of the trading places where they had *kontors* and outposts.

For Hanseatic merchants, *kontors* and outposts were the places they could feel Hanse as an institution the most. Back home, the towns' interest was strongly connected to a merchant's economic fate and was the most important guideline for his economic-political decisions. At the *kontors*, he met merchants from many other towns with their own interests. Only together could they gain the best profit and the most favorable conditions and privileges. They were forced to find a common strategy and way of handling problems. In the eyes of the local authorities, most of the time, they were no longer burghers of Kampen, Lübeck, Cologne, Danzig, or Unna. They were merchants of the German Hanse. So in looking for a common sentiment of affiliation to something called the Hanse, we have to go to the merchants at the *kontors* and outposts.

Kontors and outposts varied in their importance to the Hanseatic trade and to the local economy of their host towns. Some attracted thousands of Hansards every year, some were occupied the year round, and others were only visited by a handful of merchants in the summer. But Hanseatic merchants left their traces in all of these places and thus made the Hanse region part of an European economic culture that covered most parts of the continent and adjacent regions.

CHAPTER 5

Social Networks

Ulf Christian Ewert and Stephan Selzer

Introduction

The objective of this chapter is to give an overview of the appearance and function of social networks in the Hanseatic world during the late Middle Ages, as well as to discuss the methods used to reconstruct them. After a brief introduction to the sociological approach of network analysis, several examples will be given of social networks that emerged in Hanseatic regions. These examples will show that the social networks of the late Middle Ages can still be grasped by modern historiography, and these cases will also focus on the availability and validity of the sources used to reconstruct social networks. The two points that will finally be addressed are the importance of network formation for business purposes of Hanseatic merchants and the impact of social networks on the development of the Hanse in general.

The Paradigm: Network Analysis as a Method to Describe Social Structure

The Theoretical Concept of Social Networks

To understand social networks in the Hanse, one must understand the concepts underlying the network analysis approach.[1] Similarly to "system" and "social capital," the term "network" is very popular and widely as "social network"

1 For an introduction into social network analysis see e.g. Stephen D. Berkowitz, *An Introduction to Structural Analysis: The Network Approach to Social Research* (Toronto: Butterworths 1982); Ronald S. Burt, *Toward a Structural Theory of Action. Network Models of Social Structure, Perception, and Action* (New York: Academic Press, 1982); Franz Urban Pappi, ed., *Methoden der Netzwerkanalyse*, Techniken der empirischen Sozialforschung, vol. 1 (Munich: Oldenbourg, 1987); Barry Wellman and Stephen D. Berkowitz, eds., *Social Structures: A Network Approach* (Cambridge: Cambridge University Press, 1988); Stanley Wassermann and Katherine Faust, *Social Network Analysis. Methods and Applications* (Cambridge: Cambridge University Press, 1994); Stanley Wassermann and Joseph Galaskiewicz, eds., *Advances in Social Network Analysis. Research in the Social and Behavioral Sciences* (Thousands Oaks: Sage Publications, 1994).

 | DOI 10.1163/9789004284760_007

used in the social sciences and in history. Although because of this popularity it appears to be a well-defined and clear concept, a broad range of meanings is attributed to it. But what exactly is a social network? How can it be described? Which methods can be used to analyze it?

The social network approach claims to be both a theoretical and methodological concept. Social network theory deals with the definition and meaning of networks as being specific social configurations. Network methodology develops techniques and provides tools for the analysis of such units. First of all, a network in the exact sense of the word is a complex system of crossing lines.[2] Within a social network these crossing "lines" are relationships because they consist of "a finite set or sets of actors and the relation or relations defined on them."[3] Social networks are nonetheless distinct from groups and organizations, although these two forms could be described much the same way. However, the way the membership and relationship are defined makes the difference. An organization has formal criteria of membership, whereas social networks do not. In organizations, relationships between members are formally defined, but in social networks, relationships are informal. However, it is not informality alone that distinguishes social networks from other social units. Although in groups all members interact with everyone else, in social networks, interaction can be indirect and mediated by other members.

The beginning of social network analysis as a defined approach of social sciences dates back only to the 1970s, and it is marked by an increasing number of studies on modern networks and on the methodology of network analysis.[4] However, social network analysis follows the traditions of sociometric research and social anthropology, and the understanding of such networks is based on sociological concepts like social relationships, closeness, and interdependence. These sociological concepts had been formulated much earlier in the writings of Max Weber, Georg Simmel, and George C. Homans. For the historical sciences,

2 Franz Urban Pappi, "Einleitung: Die Netzwerkanalyse aus soziologischer Perspektive," in Id., ed., *Methoden* (see footnote 1), 11–37, 12.

3 Wassermann and Faust, *Social Network Analysis* (see footnote 1), 20.

4 Paul W. Holland and Samuel Leinhardt, "A Method for Detecting Structure in Sociometric Data," *American Journal of Sociology* 75 (1970), 492–513; Ibid., *Perspectives on Social Network Research* (New York: Academic Press, 1979); Edward O. Laumann and Franz Urban Pappi, "New Directions in the Study of Community Elites," *American Sociological Review* 38 (1973), 212–230; Ibid., *Networks of Collective Action: A Perspective on Community Influence Systems* (New York: Academic Press, 1976); Hans J. Hummell and Rolf Ziegler, *Anwendung mathematischer Verfahren zur Analyse sozialer Netzwerke* (Duisburg: Sozialwissenschaftliche Kooperative, 1977).

the study of Wolfgang Reinhard[5] on the entanglement of Roman city elites in the sixteenth and seventeenth centuries was a sort of milestone, as it was the first time that the methodology and potential of social network analysis were presented in a historical context.

A Brief Sketch of the Method of Social Network Analysis

With the formation of social network theory, formal methods to describe the structure of networks were introduced into sociological research.[6] These techniques were derived from graph theory, group theory, and matrix algebra. A set of relationships of a certain number of persons is depicted in a graph. The graph's nodes represent individuals, and its edges represent the relations found between them.[7] Two structural measures are typically calculated from such a mathematical representation of a network. The network's overall density is the actual relationships' (edges) share of the number of all relations possible.[8] The more potential connections there are between individuals, the more dense the network is. Centrality measures how easy it is for a network member to get in contact with other participants of the network. Path distances within the network are commonly used for this.[9] For example, a person who has personal relationships with every other member would obtain the highest possible degree of centrality because he can reach everyone directly. Since in sociological research, networks are often constructed using sampling and survey techniques, problems of measurement error, validity, and reliability of the data can arise. Analyses of historical social networks are naturally restricted to those pieces of social structure documented in the surviving sources. Therefore, shortcomings of the data may cause difficulties as well. As re-sampling of new data is impossible in historical research, problems that arise because of limited or biased data can only be overcome with a careful interpretation. In applying the network concept to historical networks, it is

---

5 Wolfgang Reinhard, *Freunde und Kreaturen: "Verflechtung" als Konzept zur Erforschung historischer Führungsgruppen. Römische Oligarchie um 1600*, Schriften der Philosophischen Fachbereiche der Universität Augsburg, vol. 14 (München: Ernst Vögel, 1979).

6 An overview of techniques used in social network analysis can be found in Bruno Trezzini, "Konzepte und Methoden der sozialwissenschaftlichen Netzwerkanalyse: Eine aktuelle Übersicht," *Zeitschrift für Soziologie* 27 (1998), 378–394.

7 Peter Kappelhoff, "Cliquenanalyse: Die Bestimmung von intern verbundenen Teilgruppen in sozialen Netzwerken," in Pappi, ed., *Methoden* (see footnote 1), 39–63, 39–43.

8 Pappi, "Einleitung" (see footnote 2), 28.

9 Linton C. Freeman, "Centrality in Social Networks: I. Conceptual Clarification" *Social Networks* 1 (1978/79), 215–239; Pappi, "Einleitung" (see footnote 2), 25–36.

important to know the following basic differentiations concerning scope and methodology made within social network analysis.

A structural analysis can be performed for either a global or an ego-centered network.[10] For complete or global networks, an excellent source material would be needed—a source or sources that would reveal all extant informal relationships. Criteria for differentiating between members of the network and non-members would have to be defined as well. Even in application to modern networks, neither the source problem nor the problem of membership definition can be solved satisfactorily. Instead, often ego-centered networks are analyzed. Such ego-centered or personal networks comprise the set of relationships a certain person has. This seems to be a reasonable method to approach the Hanseatic commercial exchange networks.

Networks can also be reconstructed on the empirical basis of either a single type of relationship or multiple sorts of personal connections.[11] A network that is based only on one type of relationship is called a one-mode network. However, when a person has many relations, it is called a two-mode or multi-mode network. Both approaches can describe historical, informal social structures. One example of a one-mode network is the common membership of people in the Hanseatic towns' official societies or fraternities (see below). Kinship and commercial exchange relations, for instance, would make a two-mode network out of it. Two-mode networks are "real" networks because several distinct layers of social structure are interwoven in them.

Finally, closeness within a social network can vary depending on whether the measurement of closeness is relation-based or position-based.[12] In a relation-based approach, closeness of network members is thought of as cohesiveness. Individuals are close to each other because they are located near to each other within the network and because they do have intensive personal contact. This method can be used for identifying and describing Hanseatic social networks as far as opportunities to get in contact, either personally or by letter, can be analyzed. In contrast, with a position-based approach, people are connected through structurally equivalent positions within a social network, not by personal contact. Hence, closeness is not a result of personal relationship; it stems exclusively from structural equivalence. By this approach social roles are identified, but it also goes beyond the original idea of a social network being based on social contact. The position-based approach could be

10 Trezzini, "Konzepte und Methoden" (see footnote 6), 380.

11 Trezzini, "Konzepte und Methoden" (see footnote 6), 379f.

12 Trezzini, "Konzepte und Methoden" (see footnote 6), 382f.; Kappelhoff, "Cliquenanalyse" (see footnote 7), 39–41.

used to analyze councilors and mayors of different Hanseatic towns, but even these people were connected by personal relationships as well (see below).

Social Networks within the Hanse: Examples and Corresponding Sources

Conditions of the Emerging Networks: Population Growth and Migration

The non-scientific but popular view of medieval society usually depicts it as very rigid and nearly immobile. This interpretation, however, is an oversimplification because in the high and late Middle Ages, social structure was a flexible and ever-changing matter. Such a prejudice ignores the huge demographic and social dynamics that unfolded all across Europe from the eleventh century onwards. A constant increase in population, a huge expansion of arable land, the foundation of hundreds of towns, and a sustained economic growth formed the socio-economic background of what was a significant societal take-off in the high Middle Ages. A further result of this process was the re-establishment of long-distance trade, an issue that, following the analysis of Robert S. Lopez, is referred to as the "Commercial Revolution of the Middle Ages."[13] This general economic take-off initially occurred in Western Europe and the Mediterranean, but it eventually spread over most of Europe and reached the Baltic within the first half of the twelfth century. Both political integration of the Baltic regions and conversion to Christianity of the Slavic people there were important prerequisites to a further economic development of the sparsely populated coastal areas and their hinterland. Numerous villages and towns were then founded along the Baltic coast between Lübeck and Reval until the late thirteenth century.

For people from the more densely populated Western Europe, the new settlements in the Baltic opened up much better economic opportunities and offered migrants the chance to begin a new life. Count Adolf II of Holsatia[14] founded Lübeck in 1143 by using an existing Slavic settlement. This was, in many respects, the very model of Christian expansion into the coastal areas of the Baltic. More importantly, along with the foundation of Lübeck, the Western European concept of making the classic medieval town a law-protected permanent market was transferred to the Baltic region. Based on this model, within

13 Robert S. Lopez, *The Commercial Revolution of the Middle Ages, 950–1350* (Englewood Cliffs: Prentice-Hall 1971).

14 Rolf Hammel-Kiesow, *Die Hanse* (Munich: Beck 2008), 27–30.

only a century almost every important Hanseatic town along or near the southern Baltic shore had been founded or had received municipal law—Riga (1201), Rostock (1218), Danzig (1224), Wismar (1229), Stralsund (1234), Elbing (1237), Stettin 1243, Greifswald (1250), and Königsberg (1255).[15] The first western people who settled in Lübeck were of Rhinelandian, Westphalian, and Saxon origins. Most of the other towns along the Baltic coast were founded according to the same or a similar pattern. The new arrivals joined an already settled Slavic population. The western geographic origin of settlers can be traced by their surnames. In these times last names were not yet of a specific character to the family bearing it. In their new places of residence, western immigrants were typically marked by their respective place of origin. A well-known family of municipal councilors in Lübeck, for instance, was named *Warendorp*, which was the contemporary name of a Westphalian town nowadays named "Warendorf." Quite similarly, in Torún there was a councilors' family with a surname *von Soest* ("of Soest," a Westphalian town).

Kinship Networks among Hansards

Population growth, eastern bound migration, and settlement were vital for social networks among Hansards to emerge. Another aspect of western immigration to the Baltic—a region that would become the realm of the Hanse—was that it took several generations. The migration process was prolonged as members of following generations also headed northeast, which likely promoted the foundation of many subsidiary towns. Therefore places like Wismar, Rostock, or Stralsund were not only connected to their hometown Lübeck by sharing a common municipal law, but also because of the multiple inter-town kinship relations that had emerged as byproduct of a continued eastern-bound emigration. Continuance of migration also meant that relatives of migrants would follow them after some time to their new places of residence in the Baltic. Additionally, some of the emigrants or their children would return to their western places of origin, if expectations of increasing personal wealth and improving social status there exceeded opportunities in Baltic towns. In fact, populations of those towns which would become members of the Hanse were already interrelated through a wide range of family bonds long before the Hanseatic League as an association of cities and towns had emerged. Thus, some citizens from Danzig and Hamburg very correctly claimed to have their relations in many other Hanseatic towns. Genealogical research, which is

15 And of course also the re-establishment of the newly founded town in 1159 by the Saxon duke Henry the Lion, after it had been destroyed by a fire. Hammel-Kiesow, *Hanse* (see footnote 14), 30.

often not taken serious enough, provides important and lucid insights into this kinship-based interweaving of Hanseatic town populations, which is very pertinent to the issue of Hanseatic social networks.

Kinship networks inside the Hanse can also be analyzed by way of considering the kinship relations of citizens from the older western towns instead of focusing only on relationships of citizens in the new Baltic settlements. Hereditary matters are a good source for pinpointing this. Quite often, the emigrants' relatives still living in the western towns of origin were named as their heirs. A particularly good example of this was the council of the Westphalian town of Soest, which repeatedly received letters called *Toversichtsbriefe* ("letters of confidence") from Baltic towns announcing wills of former emigrants in favor of citizens of Soest. These letters were collected and can be used as a graphic representation of the kinship relations by which many citizens of Soest were connected to citizens of other Hanseatic towns. The resultant graph—which is printed in the publication of Dösseler—has a radial appearance with edges that represent kinship relations leading from Soest to almost all the Hanseatic towns in the Baltic.[16]

An illustrative and well-documented example of a widely branched out Hanseatic kinship network is the family named *Plescow*.[17] Although the last name refers to the town of Pleskau/Pskov in North Russia and thus suggests a family of Russian origin, it seems much more likely that the family originally came from Visby on the Swedish isle of Gotland, where it can be proved that the earliest family members lived. In this particular case, *Plescow* as a surname does not indicate the family's origin but the place where most family members traded. A branch of the family then emigrated from Visby to Lübeck by the end of the thirteenth century. In Lübeck as well as in Visby, the Plescow family was part of the local ruling class. As a result, in both towns, male members of the family repeatedly held the official duty of a councilor or a mayor. Among them was the mayor of Lübeck, *Jordan Plescow*, one of the most prominent Hanseatic politicians, who died in 1425. Many additional kinship relations to families in other Baltic towns were established, mainly through marriage, from the example of the councilors's families in Stockholm.

16 Emil Dösseler, ed., *Toversichtsbriefe für Soest: Schreiben in Nachlaßangelegenheiten an die Stadt Soest 1325–1639*, Veröffentlichungen der Historichen Kommission Westfalens, vol. 31 (Münster: Aschendorff, 1969); Id., *Soests auswärtige Beziehungen, besonders im hansischen Raum*, 2 vols., Soester Zeitschrift, vol. 100 (Soest: Westfälische Verlagsbuchhandlung Mocker & Jahn, 1988).

17 Jürgen Wiegandt, *Die Plescows: Ein Beitrag zur Auswanderung Wisbyer Kaufmannsfamilien nach Lübeck im 13. und 14. Jahrhundert*, Quellen und Darstellungen zur hansischen Geschichte, vol. 29 (Cologne, Vienna: Böhlau, 1988).

The kinship-based relations between Hansards and what they meant to the structure and organization of trade will be discussed in greater detail below. The network effect on the political organization of the Hanse should be considered first. Kinship was a natural vehicle to unite councilors and mayors from various Hanseatic towns and cities, at least in particular regions of the Hanse realm.[18] A good example of such a personal kinship-based political network is that of *Arnd Sudermann*, who was a mayor in Dortmund and died in 1473.[19] His family ties were a basis for his political bonds. Like many other families in Westphalia, the *Sudermann* family had established a family branch in Thorn (Torún) in which close connections existed. Although this had happened a generation earlier, *Arnd Sudermann* and other family members in Dortmund as well as in Torún still felt as though they were part of the same clan. Apart from that, the local political network of *Arnd Sudermann* also covered his co-mayor *Christoph Hengstenberg*, who was his brother-in-law. *Hengstenberg* also had some relatives in Prussia, so beside his own relationships, *Sudermann* had a second tie between Dortmund and the eastern Hanseatic towns which could easily be activated by *Hengstenberg* if it was needed. A third dimension of network structure is the regional aspect of kinship-based relationships, since people from other towns in Westphalia and the Rhineland were also bound to the *Sudermann* family. Both *Arnd Sudermann*'s sister and his daughter were each married to mayors of the town of Soest. Moreover, by that time his cousin *Heinrich* had been a councilor several times as well as a mayor in the city of Cologne.

It is likely that since these local politicians were commissioned to represent their respective hometowns at the diets of the Hanse in Lübeck, a group of persons who met for political talks could rely on somehow firm kinship bonds. This must have had a lasting impact on Hanseatic politics and diplomacy. The kinship-based political networks worked as a sort of mediating instance. This can explain Hanseatic decision-making and enforcement better than before. For a long time, the Hanse was predominantly considered a hierarchical-bureaucratic organization. Political decisions were made at the annual Hanse diet in a quasi-parliamentary procedure. In contrast, recent studies like

18 Friedrich Bernward Fahlbusch, "Zwischen öffentlichem Mandat und informeller Macht: Die hansische Führungsgruppe," *Hansische Geschichtsblätter* 123 (2005), 43–60.

19 Friedrich Bernward Fahlbusch, "Kaufleute und Politiker. Bemerkungen zur hansischen Führungsgruppe," in: Rolf Hammel-Kiesow, ed., *Vergleichende Ansätze in der hansischen Geschichtsforschung*, Hansische Studien, vol. 13 (Trier: Porta Alba, 2002), 43–51, 47f.; Id., "Regionale Identität. Eine Beschreibungskategorie für den hansischen Teilraum Westfalen um 1470?," *Hansische Geschichtsblätter* 112 (1994), 139–159.

Dietrich W. Poeck's demonstrate how important family bonds and other informal connections between the members of the leading groups of Hanseatic towns were for the political structure of the Hanse to persist. More precisely, these politicians were the ones who, because of their mutual kinship-based connections, negotiated internal settlements between towns and got even unpopular compromises accepted in their hometowns. Those who formed the Hanseatic leading group by sticking together because of family ties became the key element of the Hanseatic political system. Interestingly enough, this group was referred to by contemporaries of the sixteenth century as *de herre der Hense* ("the masters of the Hanse").[20]

Wills as a Source of Network Reconstruction: The Case of Lübeck

Wills have been used only during the last two decades as important sources for social and economic history purposes. Prior to that time, it was up to legal historians to analyze this sort of documents. From a socio-historical perspective, wills offer insights into peoples' belief and piety, but they can also answer many other questions regarding the history of everyday life. Compared to other types of sources for the history of the Hanse, wills have survived in large numbers. By far the biggest German late medieval corpus consists of about 6,400 wills from Lübeck, all originating from before 1500.[21] The fact that they are serial

---

20 Dietrich W. Poeck, "Hansische Ratssendeboten," in Hammel-Kiesow, ed., *Vergleichende Ansätze* (see footnote 19), 97–142; Id., *Die Herren der Hanse. Delegierte und Netzwerke*, Kieler Werkstücke, vol. E8 (Frankfurt/Main: Peter Lang, 2010).

21 A good overview of the surviving material can be found in Ahasver von Brandt, "Die Hanse als mittelalterliche Wirtschaftsorganisation. Entstehen, Daseinsformen, Aufgaben," in Id. et al., eds., *Die Deutsche Hanse als Mittler zwischen Ost und West, Cologne*, (Cologne: Westdeutscher Verlag, 1963), 9–38, but also in Gerhard Jaritz, "Österreichische Bürgertestamente als Quelle zur Erforschung städtischer Lebensformen des Spätmittelalters," *Jahrbuch für Geschichte des Feudalismus* 8 (1984), 249–264; Urs Martin Zahnd, "Spätmittelalterliche Bürgertestamente als Quellen zu Realienkunde und Sozialgeschichte," *Mitteilungen des Instituts für österreichische Geschichtsforschung* 96 (1988), 55–78; and Paul Baur, *Testament und Bürgerschaft. Alltagsleben und Sachkultur im spätmittelalterlichen Konstanz*, Konstanzer Geschichts- und Rechtsquellen, N.F. 31 (Sigmaringen: J. Thorbecke, 1989), 14–35. Of the more recent studies cf. for Sitten, Hamburg, Cologne, Lüneburg, Lübeck and Stralsund, Gregor Zenhäusern, *Zeitliches Wohl und ewiges Heil. Studie zu mittelalterlichen Testamenten aus der Diözese Sitten* (Sitten: Staatsarchiv, 1992); Marianne Riethmüller, *To troste myner sele. Aspekte spätmittelalterlicher Frömmigkeit im Spiegel Hamburger Testamente 1310–1400*, Beiträge zur Geschichte Hamburgs, vol. 47 (Hamburg: Verlag Verein für Hamburgische Geschichte, 1994); Brigitte Klosterberg, *Zu Ehre Gottes und zum Wohl der Familie. Kölner Testamente von Laien und Klerikern im Spätmittelalter*, Kölner Schriften zur Geschichte und Kultur,

sources makes these documents attractive to historians. Men and women living in Lübeck—rich merchants, craftsmen, and also servants—decreed by wills how their property was to be handled after their death. Consequently, wills revealed social connections of testators, especially when they included relatives living in distant places, former trading partners, or illegitimate children. Because of such documents, it was possible to reconstruct the business relationships of a group of merchants from Lübeck and Stockholm in 1350, the year of the Black Death.[22]

Additionally, another group of people appears in almost every known will from Lübeck, the executors of wills who were called *vormund* ("guardian") or, in Latin, *provisor*. Being chosen to execute a will was a demanding and often rather tricky task. The will of *Hinrich van dem Braken*, who had died in 1413, is a good example of this. The men he had named to execute his will had to spend part of his money for devout and charitable purposes, not only in Lübeck, but also in Osnabrück and in the more distant town of Bergen. They were also requested to arrange a marriage for *Hinrich*'s daughter and to care for her until she was married. Finally, they had to administer the parts of *Hinrich*'s assets that he wanted his two sons to have after they had come of age.[23] From this example, it is clear that a testator had to be confident in his or her choice of guardian. A plausible *ad hoc* hypothesis would be to assume that testators

vol. 22 (Cologne: Böhlau 1995), Susanne Mosler-Christoph, *Die materielle Kultur in den Lüneburger Testamenten 1323 bis 1500* (Diss. phil.: Göttingen, 1998), Birgit Noodt, *Religion und Familie in der Hansestadt Lübeck anhand der Bürgertestamente des 14. Jahrhunderts*, Veröffentlichungen zur Geschichte der Hansestadt Lübeck, vol. B33 (Lübeck: Schmidt Römhild 2000), 387–401, and Ralf Lusiardi, *Stiftung und städtische Gesellschaft. Religiöse und soziale Aspekte des Stiftungsverhaltens im spätmittelalterlichen Stralsund*, Stiftungsgeschichten, vol. 2 (Berlin: Akademie Verlag, 2000).

22 Wilhelm Koppe, *Lübeck-Stockholmer Handelsgeschichte im 14. Jahrhundert*, Abhandlungen zur Handels- und Seegeschichte, vol. 2 (Neumünster: K. Wachholtz 1933); Albrecht Cordes, *Spätmittelalterlicher Gesellschaftshandel im Hanseraum*, Quellen und Darstellungen zur hansischen Geschichte, vol. 45 (Cologne: Böhlau, 1998).

23 Gunnar Meyer, ... *up dat se mynen lesten wyllen truweliken vorvullen*. "Die Werkmeister der Lübecker Pfarrkirchen als Vormünder in Testamenten," in Stephan Selzer and Ulf Christian Ewert, eds., *Menschenbilder—Menschenbildner. Individuum und Gruppe im Blick des Historikers*, Hallische Beiträge zur Geschichte des Mittelalters und der Frühen Neuzeit, vol. 2 (Berlin: Akademie Verlag, 2002), 277–294; Id., "Solidarität in der Genossenschaft: Die Lübecker Bergenfahrer des frühen 15. Jahrhunderts im Spiegel ihrer Testamente," in Antjekathrin Graßmann, ed., *Das hansische Kontor zu Bergen und die Lübecker Bergenfahrer: International Workshop Lübeck 2003* (Lübeck: Schmidt-Römhild, 2005), 187–204; Id., "*'Besitzende Bürger' und 'elende Sieche'. Lübecks Gesellschaft im Spiegel ihrer Testamente 1400–1449*," (Rostock: Schmidt-Römhild, 2010).

generally commissioned their relatives with this kind of trustful duty. In reality, the opposite was true. Relationships between testators and executors were very rarely kinship-based. By taking a closer look at the problem, it is clear that honesty and willingness were not the only requirements for a future executor or guardian to meet. A testator also had to be sure that the person he or she wanted to execute his or her will would be able to get the provisions accepted by a testator's creditors and debtors as well as by his or her possibly reluctant relatives.

Because of these requirements, analyzing the choice of guardians is very promising. First, one would naturally expect to find in such an analysis individuals who were men of high standing within their peer group. Not surprisingly, in some cases councilors and mayors were commissioned with guardianship because their affiliation with the leading social class of Lübeck was clear. Yet more interestingly, some of the executors and guardians were not chosen because of their official town duties. Instead, they were chosen because they were highly respected due to their more informal position within the society of Lübeck. The works masters of the parish churches were some of this kind, especially those at St. Mary's and St. James'.

In general, a works master managed technical problems and economic issues that arose in every day church operation. However, he was neither the master builder of the church nor the holder of the city's church administration office. The latter was officially responsible for the financial assets of the church. Usually, this office was shared by two city councilors who held it alternately. Although the churches' works masters had a lower social rank within the society, compared to city councilors or master builders, they were highly esteemed within their home parish. A really outstanding example of the linking position these works masters held is that of executor choices made in Lübeck between 1400 and 1450, as noted in Gunnar Meyer's in-depth analysis. For this particular period, the choices of citizens mostly favored *Hermann Robecke*, who was the works master of St. Mary's, and his colleague *Godeken Steenbeke*, who held the same office at St. James'. If all the choices drawn from the surviving wills are represented in a sociogramm (see Figure 5.1), the following becomes clear: only a few of the testators made mutual choices for an executor or guardian. Thus, an overall look at wills does not reveal much insight into the sketch of networks of citizens from Lübeck during the first half of the fifteenth century. However, this information indicates possible ways social networks could have been used by citizens for all kinds of purposes. Although the works masters were not in the center of a specific social group, they functioned as a sort of bridging person to connect separate networks with each other because of their high standing.

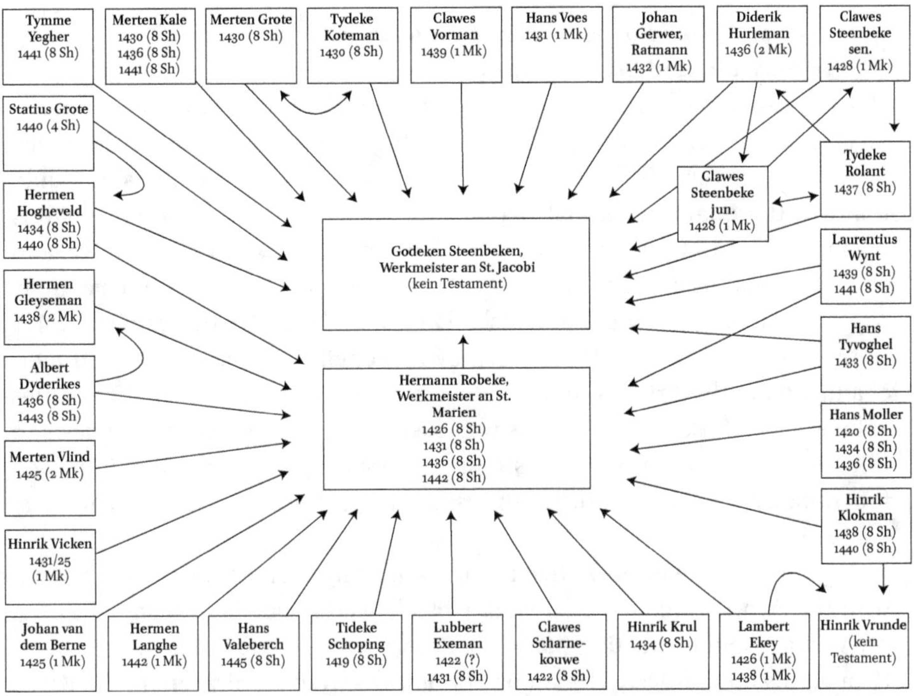

FIGURE 5.1 *Network of Guardians in Early Fifteenth Century Lübeck: Sociogram of a group of citizens in early fifteenth century Lübeck with respect to choices of guardians of their wills. As they were named in most of the wills analyzed, churches' works masters* Godeken Steenbeken *and* Hermann Robeke *stood in the center of this network.*
SOURCE: MEYER, WERKMEISTER (SEE FOOTNOTE 23), 289.

Restricting the sample to those testators already connected by professional, social, or political matters would be a much better approach to reconstructing citizens' networks on the basis of wills. Gunnar Meyer also undertook such an analysis for the group of merchants from Lübeck who had specialized in trade with Bergen. Although not all the wills belonging to the people in this group survived, the final sample consists of 109 wills, 82 of which show a testator's choice of a fellow member of this group of traders for executing one's will. The corresponding graph[24] depicts only these choices, but some of the wills do contain additional information that would be relevant to social network issues, such as business connections to other group members. Thus, testators' choices of executors would add much to the reconstruction of multi-mode social networks of merchants.

24 Meyer, "Solidarität" (see footnote 23).

Social Proximity vs. Spatial Vicinity as a Network Basis: Societies and Neighborhoods

One approach to reconstruct social networks of Hansards is to examine membership in societies and fraternities, which gives indication about the social proximity between the members of these institutions. Membership could improve the quality of social networks in Hanseatic towns because it was extremely important for the informal communication within the political and economic leading groups. A majority of the councilors of Lübeck, for example, were also members of the distinguished *Zirkelgesellschaft* ("society of circle").[25] In the Prussian towns of the Hanse, town councilors, lay assessors, and merchants met in the Artus courts[26] and were always members of the fraternities belonging to these courts, too. As was customary, they would bring guests to the meetings, and travelers and strangers were generally allowed to join such functions as well. The institution of Artus courts also enabled interurban social contacts.

A good example of how effective and enduring such contacts were is seen with the *Schwarzhäuptergesellschaft* ("black head society") of Riga. This society was a popular meeting place for experienced long-distance traders and their young apprentices. The young apprentices were usually sent to the Baltic region to learn more about the goods and practices of the Hanseatic trade with Russia. Two of these young men, *Hans Swaneke* from Danzig and *Johann van dem Springe* from Lübeck, might have met each other in 1419 in the meeting place of the *Schwarzhäuptergesellschaft*. The two of them might also have met at this time a third person, *Gerd von Borcken*, a citizen of Riga. The acquaintance of these three Hansards and especially the way they became acquainted with each other is important to better understand their business relationship, which can be verified only over a decade later. In 1430, *Gerd von Borcken* sent

25 Sonja Dünnebeil, *Die Lübecker Zirkel-Gesellschaft. Formen der Selbstdarstellung einer städtischen Oberschicht*, Veröffentlichungen zur Geschichte der Hansestadt Lübeck, vol. B27, (Lübeck: Archiv der Hansestadt Lübeck, 1996).

26 Stephan Selzer, *Artushöfe im Ostseeraum. Ritterlich-höfische Kultur in den Städten des Preußenlandes im 14. Jahrhundert*, Kieler Werkstücke, vol. D8 (Frankfurt/Main: Peter Lang, 1996); Id., "Trinkstuben als Orte der Kommunikation. Das Beispiel der Artushöfe im Preußenland (ca. 1350–1550)," in Gerhard Fouquet, Matthias Steinbrink and Gabriel Zeilinger, eds., *Geschlechtergesellschaften, Zunft-Trinkstuben und Bruderschaften in spätmittelalterlichen und frühneuzeitlichen Städten*, Stadt in der Geschichte, vol. 30 (Stuttgart: Jan Thorbecke Verlag, 2003), 73–98.

wax to *Johann van dem Springe* in Lübeck, and part of this delivery was done by order of *Hans Swaneke*.[27]

Instead of relying only on social proximity, social networks could also be based on spatial vicinity. Towns posessed quarters with either expensive or cheap lodging and therefore could be divided into commendable and disreputable neighborhoods, a fact not only relevant in modern cities.[28] Also, in Hanseatic towns, specific quarters were rated differently by citizens. In the same way that a person's clothing indicated social status, location and appearance of a dwelling were commonly seen as a status symbol. A house built of stone, for instance, elevated the owner or tenant within the town's social hierarchy over those who still lived in wooden buildings. The prestige derived from a dwelling's location inside the town was highest in the center around the market place, at the town hall or the parish church, and alongside the main streets of the town. The prestige of a dwelling place decreased as the distance to the center increased. The least reputable areas were usually found near the town wall. The differing esteem for particular locations within the town affected the social character of a specific neighborhood. A traveling Swabian noticed in 1582 that the members of Rostock's upper class spoke in a much more distinguished way than people living in Fisher's street, and that the latter again talked differently than the inhabitants of the harbor quarter of Warnemünde, the seaside port of Rostock.

Since both the purchase and sale of houses required a special juridical protection, real estate transactions were already recorded by the end of the thirteenth century. For Lübeck, these property transactions can be found in the *Oberstadtbuch*, a book in which notaries of the city council wrote down all kinds of legal transactions. Ownership can be established for each house in Lübeck from 1284 onwards based on the series of the annual records, which

---

27 Thomas Brück, "Bemerkungen zur Kaufmannschaft Rigas in der ersten Hälfte des 15. Jahrhunderts unter besonderer Berücksichtigung der Schwarzhäupter zwischen 1413 und 1424," in Niels Jörn, Detlef Kattinger and Horst Wernicke, eds., *"kopet uns werk by tyden". Beiträge zur hansischen und preußischen Geschichte. Festschrift für Walter Stark zum 75. Geburtstag* (Schwerin: Helms, 1999), 113–130, 118.

28 Dale V. Kent and Francis William Kent, *Neighbours and Neigbourhood in Renaissance Florence. The District of the Red Lion in the fifteenth Century*, Villa i Tatti, vol. 6 (New York: J.J. Augustin, 1982); Karsten Igel, "'...und schal by der Lowen namen blyven'. Identität und Selbstdarstellung städtischer Führungsgruppen im spätmittelalterlichen Hanseraum im Spiegel ihrer Häuser und Höfe," in Sünje Prühlen, Lucie Kuhse and Jürgen Sarnowsky, eds., *Der Blick auf sich und die Anderen. Selbst- und Fremdbild von Frauen und Männern in Mittelalter und früher Neuzeit. Festschrift für Klaus Arnold*, Nova Mediaevalia. Quellen und Studien zum europäischen Mittelalter, vol. 2 (Göttingen: V & R Unipress, 2007), 315–348.

survived without gaps. The records of the *Oberstadtbuch* provide historians with valuable information, such as the ups and downs of the real estate market. Also, in assessing the remains of medieval buildings, information on ownership can be useful to find former owners of fire walls or mural paintings,[29] things typically discovered in archaeological diggings. Finally, these data also offer information for socio-historical analyses. With respect to dwelling location, it becomes possible to reconstruct the spatial distances that existed between citizens, for example merchants from a particular group of traders, craftsmen, and members of a certain guild or fraternity. The results can be depicted on a street map, and such a social topography of the town helps to discover the spatial aspect of social networks.[30]

An interesting case for this pattern can be studied with data from the Pomeranian town of Greifswald around the year 1400. With the surviving administrative records, it is possible to establish the dwelling places of the members of the town's leading class and to map these locations, which recently has been done by Karsten Igel.[31] From the resulting map, it can easily be seen that town councilors and mayors lived exclusively in the eastern parts of the town. They mostly lived at the market place and in *Knopfstraße*, which was a street connecting the market place with the neighboring area. In contrast, the western areas of the town had a completely different social character because craftsmen dominated the neighborhood there. Additionally, it can be shown that a rise within the town's social hierarchy due to a person's

29 Rolf Hammel, "Hauseigentum im spätmittelalterlichen Lübeck. Methoden zur sozial- und wirtschaftsgeschichtlichen Auswertung der Oberstadtbuchregesten," *Lübecker Schriften zur Archäologie und Kulturgeschichte* 10 (1987), 85–300.

30 Matthias Meinhardt and Andreas Ranft, eds., *Die Sozialstruktur und Sozialtopographie vorindustrieller Städte*, Hallische Beiträge zur Geschichte des Mittelalters und der Frühen Neuzeit, vol. 1 (Berlin: Akademie Verlag, 2005), 123–282.

31 Karsten Igel, "Greifswald um 1400. Zur Stadtgestalt und Sozialtopographie Greifswalds im Spätmittelalter," *Baltische Studien* 88 (2002), 20–42; Id., "Zur Sozialtopographie Greifswalds um 1400. Der Greifswalder *liber herediatum* (1351–1452)," in Meinhardt and Ranft, eds., *Sozialstruktur und Sozialtopographie* (see footnote 30), 227–245; Id., "Der Raum als soziale Kategorie. Methoden sozialtopographischer Forschung am Beispiel Greifswalds um 1400," in Stefan Kroll and Kersten Krüger, eds., *Städtesystem und Urbanisierung im Ostseeraum in der Neuzeit. Urbane Lebensräume und historische Informationssysteme* (Berlin: LIT, 2006), 265–300; Id., "Wohin in der Stadt? Sozialräumliche Studien und innerstädtische Mobilität im spätmittelalterlichen Greifswald," in Jörg Oberste, ed., *Repräsentationen in der mittelalterlichen Stadt*, Forum Mittelalter-Studien, vol. 4 (Regensburg: Schnell und Steiner, 2008), 179–192; Id., *Zwischen Bürgerhaus und Frauenhaus. Stadtgestalt, Grundbesitz und Sozialstruktur im spätmittelalterlichen Greifswald*, Städteforschung, vol. A71 (Cologne, Weimar, Vienna: Böhlau, 2010).

economic success usually meant that the respective person moved from the west side to the more reputable east side of Greifswald. Therefore it seems plausible to assume that spatial vicinity or even a direct neighborhood of the councilors and mayors of the town would have increased the frequency of social contact as well as it improved the density of social networks. In terms of sheer numbers, this situation cannot be compared to modern cities because even the medieval city of Lübeck, one of the larger examples, is estimated to have had only about 25,000 inhabitants, while the population of a town like Greifswald was likely to have had only about a quarter of Lübeck's, between 5,000 and 6,000 inhabitants. Given these relatively small population figures, communication between the inhabitants of the town should have been possible, which makes the spatial social segregation in such a small town even more astonishing. And compared to Italian towns of those days, which very often were divided into separate neighborhoods each dominated by a powerful family of the town's ruling class, the social networks of Hanseatic leading families were based not only on social but also on spatial nearness within the town.

The fact that both elements—social proximity and spatial vicinity—were often combined in the social networks of Hansards, can be derived from the case of the group of those merchants from Lübeck who traveled to or traded with Bergen. The oldermen of this merchants' company, who stood in the center of a sustained social network, usually occupied also a leading political role in the city of Lübeck, and they and their descendants lived for a very long time—well into the nineteenth century—nearby to each other in only a few streets in the inner city of Lübeck.[32] A more in-depth investigation of this social network formed out of merchants who traded in the same area, which was done by Mike Burkhardt using graphical and mathematical techniques of social network analysis, reveals for the fourteenth and fifteenth centuries a strong coherence of social proximity, kinship bonds and commercial cooperation around a core of a few families, but also a visible change towards a less kinship-based trade pattern during the late fifteenth century.[33]

32 Georg Asmussen, "Die Älterleute der Lübecker Bergenfahrer (1401–1854). Eine Führungsposition in Lübeck im Vergleich über mehrere Jahrhunderte," in Stephan Selzer and Ulf Christian Ewert, eds., *Menschenbilder—Menschenbildner. Individuum und Gruppe im Blick des Historikers. Werner Paravicini zum 60. Geburtstag*, Hallische Beiträge zur Geschichte des Mittelalters und der Frühen Neuzeit, vol. 2 (Berlin: Akademie Verlag, 2002), 121–152.

33 Mike Burkhardt, *Der hansische Bergenhandel im Spätmittelalter. Handel—Kaufleute—Netzwerke*, Quellen und Darstellungen zur hansischen Geschichte, vol. 60 (Cologne, Weimar, Vienna: Böhlau, 2009); Id., "Kaufmannsnetzwerke und Handelskultur. Zur Verbindung von interpersonellen Beziehungsgeflechten und kaufmännischem Habitus

A Functional Perspective: The Economic Meaning of Social Networks

The Structure of Trade Networks and Characteristics of Commercial Exchange

Much of the Hanseatic trade was operated by self-employed merchants, family businesses, and small-scale firms. Because of their small size, complex hierarchical structures are seldom, if ever found among them. The company of *Falbrecht-Morser-Rosenfeld*,[34] which operated during the early fifteenth century in England and Hungary and the business-house *Loitz* from Stettin,[35] founded in the sixteenth century, were among these rare cases. However, the simple organizational structure of single firms was only part of the trading pattern in the late Middle Ages that can be observed in the Baltic and the North Sea region. A more complex structure of commercial exchange had emerged from the interactions between the simply structured firms. Hanseatic merchants formed trade networks of different sizes, densities, and endurances. These networks were medium-term or long-term cooperations between legally independent merchants who traded goods with each other. A spatial specialization—as it is called in organization science—was achieved because traders from different places in the Baltic could feed many different products and goods into such networks. Hanseatic merchants usually employed each other as commercial agents in distant places. As a result of many commercial exchange relations being handled in this particular manner, widely

---

im spätmittelalterlichen Ostseeraum," in Sunhild Kleingärtner and Gabriel Zeilinger, eds., *Raumbildung durch Netzwerke? Der Ostseeraum zwischen Wikingerzeit und Spätmittelalter aus archäologischer und geschichtswissenschaftlicher Perspektive*, Zeitschrift für Archäologie des Mittelalters, Beiheft 23 (Bonn: Habelt, 2012), 117–130.

34 Wolfgang von Stromer, "Der innovatorische Rückstand der hansischen Wirtschaft," in Knut Schulz, ed., *Beiträge zur Wirtschafts- und Sozialgeschichte des Mittelalters. Festschrift für Herbert Helbig zum 65. Geburtstag* (Cologne: Böhlau, 1976), 204–217; Franz Irsigler, "Hansischer Kupferhandel im 15. und in der ersten Hälfte des 16. Jahrhunderts," *Hansische Geschichtsblätter* 97 (1979), 15–35, 22–24.

35 Johannes Papritz, "Das Stettiner Handelshaus der Loitz im Boisalzhandel des Odergebietes unter besonderer Berücksichtigung seiner Beziehungen zum brandenburgischen Kurhause," (Dissertation manuscript, Berlin, 1932); Id., "Das Handelshaus der Loitz zu Stettin, Danzig und Lüneburg," *Baltische Studien* N.F. 44 (1957), 73–94; Heidelore Böcker, "Das Handelshaus der Loitz. Urteil der Zeitgenossen, Stand der Forschung, Ergänzungen," in Detlev Kattinger and Horst Wernicke, eds., *Akteure und Gegner der Hanse. Zur Prosopographie der Hansezeit. Konrad-Fritze-Gedächtnisschrift*, Hansische Studien, vol. 9, (Weimar: Böhlau, 1998), 203–218.

branched-out trade networks evolved. Since most Hanseatic merchants operated as self-employed traders, these networks were not only networks of people, but also networks of firms. Thus a further feature of such networks was that they consisted of firms of quasi-equal rank. Nevertheless, these networks did not have a formal or legal definition. They lacked formal hierarchies and showed only a small degree of formalism. Moreover, there were no headquarters, and all the trading activities had to be coordinated by means different from hierarchy. Hence it follows that the organizational form of Hanseatic trade networks cannot be judged using Max Weber's nineteenth-century-style model of bureaucratic organization.[36] As a medieval example[37] of the modern paradigm of network organization,[38] this form fits into the conceptual framework of present-day organization theory accordingly.[39] A network organization

---

36 See on the effect of Max Weber's theories on organization science Jürgen Hauschildt, "Entwicklungslinien der Organisationstheorie," *Berichte aus den Sitzungen der Joachim Jungius Gesellschaft der Wissenschaften e.V.* 5/5 (1987), 3–21.

37 See on networks of persons built to fulfil commercial purposes and networking strategies of merchants in pre-modern and modern times e.g. Gunnar Dahl, *Trade, Trust, and Networks: Commercial Culture in Late Medieval Italy* (Lund: Nordic Academic Press, 1998); Francine Rolley, "Entre économie ancienne et économie de marché: Le rôle des réseaux de parenté dans le commerce du bois au XVIIIe siècle," *Annales de démographie historique* (1995), 75–96; Claude Markovits, *The Global World of Indian Merchants 1750–1947: Traders of Sind from Bukhara to Panama* (Cambridge: Cambridge University Press, 2000); Magrit Schulte-Beerbühl and Jörg Vögele, eds., *Spinning the Commercial Web: International Trade, Merchants and Commercial Cities 1640–1939* (Frankfurt/Main: Peter Lang, 2004); Ina Baghdiantz McCabe, Gelina Harlaftis and Ioanna Pepelasis Minoglou, eds., *Diaspora Entrepreneurial Networks: Four Centuries of History* (Oxford: Berg, 2005).

38 See on the concept of network organization e.g. Walter W. Powell, "Neither Market nor Hierarchy: Network Forms of Organization," *Research in Organisational Behaviour* 10 (1990): 295–336; Joseph Galaskiewicz, "The 'New Network Analysis' and its Application to Organizational Theory and Behavior," in Dawn Iacobucci, ed., *Networks in Marketing* (Thousand Oakes: Sage, 1996), 19–31; Anne Illinitch et al., "New Organisational Forms and Strategies for Managing in Hypercompetitive Environment," *Organization Science* 7 (1996), 211–220; Richard N. Osborn and John Hagedoorn, "The Institutionalisation and Evolutionary Dynamics of Inter-organisational Alliances and Networks," *Academy of Management Journal* 40 (1997), 261–278; Thomas Ritter and Hans-Georg Gemünden, "Die netzwerkende Unternehmung: Organisationale Voraussetzungen netzwerk-kompetenter Unternehmen," *Zeitschrift für Organisation* 67 (1998), 260–265; Grahame F. Thompson, *Between Hierachies and Markets: The Logic and Limits of Network Forms of Organization* (Oxford: Oxford University Press, 2003).

39 Stephan Selzer and Ulf Christian Ewert, "Verhandeln und Verkaufen, Vernetzen und Vertrauen: Über die Netzwerkstruktur des hansischen Handels," *Hansische Geschichtsblätter* 119 (2001), 135–161; Ulf Christian Ewert and Stephan Selzer, "Wirtschaftliche Stärke durch

is defined as a loose cooperation of legally and economically independent entities. This kind of interorganizational network neither possesses hierarchical levels nor is controlled by a central authority. Thus, the cooperation between network members is thought to happen only by voluntary and flexible couplings. Such interorganizational networks are characterized by a minimal degree of formal definition.

Business transactions between the merchants of the Hanse were generally handled on a partnership basis. Several juridical forms of cooperation were used: Within the so-called *wedderleginge* (labeled also *kumpanie, vera societas*) two merchants cooperated, one of them was trading goods whereas the other only contributed part of the financial capital the first one was using for his trading operations. Profits were shared.[40] In contrast, the so-called *sendeve* was a sort of commission business. The commission agent sold the goods he had received from another merchant by order and for account of this merchant, the sender. Profits and risks remained with this sender, who had instructed the sale and had provided the commisson agent with goods.[41] Yet, by far the most important transaction type between Hanseatic merchants was the cooperation of two traders. This was different from a commission business and can be labeled a "reciprocal" business. In such reciprocal partnerships, each partner sold the other's goods, but in every case the sender pocketed the profits. However, the risk remained only with the partner who operated the sale.[42] Simultaneity of

Vernetzung. Zu den Erfolgsfaktoren des hansischen Handels," in Mark Häberlein and Christof Jeggle, eds., *Praktiken des Handels.Geschäfte und soziale Beziehungen in Mittelalter und früher Neuzeit*, Irseer Schriften, NF 6 (Konstanz: UVK Verlagsgesellschaft, 2010), 39–69, 43–50.

40 Wilhelm Ebel, *Lübisches Kaufmannsrecht vornehmlich nach Lübecker Ratsurteilen des 15./16. Jahrhunderts* (Göttingen: Göttinger Arbeitskreis, 1953); Cordes, *Gesellschaftshandel* (see footnote 22); Id., "Einheimische und gemeinrechtliche Elemente im hansischen Gesellschaftsrecht des 15.–17. Jahrhunderts. Eine Projektskizze," in Jörn, Kattinger and Wernicke, eds., *'kopet uns werk by tyden.'* (see footnote 27), 67–71; Id., *Wie verdiente der Kaufmann sein Geld? Hansische Handelsgesellschaften im Spätmittelalter*, Handel, Geld und Politik, vol. 2 (Lübeck, 2000); Hammel-Kiesow, *Hanse* (see footnote 14).

41 Cordes, *Gesellschaftshandel* (see footnote 40); Id., "Gesellschaftsrecht" (see footnote 40); Id., *Wie verdiente der Kaufmann sein Geld?* (see footnote 40).

42 Gunnar Mickwitz, "Neues zur Funktion hansischer Handelsgesellschaften," *Hansische Geschichtsblätter* 62 (1937), 24–39; Id., *Aus Revaler Handelsbüchern. Zur Technik des Ostseehandels in der ersten Hälfte des 16. Jahrhundert*, Commentationes Humanarum Litterarum, IX/5 (Helsingfors: Societas Scientiarum Fennica, 1938); Walter Stark, "Über Platz- und Kommissionshändlergewinne im Handel des 15. Jahrhunderts," in Konrad Fritze, Eckehard Müller-Mertens, and Walter Stark, eds., *Autonomie, Wirtschaft und Kultur der Hansestädte*, Hansische Studien, vol. 6 and Abhandlungen zur Handels-

reciprocal sale operations was not necessary. The striking feature of this sort of mutual transaction is that it was usually handled without a written contract. Neither written long-term agreements between two merchants, nor occasional transaction-specific written instructions existed. Even during the sixteenth century, this form of reciprocal cooperation was prevalent among Hanseatic merchants.[43] Another feature of Hanseatic commercial exchange is that the trade networks usually were also characterized by a "cooptition".[44] Since the reciprocal commercial exchange allowed merchants to cooperate with more than one trading partner and operate potentially conflicting sales with different sides, cooperation and competition could be found at the same time within one network. During the late Middle Ages, the Hanse never forbade this sort of competition.[45]

This pronounced network pattern of commercial exchange between Hansards emerged in the period of demographic expansion before 1300 when many towns in the Baltic were founded. With a simulation approach, a methodology which partly can make up for the significant lack of written sources on Hanseatic merchants in this early period, it is shown, that slow transmission of information and high transportation costs in the Baltic as well as the

und Sozialgeschichte, vol. 34 (Weimar: Böhlau, 1984), 130–146; Walter Stark, "Über Techniken und Organisationsformen des hansischen Handels im Spätmittelalter," in Stuart Jenks, Michael North, eds., *Der hansische Sonderweg? Beiträge zur Sozial- und Wirtschaftsgeschichte der Hanse* (Cologne, Weimar, Vienna: Böhlau, 1993), 191–201; Cordes, *Gesellschaftshandel* (see footnote 22); Id., *Wie verdiente der Kaufmann sein Geld?* (see footnote 40).

43 This is proved with the example of *Bertram Bene* from Oslo and his trading partners of the *Kron* family from Rostock. See on this Hildegard Thierfelder, *Rostock-Osloer Handelsbeziehungen im 16. Jahrhundert. Die Geschäftspapiere der Kaufleute Kron in Rostock und Bene in Oslo*, Abhandlungen zur Handels- und Sozialgeschichte, vol. 1 (Weimar: Böhlau, 1958), 194–197.

44 "Cooptition" is a coinage out of "cooperation" and "competition" that recently came in use in the theory of network organizations. Thilo C. Beck, "Cooptition bei der Netzwerkorganisation," *Zeitschrift für Organisation* 67 (1998), 271–276.

45 Rolf Sprandel, "Die Konkurrenzfähigkeit der Hanse im Spätmittelalter," *Hansische Geschichtsblätter* 102 (1984), 21–38, 28. An example of an explicit prohibition of competition between trading partners is that of the company formed by *Hermann Carsten, Gert vom Brocke* and *Heinrich von Kampen* in Lübeck in the middle of the sixteenth century, which nonetheless is not typical in the sense, since it was one of the later companies in which already the bureaucratic-hierarchical style had been adopted. Cf. Pierre Jeannin, "Lübecker Handelsunternehmungen um die Mitte des 16. Jahrhunderts," *Zeitschrift des Vereins für Lübeckische Geschichte und Altertumskunde* 43 (1963), 19–67, 46, 57.

exclusive trade privileges held by Hansards were important determinants of the formation of trade networks.[46]

Overlapping Circles of Family and Business

Hanseatic commercial networks consisted of several dyadic relationships between traders residing all over the Baltic and the *Kontore* of London, Bergen, Novgorod, and Bruges. The structure and composition of business networks can be determined by researching account books, letters, or, as was shown above, wills. With the exception of wills, there are not many written records about Hanseatic merchants' business practices yet available. For *Johann Pisz* from Danzig, *Vicko von Geldersen* from Hamburg, and *Hermann* and *Johann Wittenborg* from Lübeck, account books have been preserved.[47] The account book belonging to *Johann Pisz* covers a period of approximately 32 years. Moreover, account books and letters from the *Veckinchusen* family give an idea of what a Hanseatic merchant's business life must have been like in early fifteenth century.[48] Following these sources, the number of a merchant's trading partners could reach a maximum of about 40 during a period of about 30 years, and cooperation with certain partners could last up to 22 years.[49] If a single merchant cooperated with about 40 others, one could imagine that the total size of commercial networks must have been much larger, assuming

46 Ulf Christian Ewert, Marco Sunder, "Trading Networks, Monopoly and Economic Development in Medieval Northern Europe. An Agent-Based Simulation of Early Hanseatic Trade," in Kleingärtner and Zeilinger, eds., *Raumbildung durch Netzwerke?* (see footnote 33), 131–153, 145–149.

47 Hans Nirrnheim, ed., *Das Handlungsbuch des Vicko von Geldersen* (Hamburg: Kessinger Publishing, 1895); Carl Mollwo, ed., *Das Handlungsbuch von Hermann und Johann Wittenborg* (Leipzig: Dyksche Buchhandlung, 1901); Witold von Slaski, *Danziger Handel im 15. Jahrhundert auf Grund eines im Danziger Stadtarchiv befindlichen Handlungsbuches geschildert* (Doctoral Dissertation, Ruprecht-Karls-Universität Heidelberg, 1905); Walter Schmidt-Rimpler, *Geschichte des Kommissionsgeschäfts in Deutschland, vol. 1: Die Zeit bis zum Ende des 15. Jahrhunderts* (Halle: Waisenhaus, 1915); Sprandel, "Konkurrenzfähigkeit" (see footnote 45), 21–38; Stark, "Platz- und Kommissionshändlergewinne" (see footnote 42), 130–146; Id., *Untersuchungen zum Profit beim hansischen Handelskapital in der ersten Hälfte des 15. Jahrhunderts*, Abhandlungen zur Handels- und Sozialgeschichte, vol. 24 (Weimar: Böhlau, 1985); Stark, "Techniken" (see footnote 42), 191–201.

48 Wilhelm Stieda, ed., *Hildebrand Veckinchusen. Briefwechsel eines deutschen Kaufmanns im 15. Jahrhundert* (Leipzig, 1921); Franz Irsigler, "Der Alltag einer hansischen Kaufmannsfamilie im Spiegel der Veckinchusen-Briefe," *Hansische Geschichtsblätter* 103 (1985), 75–99.

49 Sprandel, "Konkurrenzfähigkeit" (see footnote 45), 21–38, 28.

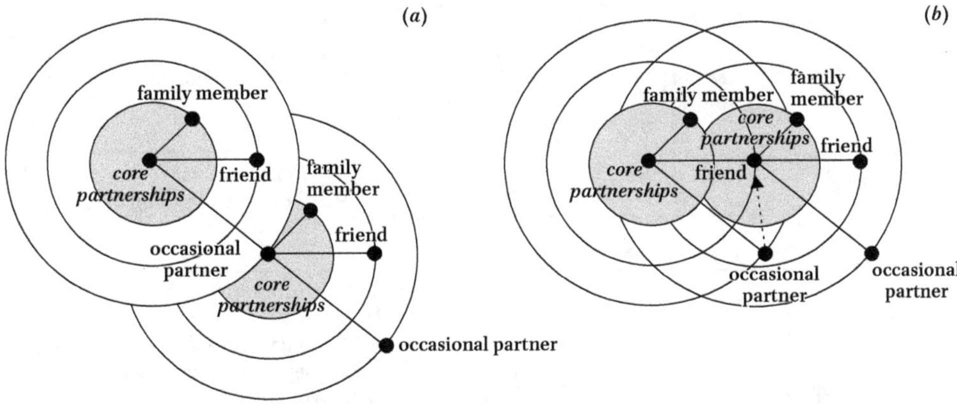

FIGURE 5.2 *Structure and Stabilization of Commercial Networks: (a) Zones of network members with respect to their classification into family members, friends, and occasional partners and overlapping personal networks; (b) An example of intensification of transactions over time after occasional partners have become friends.*
SOURCE: CREATED BY ULF CHRISTIAN EWERT AND STEPHAN SELZER.

that the density of the whole network was not complete. To a certain extent, it is an analytical drawback that sources do not provide enough information to calculate either a complete network's density or the degree of centrality of each merchant's position within a network.[50] However, it is possible to take an ego-centered network approach, and try to reconstruct only the part of an exchange network that belongs to a particular merchant.

The rare source material allows for some general conclusions to be made. The total number of a merchant's trading partners can be divided into (at least) three groups: family members, friends, and occasional partners. For each merchant, the relative position of all trading partners can be plotted on circles surrounding his own position in an ego-centered network (see Figure 5.2a). Core partnerships have a high frequency of mutual exchange and had existed for a longer period of time. In theory, family bonds and core partnerships coincide significantly.[51] In practice, there seems to be strong evidence from Hanseatic sources that core partnerships were often trading relationships with family

50 Daniel J. Brass and Marlene E. Burkhardt, "Centrality and Power in Organizations," in Nitin Nohria and Robert G. Eccles, eds., *Networks and Organizations: Structure, Form, and Action* (Boston: Harvard, 1992), 191–215.

51 Peter Ping Li, "Towards a Geocentric Framework of Organizational Form: A Holistic, Dynamic and Paradoxical Approach," *Organization Studies* 19 (1998), 829–861.

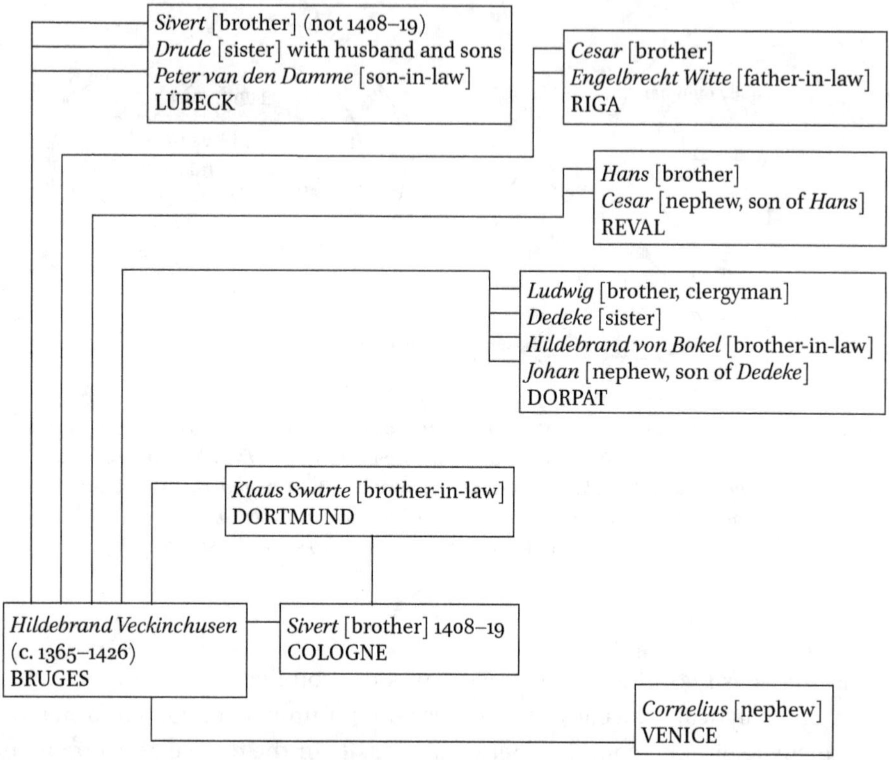

FIGURE 5.3 *The Family Network of* Hildebrand Veckinchusen*: Graph of the family network of* Hildebrand Veckinhusen *showing trading relationships and geographical diffusions of the* Veckinchusen *family.*
SOURCE: CREATED BY ULF CHRISTIAN EWERT AND STEPHAN SELZER FOLLOWING IRSIGLER, "ALLTAG" (SEE FOOTNOTE 48), 75–99, AND STARK, "TECHNIKEN" (SEE FOOTNOTE 42), 191–201.

members and friends. At the beginning of the fifteenth century, *Hildebrand Veckinchusen* traded from Bruges with some of his friends as well as with his relatives, including his father-in-law *Engelbrecht Witte* in Riga, his brother *Sivert* in Lübeck (during 1408 to 1419 in Cologne), his other brothers *Cesar* and *Hans* in Riga and Reval, his brothers-in-law *Klaus Swarte* in Dortmund and *Hildebrand von Bokel* in Dorpat, his son-in-law *Peter van den Damme* in Lübeck, and his nephews in Lübeck, Reval, Dorpat, and even Venice (see Figure 5.3).[52]

Once established, a commercial network became more and more dense (see Figure 5.2b) as it was a common strategy of merchants to make occasional

52 Irsigler, "Alltag" (see footnote 48), 75–99; Stark, "Techniken" (see footnote 42), 191–201; Cordes, *Gesellschaftshandel* (see footnote 22).

partners friends and friends relatives. *Engelbrecht Witte* from Riga, the later father-in-law of *Hildebrand Vechinchusen*, married his daughter into the *Veckinchusen* family with a clear aim at becoming friends with that family.[53] Hence, Hanseatic trade networks appear to have been a so-called "small world",[54] as they allowed each member to contact any other participant through only a few mediating persons, despite having a weak overall density and having been fragmented into separate subgroups.

Coordination Mechanisms to Make Business Networks Working

In networks like the multiple Hanseatic business partnerships, problems like free-riding and cheating often arose,[55] especially if a considerably large number of members were involved.[56] With a lack of written contracts, it seems as though it must have been very easy to participate in a commercial network of Hanseatic merchants and take personal benefits for free. In principle, this was possible if a merchant refused to contribute substantially to the diffusion of goods within the network. For example, a merchant would sell another merchant's goods and pocket the profit, without sending goods back for recompensation, as it was usually done in reciprocal trade. However, a fair exchange between merchants within these business networks could be guaranteed by different mechanisms—culture, trust, and reputation.

Coordination by culture[57] was essential to make business networks run smoothly. In general, when merchants shared common values, mutual cooperation was facilitated. The spread of common values across the Baltic and the creation of a Hanseatic cultural identity were more or less a by-product of migration, as shown earlier. First, the common Lower German language

---

53 Irsigler, "Alltag" (see footnote 48), 81; Id., "Der hansische Handel im Spätmittelalter," in Jörgen Bracker, ed., *Die Hanse: Lebenswirklichkeit und Mythos. Katalog der Ausstellung im Museum für Hamburgische Geschichte 1989* (Lübeck: Schmidt-Römhild, 1989), 518–532, 530.

54 Duncan Watts, "Networks, Dynamics, and the Small-World Phenomenon," *American Journal of Sociology* 105 (1999), 493–527, 495–498.

55 Leigh Tesfatsion, "A Trade Network Game with Endogenous Partner Selection," in Hans Amman, Berc Rustem, and Andrew Whinston, eds., *Computational Approaches to Economic Problems*, Advances in Computational Economics, vol. 6 (Dordrecht, Boston, London: Kluwer Academic Publishers, 1997), 249–269, 252.

56 Andreas Diekmann, "Soziale Dilemmata: Modelle, Typisierungen und empirische Resultate," in Hans-Jürgen Andreß et al., eds., *Theorie, Daten, Methoden: Neue Modelle und Verfahrensweisen in den Sozialwissenschaften. Theodor Harder zum sechzigsten Geburtstag* (Munich: Oldenbourg, 1992), 177–203.

57 Gareth R. Jones, "Transaction Costs, Property Rights, and Organizational Culture: An Exchange Perspective," *Administrative Science Quarterly* 28 (1983), 454–467.

fostered a tight bond between the Hanseatic merchants.[58] Cultural identity also appeared in marriage patterns, festivities, and law habits. As the municipal law of Lübeck became predominant in the Baltic, almost all Hanseatic merchants acted on the grounds of a commonly known and practiced law,[59] despite coming from different towns. Given all of this, merchants that spoke the same language and were often also closely related to each other were present all across the Baltic. This made finding ways to organize commercial exchange easier.

Therefore, culture was important within the core partnerships of merchants, that is, in commercial exchange with relatives and friends. Cheating or betraying a family member or a friend not only meant losing a particular mutual transaction relationship, it was also likely a reason of being excluded from the entire network. Cultural bonds of network members were continuously revived by institutions and social events which enabled network members to socialize with each other. The previously mentioned Artus courts or the *Zirkelgesellschaft* are good examples of such institutions. The meeting halls of these societies were places where business information was exchanged and commercial transactions were arranged. Members, usually the city's rich merchants and political leaders, came together with guests from other towns and celebrated festivities which helped facilitate all kinds of business exchanges.

Like culture, trust was also important for coordinating network activities,[60] especially because it was essential to cooperation whenever traders were not members of the same family. The network pattern is commonly called a "total-trust" organization, thereby putting it in sharp contrast to the model of a "zero-trust" bureaucratic-hierarchical organization in which control is achieved by instructions.[61] Trust between Hanseatic traders usually increased when a mutual relationship endured a long period of time. By reciprocity of

---

58 Dick E.H. de Boer et al., eds., '... *in guete freuntlichen nachbarlichen verwantnus und hantierung*...' *Wanderung von Personen, Verbreitung von Ideen, Austausch von Waren in den niederländischen und deutschen Küstenregionen vom 13. bis 18. Jahrhundert*, Oldenburger Schriften zur Geschichtswissenschaft, vol. 6 (Oldenburg: Bibliotheks- und Informationssystem der Universität Oldenburg, 2001).

59 Ebel, *Lübisches Kaufmannsrecht* (see footnote 40).

60 Tanja Ripperger, *Ökonomik des Vertrauens. Analyse eines Organisationsprinzips* (Tübingen: Rainer Hampp Verlag, 1998); John Child, "Trust—The Fundamental Bond in Global Collaboration," *Organizational Dynamics* 29 (2001), 274–288; Chris Grey and Christina Garsten, "Trust, Control and Post-bureaucracy," *Organization Studies* 22 (2001), 229–250.

61 Michael I. Reed, "Organization, Trust, and Control: A Realist Analysis," *Organization Studies* 22 (2001), 201–228, 203.

actions—sending goods to a partner if goods were obtained from him, selling the goods received if the partner also sells the goods sent to him, etc.—potential free-riding could be avoided even without hierarchy and without a powerful legal system. Nevertheless, trust had to be built up over a long time. A step-by-step approach had to be taken by the merchants in the early stages of mutual relationship or in case of trading with occasional partners. In game theory this phenomenon is generally described as Tit-for-Tat strategy.[62] The growing volume of the transactions between *Hildebrand Veckinchusen* and *Gerwin Marschede* is an example of how a bond of trust formed over time, similar to many other Hanseatic commercial networks.[63] Very often, partners also tried to tighten personal relationships by mutual gift giving.[64]

Simultaneously with both culture and trust, reputation played a fundamental role in enforcing fair conduct between network members. This can easily be shown by using a game-theoretical approach. Following Avner Greif's idea, a trade relationship is modeled as a one-sided sequential prisoner's dilemma.[65] Within this framework, the form of reciprocal trade, which was predominant among Hanseatic merchants, does not create incentive for the participants to act fair. In a simple one-shot situation, for the partner who was selling the other's goods, gaining a *P* by cheating would have been bigger than a zero return from fair behavior (see Figure 5.4a). In a more realistic scenario, where

62 Robert Axelrod, *The Evolution of Cooperation* (New York, 1984); Håkan Håkansson and D. Deo Sharma, "Strategic Alliances in a Network Perspective," in Iacobucci, ed., *Networks in Marketing* (see footnote 38), 108–124, 116f.

63 Stark, *Untersuchungen zum Profit* (see footnote 47).

64 See for examples from Riga, Königsberg, Oslo and Rostock Wilhelm Stein, "Handelsbriefe aus Riga und Königsberg von 1458 und 1461," *Hansische Geschichtsblätter* 9.2 (1898), 59–125, 89–91, Nr. 10, 93–97, Nr. 13, and 114, Nr. 21; Stark, "Platz- und Kommissionshändlergewinne" (see footnote 42), 141; Thierfelder, *Rostock-Osloer Handelsbeziehungen* (see footnote 43), 209.

65 Avner Greif, "The Fundamental Problem of Exchange: A Research Agenda in Historical Institutional Analysis," *European Review of Economic History* 4 (2000), 251–284, 254–256. Here, each of the two partners involved in mutual exchange would be at the same time a "principal", who is sending goods to the partner, as well as an "agent," who is receiving goods and selling them for the sender. While playing these roles merchants are assumed to have a choice: as "principal" they can decide upon sending their goods; as "agent" they can decide whether to cooperate or not. See on this model in more detail Ewert and Selzer, "Wirtschaftliche Stärke durch Vernetzung" (see footnote 39), 50–60. On game-theoretical approaches to the history of medieval trade see also Avner Greif, *Institutions and the Path to the Modern Economy: Lessons from Medieval Trade* (Cambridge: Cambridge University Press, 2004).

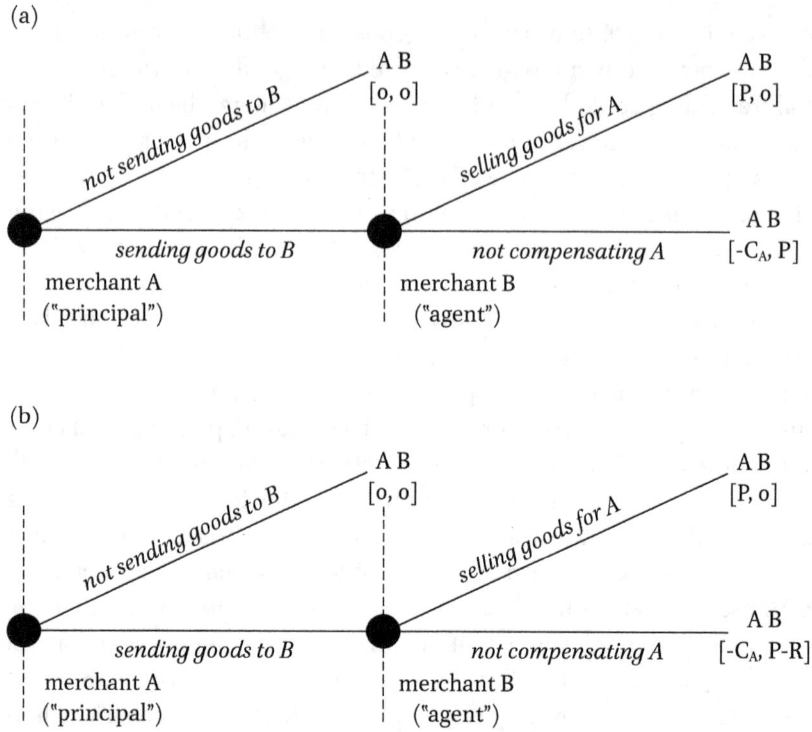

FIGURE 5.4 *Game Theoretical Analysis of Hanseatic Reciprocal Trade: Game-theoretical model of reciprocal trade:* P = *profit of sale;* C_A = *costs of sending goods to B;* R = *Reputation* (R > P). *(a) One-shot situation without incentives for B to act fair; (b) situation of repeated games with accounting for B's losses of reputation in the event of cheating A.*
SOURCE: CALCULATED AND CREATED BY ULF CHRISTIAN EWERT AND STEPHAN SELZER.

trading activities could be repeated infinitely,[66] this defect in principle could be removed by common cultural bonds and mutual trust, because reputation *R* of merchants was an even stronger means to enforce a reciprocal fair comportment (see Figure 5.4b).

Therefore, being a reliable trader of high standing was essential to all members of a network. Keeping this reputation was a strong incentive to follow the network rules. Losing it by cheating or betrayal not only undermined a particular bilateral relationship, it also automatically meant losing access to an entire network and thus losing possible future partnerships as well. Because of

66 Assuming infinity of repetitions is plausible insofar as both partners in reality do not know when exactly their exchange relationship would come to an end.

this multilateral reputation mechanism,[67] the Hanseatic network trade was a self-enforcing institution. Hanseatic societies and institutions creating opportunities to socialize contributed greatly to the reputation mechanism. It was in the societies' functions and informal meetings that participants were regularly provided with information regarding the reputation of other network members.[68] For example, there is plenty of evidence that the names of those who were no longer allowed to share the privileges of the Hanseatic League in Bruges were published in the Artus courts.[69] Joint membership of merchants and councilors in societies or fraternities as well as closeness within a town helped merchants make city councilors an instrument in advocating commercial interests. Thus, design and functionalism of trade networks do verify that commercial purposes and social practices of Hanseatic merchants overlapped to a great extent.

Benefits and Long-range Consequences of Networking

Using networks for commercial purposes was certainly beneficial for Hanseatic merchants, but in the long run, this also had some ambiguous consequences for the competiveness of the Hanse as a whole. Individual level benefits of networking can be derived from the transaction costs approach, which was developed by Coase and Williamson.[70] First, "networking" produced many costs instead of saving them. Since merchants were engaged in medium-term or even long-term partnerships, they had to account for the individual costs that

67 See on the impact of reputation-based institutions in medieval trade Avner Greif, "Institutions and International Trade: Lessons from the Commercial Revolution," *American Economic Review, Papers and Proceedings* 82 (1992), 128–133, 130; Id., "Contract Enforceability and Economic Institutions in Early Trade: The Maghribi Traders' Coalition," *American Economic Review* 83 (1993), 525–548, 531–535; Id., Paul Milgrom and Barry R. Weingast, "Coordination, Commitment, and Enforcement: The Case of the Merchant Guild," *Journal of Political Economy* 41 (1994), 745–776; Id., "Fundamental Problem of Exchange" (see footnote 65), 260–272; Jochen Streb, "Die politische Glaubwürdigkeit von Regierungen im institutionellen Wandel. Warum ausländische Fürsten das Eigentum der Fernhandelskaufleute der Hanse schützten," *Jahrbuch für Wirtschaftsgeschichte* 2004/1, 141–156; and quite recently Yadira Gonzáles de Lara, "The Secret of Venetian Success: A Public Order, Reputation-based Institution," *European Review of Economic History* 12 (2008), 247–285.

68 Selzer, "Trinkstuben" (see footnote 26), 84, 96–97.

69 Selzer, *Artushöfe* (see footnote 26), 105.

70 Ronald H. Coase, "The Nature of the Firm," *Economica* NS 4 (1937), 386–405; Id., "The New Institutional Economics," *Journal of Institutional and Theoretical Economics* 140 (1984), 229–231; Oliver E. Williamson, "Transaction-Costs Economics: The Governance of Contractual Relations," *Journal of Law and Economics* 22 (1979), 233–261.

were due to these commitments. Common costs could be produced because single members of a commercial network could attempt to take the network services for free and to externalize private costs to the network community. Why did Hanseatic merchants prefer this pattern of trade? By participating in a commercial network, each must have gained personal profits, at least in the long run; otherwise there would not have been any incentive for participation at all. Choosing a network structure for trade reduced the costs significantly.[71] This saving can be split into reductions of transaction, information, and organization costs. And with reciprocal trade, Hansards had a powerful tool against the classic problems that occur in principal-agent relationships, also known as "adverse selection" and "moral hazard".[72]

Probably the best-known benefit of a network structure is its ability to decrease transaction costs significantly. This cost reduction mainly stemmed from network members acting in accordance with the same set of norms; even more so because many of them were members of the same family or were just friends. Mutual commercial transactions were facilitated. Stable sets of partnerships reduced transaction costs as well because merchants then already knew what could be expected from a particular trading partner. Due to the commercial networks' core principle of construction, legally independent merchants had to voluntarily cooperate. In general, each partner had the same interests and they could trust each other's determination to keep to the partnership.

---

71 The role particular institutions played for the reduction of transaction costs and thus could enhance trade and economic growth in medieval Europe was analyzed in numerous studies, for example by North and Greif. Douglass C. North, *Structure and Change in Economic History* (New York: Norton, 1981); Id., "Transaction Costs in History," *Journal of European Economic History* 14 (1985), 557–576; Id., *Institutions, Institutional Change and Economic Performance* (Cambridge: Cambridge University Press, 1990); Id., "Institutions and Credible Commitment," *Journal of Institutional and Theoretical Economics* 149 (1993), 11–23; Avner Greif, "Institutions and Impersonal Exchange: From Communal to Individual Responsibility," *Journal of Institutional and Theoretical Economics* 158 (2002), 168–204; Id., *Institutions and the Path to the Modern Economy: Lessons from Medieval Trade* (Cambridge: Cambridge University Press, 2006). See also John H. Munro, "The 'New Institutional Economics' and the Changing Fortunes of Fairs in Medieval and Early Modern Europe: the Textile Trade, Warfare, and Transaction Costs," *Vierteljahrschrift für Sozial- und Wirtschaftsgeschichte* 88 (2001), 1–47.

72 Selzer and Ewert, "Verhandeln und Verkaufen" (see footnote 39), 135–161, 151–152; Iid., "Die Neue Institutionenökonomik als Herausforderung an die Hanseforschung," *Hansische Geschichtsblätter* 123 (2005), 7–29, 28; Ewert and Selzer, "Wirtschaftliche Stärke durch Vernetzung" (see footnote 39), 55, 58–59.

A second block of costs contained all costs arising from collecting and processing information. Being a member of a network helped Hanseatic merchants find partners in whom they could trust. The network provided them with all the necessary information on the reputation of a potential trading partner, either by its kinship, or by character social institutions. The risk of "adverse selection," that is, choosing the wrong trading partner, was minimized. With networks based on reciprocal trade, the costs of market information decreased. In long-term partnerships, the information about market conditions at distant places where a partner sold a trader's goods did not necessarily have to be gathered by the sending merchant himself. Because of the multilateral reputation mechanism, the partner who handled the sale had strong incentives to do so in the best interest of the sender. Therefore, it was sufficient if only the seller had the relevant information at his disposal.

The reduced costs of organization were probably the biggest profit that could be made from operating in commercial networks. The networks' structural element of employing each other mutually as commercial agents implied that many of the core functions of trade organizations could simply be delegated to a trading partner. As a consequence, Hanseatic businesses remained relatively small and simply organized. This enabled merchants to save most of the costs which otherwise would have been spent on a hierarchical control of commercial transactions. Moreover, since the transmission of information was slow due to the immense geographical extent that had to be bridged by trade in the Baltic, instructing and controlling employed business agents at distant market places on a regular basis was almost impossible. By using trading partners as agents, transactions could be handled much more easily and safely. Because of the potential threat to their reputation if they acted otherwise, both partners acted primarily in the other partner's interest. A fairly responsible conduct was also enforced by judicial practice. In lawsuits concerning trading activities, arbitration usually pointed to the principle that each party had to act in such a manner that also its own interest would have been guaranteed. The formula *to synem besten to verkopen* ("to sell something for his best interest") can be found again and again in various sources, accordingly.[73] Therefore, the network structure also provided the Hansards with a solution to the well-known problem of "moral hazard," and a coverage of commercial transactions by written contracts in most cases was unnecessary.

Although the form of trade through networks was adapted to specific conditions of commercial exchange within the Hanseatic world, information was generally transmitted slowly and the legal institutions were rather weak.

73 Ebel, *Lübisches Kaufmannsrecht* (see footnote 40), 84.

In the late fifteenth century, this pattern itself turned into a hindrance to both the expansion and competitiveness of the Hanse.[74] The Hanse was in a sense a "small world," but only for Hansards. To strangers it must have appeared as a closed society, nearly impossible to reach, and in fact it was. The negative effect of self-containment is quite typical for networks based on cultural identity. The Florentine banker *Gherardo Bueri* is one of the rare exceptions to this rule because he managed to settle with his business in Lübeck. Only after he had married into a rich family from Lübeck he could join a Hanseatic network.[75] Since Hanseatic merchants very strictly held on to the privileges of the Hanse in London, Bruges, Bergen, and Novgorod, and since the multilateral reputation mechanism only worked to perfection in smaller or medium-size networks, it was difficult to expand beyond the borders of a settled network-based trading system, which had been working for so many generations with great success.

Additionally, the Hanseatic capital market was underdeveloped, according to the standards of the time. This again was a result of networking because the normal reciprocal trade through networks had allowed Hanseatic businesses to remain small and to operate with little capital. Networks became a safety net; something to make merchants independent of the high interest rates that were usually paid in the Baltic. Yet, this protective function of networks prevented Hanseatic merchants from engaging in ventures that would have needed risk capital. It also prevented the capital market from developing into a powerful financial institution by which the merchants could have been provided with this risk capital.[76] The Hanse's inability to expand and its decreasing competitiveness at the turn of the fifteenth century were, in part, triggered by a trading system that predominantly relied on networks.

---

74 Ulf Christian Ewert and Stephan Selzer, "Netzwerkorganisation im Fernhandel des Mittelalters: Wettbewerbsvorteil oder Wachstumshemmnis?," in Hartmut Berghoff and Jörg Sydow, eds., *Unternehmerische Netzwerke: Eine historische Organisationsform mit Zukunft?* (Stuttgart: Kohlhammer, 2007), 45–70.

75 Gerhard Fouquet, "Ein Italiener in Lübeck: Der Florentiner Gherardo Bueri (gest. 1449)," *Zeitschrift des Vereins für Lübeckische Geschichte und Altertumskunde* 78 (1998), 187–220.

76 For more detail, see Mark Schonewille, *Hanse Theutonicorum* (Groningen, 1997); Id., "Risk, Institutions and Trade: New Approaches to Hanse History," (Working Paper, Nijmwegen, 1998).

Conclusion

This chapter has been dedicated to the description of Hanseatic networks and the economic function of these social configurations. Unfortunately, the number and quality of Hanseatic sources do not allow an application of more sophisticated methods of social network analysis. The sociological concept of network nevertheless helps identify clusters of persons and types of relationships. It has also been shown that kinship networks have evolved through eastern bound migration, whereas friendship networks have developed from a common economic interest. Interurban connections of family members, wills, membership in societies, and the social topography of Hanseatic towns are points of departure for reconstructing the social networks. It turns out that commercial exchange networks and social networks overlapped to a great extent. This result is significant because it proves that the Hanseatic trading system relied mainly on a network pattern. Therefore, social networks should not be viewed as a sociological phenomenon only, but also as an essential component to make the typical Hanseatic system based on reciprocal trade relationships work.

CHAPTER 6

The Baltic Trade

Carsten Jahnke

The Baltic Trade: A General Introduction

From the beginning of the League, the trade along the coasts of the Baltic Sea was the backbone of all sea-going Hanseatic activities. Products from the regions on the farthest east of the Baltic Sea were of such high interest that from Roman times onwards merchants accepted the risks of a long and troublesome journey to sell western and to buy eastern products at both ends of the Baltic. The German merchants who came to the Baltic in the eleventh century and who would become the later Hanse did not create a new trade route; they intensified and developed the old and well-rehearsed northern axis of European trade. (See Chapter 1).

The Hanseatic trade in the Baltic was not static: in the course of time some towns developed a greater importance for trade than others, as some trading goods changed their importance and appeared or disappeared from the international stock lists. The trade and trade system of the Baltic were in a constant flux, but the east coast of the Baltic Sea was the most important economic center of this area throughout the period. Wax and fur were two of the most important trading goods from the eleventh to the sixteenth centuries.

The Baltic Sea trade was not only of interest because of wax, fur and other trading goods, but also because this sea was one of the most important commercial connectors in northern Europe. From the tenth century onwards, the Baltic Sea constituted one of the most important trade routes, connecting not only the individual shores of the Baltic, but also tying the Russian, Polish, Hungarian and middle German production centers to international trade-routes via river and overland transport. Therefore, the Baltic was not predominantly a production center of European scope, but first and foremost one of the most important European zones of contact and trade.[1]

1 Carsten Jahnke, "Der Ostseeraum und seine Produktion bis 1400." In *Der Ostseeraum bis 1400*, ed. Thomas Riis (Tönning: Der andere Verlag forthcoming); Henryk Samsonowicz, "Les foires en Pologne au XVe et XVIe siecle sur la toile de fond de la situation économique en Europe." In *Der Außenhandel Ostmitteleuropas, 1450–1650. Die ostmitteleuropäischen Volkswirtschaften in ihren Beziehungen zu Mitteleuropa*, ed. Ingomar Bog (Cologne, Vienna: Böhlau, 1971),

 | DOI 10.1163/9789004284760_008

The Main Trade Routes

The connecting function constituted the basic element of the Baltic trade system. Traffic from the east to the west of the Baltic Sea was the major task of the Hanseatic trade in this area. Merchants brought their goods inland to the great entrepôts, mainly at the eastern and southern coasts, where they were consolidated into larger cargoes and then shipped to the west.

The Hanseatic merchants preferred two main westward routes. The first, from the middle of the thirteenth[2] up until the fifteenth century, was the route via Lübeck and Hamburg. This route was the most secure but also one of the most expensive routes in and out of the Baltic Sea. In this case, goods were shipped to the harbor of Lübeck, repacked to carts, brought onto Hamburg by land, or from 1398 by smaller boats with a voyage of about 97 km on the Stecknitz channel to the river Elbe and to Hamburg harbor, from where they were send to their final destinations in the west. This route was very secure because Lübeck and Hamburg controlled both routes and provided for the security of the merchants. But it was so expensive to load and unload three times on the way to the west that mainly luxury goods and only a few bulk goods were sent by this route.

The other route was the only sea route to the Baltic, the waterway around the Skaw (Cape Skagen), the so-called "*ummelandfart*," which was used for transport from the beginning of the thirteenth century also. This route was two hundred kilometers longer but cheaper and more practical, particularly because it could accommodate the bigger ships with higher tonnage that were developed in the beginning and the middle of the thirteenth century. But the seaway west of the Skaw was one of the most dangerous in Europe until the end of the nineteenth century and remained one of the greatest graveyards for ships until modern times. Therefore, in the beginning this route was only used for bulk cargos and developed later into a full-fledged—albeit very perilous—alternative to the Lübeck route. This seaway was first mainly used as a connection between the Scanian markets and the west,[3] but from the end of the fourteenth century, it was used as a connection between the Dutch and the

---

246–259; Antoni Mączak and Henryk Samsonowicz, "La zone Baltique: L'un des éléments du marché Européen." *Acta Poloniae Historica* 11 (1965): 71–99.

2 Carsten Jahnke, "Handelsstrukturen im Ostseeraum im 12. und beginnenden 13. Jahrhundert. Ansätze einer Neubewertung", in: *Hansische Geschichtsblätter* 126 (2008): 145–185.

3 Carsten Jahnke, *Das Silber des Meeres. Fang und Vertrieb von Ostseehering zwischen Norwegen und Italien (12.–16. Jahrhundert)* (Cologne: Böhlau, 2000), 69ff.

Prussian and Livonian cities and, by beginning of the sixteenth century, grew into the main route in and out of the Baltic.[4]

The way to the Skaw led from the Baltic through the Sound as the main seaway, where the Danish kings levied a custom beginning in 1429,[5] or through the Danish Belts, where the kings of Denmark also tried to levy a similar custom from all passing ships. So the kingdom of Denmark gained a key position in the political and economic considerations of the Hanseatic League, because it was very easy for the Danish kings to close the Sound and the Belts and thereby strangle Hanseatic trade, even though the royal exchequer got most of its income from the custom at the Sound.

But international trade to and from the Baltic was only one side of the coin. On the other side were regional and sub-regional business areas along the Baltic Sea. Because of the Baltic's geography, the line between Scania and Pomerania ran between the Jutish-Danish-Wendian and the Prussian-Swedish trade-area, while the Gulf of Bothnia together with the Gulf of Finland and Estonia comprised another area. These different areas had their own trade centers and rhythms as well as their particular products. Certainly these areas were not strictly separated from each other, but instead often overlapped as they took part together in supplying the international trade and worked as sub-distribution centers for imported goods.

All in all, these areas acted as well-rehearsed components of the great northern European and Hanseatic trade: The hinterland supplied the regional sub-centers with commercial goods, where they were then sent to the closest center and then to the great entrepôts. In this system, the goods were bundled into larger and larger units until they could be formed into international cargoes in the big sea harbors. On the other way around the large cargoes were broken up on their way from the entrepôt to customers in the hinterlands. The result was that international trade and the regional trade areas of the Baltic were merged together seamlessly.

---

4 Carsten Jahnke, Netzwerke in Handel und Kommunikation an der Wende vom 15. zum 16. Jahrhundert am Beispiel zweier Revaler Kaufleute (Unprinted Habilitation: University of Kiel, 2004).

5 Kai Hørby, "Øresundtolden og den Skånske Skibstold." In *Middelalderstudier, Tilegnede Aksel E. Christensen på Tresårsdagen, 11. September 1966*, (Copenhagen: Munksgård, 1966), 245–272.

The Main Trade Centers

In the course of time some places on the Baltic developed into important trading-centers at the cost of other, mostly older places from the Viking age. One might say *cum grano salis* that since the end of the twelfth century one type of trading place was the most successful: the harbor-town with German municipal law and a central market with main church and guildhall. This kind of town—which in the older tradition wrongly was called "*Gründungsstadt*"—was the future model of all Baltic town constructions. The most important "new" towns were not established in the open countryside, but based on older and well-known trading centers. The first example of this kind of town was Lübeck, an older Slavonian settlement which was granted German rights in 1158/59, and shortly thereafter Slesvig, which was remodeled at the end of the century. (See Chapter 1 in this volume). Emanating from Lübeck, this type of town law and construction spread to the whole Baltic area, mostly to the south and east coast, but also to the north. The number of these "new" cities increased to 204 in the thirteenth century from 38 cities before 1200.[6] Beginning with Riga in 1201, the deltas of the most important rivers developed into trading centers as did the endpoints of the main inland roads at the most important bays and fjords. A tightly woven network of merchant towns had thus developed by the middle of the thirteenth century around the Baltic: Reval (Tallinn) since 1230, Pernau (Pernü) 1251, Dorpat (Tartu) after 1224, Altstadt Königsberg (Kaliningrad) 1255, Danzig (Gdańsk) 1238, Thorn (Toruń) 1231, Elbing (Elbląg) 1241, Stettin (Szczecin) 1237, Greifswald 1241, Demmin around 1231, Rostock 1218, Wismar 1228, Kiel between 1232 and 1242, Flensburg latest 1284, Næstved at the end of the twelfth century, Køge 1288, Copenhagen 1254 and Stockholm around 1250 were only some of the many new modeled towns that opened their gates for an extended trade.[7]

The remodeling of the old trading centers went along with a change in the religious, social and ethnological structure of the whole area. Parallel to the movement of merchants, German farmers also moved east, in the German tradition called "*Ostkolonisation*," changing the methods of agricultural

6 Konrad Fritze, "Zur Entwicklung des Städtewesens im Ostseeraum vom 12. bis zum 15. Jahrhundert." In *Der Ost- und Nordseeraum. Politik—Ideologie—Kultur vom 12. bis zum 15. Jahrhundert*, ed. K. Fritze, E. Müller-Mertens and J. Schildhauer (Weimar: Böhlau, 1986), 9–18.

7 Philippe Dollinger, *Die Hanse*, (Stuttgart: Körner, 1989), 49–52; Thomas Riis, "Die Urbaninisierung Dänemarks im 12. und 13. Jahrhundert." In *Die Stadt im westlichen Ostseeraum. Vorträge zur Stadtgründung und Stadterweiterung im Hohen Mittelalter, 1*, ed. Erich Hoffmann and Frank Lubowitz (Frankfurt a.M.: Lang, 1995), 195–213, Kieler Werkstücke, A, 14.

cultivation and beginning to produce more and more saleable surpluses in a wide hinterland of the southern Baltic region. This movement was supported by the Teutonic Order, which came to Prussia in 1226/1230. The Teutonic Order not only "founded" new cities, beginning with Kulm (Chełmno) in 1230, and settled German farmers in its newly conquered lands, but also collected surpluses to exchange for western luxury goods, so it is evident that the Order had a genuine interest in international trade. Another equalizing factor was the Christianization of the whole area, beginning in Holstein and Scandinavia around 850 and slowly spreading eastwards until Lithuania was Christianized in 1385/86.

Hanseatic trade operated as a stabilizing factor in the development of German colonization, because of the constant inflow of western culture and goods and the fact that the Hanseatic language, Lower German, became the lingua franca of this area.

The trading system which the Hanse established around 1250 was not static and can be divided into several major phases. In the first phase, from ca. 1200/1250 until 1370, the western Hanseatic towns, and most importantly Lübeck, dominated trade in and out of the Baltic. The route between Lübeck and Hamburg was for the Hanseatic merchants the eye of the needle. Most goods had to pass through there, so became Lübeck the key of the Baltic trade. But after the peace of Stralsund and the installation of a Hanseatic government at the Scanian markets, the system changed. The Prussian and Dutch cities developed their own overlapping interests by excluding Lübeck more and more from their trade, slowly in the fifteenth century and with increasing intensity in the sixteenth century. Lübeck did not lose its importance for the Baltic trade, but the city of Danzig became more important and wealthier than its old sister at the Trave.[8] From the beginning of the sixteenth century, Baltic trade was more affected by the trade between Danzig and Amsterdam than by the old route between Lübeck and Hamburg, even though this route did not lose its importance entirely until modern times.[9]

---

8 Jahnke, Netzwerke, *passim*. Rolf Hammel-Kiesow, "Vom Koggen zum RoRo-verkehr. Die Lübecker Handelsflotte vom Mittelalter bis zum Ende des 20. Jahrhunderts." In *Seefahrt, Schiff und Schifferbrüder. 600 Jahre Schiffergesellschaft zu Lübeck, 1401–2001*, ed. R. Hammel-Kiesow (Lübeck: Schiffergesellschaft, 2001), 83–90; Pierre Jeannin, "Les relations économiques des villes de la Baltique avec Anvers au XVIe siècle, I." In *Vierteljahrsschrift für Sozial- und Wirtschaftsgeschichte* 43 (1956), 193–217, here 193–202.

9 Johannes Schildhauer, "Zur Verlagerung des See- und Handelsverkehrs im nordeuropäischen Raum während des 15. und 16. Jahrhunderts, Eine Untersuchung auf der Grundlage der Danziger Pfahlkammerbücher." In *Jahrbuch für Wirtschaftsgeschichte* IV (1968), 187–211; A. Mączak and H. Samsonowicz, "La zone Baltique," 75–85, with similar phases.

In summary, one can say that these developments in the thirteenth century were the crucial point for the economic future of the Baltic. During this century the economic structure was built up; a structure that lasted until the nineteenth century and the Hanseatic League was one of the main factors that strengthened the new circumstances. As a result, the center of gravity within this structure changed to the south east with Danzig as the new leading city from the west and Lübeck.

The Cities and Their Hinterland Connections

One of the main characteristics of the Baltic merchant cities is that they mainly—as opposed to those in Flanders or in the Netherlands—did not produce for the international market. This does not mean that they were without their own "industries," but their commercial activities were primarily based on intermediate trade and not on the sale of "domestic" products. This means that every important town in the Baltic had its own and very specific hinterland.[10] Reval, Dorpat and Riga were the great ports to Russia, especially to the Hanseatic *kontors* of Novgorod, Pleskau/Polosk and Smolensk. Reval was also in a broader sense connected by the Neva River to the Volga and by this to the Black, White, and Caspian Seas and the Sea of Azov. Riga had via the Daugava and Kasplja Rivers a connection to the Dniepr and thence to an enormous hinterland.[11]

Königsberg connected the international trade with Kaunas. Danzig and Thorn connected to the Vistula River and looked out on a trading area from Lviv to Craków and Breslau (Wrocław), and included the Polesia, which was the most important wood producing area in Europe, and the Hungarian mining areas.[12] At the same time, Danzig also had interests at the Nemen River, where merchants from this town founded a filial in Kaunas and later in Vilnius, where Danzig had a connection to the Russian market in Polotsk.[13]

10 Carsten Jahnke, "Der Ostseeraum," forthcoming, chapt. I and III.

11 Norbert Angermann, "Die Bedeutung Livlands für die Hanse." In *Die Hanse und der Deutsche Osten*, ed. Norbert Angermann (Lüneburg: Nordostdeutsches Kulturwerk, 1990), 97–115, here 103.

12 See in general Jan Rutkowski, *Histoire économique de la Pologne avant les Partages* (Paris: Libraire ancienne Honoré Champion, 1927), 53–72.

13 Artur Attman, Den Ryska Marknaden i 1500-talets Baltiska politik 1559–1595 (Lund: Lindstedt, 1944), 41f; Theodor Hirsch, Danzigs Handels- und Gewerbegeschichte unter der Herrschaft des Deutschen Ordens (Leipzig: S. Hirzel, 1858), 164ff.

Stettin, which was situated at the Oder River, was the entrepôt to Silesia, Saxony and Brandenburg, and the surrounding areas. The hinterland of Greifswald, Stralsund, Rostock and Wismar was much smaller, including Pomerania, the Brandenburg Mark, the Altmark and the mining areas at the Harz. The same small hinterland had the towns in Holstein, Schleswig and Denmark/Scania, whereas Stockholm and Söderköping where the main ports of disembarkation for Swedish iron and copper.

The city of Lübeck possessed an extraordinary role in the whole system.[14] Conceived as a Baltic Sea harbor for Westphalian merchants, this city at the river Trave grew after 1188 into a key position in the Baltic trade when the city of Hamburg expended to the River Elbe and thus became Lübeck's "western port"[15] (see chapter 1 in this volume). The Lübeckian/Hamburger hinterland extended from the Brandenburg Mark and Altmark south to Frankfurt, Westphalia and Lower Saxony, but the major task of this town and its merchants was the transfer of goods from the Baltic to the North Sea and not to expand the market for its own products.

Products from the Baltic General Region

The starting point of this development was the fact that the nearer Baltic area, in the geographical sense of the word, was only able to offer a few goods of interest to Western Europe. The oldest of these goods was certainly amber, known and used throughout the whole European world since Roman times.[16] Since the end of the eleventh century, and increasingly in the Hanseatic period, western Baltic herring was the next important trading good to central European people, as was iron and copper from the big Swedish mines in Falun and Norraskog. The export of grain from Prussia and Livonia is a phenomenon of the late fifteenth

14 Carsten Jahnke, "Der Aufstieg Lübecks und die Neuordnung des südlichen Ostseeraumes im 13. Jahrhundert," in Roman Czaja and Carsten Jahnke, eds., *Städtelandschaften im Ostseeraum im Mittelalter und in der Frühen Neuzeit*, Towarzystwo Naukowe w Toruniu, Wyd. 1. Ark. wyd. 12, (Torun: Towarzystwo Naukowe w Toruniu 2009), 29–72.

15 Carsten Jahnke, "... und er verwandelte die blühende Handelsstadt in ein unbedeutendes Dorf," "Die Rolle Schleswigs im internationalen Handel des 13. Jahrhunderts." In *Von Menschen, Ländern Meeren, Festschrift für Thomas Riis zum 65. Geburtstag*, ed. Gerhard Fouquet et al. (Tönning: Der andere Verlag, 2006), 251–268; C. Jahnke, *Handelsstrukturen*.

16 Audronė Bliujienė, *The Northern Gold. Amber in Lithuania* (*c. 100 to c. 1200*), (Leiden: Brill, 2011).

and early sixteenth centuries, but grain export from the whole Baltic area was known from the thirteenth century onwards. More important than the export of grain was the export of beer. Contrary to the accepted older opinion, Hamburg was not the center of Hanseatic beer production. The so-called Wendian quarter, with the cities of Lübeck, Wismar and Rostock, held that honor. The western Baltic was the focal point of the Hanseatic beer production and connected with a large area of wheat and hops cultivation.

Imports via the Baltic

But the Baltic was not known primarily because of its amber, herring and beer, but of other items of trade. These goods—even if they were called Baltic goods—were not produced in the Baltic geographical area, but in a zone we can call the Baltic economic zone. This area spans the whole western part of Russia and Ukraine, the Polesia, Hungary with its Slovakian parts, and had connection to Asia, Arabia and in some parts to southern Europe also.

The most recognizable and important trading good of the Baltic was definitely fur, mainly fine fur from Russian suppliers. The same is true for wax and to a lesser extent for honey. Next to these was wood and wood-products from Poland and Polesia, which were increasingly important for the European market, especially for the developing English and Dutch fleets. These products were exported mainly via Thorn and later Danzig and maintained their importance until the end of the nineteenth century. But Hanse merchants did not only identify each of these cities as "house of wood" (*Holzhaus*), but also the "house of metal" (*Kupferhaus*). The Hungarian-Slovakian copper, iron and silver mines lay on the north side of the Carpathian Mountains and the best export route was via the Vistula River and north to the Baltic Sea. With this route, Hungary became a part of the Baltic economic zone.

In addition to the primary Baltic trade goods of fur, wax, copper and iron, merchants dealt in luxury goods like spices and silk. Until 1400, these goods were imported from Asia and Arabia via Lviv and Thorn and were a complement to imports via Venice and Bruges. These main products together with many others, made the Baltic one of the most important European economic zones from the eleventh century onwards. The main purpose of the Hanseatic League was to serve as agents for these goods between the producers in the east and the consumers in the west and to exchange these products with western cloth and other luxury articles.

The Intra-Baltic Trade

The Baltic was certainly not only the main route for international trade between Bruges and Reval/Danzig. Baltic trade was also made up of many other trading activities, both big and small, within this area. This Intra-Baltic trade had many components. Some were of supra-regional relevance, like the trade in salt, Baltic cloth, hops, stone products or Baltic wine. Others had only regional relevance, like that of Estonian gloves or Swedish salmon. All these activities together distinguished Hanseatic trade and it is its multiplicity that was the primary hallmark of this trade. The Hanseatic merchant was not a monolithic wholesaler, but a multitasking all-rounder with many connections and interests. He was acting on the international level as well as on the supra-regional level and the regional level from many places at the same time.

The Organization of Baltic Trade

One of the biggest problems of the Baltic trade was the long distances between its trading centers and the seasonal problems of shipping and communication. It took between four weeks, depending on the weather conditions, and, during the winter, up to three or four months to get from Reval to Lübeck, so it was not possible to communicate rapidly with factors at other places. To resolve this problem, the Hanseatic merchants in the Baltic developed their own system of trade. Instead of organizing their companies after the Italian example, with strong headquarters and dependant subalterns at other markets, the Baltic merchants pinned their hope on decentralization. The Hanseatic companies operating in the Baltic were designed by a consortium of independent merchants, which dealt with their own goods in the same manner as they did with the goods of their partners (see the chapter by Christian Selzer and Ulf Ewert). As a result, the distance between the different places did not matter, because every merchant knew that his partner would act as carefully and responsibly as he did—and without any additional charges. This system was extremely inexpensive and reliable and tailor-made for the conditions around the Baltic Sea, but there was one downside: because of the absence of a general headquarters, Hanseatic merchants were not able to calculate their earnings and losses continuously. Rather, merchants had to wait until all trading activities with all partners in the particular company were completed.

As a result of this system, Baltic merchants were individually rich, but experienced poor cash flow over long stretches of time and therefore made no investments in productive industries. This aggravated the tendency for the Baltic area to be more a contact zone than a zone of productivity, even if the earnings of Hanseatic merchants were at least as high as those of their Italian or South German counterparts.[17]

Research on the Baltic Trade: Mainstreams, Controversies, Problems and New Directions

The history of the Baltic trade has been a focus of interest since the nineteenth century. But the historical circumstances and the different fashions in historiographies created some special points of view and many problems that still appear today.

The beginning of historical research into the Baltic trade had its origin in the national-romantic movement in Northern Europe. The return to national histories and the growing interest in archives and historical monuments established the basis for our current knowledge. Many of the main collections of sources ("*Urkundenbücher*") were found in this period, like the Lübeckische Urkundenbuch in 1843, the Mecklenburgische Urkundenbuch in 1863, the Preußische Urkundenbuch in 1882, the Liv-, Esth- und Kurländische Urkundenbuch in 1853 or the Danske Magazin in 1745/1843. At the same time the first standard opera dedicated to the history of trade in the Baltic, like Theodor Hirschs "Handels- und Gewerbegeschichte Danzigs unter der Herrschaft des Deutschen Ordens" from 1858[18] or Dietrich Schäfers "Die Hansestädte und König Waldemar von Dänemark" from 1876,[19] emerged. After the German wars of 1864 and 1870/71 historical research came under the strong influence of nationalistic tendencies and political propaganda. The history of the Hanse, and primarily the "pride history" of Lübeck and Danzig, provided the justification for the new German armament at sea: The proud German merchant, overruling all competition from north, east and west was the historical archetype for the new generation of Germans and the new German position in the nationalistic world.[20]

---

17 Carsten Jahnke, Geld, Geschäfte, Informationen. Der Aufbau hansischer Handelsgesellschaften und ihre Verdienstmöglichkeiten, Handel, Geld und Politik, vol. 10 (Lübeck: Schmidt Römhild, 2007); Carsten Jahnke, Netzwerke in Handel und Kommunikation.

18 Th. Hirsch, "Handels- und Gewerbegeschichte."

19 Dietrich Schäfer, Die Hansestädte und König Waldemar von Dänemark (Jena, 1879).

20 Thomas Hill, "Vom öffentlichen Gebrauch der Hansegeschichte und Hanseforschung im 19. und 20. Jahrhundert." In *Ausklang und Nachklang der Hanse*, ed. Antjekathrin Graßmann, Hansische Studien, XII (Trier: Porta Alba, 2001), 67–88.

In that climate and under that condition most of the important works on the Baltic trade emerged. Around 1900, Dietrich Schäfer led one of the most important scientific schools in the field of Hanse studies. His books "Die deutsche Hanse"[21] and "Das Buch des lübeckischen Vogts auf Schonen"[22] set the pattern for future generations. This scientific tradition and the idea of German and Hanseatic dominance continued until 1945. All leading works like Goetz' "Deutsch-russische Handelsgeschichte"[23] or of E.R. Daenell, F. Rörig and A.V. Brandt and their schools, who were very productive in the 1930s and later on, stood more or less on Schäfer's shoulders. The predominant interpretation was formulated by Fritz Rörig in 1932 and reprinted in 1955:

> The deeper sense of the development of the urban landscape in the Baltic Sea Area [was given by the Hanseatic League.] The whole existed earlier than the parts. The development of the proud Hanseatic cities in the Baltic Sea Area [...] was not a whim of fate, but was the consequence of a willful economic program: the economic dominance of the Baltic Sea by German merchants.[24]

This concept contained no space for alternate interpretations and certainly also no space to correspond and hold discussions with foreign colleagues from equally proud nations. Therefore, German researchers of the 1950s engaged in a feud with their colleagues from Denmark, such as Aksel E. Christensen, or Sweden, in the case of Erik Lönnroth, which meant that there could not be fruitful dialogue for a long time.[25] Aksel E. Christensen's attempt to create a new definition of the Baltic trade,[26] for example, had no impact in Hanse research of the next few decades.

Another problem from the 1950s up to the 1990s was the outcome of the Second World War. Some important archives, like the Lubeckian, were spread

---

21 Dietrich Schäfer, *Die Deutsche Hanse* (Bielefeld, 1903).

22 Dietrich Schäfer, *Das Buch des lübeckischen Vogts auf Schonen*, Hansische Geschichtsquellen, N.F. Vol. IV (Lübeck²: Hansischer Geschichtsverein, 1927).

23 Leopold Goetz, Deutsch-russische Handelsgeschichte des Mittelalters (Lübeck: Waelde, 1922).

24 Fritz Rörig, *Die europäische Stadt und die Kultur des Bürgertums im Mittelalter*, ed. Louise Rörig (Göttingen: Vandenhoek & Ruprecht, 1955), 19f.

25 Lennart Bohman, "Hanseväldet ur nordisk synvinkel." *Gotländskt arkiv* XXX (1958), 39–52.

26 Aksel E. Christensen, "La Foire de Scanie." In: *Danmark, Norden og Østersøen, Udvalgte Afhandlinger* (Copenhagen: Dansk historisk forening, 1976), 98–117.

over the GDR and the Soviet Union, and others lay suddenly behind the other side of the iron curtain like the one in Gdańsk or Reval/Tallinn (at that time in Göttingen/Germany), while yet others were disputed between states, like that of Stettin, or destroyed, like that of Wismar. Opportunities for research were greatly reduced during this time, and communication between colleagues was affected by ideological and political conditions and the ideologization of historical events (for example, whether the city of Danzig/Gdańsk had belonged to the German or Polish nationality), or the different valuation of the bourgeoisie.

It is apparent that research on Baltic trade was regionalized in the decades between the Second World War and the fall of the iron curtain.[27] There was no common discourse about this in the Baltic, and the dogma of the German/Hanseatic monopoly in trade dominated the research unquestioned and still encumbers the discussion today.

After the fall of the iron curtain, the situation of the archives improved, especially in towns such as Lübeck. A new generation of researchers started to examine some of the old items again. In 1997 Dieter Seifert picked up the relationship between the Hanse and the Netherlands,[28] in 1995/1998 it followed the colloquium of the 625th anniversary of the peace of Stralsund,[29] in 1999 Detlef Kattinger published his analysis about the German merchants of Gotland,[30] 2000 saw the publication of Carsten Jahnke's book about the Scanian markets,[31] 2002 Milja van Tielhof's substantial work about the Baltic

27 One of the few exceptions are Walter Starks book *Lübeck und Danzig in der zweiten Hälfte des 15. Jahrhunderts. Untersuchungen zum Verhältnis der wendischen und preußischen Hansestädte in der Zeit des Niedergangs der Hanse*, Abhandlungen zur Wirtschafts- und Sozialgeschichte, XI (Weimar: Böhlau, 1973).

28 Dieter Seifert, *Kompagnions und Konkurrenten. Holland und die Hanse im späten*, Quellen und Darstellungen zur hansischen Geschichte, N.F., Vol. 43 (Cologne: Böhlau, 1997).

29 Nils Jörn, Ralf-Gunnar Werlich, Horst Wernike eds., *Der Stralsunder Frieden von 1370*, Quellen und Darstellungen zur hansischen Geschichte, N.F., Vol. 46 (Cologne: Böhlau, 1998).

30 Detlef Kattinger, *Die gotländische Genossenschaft. Der frühhansisch-gotländische Handel in Nord- und Westeuropa*, Quellen und Darstellungen zur hansischen Geschichte, N.F., Vol. 48 (Cologne: Böhlau, 1999).

31 Carsten Jahnke, *Das Silber des Meeres. Fang und Vertrieb von Ostseehering zwischen Norwegen und Italien (12.–16. Jh.)*, Quellen und Darstellungen zur hansischen Geschichte, N.F., Vol. 49 (Cologne: Böhlau, 2000).

grain trade,[32] and 2005 Wolfgang Frontzek's groundbreaking analysis of the Wendian beer-production.[33]

Therefore, it can be stated that the research of the Baltic trade is presently in its infancy, and until now, a common overview and international discussion has been missing. In 1996 the "Ständige Konferenz der Historiker des Ostseeraumes" was founded, in 2005 the "International Commission for the History of the Baltic Sea Region" and in 2006 the first conference on the "Baltic until 1400" took place at Kiel University, but its minutes were not released until now.[34] This conference underlined the fact, that the research of the medieval Hanseatic trade in the Baltic faces more and bigger problems than before. The regionalization in the Baltic and the current lack of a common scientific language in this area makes it nearly impossible to analyze the whole situation without the help of international projects and members from different areas and who speak different languages.

Beyond this, there are many problems with regard to medieval Baltic trade. We are still missing an analysis of the interaction between international and regional trade in general, for example in the trade with wood, cloth or other regional products. In most cases regional research is either missing or is outdated as in Danzig, where Hirsch's work from 1858 is still unsurpassed. The terminology of trade in the Baltic is still understudied, as is the history of money and rates of exchange.[35]

Another problem is the dominance of German sources in the research. As long as we are unable to find adequate non-German sources about the trade in the Baltic, our picture will be fragmentary. We have to challenge the alleged Hanseatic monopoly of trade, otherwise we will fall back to the nationalistic point of view. Had Hanseatic merchants no companions in Denmark or other places? Certainly not, as the example of the Malmogian merchant Ditliv Enbecke from the sixteenth century shows.[36] But these connections over the Hanseatic borders have not been analyzed until very recently.

---

32 Milja van Tielhof, The mother of all trades: the Baltic grain trade in Amsterdam from the late sixteenth to the early nineteenth century, The Northern World, vol. 3 (Leiden: Brill, 2002).

33 Wolfgang Frontzek, *Das städtische Braugewerbe und seine Bauten vom Mittelalter bis zur frühen Neuzeit*, Häuser und Höfe in Lübeck, vol. 7 (Neumünster: Wachholtz, 2005).

34 Thomas Riis ed., *Der Ostseeraum bis 1400*, forthcoming.

35 See the first attempt by Carsten Jahnke, *Wechselkurse und Gewichtsrelationen im hansischen Wirtschaftsraum bis 1600*, http://www.histosem.uni-kiel.de/lehrstuehle/land/waehrung/Katalog.html, September 12 2007.

36 Emilie Andersen, Malmøkøbmanden Ditlev Enbeck og hans regnskabsbog: Et bidrag til Danmarks handelshistorie i det 16. århundrede (Copenhagen: Munksgård, 1954).

Furthermore the research on Baltic trade is mostly concentrated on the Lubeckian point of view. This is understandable with regard to the exceptional situation in the archives of Lübeck during the post-war years, but this distorts the picture. There are, beside the groundbreaking doctoral dissertation from Angela Huang from 2013,[37] for example missing analyses of the inland trade routes of the Baltic and their connection to and interaction with the international trade;[38] and the same can be said of the relationship of inland-towns to the international trade at and along the Baltic. We know that the city of Breslau in Silesia was connected to the west by its trade via the Oder and the Baltic Sea,[39] but what about Kraków, Lviv, Leipzig or Berlin? This and many other questions remain unanswered.

In summary, one can say that modern research about the Hanseatic trade in the Baltic is in its fledgling stages. Since 1989, new sources of information have arrived which are now stimulating new research.

Products of the Hanseatic Trade in the Baltic

Amber

One of the oldest Baltic products with international fame is amber, which was mentioned in the Epic of Gilgamesh and the Old Testament,[40] as well as the writings of Dionysius Halicarnassus and Tacitus, who reported the export of

37 Angela Huang, *Die Textilien des Hanseraums. Produktion und Distribution einer spätmittelalterlichen Fernhandelsware* (Copenhagen: University of Copenhagen, Faculty of Humanities 2013).

38 See the first attemps of Gerhard Theuerkauf, "Binnen- und Seehandel zur Hansezeit am mecklenburgischen Beispiel." in *Zwischen Lübeck und Novgorod. Wirtschaft, Politik und Kultur im Ostseeraum vom frühen Mittelalter bis ins 20. Jahrhundert*, Norbert Angermann zum 60. Geburtstag, ed. Ortwin Pelc and Gertrud Pickhan (Lüneburg: Inst. Nordostdt. Kulturwerk, 1996), 179–189.

39 Krzysztof Wachowski and Jacek Wittkowski, "Wrocław wobec Hanzy." *Archaeologia Polski* XLVIII, 1–2, (2003), 201–221; Hugo Weczerka, "Die Südostbeziehungen der Hanse." In *Die Hanse und der deutsche Osten*, ed. Norbert Angermann (Lüneburg: Verlag Nordostdeutsches Kulturwerk, 1990), 117–132.

40 Joan Markley Todd, "Baltic Amber in the ancient Near East: A preliminary investigation," *Journal of Baltic Studies* 16 (1981/1985), 292–301.

amber from the "Svevician Sea", which was part of the later Prussian Sambia, to Rome.[41] This trade continued uninterrupted until medieval times.[42]

In the high Middle Ages the local dukes of Pomerelia monopolized the trade in amber for ducal regalia.[43] This practice continued unchanged when the Teutonic Order occupied Pomerelia between 1240 and 1260. Later in the fourteenth century the possession of raw amber was forbidden to all Prussians. All amber collected by the subjects of Order had to be delivered to the local *Bernsteinmeister* (master of the amber), who had to collect the material and had to send it further to the *Großschäffer* in Königsberg. The *Großschäffer* of the Teutonic Order in Königsberg pulled the strings of the whole amber-trade in the Baltic area and it was his ambition to sell the raw material for the best price possible.[44] The prohibition of the possession of raw amber and the commercial interests of the Order implied that amber was not processed in Prussia, but was exported instead.[45] In the course of time the *Großschäffer* concentrated the trade with amber in three cities: in the east in Lviv,[46] at the Baltic coast in Lübeck and in the west in Bruges,[47] where he bought Flemish cloth and other luxury products.

The trade with Lviv went via Thorn. At this place and in Lviv clerks of the *Großschäffer*, the so called Lieger, sold the raw material to local merchants and those from Armenia, Genoa, Venice, Russia, and Tatars, and bought eastern

---

41 A. Bliujienė, *The Northern Gold.*

42 See for example P. Petrequin, C.W. Beck, J.F. Pningre, P. Hartmann and S.R. de Simone, "L'importation d'ambre Balte: un échantillonnage chronologique de L'est de la France," *Revue Archéologique de L'Est et du Centre-Est* XXXVIII, Fasc. 1–2 (1987), 273–284.

43 Wilhelm Tesdorpf, Gewinnung, Verarbeitung und Handel des Bernsteins in Preußen von der Ordenszeit bis zur Gegenwart. Eine historisch-volkswirtschaftliche Studie, Staatswissenschaftliche Studien, I. Band, 5. Heft, 7. (Jena: Gustav Fischer, 1887).

44 Fritz Renken, *Der Handel der Königsberger Großschäfferei des Deutschen Ordens mit Flandern um 1400*, Abhandlungen zur Handels- und Seegeschichte, Band V (Weimar: Böhlau, 1937), 38.

45 See the source-edition *Schuldbücher und Rechnungen der Großschäffer und Lieger des Deutschen Ordens in Preußen*, especially vols. 1–2. Großschäfferei Königsberg, ed. by Jürgen Sarnowsky, Christina Link and Joachim Laczny (Cologne: Böhlau 2008 and 2013). *Veröffentlichung aus den Archiven Preussischer Kulturbesitz*, vol. 62, 1–2, Quellen und Darstellungen zur Hansischen Geschichte, vol. LIX, 1–2.

46 The amber-trade with Breslau and Liegnitz is not investigated until now. See Jan A. van Houtte, "Ambernijverheid en paternostermakers te Brugge gedurende de XIVe en XVe eeuw." In the same, *Essays on medieval and early modern economy and society*, Symbolæ, facultatis Litterarum et Philosophiæ Lovaniensis, Series A, Vol. 5, 49–80 (Leuven: University Press, 1977), here 53 note 21.

47 Renken, *Handel*, 42ff.

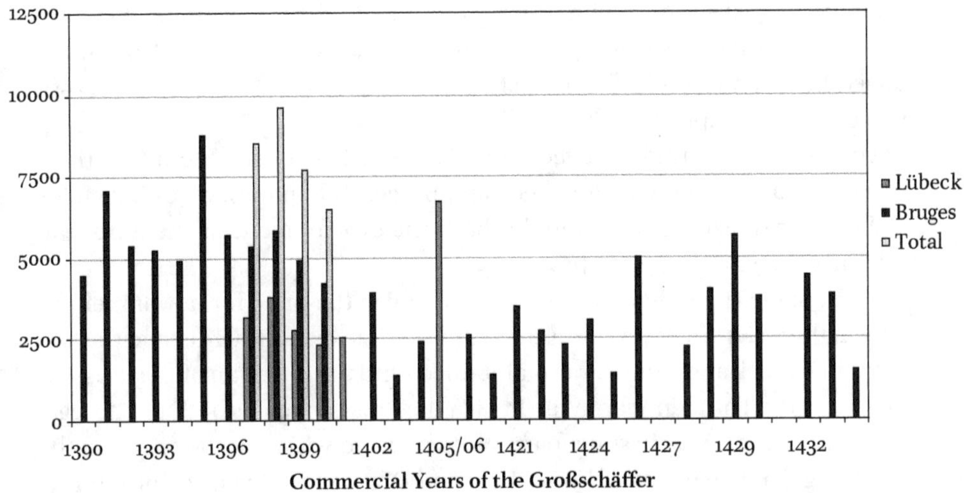

FIGURE 6.1 *Export of Amber to the West.*
F. RENKEN, HANDEL DER KÖNINGSBERGER GROSSSCHÄFFEREI, 54
C. JAHNKE, DER OSTSEERAUM BIS 1400, FORTHCOMING.

and southern goods at the same time.[48] The trade with Lübeck and Bruges was more monopolized. In Lübeck the guild of the *Paternostermaker*, (the makers of rosaries),[49] bought the all imports by contracts with the Order late in the fourteenth century.[50] From Lübeck the amber-rosaries were sold farther to the south, to Venice, Nuremberg or Frankfort. The same system existed in Bruges also, where the local guild of rosary-makers had to produce one quota of rosaries for the Order without any costs.[51] From Bruges the rosaries were delivered to Venice and also to Spain.[52]

Because of the monopoly of the Teutonic Order, we have the ability to determine some figures of the export of amber from Prussia in the period 1397–1405/06 and 1419 to 1434.

It can be seen from this table that the export of amber from the Baltic was not constant at all. Annual fluctuations and differences between the two

48 Renken, *Handel*, 42–45.
49 To the history of rosaries see Jan A. van Houtte, "Ambernijverheid," 49–51.
50 UBStL IV, 657, 743 f. See also the Archives of the Teutonic Order, Geheimes Preußisches Staatsarchiv Berlin, GPStA PK, HA XX, OBA, 1532. See also J. Warncke, "Bernsteinkunst und Paternostermaker in Lübeck." *Nordelbingen* 10 (1934), 428–464.
51 J. van Houtte, "Ambernijverheid," 54–80. F. Renken, *Handel*, 53–61.
52 J. van Houtte, "Ambernijverheid," 57f.

destinations make it nearly impossible to estimate the average-rate of export. In the four years between 1397 and 1400 the total western export of amber ranged between 6.000 and 8.000 m.l., in 1498 the revenue of amber was estimated by 4,400 m.pr. (c. 4.986 m.l.).[53]

Around 1400 the trade between Prussia and Lviv ended.[54] From that time, amber was only exported via Lübeck and Bruges. But in both cities the guilds of the rosary-makers smarted under both the development of the European fashion and some marketing problems.[55]

At the same time the Order tried to maximize the price for raw amber initially in the years after 1410.[56] But the symbiosis between the Order and the two guilds in Lübeck and Bruges was maintained until the rebellion of the Prussian towns and the Thirteen Years' War. In 1454 the Prussian towns became the legal successor of the Order in some parts of Prussia and with that they got also the amber regalia. The towns of Königsberg and Danzig took over the former rule of the Order. Certainly they restricted the trade not only to the export of raw amber, and in 1477 a guild of Bernsteindreher, maker of amber products, was founded in Danzig.[57]

After the wars between the Prussian towns and the Order, and especially after 1525, the duke of Prussia entrusted single merchants or companies with the distribution of amber. In 1495–96 Augsburgian merchants, in the beginning of the sixteenth century Königsberger,[58] and in 1533–1545 three Danzig merchants together with the Antwerp merchant Heinrich von Achelen were all entrusted with this privilege.[59] The proceeds of the sale of amber fluctuated greatly, as can be seen by the following diagram.[60]

Nevertheless, these proceeds made a great part of the income of the Grand Master of the order, from 35.6% of his total budget in 1500 to 57.6% of the

53 Tesdorpf, *Gewinnung*, 11. Conversion rate by Carsten Jahnke, *Wechselkurse und Gewichtsrelationen im hansischen Wirtschaftsraum bis 1600, Sammelkatalog*, http://www.histosem.uni-kiel.de/lehrstuehle/land/waehrung/Kurse.html, September 5th 2007.

54 The reason for this is unknown until now, but see R. Rutkowski, *Histoire économique*, 61f.

55 Between 1398 and 1440 the number of Bernsteindreher in Lübeck sank from 40 to 10. Warncke, "Bernsteinkunst," 431f. The same for Bruges J. van Houtte, "Ambernijverheid," 61.

56 J. van Houtte, "Ambernijverheid," 61.

57 Tesdorpf, *Gewinnung*, 37ff. The guilds in Elbing and Königsberg were founded in 1539 and 1641.

58 Oliver Volckart, "Kartelle und Monopole im Ordensland Preußen zu Beginn des 16. Jahrhunderts: Bernsteinregal und Münze in der Sicht des rent-seeking-Ansatzes." *Vierteljahrsschrift für Sozial- und Wirtschaftsgeschichte* 84/1 (1997), 1–32.

59 Tesdorpf, *Gewinnung*, 13.

60 Exchange rate: 60 m.pr. = 80 m. rig. and 100 mk. rig. = 85 m.l.

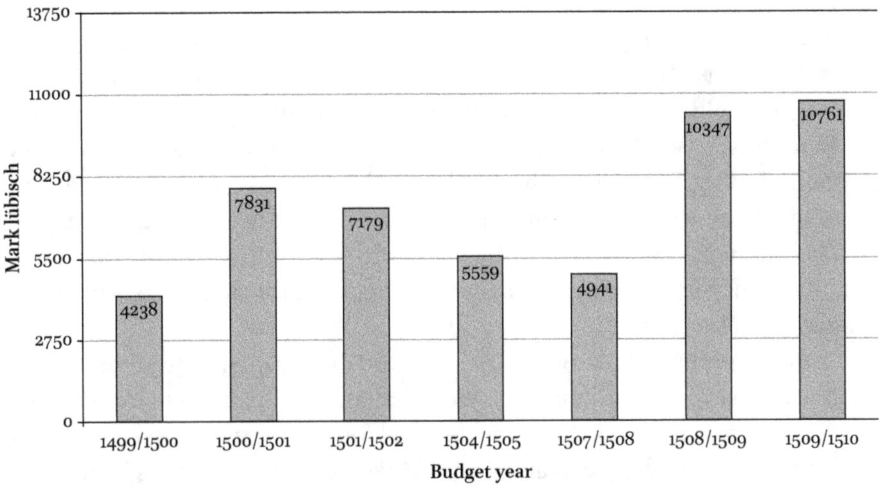

FIGURE 6.2 *Proceeds of the Grand Master of the Teutonic Order in the sale of amber.* FIGURES BY L. DRALLE, DER BERNSTEINHANDEL DES DEUTSCHEN ORDENS, 70.

budget of the year 1501/02.[61] From 1550 on and for the next one hundred years, the family Koehn von Jaskis held nearly a monopoly in the amber-trade among the Prussian dukes, paying for this privilege between 20.000 to 30.000 m.pr. annually to the ducal treasurer.[62] After the Reformation, the sale of amber met a market break. Subsequently, amber was used solely for the creation of luxury items and even then was rivaled by other raw materials.

Baltic Herring

By the year 1000, salt and herring, (*salt eđa síld*), had already become two of the main trading products in the Baltic Sea. In the autumn, farmers from all over Scandinavia assembled at the shores of Scania, the Danish islands, the islands of Bornholm and Rugia, to catch *clupeus harengus*, the herring, for winter stock. The best method to prepare and to conserve this fish is salting, a process known since the Viking age.[63]

---

61 Lothar Dralle, "Der Bernsteinhandel des Deutschen Ordens in Preußen, vornehmlich zu Beginn des 16. Jahrhunderts." *Hansische Geschichsblätter* 99 (1981), 61–72.

62 Tesdopf, *Gewinnung*, 14f.

63 Ingrid Bødker Enghoff, "Denmarks's first fishing industry?" *Maritime Newsletter from Roskilde, Denmark* 6 (May 1996), 2–4; Ingrid Bødker Enghoff "Fishing in the Baltic Regions from the 5th century BC to the sixteenth century AD: Evidence from Fish Bones," *Archaeofauna* 8 (1999), 41–85.

Salted herring gained increased importance throughout Europe with the spread of Christianity. By 1300, the Christian fasting rules claimed 120 to 182 days a year without meat[64] and herring was the ideal substitute because of its durability, ease of sale, and the fact that it was a permissible food under Catholic fasting laws. From the tenth century onwards we have evidence of herring on the cathedral island of Breslau[65] and from 1035 in the cloister of St. Gall in Switzerland.[66] It can be stated from these discoveries that by the middle of the eleventh century, salted herring from the Baltic was widely consumed in Western Europe.

At the beginning of the twelfth century, the Rugian fishing grounds were the main supplier of western markets. Westphalian and Saxonian merchants traveled to that pagan island, driven by demand for herring, even paying tribute to the pagan priest at the local sanctuary of Arkona.[67] After the transformation of the city of Lübeck into a town with German law in 1158/59, the new immigrated Westphalian merchants went to the nearby situated island to buy fish there instead. The new Lubeckian merchants had two crucial advantages: because of the situation of their city they could easily buy and distribute their products, and they also possessed the best connection to the Luneburgian saline, which produced the best salt in the Baltic region.

The Lubeckian merchants focused on concentrating the salt-herring trade in their town and through their efforts they were able to acquire special privileges at the Rugian herring markets.[68] Later, at the end of the twelfth century, Lubeckian merchants went further north, supplying the Scandinavian farmers fishing in the Sound area with salt and other products too.

64 Richard C. Hoffmann, *Fishers' Craft and Lettered Art. Tracts on Fishing from the End of the Middle Ages* (Toronto: University of Toronto Press, 1997), 18; C.M. Woolgar, "Fish production, trade and consumption, c1300/1530, 'Take this Penance now, and afterwards the Fare will improve': Seafood and Late Medieval Diet." In: *England's Sea Fisheries. The commercial Sea Fisheries of England and Wales since 1300*, ed. David J. Starkey, Chris Reid and Neil Ashkroft (London: Chatham Publishing, 2000) 36–44, here 37.

65 Bødker Enghoff, "Fishing in the Baltic," 69.

66 Carsten Jahnke, "Wege und Absatzmärkte im Handel mit Ostseehering, 1100–1600. Kontinuität und Wandel," in *Der Ostseeraum und Kontinentaleuropa, 1100–1600*, ed. Detlef Kattinger, Jens E. Olesen and Horst Wernicke, Culture Clash or Compromise VIII (Schwerin: Thomas Helms Verlag, 2004) 131–136, 132.

67 Carsten Jahnke, Silber des Meeres, 20 f. Carsten Jahnke, "The Medieval Herring Fisheries in the Baltic Sea," in Louis J. Sicking and Darlene Abreu-Ferreira, eds., *The North Atlantic Fisheries in the Middle Ages and early Modern Period. Interdisciplinary approaches in history, archaeology and biology*. The Northern World vol. 41 (Leiden: Brill, 2009), 157–186.

68 Carsten Jahnke, *Silber des Meeres*, 69–75.

At the traditional meeting places of the farmers at Skanör on the peninsula of Falsterbo, at Dragør on the island of Amager, or later Malmö, the early Hanseatic merchants met a big and rich crowd, desirous to buy western goods and to sell herring. The allure of that trade was so great for merchants that in 1201 the entire Lubeckian elite assembled there—which proved to be an easy prey for the Danish king, who successfully brought the town under his rule.

Between 1201 and 1224, Lübeck was part of the Danish empire, and during this period its merchants were able to transfer their Rugian market privileges to the Scanian markets. These early privileges secured four central points: first, the security of merchants and merchandizing in Denmark and on the ways to and from the fairs in the case of jettison or shipwreck, second, stable and calculable customs, third, affording of own jurisdiction to the merchants, including the jurisdiction of their home-town, and fourth, exemption from the rule discouraging any activity to disturb the quietness of Sundays and holydays. (See the chapter of Mike Burkhardt).

But the Scanian Markets were not only herring fairs. They also got their importance from the fact that at the beginning of the thirteenth century, merchants from England, the Low Countries, and other western nations perceived that they could deal with their Baltic partners directly at the markets under very propitious conditions. As a result, the Scanian markets developed into Northern Europe's most important trading fair in the beginning of the thirteenth century. At this place western cloth and luxury goods were traded with fur, wax and eastern products, including top-quality Scanian herring.

Until the end of the thirteenth century, the Scanian markets were so important, that the Lubeckians neglected the Rugian fairs and the sale of any herring other than Scanian herring was forbidden in the Netherlands to control the quality of herring imports. The height of the Scanian markets lasted until 1370, when the Hanseatic regiment at this place disturbed the interchange between west and east.[69] (See the chapter of Jurgen Sarnowsky). After this time, the Wendian merchants tried to expel their competitors from the market. As a result of this political decision, the English and Dutch recovered their old fishing grounds at the Dogger Bank and the triumph of the Dutch *Matjes* began in the fifteenth century.

Because of the diversity of fishing places and commercial partners at the Scanian Fairs we are not able to estimate concrete figures of the herring export from the Baltic. But we can calculate a minimum trade between the Scanian Markets and Lübeck for some years of the fourteenth century:[70]

---

69 Carsten Jahnke, *Silber des Meeres*, 90–103.

70 Carsten Jahnke, *Silber des Meeres*, 421.

TABLE 6.1 *The import of Scanian herring in the harbor of Lübeck in Rostocker Barrel*

Port of Origin	*1384/85*	*1398*	*1399*	*1400*
Malmö		32.636¼	27.289	29.142
Skanör/Falsterbo		26.425	32.243¾	28.340
Dragør		8.082½	10.965½	6.885½
Ystad	5.988	3.354½	9.258¼	3.072
Trelleborg	6.493	732	1.416	2.536
Summa	?	71.230¼	81.199½	69.975½

C. Jahnke, Silber des Meeres, 421

Table 6.1 shows only a small part of the Hanseatic and non-Hanseatic herring trade from the Scanian Markets. From the Sound area this fish was distributed throughout Europe from Novgorod aud Lviv in the east, to Italy and Spain in the south, and England and Scotland in the west. The Scanian herring was by this time one of the main Hanseatic products and remained so until the Atlantic herring surpassed the Scanian variety at the end of the fifteenth century.

Cereals and Hemp

The discovery of the Scanian markets by western merchants opened the gate for a direct trade between the Baltic east and the Western Seas, even if the trade around the Skaw was very dangerous. One of the Baltic products demanded throughout Western Europe was grain. Since the seventeenth century, the trade in grain has held the status of "the mother of all trade". However, it is questionable whether this appellation is also valid for the Middle Ages.[71] It is apparent that in the thirteenth century Baltic grain was exported to the West, for example to England, where the city of London was salvaged from a great famine by Baltic grain in 1258.[72] Also, Norway was another receptor

71 Nils Hybel, "The foreign grain trade in England, 1250–1350." In *Cogs, Cargoes, and Commerce. Maritime Bulk Trade in Northern Europe, 1150–1400*, ed. Lars Berggren, Nils Hybel and Annette Landen, Papers in Medieval Studies, vol. 15 (Toronto: Pontifical Institute, 2002), 212–241.

72 Eleanor Carus-Wilsen, "Die Hanse und England." In *Die Hanse in Europa. Brücke zwischen den Märkten, 12.–17. Jahrhundert, Katalog des kölnischen Stadtmuseums* (Cologne: Stadtmuseum, 1973), 85–106, here 96. See also Rolf Hammel-Kiesow, "Lübeck and the Baltic trade of bulk goods for the North Sea region 1150–1400." In *Cogs, Cargoes and*

of Baltic grain, even if this import did not lead to that country's dependency on Hanseatic merchants.[73] Only 20 to 25 percent of the demand of the whole Norwegian population was satisfied by Hanseatic imports, which as stated earlier is significant but not a monopoly.

Generally, it can be said that until 1400 the entire Baltic region exported grain to the West and the North. Because of its economic system, the Teutonic Order relied solely on exports, but Hansard merchants all over the Baltic also seized the opportunity. After 1402 the picture changed, as Danzig and Thorn grew into the main entrepôts of grain trade in the Baltic as the Western Baltic developed into one of the greatest grain-consumers of the region. The reasons for the rise of Danzig and Thorn are explained by the special agricultural system of Poland, Prussia and the German East. In these regions, great manors produced saleable surpluses, which were exported via the Vistula River.[74] At the same time, the breweries of the Wendian quarter developed a rising demand of grain that consumed the whole regional surplus. This meant that the Lubeckian brewers needed in the fourteenth and fifteenth centuries alone 10,000,000 kg grain per year, not including the demand of their Rostockerian and Wismarian colleagues.[75]

At the end of the fifteenth century, the importance of the grain-trade between the Baltic East and the Netherlands increased.[76] The growing demand of the Dutch and Flemish towns and the cheap supply of Polish, Prussian, and Livonian grain was an ideal connection. Both areas developed their own, special interests in trade which existed contrary to, for example, the interests of Lübeck and the other Wendian cities.[77] The grain export from the eastern Baltic, which was simply one export among others before this development,

---

Commerce. Maritime bulk trade in Northern Europe, 1150–1400, ed. Lars Berggren, Nils Hybel and Annette Landen, Papers in Medieval Studies, vol. 15 (Toronto: Pontifical Institute 2002), 53–91. Richard W. Unger, "Feeding the Low Countries Towns: The grain trade in the fifteenth century." *Revue belge de philologie et d'histoire* 77/2 (1999), 329–358, here 333f.

73 Kåre Lunden, "Hanseatane og norsk økonomi i seinmellomalderen. Nokre merknader." *Norsk Historisk Tidsskrift* 46 (1967), 97–129.

74 A. Mączak and H. Samsonowicz, "La zone Baltique," 78f.

75 W. Frontzek, Braugewerbe, 20.

76 M. van Tielhof, *The mother of all trades*, 6f; R.W. Unger, "Feeding the Low Countries Towns," 334f; Marie-Jeanne Tits-Dieuaide, "The Baltic grain trade and cereal prices in Flandres at the end of the Middle Ages: some remarks." In *The Baltic grain trade, five essays*, ed. Walter Minchinton (Exeter: Association for the History of the Northern Seas, 1985), 11–20; The same, *La formation des prix céréaliers en Brabant et en Flandre au XVe siecle* (Brussels: Editions de l'Universite de Bruxelles, 1975), 214–242.

77 M. van Tielhof, *The mother of all trade*.

rose from a minimum of 8,473 lasts in the 1490s to 30,000 lasts in the 1550s up to 95,000 lasts annually in the 1640s. The Baltic became the main distributor of grain during this time to the Netherlands.[78]

More and more, the growing grain-trade of the fifteenth and sixteenth century developed the potential to destroy the old Hanse and the political and economical union between the Baltic East and the West. Additionally, the old Hanseatic trading system was no longer practical for bridging the gap between Danzig and Amsterdam. Because of this, Hanseatic merchants developed a new trading system with a strong central and salaried personal at the other trading places. In this new system, the old flow of money didn't work any longer, so the Baltic merchants began to be in need of banks to transfer their money from the East to the West, a service which had previously been done by their colleagues and companions.[79]

Along with grain, hemp became another important export-product from the Baltic region. Hemp was mainly produced in the area of Novgorod, Pskov, Smolensk, Polatsk, Livonia, and Prussia.[80] This product was primarily used to produce hemp-rope for ships and thus had an important role in the creation and maintenance of the Dutch and English navies, at least in the period after the Navigation Act and the building of the Dutch merchant-fleet. Hemp was exported in two fashions—as a raw material, pressed in tons, and also as semi-finished products, called *Kabelgarn*.[81]

Beer

Traditionally, Hamburg is known as the Hanseatic house of beer (*Bierhaus*), because of its exports to the Netherlands and the long known struggle at the

78 M. van Tielhof, *The mother of all trade*, 7f; M.-J. Tits-Dieuaide, "Grain trade," 20.

79 Carsten Jahnke, "Lübeck, der Bankenplatz des Nordens?, Lübecker Banken des 15. Jahrhunderts als Indikatoren eines neuen Kommunikationsmodells und eines sich ausweitenden Handelsraumes." In *Beiträge der Sektion Beschleunigung und Ausdehnung—Konturen der Bankgeschichte vom 15.–20. Jahrhundert des Historikertages 2004*, ed. S. Elkar aud A. Denzel, Scripta Mercaturia, 149–168; Carsten Jahnke, *Die Hanse* (Stuttgart: Reclam 2014), 182–208. See also Carsten Jahnke, Mit Strukturen von gestern auf Märkte von morgen? Hansische Kaufleute und deren Handelsorganisation an der Wende vom 15. zum 16. Jahrhundert, forthcoming.

80 A. Attman, *Den Ryska Marknaden*, 9ff. and Bilag 2.

81 Paul Johansen and Heinz von zur Mühlen, *Deutsch und Undeutsch im mittelalterlichen und frühneuzeitlichen Reval* (Cologne, Vienna: Böhlau, 1973). Ostmitteleuropa in Vergangenheit und Gegenwart, xv. Wilhelm Stieda, "Kabelgarn und Steine, zwei Revaler Ausfuhrartikel." *Beiträge zur Kunde Est-, Liv- und Kurlands* 7 (1910), 153–208, here 161–166.

Dutch beer-market. But as new research has shown, this idea has not always been the reality.[82]

Beer was usually brown in Europe, but hopped beer in good quality was exclusively brown in the northern German towns.[83] The deciding factors of this success were the availability of good fresh water and especially the constant supply of barley, malt and hop. The only places that possessed these requirements were the north German harbor towns: here there was a wide grain-producing hinterland which was close to the big hop-areas of Mecklenburg and Brandenburg.[84] Normally Eimbeck in Lower Saxony is recognized as one of the most important brewhouses, but the annually export of Eimbeck was minimal compared to that of Lübeck, Wismar, or Rostock.[85]

In German towns brewery was a privileged craft, but the number of brewers in a town is not necessarily correlated with the amount of beer exported from a town. In the fifteenth century, the 270 Hamburgian brewers exported more beer in one year than the 700 brewers in Eimbeck in ten years.[86] During the fourteenth and fifteenth century, Hamburg exported 90,000 tons of beer annually, Lübeck 80,000 tons (120,000 hl), followed by Rostock and Wismar. In contrast, Eimbeck exported about 5,000 tons *per annum*, which was half of the annual production of one Lubeckian brewer.[87]

The export of western Baltic beer is a phenomenon from the beginning of the fourteenth century onwards.[88] Its importance increased in the course of the thirteenth, fourteenth and fifteenth century and declined again in the sixteenth and seventeenth century.[89] The increasing export of beer can be logically associated with the decline of grain exports from the western Baltic during

---

82 W. Frontzek, Braugewerbe.

83 Christine von Blanckenburg, *Die Hanse und ihr Bier. Brauwesen und Bierhandel im hansischen Verkehrsgebiet* Quellen und Darstellungen zur Hansischen Geschichte, 51 (Cologne, Weimar, Vienna: Böhlau, 2001), 255.

84 C. Jahnke, "Der Ostseeraum," chapter β, forthcoming; Blanckenburg, *Die Hanse*, 196–204; Friedrich Techen, "Das Brauwerk in Wismar." *Hansische Geschichsblätter* 41 (1915), 263–352; Wilhelm Stieda, "Studien zur Gewerbegeschichte Lübecks, Teil 3, Hopfenanbau." *Mitteilungen des Vereins für Lübeckische Geschichte und Alterthumskunde* 3. Heft (1887), Nr. 1–2, 1–16.

85 W. Frontzek, *Braugewerbe*, 16f.

86 W. Frontzek, *Braugewerbe*, 26.

87 W. Frontzek, *Braugewerbe*, 16f. and 64.

88 See in general Richard W. Unger, "Beer: A new bulk good of international trade." In *Cogs, cargoes and Commerce. Maritime bulk trade in Northern Europe, 1150–1400*, ed. Lars Berggren, Nils Hybel and Annette Landen (Toronto: Pontifical Institute, 2002), 113–127.

89 W. Frontzek, *Braugewerbe*, 64–73.

this time. Wendian beer was exported to the west in addition to Hamburgian brews, and also found a significant outlet in the three northern kingdoms, and primarily at the *kontor* of Bergen.

Products Imported via the Baltic

Wax and Honey

One of the staples that kept the Baltic trade going was wax and its related product honey. Wax was increasingly demanded in Europe because of the Christian veneration of saints with candles and bells in addition to all the offices that were in need of material to seal their documents. Wax is a by-product of apiary, which was practiced all over Europe, but the eastern and southeastern hinterland of the Baltic produced the most wax of the best quality. The area from Lviv to Warsaw and from Smolensk to Novgorod was one of the most important wax-producing areas beside the areas around Kazan and Ryazan.[90] Here, most of the wax consumed in medieval Europe was produced, and it was the Hanse who organized the trade between the producers in the east and the consumers in the west. The most important transfer points of wax trade were the *kontors* in Novgorod and Polozk and, after the closing of the Novgorodian *kontor* in 1494, Reval, Dorpat and Narva, besides Warsaw and Thorn. At these transfer points the direct trade between producer and Hanseatic merchants took place, the quality of the greenware was controlled, and the wax was remelted, sealed and brought to western European packaging units and standards.[91]

Until now it has not been clear how much wax was exported via Novgorod/Polozk and Kowno/Warsaw/Thorn. But it is evident that the exports travelling on the Vistula were important to the trade as was the famous wax-route Novgorod-Dorpat/Narva-Reval. Merchants in Thorn declared to customs in 1362/63 1,225 pieces of wax in a value of 41.620 m.l. and in 1369 1,666 pieces in the value of 46,070 m.l.[92] However, it is impossible to give complete

---

90 A. Attman, *Den ryska Marknaden*, 10f. and Bilag 4.

91 Stuart Jenks, "Die mittelalterlichen Schraen des hansischen *Kontor*es in Nowgorod, CD-rom." In *Das Gedächtnis der Hansestadt Lübeck. Festschrift für Antjekathrin Graßmann zum 65. Geburtstag*, ed. Rolf Hammel-Kiesow and Michael Hundt (Lübeck: Schmidt-Römhild, 2005), IV.97; Leopold Karl Goetz, *Deutsch-Russische Handelsgeschichte des Mittelalters*, Quellen und Darstellungen zur Hansischen Geschichte, N.F., Band V (Lübeck: Waelde, 1922), 261–269.

92 C. Jahnke, "Der Ostseeraum," chapter VII. β, forthcoming; Karl-Otto Ahnsehl, *Thorns Seehandel und Kaufmannschaft um 1370*, Wissenschaftliche Beiträge zur Geschichte und Landeskunde Ost-Mitteleuropas, No. 53 (Marburg: Herder Institut, 1961), 21–25. For later

TABLE 6.2 *Import of wax in English harbors between 1303 and 1311*

Customs year from Michaelmas to Michaelmas	London	Southampton	Sandwich	Ipswich	Yarmouth	Lynn	Newcastle	Hull	Boston	In total
From February 1303	231¾		159⅜	22½	11¼	33½			312¾	770⅞ (39.162¼ kg)
1303–1304	1425	1½†	194⅝	123	16⅞	87½†		22⅛†	212¾	2083⅜ (105.840⅓ kg)
1304–1305	1037¾	8⅛	170¼	243	10⅝	5½	5½	40¼	317⅝	1838⅝ (93.406½ kg.)
1305–1306	708¾	15	414⅝	24½	70¼	17¾	13⅙	181¾	489⅛	1934¾ + ⅙ (98.298⅓ kg.)
1306–1307	976½	7	676¼	3	58¾	30	2	317	386	2456½ (124.796 kg.)
1307–1308	1228⅞	40†	183½		48½	4	9	153	216½	2067⅜ (105.027½ kg.)
1308–1309	564¾	44†	38½	9	76¾	20†		50½	148¾†	952¼ (48.376½ kg.)
1309–1310	77					5†			126½	208½ (10.592¼ kg.)
1310–1311	765	4	91¼†	42††	37½††	30††			248	1217¼ (61.839 kg.)

By the table edited by St. Jenks, The Enrolled Customs Accounts, Part 1
Source: [1] *The Enrolled Customs Accounts* (TNA:PRO E 356, E 372, E 364) 1279/89–1508/09 (1523/1534), ed. Stuart Jenks, Part 1 (Kew: List and Index Society 2004).
Data in Quintalli à 112 lb.
† These *rotuli* do not cover the whole period.
†† The custom was levied until October 9th 1311 (5 EDW II).

figures regarding the wax export of the Baltic in Hanseatic times, because figures for the exports from Novgorod and Polozk are missing.[93] What is possible is to describe the import of Baltic wax in England using the Enrolled Customs Accounts from the beginning of the fourteenth century.

It is clear that the import of wax in the English harbors had an enormous impact. In the year 1303/1304 alone, 105,840½ kg and in 1306/1307 124,796 kg wax was imported. That this wax came from the Baltic became clear in 1309/10, when the import went down to 10,592¼ kg. The crown impeached the Hanseatic merchants on charges of conspiracy against the king of England by creating an artificial shortage of this product, an accusation the merchants were only narrowly acquitted of.[94]

The wax-trade was one of the foundation pillars of the Hanseatic trade from the beginning and continued to be so after the Reformation. The customs-lists in the Sound in 1566 register an export of 4,926½ *Schiffspfund* wax from the Baltic, which is about 787,490½ kg.[95] These exports came—though our sources are suspect—from the same areas as in the times before the Reformation: 68.9% came from Danzig, 23.2% from Narva, 4.4% from Riga, 2% from Königsberg and 1.5 % from other harbors. It is evident—even if we have to deal with the fact of some customs-defraud—that Danzig and not Narva/Reval formed the main harbor of export for this product.

Fur

In addition to wax, fur was just as important if not more so to the Hanseatic trade. In the boreal zone in the hinterland of the Baltic[96] fur-bearing animals develop a thick and valuable winter coat, which is demanded as a luxury product all over Europe.

The main trade center for fur was, after the Russian merchants no longer came to the Western Baltic at the end of the twelfth century,[97] the Baltic east

---

times see W. Stark, *Lübeck und Danzig*, 118–125, and Marian Biskup, "Z problematyki handlu polsko-gdańskiego drugiej połowy Xv wieku." *Przegląd Historyzcny* 45 (1954), 393ff.

93 L. Goetz, *Handelsgeschichte*, 270f.

94 Ph. Dollinger, *Die Hanse*, 82f.

95 A. Attman, *Den ryska Marknaden*, 50. 1 Schiffpfund is equivalent to 159,783 kg. Klaus-Joachim Lorenzen-Schmidt, *Kleines Lexikon alter schleswig-holsteinischer Gewichte, Maße und Währungseinheiten* (Neumünster: Wachholtz, 1990), 58f.

96 See the map in A. Attman, *Den ryska marknaden*, Bilag 5.

97 Carsten Jahnke and Anton Englert, "The state of historical research on merchant seafaring in Danish waters and in the Western Baltic Sea 1000–1250." In *Large Cargo Ships in Danish Waters 1000–1250. Evidence of professional merchant seafaring prior to the* Hanseatic *Period*, ed. Anton Englert et al., Ships and Boats of the North Vol. NN (Roskilde: 2015 in

coast, specifically the *kontors* in Novgorod, Polozk, Pskow, Smolensk[98] and the Hanseatic cities, foremost Riga, but also Dorpat and Reval. Warsaw and Thorn were also centers of the Hanseatic fur trade.[99]

At these entrepôts Russian boyars and Karelian hunters brought their catch, usually white and grey squirrel,[100] to the Hanseatic merchants, who traded directly with them.[101] To secure their dominance at these markets Hanseatic merchants jealously did everything they could to ensure that their non-Hanseatic competitors could not learn Russian or even get contact with the Russian hunters.[102] At the *kontors* the furs were inspected (*gewrackt*),[103] divided into the multitudinous categories of quality and sorts[104] and packed in barrels for the international transport.

From the Baltic East, from the *kontors* but also from Thorn, fur was exported by Hanseatic merchants to Western Europe. Despite the importance of the

---

preparation); E.A. Rybina, "Beziehungen zwischen Novgorod und der Hanse." In *Beiträge zur hansischen Kultur-, Verfassungs- und Schiffahrtsgeschichte*, ed. Horst Wernicke and Nils Jörn, Hansische Studien, x (Weimar: Böhlaus Nachfolger, 1998), 323–330, here 325.

98 Raymond Henry Fisher, *The Russian fur trade, 1550–1700* (Berkeley: University of California Press, 1943), 7f.

99 See the map in Robert Delort, *Le commerce des fourrures en occident à la fin du moyen age (vers 1300–vers 1450)*, II Vol., (Paris: École Française de Rome, 1978), LXVII and pages 1037–1065; M.P. Lesnikov, "Der Hansische Pelzhandel zu Beginn des 15. Jahrhunderts." In *Hansische Studien, Heinrich Sproemberg zum 70. Geburtstag*, ed. Gerhard Heitz and Manfred Unger (Berlin: Akademie-Verlag 1961), 219–272, here 240–258.

100 I am very gratefully to Prof. Dr. John Lind, Odense/Denmark, about his comments and the assignment of a manuscript of a forthcoming article about fur-trade.

101 Janet Martin, *Treasure of the Darkness. The fur trade and its significance for medieval Russia* (Cambridge: University Press, 1986), 68–81. Anna Leonidovna Choroškevič, "Der deutsche Hof in Novgorod und die deutsche Herberge (Fondaco die Tedeschi) in Venedig im 13./14. Jahrhundert. Eine vergleichende Studie." In *Zwischen Lübeck und Novgorod. Wirtschaft, Politik und Kultur im Ostseeraum vom frühen Mittelalter bis ins 20. Jahrhundert, Norbert Angermann zum 60. Geburtstag*, ed. Ortwin Pelc and Gertrud Pickhan (Lüneburg: Inst. Nordostdt. Kulturwerk, 1996), 67–87, here 74f; R.H. Fisher, *Fur trade*, 3–7; K.L. Goetz, *Handelsgeschichte*, 248f.

102 In terms of the language of the Russian merchants see Elisabeth Timmler, *Die Sprache der Kaufleute in Novgorod des 12. bis 15. Jahrhunderts*, (Phil. Diss: Berlin, 1991).

103 Jenks, Novgoroder Schra, II L, 63. II K, 65. II R, 63. III, 2a. IV, 56. IV, 58f. V, 66.

104 Until now the best overview over sorts and qualities is in Wilhelm Stieda, *Revaler Zollbücher und—quittungen des 14. Jahrhunderts*, Hansische Geschichtsquellen, V (Halle a.S.: Buchhandlung des Waisenhauses, 1887), CII. See also in a broader European perspective R. Delort, *Les commerce des fourrures*, 9–92 and M.P. Lesnikov, "Hansischer Pelzhandel," 222–240.

fur trade to the Hanse, no research into it has been conducted until recently.[105] One reason could be that we are missing evidence for the value of exported fur from the Baltic. The custom-lists normally used to quantify exports listed fur only sporadically,[106] so we do not know the position of fur in the Baltic trading system even though we can state that this trading-good was important and expensive. In 1406, English pirates captured three ships from Riga alone with 394,864 pieces of fur on board in a value of £ 3,373 16 ß and 4 den. (after a later exchange rate c. 33,730 ml.), and R. Delort, together with M.P. Lesnikov, estimated for the same time an export of 1,500,000 pieces of fur annually from the Eastern Baltic.[107]

What is known is that at the end of the fifteenth century[108] and in the middle of the sixteenth century the trade in fur shifted to the North and the South of the Baltic. The Novgorodian fur trade system disintegrated in the third quarter of the fifteenth century, which was caused by Hanseatic reluctance to import silver to Novgorod and a change in consumption patterns.[109] In the next decades the fur trade relocated in the Estonian and Livonian towns Dorpat, Reval, and Riga.[110] In the second half of the fifteenth century, Dutch merchants tried to buy fur in Arkhangelsk and other northern Russian entrepôts,[111] and beginning in the end of the fifteenth century the Leipzigan fairs became more and more important to the fur trade.[112] So it is no wonder that in 1558/59 Hanseatic merchants only exported furs in the value of 26,606 m.l. from Russia via Viborg compared to wax in a value of 81,580 m.l.[113]

---

105 In general see R. Delort, *Le commerce des fourrures* and M.P. Lesnikov, "Hansischer Pelzhandel," 219–222.

106 K.L. Goetz, *Handelsgeschichte*, 256 f; Georg Lechner (ed.), *Die hansischen Pfundzollisten des Jahres 1368*, Quellen und Darstellungen zur Hansischen Geschichte, N.F., X (Lübeck: Verl. des Hansischen Geschichtsvereins, 1935), 53.

107 R. Delort, *Le commerce des fourrures*, 1042f.

108 For the Russian development see R.H. Fisher, *Fur trade*, 9–16.

109 J. Martin, *Treasure of the Land*, 81–85.

110 Norbert Angermann, "Zum Rußlandhandel von Dorpat/Tartu in der Zeit seiner höchsten Blüte (Mitte des 16. Jahrhunderts)." In *Die baltischen Länder und der Norden, Festschrift für Helmut Piirimäe zum 75. Geburtstag*, ed. Mati Laur and Enn Küng (Tartu: Akadeemiline Ajalooselts, 2005), 82–93.

111 A. Attman, *Den ryska marknaden*, 58f.

112 Herbert Eiden, "Die Hanse, die Leipziger Messen und die ostmitteleuropäische Wirtschaft," *Hansische Geschichsblätter* 120 (2002), 73–95; Manfred Unger, "Die Leipziger Messe und die Niederlande im 16. und 18. Jahrhundert," *Hansische Geschichsblätter* 81 (1963), 20–38.

113 Gunnar Mickwitz, "Die Hansekaufleute in Wiborg 1558/1559," *Historiallinen Arkisto, Toimittanut Suomen Historiallinen Seura* XLV (1939), 107–193, here 116. By an exchange rate of 10 ß l. of 1 m.l.

It appears as though the Hanseatic trade in fur lost its importance in the course of the fourteenth century—but it is difficult to determine considering the state of our sources.[114]

Wood and Wood-products

The importance of the Baltic trade was based not only on luxury products like wax and fur, but also on bulk goods, wood, wood-products and also metals, as discussed in the next chapter. Wood export was a main pillar of the Baltic trade from the middle of the thirteenth century until the end of the nineteenth century. But this trade poses one main question: Why was wood transported along the great distance from Belarus to England, when Scandinavia is so much closer? The answer to this is threefold. Until the middle of the thirteenth century England had indeed imported wood from Scandinavia, but thereafter the relation shifted.[115] This can be seen with the intensifying of the shipping traffic around the Skaw, but does not explain the entire issue. The price relationship between the Baltic and the West must have been good enough to be profitable to ship this bulk cargo such a long way. The reasons for this are unknown until now. The old thesis, that Hanseatic ships were bigger and therefore more profitable[116] is wrong, as A. Englert has shown recently.[117] But there must have been a connection between the rising traffic and the beginning of the Baltic wood trade. Perhaps another explanation can be seen in the different supply of Scandinavia and the Baltic East. Scandinavia delivers primarily softwood, which is not suitable for constructing big ships, whereas the Baltic East has a supply of prime oak tree.[118] A third explanation can be seen in the intrusion of Hanseatic merchants in the Norwegian trade with England, which disregarded the old Norse wood-trade in place of other products.[119] Under this light the trade in wood between the Eastern Baltic and the west can be seen as an artificial market, made by the interests of merchants at this time and not by the geographically best possibilities.

---

114 But see J. Martin, *The treasure of the Land*, 84f.

115 Wendy R. Childs, "Timber for Cloth: Changing comodities in Anglo-Baltic trade in the fourteenth century." In *Cogs, Cargoes, and Commerce. Maritime Bulk Trade in Northern Europe, 1150–1400*, ed. Lars Berggren, Nils Hybel and Annette Landen, Papers in Medieval Studies, 15 (Toronto: Pontifical Institute, 2002), 181–211, here 191–196.

116 W. Childs, "Timber for cloth," 203.

117 Anton Englert, *Large cargo vessels in Danish waters*, (Diss. Masch: Kiel, 2000).

118 Friedrich Mager, *Der Wald in Altpreußen als Wirtschaftsraum*, 2 volumes, Ostmitteleuropa in Vergangenheit und Gegenwart, Band 7/I–II (Cologne, Graz: Boehlau, 1960), 25–28, map I, 55–71.

119 W. Childs, "Timber for cloth," 203.

The transport of wood is very complex. Because of this, sea- and river-transport is the best and cheapest possibility, so wood predominantly came from forests connected to the big river systems. In the Vistula area the wood came from the big Polish, Galician, Volhynian, and Lithuanian forests connected to the Vistula water-system. The felled trees were bundled in the forests and floated to the main entrepôts such as Thorn or Danzig.[120]

Finally, the wood was processed in Danzig—whole trees were not exported to the west but completed products; some of the Prussian specialities were wainscot, tunhold and bowstaves, used to build ships or barrels or for military purposes.[121] The entire English, Hanseatic, and later the Dutch fleet was as dependent on the supply of Baltic wood, as were the archers in the armies, the west European cathedral architects, and Dutch painters like Rembrand or Breughel. The wood trade, especially the Hanseatic portion of it, between the East and the West was the lifeblood of the late medieval trade.

In the area of the wood trade, there is also a lack of evidence to enumerate the total quantity of exported wood. What we can estimate, however, is the amount of floated wood on the Vistula in the years 1464 and 1465, as shown in the following graph.[122]

The main product floated on the Vistula during this time was wainscot, fine, knobfree and sawed oak-wood of finest quality. This wood was used for all building purposes, from ships to cathedrals, all over the West, and this wood made the Baltic famous. And so it should be no wonder that in 1464 that of the 983,066 pieces of wood floated on the Vistula, 739,718 were wainscot.[123]

Not only was raw wood exported to the West, but also wood-products. Among these products, alkaline materials played a large role because of the growth of the English, Flemish and Dutch cloth industries, which needed more and more potash and dyer's weed-ash to dye. The producing of potash is a typical byproduct of the wood-trade, created when wasted wood was burned at very low

120 H. Oesterreich, "Die Handelsbeziehungen der Stadt Thorn zu Polen. Von der Gründung der Stadt bis zum Ende des sechzehnten Jahrhunderts, 1232–1577, Teil I," *Zeitschrift des Westpreussischen Geschichtsvereins* Heft XXVIII (1890), 1–92, here 87.

121 W. Childs, "Timber for cloth," 194.

122 Marian Biskup, "Handel Wiślany w latach 1454–1466," *Roczniki dziejów społecznych i gospodarczych, Annales d'Histoire, sociale et économique* XIV (1952), 155–202, here 180f.

123 Contrary to Marian Biskup, "Handel Wiślany," 180, Note 16, these numbers are calculated at the basis of the grand Großhundert à 120 pieces, which are coharent to the division in "sostich" and "quarter". According to Biskups calculations with the minor Großhundert à 96 pieces the grand total is 954.787 pieces.

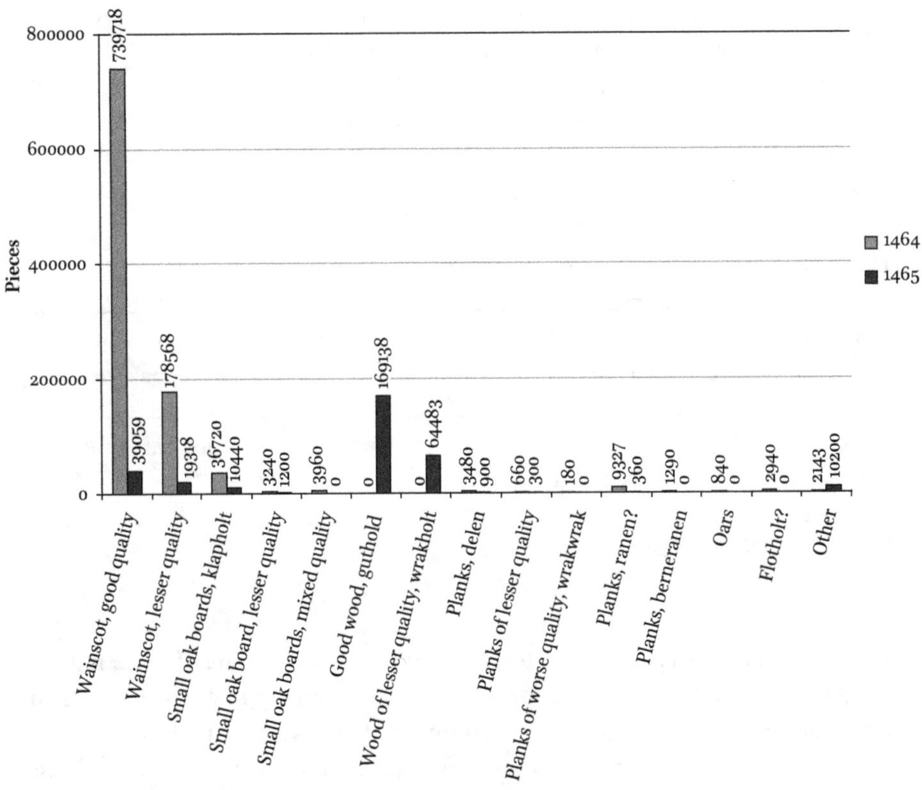

FIGURE 6.3 *Floated wood on the Vistula River.*
M. BISKUP, HANDEL WIŚLANY, 180F.

temperatures.[124] Ashes were produced in the felling-areas and from there transported to the overseas centers, like Danzig, Thorn, Elbing, Königsberg-Kneiphof but also to Riga and Pernau. At these places the ashes were examined (*gewrackt*) and got a special seal guaranteeing the quality of this product.[125] Not only the Prussian cities but also the Hanseatic *kontors* played a great role in the ash-trade, as did the Teutonic Order, which produced a huge amount in their own forests in

124 Rolf Gelius, "Waidasche und Pottasche als Universalalkalien für die chemischen Gewerbe des Ostseeraumes im 16./17. Jahrhundert." In: *Der Ost- und Nordseeraum. Politik—Ideologie—Kultur vom 12. bis zum 17. Jahrhundert*, ed. Konrad Fritze, Eckhard Müller-Mertens and Johannes Schildhauer, Abhandlungen zur Handels- und Sozialgeschichte, Band 25, zugl. Hansische Studien, Band VII (Weimar: Böhlaus Nachf., 1986), 91–107.

125 Th. Hirsch, *Handelsgeschichte*, 165f. and Beilage VIII, 282f.; F. Mager, *Der Wald*, II, 42.

Masovia.[126] The Teutonic Order exported the ash directly to Flanders, where the Order in the port of Damme had rented three booths for ash.[127]

It is not possible to give the whole quantity of exported ash from the Baltic, but figures can be given from the years 1464 and 1465, which can give clues as to their value.

TABLE 6.3 *Ash transported on the Vistula River*

Year	Ash, 1st quality asche gud	Ash, 2nd quality asche wrak	Ash, 3rd quality asche wrak wrak
1464	1957 barrels	2902 barrels	1207 barrels
1465	1164 barrels	–	–

M. Biskup, Handel Wiślany, 181

The value of the ash is not clear, but in 1362/63 ash had a value of 2,684 m.l. and in 1369/71 of 5,066 m.l. was declared in Thorn,[128] but we have to consider the fact that ash was a very cheap good compared to its weight and lastings.

Another byproduct of the wood-trade was pitch and tar, used in shipbuilding and also for military purposes. These products were produced from the stubs of the felled trees used for wood and thus belong in the same category as other wood-products.[129] The demand on these products was enormous, mainly because of growing shipbuilding throughout Europe. Modern archaeological practices demonstrate that a new ship of 25 tons needed in the first two years two coatings with tar annually and one coating annually afterwards, with 10 l barrels reckoned per coating.[130] Considering the fact that the average size of a medieval fleet was many times bigger than 25 tons, we can only estimate how many barrels of tar and pitch were used annually.

We are missing total numbers of export for this trade as well, but we do have a first lead from the Vistula area in 1463, 1464 and 1465.

126 K. Goetz, *Handelsgeschichte*, 514f.; C. Sattler, *Handelsrechnungen des Deutschen Ordens* (Leipzig: Duncker & Humblot, 1887), XVIIf. and XXXIIf.

127 C. Sattler, *Handelsrechnungen*, 18.

128 K.-O. Ahnsehl, *Thorns Seehandel*, 34f.

129 Rolf Gelius, "Teer und Pech im Seehandel der Ostseeländer im letzten Jahrhundert der Hanse (1550–1650)," *Hansische Geschichsblätter* 120 (2002), 181–203.

130 C. Jahnke, "Der Ostseeraum," forthcoming.

TABLE 6.4 *Tar and pitch transported on the Vistula River*

Year	Tar and pitch together	Tar	Pitch
1463	– (no numbers)	–	1524 barrels
1464	9309 barrels	1109 barrels	696 barrels
1465	486 barrels	–	–

M. Biskup, Handel Wiślany, 181

Metals

Copper

The Baltic Sea area was not only famous for its wood, but also for "its" copper, even if only one of Northern Europe's important mining areas laid in the geographic area of the Baltic. To understand this problem, we can glance at the Hanseatic custom lists from 1362 up till 1370. The noted copper trade in the Baltic dispersed as follows:

TABLE 6.5 *Copper trade in the Baltic, noted in the Custom Lists*

Year	*Sweden (via Lübeck)*	*Hungary (via Thorn)*	*Harz (via Hamborg)*
1362/63	–	32.780½ m.l.	–
1368	4.500 m.l.	–	–
1369	5.500 m.l.	9.150 m.l.	1.520 m.l.
1370	–	9.450 m.l.	-

K.-O. Ansehl, Thorns Seehandel, 51

As it can be seen, most of the "Baltic copper" came from Hungary, followed by the export of the Swedish mines.[131] The Harz-area in lower Saxony contributed only a small amount to this trade and therefore shall be neglected in this context.

The term "Hungarian copper" denotes metals from the north-east Slovakian mining-areas of the Carpathian Mountains, which belonged to the Kingdom of Hungary. Most of the metals in this area came from the cities of Schmölnitz,

131 K.-O. Ahnsehl, *Thorns Seehandel*, 51.

Göllnitz, Bartfeld, Letschau,[132] Libethen, Neusohl and the region Spiš/Zips in The High Tatras, where copper had been extracted since the thirteenth century.[133] Sixty percent of all European copper in the late Middle Ages was derived from these regions,[134] and some Hanseatic merchants, like the Fahlbrecht from Danzig, invested capital in these mines.[135] Because of the geographical situation, one of the best trading-possibilities for these areas was the sea-way at the Vistula River, used since the end of the thirteenth century.[136] Since 1306 Thorn was, beside Cracow, the Hanseatic house of copper (*Kupferhaus*), the official staple for all Slovakian/Hungarian copper, traded towards the north.[137] From Thorn the metal was exported directly to Flanders and also to Brunswik, two of the most important copper-processing areas.[138]

In the second half of the fourteenth century Thorn's privileges in copper trade came under pressure by the cities of Cracow and Danzig also tried to get into the lucrative trade. Cracowian merchants explored the trade route via the Oder River and Stettin and took so part of the Slovakian export to the west via Silesia instead of Prussia.[139]

But in the course of the fourteenth and fifteenth centuries, more and more European mines became flooded because of climate- and geographically-related reasons.[140] The production of the Slovakian mines, which in Schmöllnitz was around 4,303 *centner* and in Libethen around 6,666 *centner* at the beginning of the fifteenth century[141] decreased and the end of the

---

132 H. Oesterreich, "Handelsbeziehungen der Stadt Thorn," Part 1, 86.

133 Ondrej R. Halaga, "Kaufleute und Handelsgüter der Hanse im Karpartengebiet," *Hansische Geschichsblätter* 84 (1966), 59–86, here 65f; Josef Vlachović, "Die Kupfererzeugung und der Kupferhandel in der Slowakei vom Ende des 15. bis zur Mitte des 17. Jahrhunderts." In *Schwerpunkte der Kupferproduktion und des Kupferhandels in Europa 1500–1630*, ed. Hermann Kellenbenz (Cologne: Böhlau Verlag, 1973), 148–171.

134 Wolfgang von Stromer, "Die ausländischen Kammergrafen der Stephanskrone—unter den Königen aus den Häusern Anjou, Luxemburg und Habsburg—Exponenten des Großkapitals." *Hamburger Beiträge zur Numismatik* 27/29 (1973), 85–106, here 86.

135 W.v. Stromer, "Kammergrafen," 96.

136 O. Halaga, "Kaufleute," 12; H. Oesterreich, "Handelsbeziehungen," 12 and *passim*.

137 H. Oesterreich, "Handelsbeziehungen," 21–27.

138 Franz Irsigler, "Hansischer Kupferhandel im 15. und in der ersten Hälfte des 16. Jahrhunderts," *Hansische Geschichsblätter* 97 (1979), 15–35.

139 F. Irsigler, "Kupferhandel," 21f.

140 Georg von Stromer, "Wassernot und Wasserkünste im Bergbau des Mittelalters und der frühen Neuzeit." In *Montanwirtschaft Mitteleuropas vom 12. bis 17. Jahrhundert. Stand, Wege und Aufgaben der Forschung*, ed. Werner Kroker and Ekkehard Westermann (Bochum: Vereinigung der Freunde von Kunst und Kultur im Bergbau 1984), 50–72.

141 Peter Ratkoš, "Das Kupferwesen in der Slowakei vor der Entstehung der Thurzo-Fuggerschen Handelsgesellschaft." In *Der Außenhandel Ostmitteleuropas, 1450–1650. Die*

Slovakian copper-production began. In this situation, south German high financiers invested a lot of money in then-modern engineering to drain the mines and to monopolize the trade with metals. In the case of the Slovakian mining areas the Augsburgian Fugger, together with Johann Thurzo, got a privilege from King Mathias Corvinus of Hungary for mining, successfully drained the flooded mines, and obtained from 1472 to 1475 a *de facto* monopoly in the copper trade of Slovakia.[142] The Thurzo-Fugger company exported one part of the output to Saxony and to Italy, but sent the other part via the Baltic to the Netherlands. With their records, we are able to ennumerate the quantities of exported Slovakian copper around 1500.

Between 1510 and 1513, the annual export of copper was around 43,140 *centner*—of which 25,911 *centner* were exported via the Baltic. The old Hanseatic trade route maintained its importance even if the Hanseatic merchants—to their disappointment—received no part in this trade.[143]

The situation in Sweden was somewhat better from the Hanseatic point of view. Here, copper was extracted only in the famous mountain of Falun in Dalarna. At the so called "big-copper-mountain", copper had been mined since the second half of the eleventh century and the city of Falun developed into Sweden's most important center for metal trade.[144] In the Middle Ages the copper-mountain was partitioned in interests, which were saleable and devisable. Shareholders included the Swedish king and the regional bishop of Westerås but also Hanseatic merchants, who were primarily Lubeckians.[145]

---

ostmitteleuropäischen Volkswirtschaften in ihren Beziehungen zu Mitteleuropa, ed. Ingomar Bog (Cologne, Vienna: Boehlau, 1971), 584–599.

142 Stanisław Gierszewski, "Słowackie zaplecze portu gdańskiego w końcu XV i w pierwszej połowie XVI w." In Strefa bałtycka w XVI–XVIII wieku, polityka—społeczeństwo—gospodarka, Ogólnopolska sesja naukowa zorganizowana z okazji 70-lecia urodzin Professora Edmunda Cieślaka, ed. Jerzy Trzoska (Gdańsk: Komisja Historyczna, 1993), 123–133; Max Jansen, Jakob Fugger der Reiche. Studien und Quellen, Studien zur Fuggergeschichte, 3 (Leipzig: Duncker & Humblot, 1910); Friedrich Dobel, "Der Fugger Bergbau und Handel in Ungarn," Zeitschrift des Historischen Vereins für Schwaben und Neuburg 6 (Augsburg 1879), 33–50.

143 Pierre Jeannin, "Le cuivre, les Fugger et la Hanse." *Annales* 10 (1955), 229–236 contrary to Götz Freiherr von Pölnitz, *Fugger und die Hanse. Ein hundertjähriges Ringen um Ostsee und Nordsee*, Schwäbische Forschungsgemeinschaft bei der Kommission für bayerische Landesgeschichte, R. 4, Vol. 5, Studien zur Fuggergeschichte, Vol. 11 (Tübingen: Mohr, 1953).

144 Bertil Boëthius, Kopparbergslagen fram till 1570-talets genombrott. Uppkomst, medeltid, tidig vasatid (Uppsala: Almqvist & Wiksell, 1965), 22. Tom Söderberg, Stora Kopparberget under Medeltiden och Gustav Vasa (Stockholm: Petterson, 1932), 66.

145 T. Söderberg, *Stora Kopperberget*, 71; Wilhelm Koppe, *Lübeck-Stockholmer Handelsgeschichte im 14. Jahrhundert* (Neumünster: Wachholtz, 1933), 21f. and 29f.

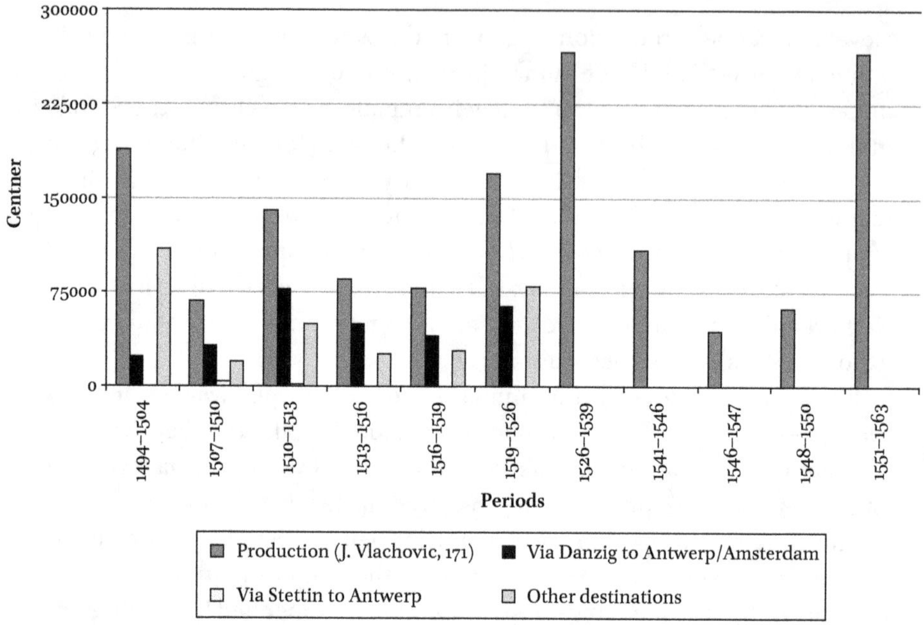

FIGURE 6.4 *Production and Export of Slovakian Copper.*
M. JANSEN, JAKOB FUGGER DER REICHE, 156–158 J. VLACHOVIĆ, KUPFERERZEUGUNG, 171.

Certainly, the Lubeckian investment secured some kind of Hanseatic influence at the copper mines, but this cannot be interpreted in the sense that the Germans had initiated the Swedish copper-mining.[146]

From Falun the copper was exported via Stockholm and Lübeck to Bruges, where for the most part, the trade laid in the hands of Hanseatic, Stockholmian and Lubeckian merchants.[147] It is not possible to estimate the quantity of copper exported to the West in Hanseatic times.[148] Generally, the Falun mines boomed in the sixteenth and seventeenth century, even if their importance in Hanseatic times is indisputable.[149]

146 B. Boëthius, *Kopparbergslagen*, 22.

147 W. Koppe, *Handelsgeschichte*, 21f.

148 Kjell Kumlien, "Staat, Kupfererzeugung und Kupferausfuhr in Schweden 1500–1650." In *Schwerpunkte der Kupferproduktion und des Kupferhandels in Europa 1500–1630*, ed. Hermann Kellenbenz (Cologne: Böhlau Verlag, 1973), 241–251, here 245f.

149 Björn Ivar Berg, "Krisen und Konjunkturen im skandinavischen Bergbau bis 1800." In *Konjunkturen im europäischen Bergbau in vorindustrieller Zeit*, ed. Christoph Bartels and Markus A. Denzel, Festschrift für Ekkehard Westermann zum 60. Geburtstag (Stuttgart: Steiner, 2000). VSWG, Beihefte, 155, 85–101, here 87ff.

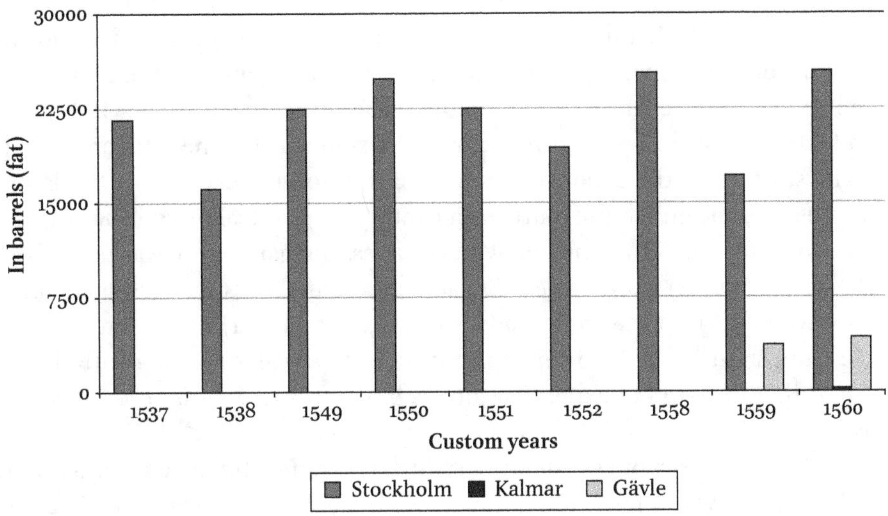

FIGURE 6.5 *Swedish copper-export.*
S. LUNDKVIST, GUSTAV VASA, 397FF.

From the times of Gustav Vasa onwards, the production and export of Swedish copper assumed dimensions of international importance. This was increasingly the result of a new Swedish politic under the kings of the House of Vasa and changing circumstances at the European market. The quantity of this late medieval and early modern export can be seen in the Swedish export statistics of the 1530's onwards.[150]

Iron

The second important metal of the Baltic was iron, and just as in the case of copper, we can also trace the same pattern of geographical distribution. One part of the Baltic iron came from Sweden, the other from the Slovakian mining area. But unlike copper, the export of iron from the Baltic in medieval times was not as important as the export of the Basque Country.[151]

Since the thirteenth century the region Spiš in Hungary was, beside Kaschau, very involved in the iron trade. In the same manner, the Teutonic Order, which exported the iron towards England and Flanders, was engaged in this trade

150 Sven Lundkvist, Gustav Vasa och Europa. Svensk handels- och utrikespolitik, 1534–1557 (Uppsala: Svenska Bokförlaget, 1960), 397ff.

151 R.H. Bautier, "Notes sur le commerce de fer en Europe occidentale du XIIIe au XVIe siècle", *Revue d'histoire de Sidérurgie*, part I, IV (1960), 7–35, part II, IV (1963–1), 35–61, here II, 35. and 52f.

also.[152] The Slovakian iron used the same route as the copper, and all northbound iron had to be stapled in Thorn.[153] But in the course of the fourteenth century Cracowian merchants developed the route on the Oder via Breslau and Stettin as well, in concurrence with the staple in Thorn.[154] It can be generally stated that the export of Hungarian iron to markets west of the Baltic increased at the end of the fourteenth century for political reasons but experienced a backlash during the following decades. Hungarian iron was part of the Hanseatic trade in Flanders and England and traded by the Dutch merchants also, even if its importance in trade is not clear at all.[155] The total amounts for the Hungarian/Slovakian iron-export have been unclear until recently, but it seems that this kind of export was not as important as the iron production in Sweden.

Contrary to the copper-production which was concentrated at the mountain of Falun, iron was mined in many Swedish regions, on the islands of Gotland and of Utö near Stockholm, in Dalarna, at the Norberg and Skinnskatteberg in Västermanland, in Uppland and Södermannland[156] and in the important mountain region of Örebro, called *Nor(r)askog* (The northern forest).[157]

The iron-mining industry in Sweden had developed a long tradition parallel to the copper-industry and under the influence of Hanseatic merchants.[158] Around 1340, we have the first written evidence for this industry[159] and the annual production for Noraskog at this time is estimated by 2,400 *Schiffspfund* (c. 324,794½ kg) iron annually.[160]

In Sweden the cities of the Mälardelta, primarily Arboga and Örebro, tried to concentrate the iron-trade in their walls. The metal was then sent further

152 Josef Vozár, "Die Eisenproduktion und der Eisenhandel in den Städten der Slowakei." In *Stadt und Eisen*, ed. Ferdinand Opll, Beiträge zur Geschichte der Städte Mitteleuropas, Band XI (Linz an der Donau: Österreichischer Arbeitskreis für Stadtgeschichtsforschung, 1992), 97–109; R.H. Bautier, "Notes," II, 52f. and 55.

153 H. Oesterreich, "Handelsbeziehungen," 27.

154 R.H. Bautier, "Notes," II, 54f.

155 R.H. Bautier, "Notes," II, 55–59.

156 Lars Magnusson, *Sveriges ekonomiska historia* (Stockholm: Prima, 1996), 133; B. Boëthius, *Kopparbergslagen*, 256–259.

157 Johan Johansson, *Om Noraskog. Äldre och nyere Anteckningar*, Part I (Stockholm: Ivar Haegeströms Boktryckeri, 1875), Part II (Stockholm: Ivar Haegeströms Boktryckeri, 1881–1882) here I, 111f. See also Eli F. Heckscher, *Sveriges ekonomiska Historia från Gustav Vasa* (Stockholm: Albert Bonnier Förlag, 1935–1949), here I, Bilag 1.

158 J. Johansson, *Om Noraskog*, I, *passim*; R.H. Bautier, "Notes," II, 37–40.

159 Gunnar Larsson, Bergsbruket som Kolonisationsfaktor i Bergslagen, speciellt Noraskog och Linde Bergslaget, Uppsats för D1 i arkeologien Umeå 1984, 26ff.

160 J. Johansson, *Om Noraskog*, II, 73f.

to Stockholm as the main entrepôts but also to Söderköping.[161] From there, iron was distributed in the middle of the thirteenth century all over the Baltic and the West, but in contrast to copper, iron was not entirely exported to the west, but was consumed in the Baltic region also.[162] One of the destinations of Swedish iron was England, where it was named under its Swedish denomination *osemund*, and where the original barrels were used as units of measurement instead of £.[163] Also in this case it can be stated that the amount of imported Swedish iron in England was modest and laid around 170 to highest 300 tons annually.[164]

The export of Swedish iron was generally not especially high. At the end of the Middle Ages, between 1492 and 1496, Sweden exported from Stockholm, Söderköping, Nyköping, Westerwik and Kalmar between 1,000 t. and 1,300 t. annually towards Lübeck,[165] and at the beginning of the sixteenth century around 27.000 *Schiffspfund* (c. 4,314 tons) iron annually to the whole Baltic.[166] This export rose first in the 1560's and later on.[167] Whether these low values are a result of the many wars and revolutions in the second half of the fifteenth century or of a lack of capacity is unclear.[168]

Other Products Imported via the Baltic

Within the narrow limits of this chapter, it is certainly not possible to mention all products that were part of the trade in the Baltic Area. This concerns not only the trade in metals and agrarian products, where alaun,[169] lead,[170] green

161 Gustaf Jonasson, *Medeltidens Örebro* (Malmö: Liber, 1984), 65–69. Örebro Studies, 3. W. Koppe, *Handelsgeschichte*, 32f.

162 W. Koppe, *Handelsgeschichte*, 35 and relativizing Koppes enthusiasm R.H. Bautier, "Notes," II, 42f.

163 Wendy R. Childs, "England's iron trade in the fifteenth century," *The Economic History Review*, New Series, 34, 1 (Feb. 1981), 25–47, here 33f.

164 W.R. Childs, "Iron trade," 36ff.

165 R.H. Bautier, "Notes," II, 43f.

166 E. Heckscher, *Historia*, 156f.

167 E. Heckscher, *Historia*, 156ff and Diagram VI.

168 Rolf Sprandel, *Das Eisengewerbe im Mittelalter* (Stuttgart: Anton Hiersemann, 1968), 206–211.

169 Rolf Gelius, "Färbewaren im Seehandel der Ostseeländer," *Hansische Geschichsblätter* 121 (2003), 93–122, here 102ff.

170 Danuta Molenda, "Der polnische Bleibergbau und seine Bedeutung für den europäischen Bleimarkt vom 12. bis 17. Jahrhundert." In *Montanwirtschaft Mitteleuropas vom 12. bis 17. Jahrhundert, Stand, Wege und Aufgaben der Forschung*, ed. Ekkehard Westermann

vitrol[171] and quicksilver[172] played a part, as did flax,[173] hemp,[174] tallow, skins[175] or dairy products, like butter, or luxury goods like silk or spices.[176] But it can be generally noticed that the axis from Danzig to Thorn-Lviv served until 1400 as a pendant to the much better known route from Lübeck to Bruges. Luxury products such as silk or spices or rare products like alaun came from both directions into the Hanseatic trade.

In summary, the Baltic connected a wide hinterland from the Ural to Arabia with the north and west European trade. The Baltic was the main transport-route but also the main market for some of the most important European trading goods and acted as an important part of the European economy. The Hanseatic merchants acted as negotiators between the east and the west. They possessed the necessary connections and the knowledge of the different market systems and they had the techniques to bridge the very long distances between such cities as Novgorod, Lviv, and Cracow in the east and Bruges, London, and Antwerp in the west. This was the special function and role that the Hanseatic merchants had in the medieval economy.

The Inner Baltic Trade

In contrast to the old opinion,[177] Hanseatic trade is today defined as trade done by Hanseatic merchants, between or from towns which were members of the Hanseatic League. This definition is important, because the Hanseatic trade was not only the high speed trade between Riga and Amsterdam but also the small scale traffic between Reval and Viborg or between Stockholm and Wismar.

---

and Werner Kroker (Bochum: Vereinigung der Freunde von Kunst und Kultur im Bergbau 1984), 1876–198. Der Anschnitt, Beiheft; Th. Hirsch, *Danzigs Handelsgeschichte*, 181 and 186.

171 R. Gelius, "Färberwaren," 104f.

172 H. Oesterreich, "Handelsbeziehungen," 86; K.-O. Ahnsehl, *Thorns Seehandel*, 54.

173 A. Attman, *Den ryska marknaden*, Bilag 1.

174 A. Attman, *Den ryska marknaden*, 9 and Bilag 2.

175 A. Attman, Den ryska marknaden, 12.

176 F. Renken, *Der Handel*, 137f; K.-O. Ahnsehl, *Thorns Seehandel*, 56f.

177 See for example Rolf Hammel-Kiesow, "Wer kaufte die Waren des hansischen Handels? Eine Annäherung an die Endverbraucher." In "*kopet uns werks by tyden*", *Beiträge zur hansischen und preußischen Geschichte*, ed. Nils Jörn, Detlef Kattinger and Horst Wernicke (Schwerin: Thomas Helms Verlag, 1999), 73–80, here 73.

Within this inner Baltic trade all kinds of goods were trafficked, but we can enumerate some goods which have interregional importance for the whole Baltic area and for the Hanseatic trade as well.

In the field of the agrarian products hop and wine were two of these important inner Baltic goods. Hopped beer is one of the famous Hanseatic products and it can be assumed that the German colonists learned the use and cultivation of hop from the Slavonian population at the Baltic coasts.[178] The most famous hop producing areas at the Baltic laid in Mecklenborg, Brandenborg, and also in Prussia.[179] The demand of the Hanseatic brewers was very high, so the brewers of the city of Wismar, for example, needed 72,000 *Scheffel* above hop annually,[180] which demonstrates that the market was big and lucrative. The hop was brought from the inland in the Hanseatic towns at the sea and was distributed to the brewer cities along the Baltic coast. Beyond this, hop was also an important export good in the trade with Russia.[181]

It is not well known that the Baltic is a wine producing area, and was so in Hanseatic times as well as today.[182] In the Middle Ages wine was blended with spices and honey and because of this practice, people had other uses for that product than they typically do today.[183] The wine-producing area in the Baltic extended from Holstein and Lauenburg in the west via Mecklenburg and Brandenburg to Prussia in the east.[184]

---

178 W. Frontzek, *Braugewerbe*, 40f.

179 Jürgen Sarnowsky, "Die Entwicklung des Handels der preußischen Hansestädte im 15. Jahrhundert." In *Die preußischen Hansestädte und ihre Stellung im Nord- und Ostseeraum des Mittelalters*, ed. Zenon H. Nowak and Janusz Tandecki (Toruń: Wydawn. Uniwersytetu Mikolaja Kopernika, 1998), 51–78, here 58; Gerhard Theuerkauf, "Binnen- und Seehandel zur Hansezeit am mecklenburgischen Beispiel." In *Zwischen Lübeck und Novgorod. Wirtschaft, Politik und Kultur im Ostseeraum vom frühen Mittelalter bis ins 20. Jahrhundert, Norbert Angermann zum 60. Geburtstag*, ed. Ortwin Pelc and Gertrud Pickhan (Lüneburg: Inst. Nordostdt. Kulturwerk, 1996), 179–189, here 187 f; Friedrich Techen, "Das Brauwerk in Wismar," *Hansische Geschichsblätter* 41 (1915), 263–352, here 319ff.

180 W. Frontzek, *Braugewerbe*, 43.

181 K.L. Goetz, *Handelsgeschichte*, 517.

182 C. Jahnke, "*Ostseeraum*," chapter VI.8, forthcoming.

183 Klaus Militzer, "Der Wein des Meisters. Die Weinversorgung des Hochmeisters des Deutschen Ordens in Preußen." In *Zwischen Lübeck und Novgorod. Wirtschaft, Politik und Kultur im Ostseeraum vom frühen Mittelalter bis ins 20. Jahrhundert*. Norbert Angermann zum 60. Geburtstag (Lüneburg: Inst. Nordostdt. Kulturwerk, 1996), 143–155, here 151f.

184 C. Jahnke, "*Ostseeraum*," chapter VI.8, forthcoming.

Latest in the thirteenth century these areas, primarily the Brandenburgian cities and Prussia, exported wine, and in Prussia the cultivating of wine was intensified after the conquest of the Teutonic Order, even if the order did not introduce the cultivation of wine to that country.[185] The acreage in Prussia covered around 500 ha. alone[186] but the dimensions of the other areas is unknown, as well as the volume of all produced wine. But nevertheless wine has appeared as a trading good in our sources, even if its importance has been unknown until now.

Beside the agrarian products, salt was one of the most demanded products in the Baltic and in the trade with Russia. In the Baltic, the east was saltless and the west was rich in salt springs.[187] In the west the Luneburgian salt springs had been the most important since 956,[188] and the fame of the city of Lübeck was based on the export of this product. As a result, this city exported in 1368 56,000 tons salt[189] with a value of 61,625½ m.l. to the Baltic alone.[190] Beside

185 Janusz Tandecki, "Weinbau im mittelalterlichen Preußen." *Beiträge zur Geschichte Westpreußens* 12 (1991), 83–99.

186 J. Tandecki, "Weinbau," 89–91.

187 Stuart Jenks, "Der hansische Salzhandel im 15. Jahrhundert im Spiegel des Danziger Pfundzollbuchs von 1409." In *"Vom rechten Maß der Dinge", Beiträge zur Wirtschafts- und Sozialgeschichte, Festschrift für Harald Witthöft zum 65. Geburtstag*, ed. Rainer S. Elkar, Cornelius Neutsch, Karl Jürgen Roth and Jürgen H. Schawacht Vol. 1, Sachüberlieferung und Geschichte vol. 17 (St. Katharinen: Scripta-Marcaturae-Verlag, 1996), 257–284, here 258.

188 Harald Witthöft, "Der Export Lüneburger Salzes in den Ostseeraum während der Hansezeit." In *Die Hanse und der deutsche Osten*, ed. Norbert Angermann (Lüneburg: Nordostdeutsches Kulturwerk, 1990), 41–65; Harald Witthöft, "Struktur und Kapazität der Lüneburger Saline seit dem 12. Jahrhundert," *Vierteljahrschrift für Sozial- und Wirtschaftsgeschichte* 63 (1976), 1–117.

189 That are 7.600 metric tons.

190 Rolf Hammel-Kiesow, "Lübeck and the Baltic trade of bulk goods for the North Sea region 1150–1400." In *Cogs, Cargoes and Commerce. Maritime bulk trade in Northern Europe, 1150–1400*, ed. Lars Berggren, Nils Hybel and Anette Landen, Papers in Medieval Studies, Vol. 15 (Toronto: Pontifical Institute, 2002), 53–91, here 83. See also Rolf Hammel-Kiesow, "Salzzoll und Grabenzoll—Konjunkturen des Salzhandels und des Transithandels auf dem Stecknitzkanal im 16. Jahrhundert." In *"Vom rechten Maß der Dinge", Beiträge zur Wirtschafts- und Sozialgeschichte, Festschrift für Harald Witthöft zum 65. Geburtstag*, ed. Rainer S. Elkar, Cornelius Neutsch, Karl Jürgen Roth and Jürgen H. Schawacht, Vol. 1 (St. Katharinen: Scriptra-Mercaturae-Verlag, 1996), 285–305; Walter Fellmann, "Die Salzproduktion im Hanseraum." In *Hansische Studien, Heinrich Sproemberg zum 70. Geburtstag*, ed. Gerhard Heitz and Manfred Unger (Berlin: Akademie-Verlag, 1961),

Lüneburg/Lübeck, the city of Kolberg was also famous for its salt springs[191] and in fact, this town was the oldest salt-city in the inner Baltic trade.

But not only Lüneburg and Kolberg contributed to the salt supply of the Baltic, but also the Polish salt mines in Cracow, Salzberg, and Groß Salze. At these mines rock salt was extracted, which from 1329 had to be stapled in Cracow.[192]

These three main sources of salt secured the constant supply of salt in the Baltic, and the Scanian Fairs served as the central salt-market at this area. For example, the City of Danzig exported in 1409 2,148½ tons of salt to Scania but purchased in return 10,967 tons of Luneburgian salt, which meant that a quarter of all salt-imports came from there.[193] Besides Lübeck and Scania, Danzig was the third important center of salt-trade in the Baltic. Danzig was not only an entrepôts for Luneburgian salt but also ceased importing cheaper Western sea-salt from the Baie de Bourgneuf and from the Iberian Peninsula, had been distributed to other cities in the eastern Baltic like Thorn, Riga or Reval or further to Russia.[194] In Russia salt functioned alongside silver as one of the most important goods in the trade with Novgorod and the other Hanseatic *kontors*.

Until the end of the fourteenth century the Baltic salt-market from Lübeck to Russia was dominated by Luneburgian salt. In the next centuries this dominance was challenged by an increased import of cheaper western sea-salt, so that the Luneburgian trade lost its dominance late in the sixteenth century.[195] But nevertheless the trade in regional salt was one of the important main pillars of the Hanseatic trade in the Baltic.

The last item that will be mentioned is Baltic cloth and linen. Previous research focused only on the import of expensive Flemish and English cloth to the Baltic. But if we examine the inner Baltic customs accounts, we can find

---

56–71; Hermann Heineken, *Der Salzhandel Lüneburgs mit Lübeck bis zum Anfang des 15. Jahrhunderts*, Historische Studien, Heft LXIII (Berlin: Ebering, 1908).

191 Peter Tepp, Untersuchungen zur Sozial- und Wirtschaftsgeschichte der Hanse- und Salzstadt Kolberg im Spätmittelalter (Diss. masch.: Hamburg, 1980).

192 Józef Piotrowicz, "Die Versorgung der Krakauer Salinen mit Roh- und Hilfsstoffen sowie Lebensmitteln als Faktor des Aufschwungs des Lokal- und Fernhandels vom 13. bis 16. Jahrhundert." In *Bergbaureviere als Verbrauchszentren im vorindustriellen Europa, Fallstudien zu Beschaffung und Verbrauch von Lebensmittel sowie Roh- und Hilfsstoffen (13.–18. Jahrhundert)*, ed. Ekkehard Westermann (Stuttgart: Steiner, 1997), 331–343, here 331 and 342f.; VSWG, Beihefte, 130; J. Rutkowski, *Histoire économique*, 60f.

193 St. Jenks, "Hansischer Salzhandel," 270f.

194 St. Jenks, "Hansischer Salzhandel," 272f.

195 See the maps in W. Fellmann, "Salzproduktion."

many other types of cloth than the western styles and some linen production. So it is legitimate to mention this trade too, even if most of the research is missing.

Almost every city in the Baltic sheltered weavers, woolen or linen weavers and other kinds of cloth-producing industries. These cloth-makers produced primarily for the regional market but additionally made cloth meant for inter-regional export. For example, the Prussian weavers were known in Danzig, Kulm, Marienburg and Elbing,[196] or the weavers in Brunswik and Gottingen.[197] Like the Flemish, these weavers marked their products with a lead seal, a seal that was so important that it was falsified by other Polish towns. Beside Prussia, the cities of Breslau, Schweidnitz/Świdnica and Beitsch/Biecz in Silasia and Cracow were centers of cloth making,[198] as were the Brandenburgian cities from Kyritz to Osterburg and Berlin.[199] The cloth production of the Wendian and Saxonian quarter of the Hanseatic League is also known.[200]

From all these cities cloth was exported not only to the nearer lands, but also to the whole Hanseatic region, and even to Russia and Hungary. The value of this trade is likewise unknown as is the significance of this product compared to the Flemish and English imports.

---

196 Jerzy Maik, "Stand und Notwendigkeit der Forschungen über die mittelalterliche Wollweberei auf dem südlichen Ostseegebiet." In *Northern Archaeological Textiles, NESAT VII, Textile Symposium in Edinburgh, 5th–7th May*, ed. Frances Pritchard and John Peter Wild (Oxford: Oxbow Books, 2005), 84–92; Rudolf Holbach, "Zur Handelsbedeutung von Wolltuchen aus dem Hanseraum." In *Der hansische Sonderweg? Beiträge zur Sozial- und Wirtschaftsgeschichte der Hanse*, ed. Stuart Jenks and Michael North, Quellen und Darstellungen zur hansischen Geschichte, N.F., Band XXXIX (Cologne: Böhlau, 1993), 135–190; Jerzy Maik, *Sukiennictwa Elbląskie w Średniowieczu* (Łódź: Polska Akademia Nauk, 1997); Acta Archaeologica Lodiziensia, Nr. 41; Bruno Widera, "Tucherzeugung und Tucheinfuhr Polens und der Rus vom 10.–13. Jahrhundert im Lichte technologischer Untersuchungen. Materialien aus Danzig und Novgorod," *Zeitschrift für Geschichtswissenschaft* 9 (1961), 944–948; Th. Hirsch, *Handelsgeschichte*, 329.

197 A. Huang, *Die Textilien*, 301–310.

198 Jerzy Wyromzumski, "The textile trade of Poland in the Middle Ages." In *Cloth and Clothing in Medieval Europe. Essays in memory of Professor E. M. Carus-Wilson*, ed. N.B. Harte and K.G. Ponting (London: Heinemann and The Pasold Research Fund, 1983), 249–258.

199 R. Holbach, "Zur Handelsbedeutung", 170ff; Herbert Helbig, *Gesellschaft und Wirtschaft der Mark Brandenburg im Mittelalter*, Veröffentlichungen der Historischen Kommission zu Berlin vol. 41 (Berlin, New York: de Gruyter, 1973), 143f.

200 A. Huang, *Die Textilien*, 301–310.

General Conclusion: The Baltic Trade and Its Purpose in the Hanseatic Trade System

Certainly, the Baltic trade was only one part of the Hanseatic system. However, it was the initial point of the sea-going Hanseatic trade in the twelfth and thirteenth centuries, and the changing conditions of the Baltic trade led *inter alia* to the end of the Hanseatic League in the fifteenth and sixteenth centuries. Therefore, the Baltic trade can justly be described as the alpha and the omega of the se-going Hanseatic system.

The Hanseatic trade in the Baltic bridged the gap between the suppliers of cloth and luxury goods in the west and the producers of wax and fur in the east. In between these areas, the Baltic Sea was the most practical medium of transport. The Hanseatic merchants developed their own very successful trading system between these two points because: they had knowledge of eastern languages and customs, they had survey over supply and demand and—most importantly—they had developed a structure of trade and companies which could bridge the long distances between Novgorod, Lviv, and Bruges.

In the very beginning, the exchange of cloth/luxury goods vs. wax/fur took center stage. But when the city of Lübeck opened the gate for the inflow of Luneburgian salt, the picture changed. In addition to the cloth-wax trade other branches like the salt-herring trade appeared. These changes economically rearranged the Baltic Sea area. From the middle of the thirteenth to the end of the fourteenth century the Baltic was divided into four economic zones: First, the old long-term routes with direct trade between the eastern *kontors* and the west via Lübeck, second, the medium-distance trade between the west and the distribution-centers along the Baltic Sea, third, the trade at the connection points where the trade of the west and the east met, at Hamborg/Lübeck and at the Scanian Fairs, and fourth, the regional trade of the Baltic. In this system, the connection points between the west and the east developed into key positions economically and politically.

The trade between the European west and the Baltic east, especially with Russia, was very lucrative but also contained special risks. Because of the long and troublesome journey, which included the perils of the sea and the differences between Hansard and Russian culture and manners, the Hanseatic merchants were not able to offer enough goods to adjust the balance of trade. Because of this imbalance, a perpetual stream of western silver flowed to Russia and Poland-Lithuania and from there on to Persia.[201] The Russian Empire

201 Michael North, "Bilanzen und Edelmetall im hansischen Rußlandhandel." In Zwischen Christianisierung und Europäisierung. Beiträge zur Geschichte Osteuropas im Mittelalter

was able to rake off enormous earnings, and the European west received for its input of silver only non-durable goods, which had consequences for the European economy.

At the end of the fourteenth century the system changed. The direct trade between the west and the eastern Baltic harbors grew in importance and as a result, the connection points lost their leading rule as the eastern *kontors*. At the same time the spectrum of traded goods changed. In addition to wax, new bulk goods such as wood, copper, and not least grain grew in importance while the importance of fur declined. Also, these new goods were products of the Baltic east, which meant that the western Baltic could enter the lee side of international trade.

The cities of the Wendian quarter were partly able to absorb this development by their privileged trade with the Hanseatic *kontors*, by the trade with their own products, primarily beer and perhaps cloth, and by their position in the regional and interregional trade.

In the Hanseatic trade-system of the Baltic the function of the inner Baltic regional and supra-regional trade cannot be overestimated. The big cargos of the east-west trade were bundled and cleaved for this regional trade, while the constant influx of goods secured the supply and distribution of the goods of international trade. The Hanseatic trade comprised not only the large-scale trade between Novgorod and Bruges, but also the small traffic in the Baltic and with the Baltic hinterland. The palette of goods in trade was composed of a blended assortment of international, supra-regional and regional goods. The Hanseatic merchants of the Baltic can be characterized by their ability to blend the various spheres and operate in the large as well as in the small, at the long distances as well as in the short.

und Früher Neuzeit. Festschrift für Peter Nitsche zum 65. Geburtstag, ed. Eckhard Hübner, Ekkehard Klug and Jan Kusber, Quellen und Studien zur Geschichte des östlichen Europa vol. 51 (Stuttgart: Steiner, 1998), 415–422; Artur Attman, The Russian and Polish markets in international trade 1500–1650 (Göteborg: The Swedish Council for Social Science Research, 1973), 103–193, and A. Attman, Den ryska marknaden, 107–117.

Bibliography

Aaslestad, Katherine. "Paying For War: Experiences of Napoleonic Rule in the Hanseatic Cities." *Central European History* 39 (2006): 641–675.

Abraham-Tisse, Simone. "Les relations Hispano-Hanséates au bas Moyen Âge." *En la España medieval* 14 (1991) 131–61, and 15 (1992), 249–95.

Ahnsehl, Karl-Otto. *Thorns Seehandel und Kaufmannschaft um 1370*. Marburg/Lahn: Johann Gottfried Herder-Institut, 1961.

Amman, Hans M., Berc Rustem and Andrew B. Whinston, eds. *Computational Approaches to Economic Problems*. Advances in Computational Economics; Vol. 6. Boston: Kluwer Academic Publishers, 1997.

Andermann, Kurt and Peter Johanek. *Zwischen Nicht-Adel und Adel.* Stuttgart: J. Thorbecke, 2001.

Andermann, Ulrich. *Ritterliche Gewalt und bürgerliche Selbstbehauptung. Untersuchungen zur Kriminalisierung und Bekämpfung des spätmittelalterlichen Raubrittertums am Beispiel norddeutscher Hansestädte*. Frankfurt: Peter Lang, 1991.

Andersen, Emilie and Ditlev Henriksen Enbeck. *Malmøkøbmanden Ditlev Enbeck og Hans Regnskabsbog: Et Bidrag til Danmarks Handelshistorie I det 16. århundrede.* Copenhagen: I Kommission hos Munksgaard, 1954.

Andersson, Espen Bowitz, ed. *Bryggen. The Hanseatic Settlement in Bergen*. Bergen: Hanseatiske Museums, 1982.

Andreß, Hans-Jürgen. *Theorie, Daten, Methoden: Neue Modelle und Verfahrensweisen in den Sozialwissenschaften*. Munich: Oldenbourg, 1992.

Angermann, Norbert and Klaus Friedland. *Novgorod: Markt und Kontor der Hanse.* Quellen und Darstellungen zur hansischen Geschichte. Cologne: Böhlau, 2002.

Angermann, Norbert. *Die Hanse und der deutsche Osten*. Lüneberg: Verlag Nordostdeutsches Kulturwerk, 1990.

———. "Die Hanse und Rußland in den Jahren 1584–1603." Hansische Geschichsblätter 102 (1984): 79–90.

Ashcroft, Neil, David J. Starkey and Chris Reid, eds. *England's Sea Fisheries: The Commercial Sea Fisheries of England and Wales since 1300*. London: Chatham, 2000.

Asmussen, Georg. *Hansekaufleute in Brügge*, Vol. 2. *Die Lübecker Flandernfahrer in der zweiten Hälfte des 14. Jahrhunderts (1358–1408)*. Frankfurt: Peter Lang, 1999.

Attman, Artur. *The Russian and Polish Markets in International Trade, 1500–1650*. Göteborg: Institute of Economic History of Gothenburg University, 1973.

———. *Den Ryska Marknaden I 1500-Talets Baltiska Politik, 1558–1595*. Lund: A.-b. P. Lindstedts, 1944.

Ausgabe, Franz. *Les Allemands en Europe centrale et orientale au Moyen Âge*. Paris: Aubier, 1989.

Axelrod, Robert M. *The Evolution of Cooperation*. New York: Basic Books, 1984.

Baasch, Ernst. *Die Islandfahrt der Deutschen, namentlich der Hamburger von 15. bis 17. Jahrhundert*. Hamburg: Herold'sche Buchhandlung, 1889.

Barüske, Heinz. *Erich von Pommern: Ein nordischer König aus dem Greifengeschlecht*. Rostock: Hinstorff, 1997.

Bately, Janet and Anton Englert. *Ohthere's Voyages: A Late Ninth-Century Account of Voyages Along the Coasts of Norway and Denmark and its Cultural Context*. Roskilde: Viking Ship Museum, 2007.

Baur, Paul. *Testament und Bürgerschaft: Alltagsleben und Sachkultur im spätmittelalterlichen Konstanz*. Konstanzer Geschichts- und Rechtsquellen, Vol. 31. Sigmaringen: J. Thorbecke, 1989.

Bautier, R.H. "Notes sur le commerce de fer en Europe occidentale du XIIIe au XVIe siècle." *Revue d'histoire de Sidérurgie*. Part 1, I (1960): 7–35, and Part 2, IV (1963): 35–61.

Beck, Thilo C. "Cooptition bei der Netzwerkorganisation." *Zeitschrift für Organisation* 67 (1998): 271–76.

Berggren, Lars, Nils Hybel Annette Landen, eds. *Cogs, Cargoes, and Commerce: Maritime Bulk Trade in Northern Europe, 1150–1400*. Papers in Mediaeval Studies, Vol. 15. Toronto: Pontifical Institute of Mediaeval Studies, 2002.

Berghoff, Hartmut and Jörg Sydow. *Unternehmerische Netzwerke: Eine historische Organisationsform mit Zukunft?* Stuttgart: Kohlhammer, 2007.

———. "Vertrauen als ökonomische Schlüsselvariable: Zur Theorie des Vertrauens und der Geschichte seiner privatwirtschaftlichen Produktion" in: Karl-Peter Ellerbrock et al., eds., *Die Wirtschaftsgeschichte vor der Herausforderung durch die New Institutional Economics*, Dortmund: Gesellschaft für Westfälische Wirtschaftsgeschichte, 2004.

Berkowitz, Stephen D. *An Introduction to Structural Analysis: The Network Approach to Social Research*. Toronto: Butterworths, 1982.

Bendixen, B.E. and W.D. Krohn, eds., *Dat Gartenrecht in den Jacobsfjorden unndt Bellgarden med oversættelse*, Skrifter udgivne af Bergens Historiske Forening, Vol. 1, Bergen, 1895.

Benninghoven, Friedrich. "Die Gotlandfeldzüge des deutschen Ordens 1398–1408." *Zeitschrift für Ostforschung* 13 (1964): 421–77.

Bes, Lennart, Edda Frankot and Hanno Brand, eds. *Baltic Connections. Archival Guide to the Maritime Relations of the Countries around the Baltic Sea (including the Netherlands)* 3 Vols. Leiden: Brill, 2007.

Beutin, Ludwig. "Das Reich, die Hansestädte und England (1590–1618)." (Doctoral Dissertation, Philipps-Universität zu Marburg, 1929).

———. *Hanse und Reich im Handelspolitischen Endkampf Gegen England*. Studien zur Geschichte der Wirtschaft und Geisteskultur. Berlin: K. Curtius, 1929.

Biskup, Marian. "Z Problematyki Handlu Polsko-Gdanskiego Drugiej Polowy Xv Wieku." *Przegląd Historyzcny* 45 (1954): 393

Bjork, David K. "Piracy in the Baltic." *Speculum* 18 (1943): 39–68.

Blanckenburg, Christine von. *Die Hanse und ihr Bier: Brauwesen und Bierhandel im hansischen Verkehrsgebiet.* Quellen und Darstellungen zur hansischen Geschichte. Cologne: Böhlau, 2001.

Blickle, Peter, and Elisabeth Müller-Luckner. *Theorien Kommunaler Ordnung in Europa.* Munich: Oldenbourg, 1996.

Bliujienė, Audronė. *The Northern Gold. Amber in Lithuania (c. 100 to c. 1200).* Leiden: Brill, 2011.

Bloch, Hermann, ed. *Annales Marbacenses.* Hannover: Hahnsche Buchhandlung, 1907.

Blomkvist, Nils. *The Discovery of the Baltic: The Reception of a Catholic World-System in the European North (AD 1075–1225)* Northern World, v. 15. Leiden: Brill, 2005.

Boëthius, Bertil. *Kopparbergslagen Fram till 1570-Talets Genombrott. Uppkomst, Medeltid, Tidig Vasatid.* Uppsala: Almqvist & Wiksell, 1965.

Boer, Dirk E.H. de, Gudrun Gleba, and Rudolf Holbach. *"—in Guete Freuntlichen Nachbarlichen Verwantnus und Hantierung—": Wanderung von Personen, Verbreitung von Ideen, Austausch von Waren in den niederländischen und deutschen Küstenregionen vom 13.–18. Jahrhundert.* Oldenburg: Bibliotheks- und Informations system der Universität Oldenburg, 2001.

Boer, Dirk E.H. de. "Looking for Security: Merchant Networks and Risk Reduction Strategies." in Hanno Brand, ed., *The German Hanse in Past & Present Europe: A Medieval League as a Model for Modern International Cooperation?* Groningen: Castel International Publishers, 2008.

Bog, Ingomar. *Der Aussenhandel Ostmitteleuropas 1450–1650: Die östmitteleuröpaischen Volkswirtschaften in ihren Beziehungen zu Mitteleuropa.* Cologne: Böhlau, 1971.

Bøgh, Anders. *Sejren I Kvindens Hånd: Kampen om Magten I Norden Ca. 1365–89.* Aarhus: Aarhus Universitetsforlag, 2003.

Bohman, Lennart. "Hanseväldet ur Nordisk Synsvinkel." *Gotländskt arkiv* XXX (1958): 39–52.

Böhmer, Johann Friedrich, Ferdinand Opll and Hubert Mayr, eds. *Die Regesten des Kaiserreiches unter Friedrich I, 1152 (1122)–1190.* Regesta Imperii, Vol. 4. Vienna: Böhlau, 2001.

Bosau, Helmold von. *Slawenchronik.* Transcribed and explained by Heinz Stoob. Ausgewählte Quellen zur deutschen Geschichte des Mittelalters, vol. 19. Darmstadt: Wissenschaftliche Buchgesellschaft, 1973.

Bourdieu, Pierre. "Das ökonomische Feld" in *Der Einzige und sein Eigentum.* Schriften zur Politik und Kultur, Vol 3. Hamburg: Philipp, 1998.

Bracke, Niels. *Die Regierung Waldemars IV. Eine Untersuchung zum Wandel von Herrschaftsstrukturen im spätmittelalterlichen Dänemark.* Kieler Werkstücke, vol. 21. Frankfurt: Peter Lang, 1999.

Bracker, Jörgen, Volker Henn and Rainer Postel, eds. *Die Hanse: Lebenswirklichkeit und Mythos*. Lübeck: Verlag Schmidt-Römhild, 2006.

Bracker, Jörgen. *Gottes Freund—Aller Welt Feind: Von Seeraub und Konvoifahrt. Störtebeker und die Folgen*. Hamburg: Zertani, 2001.

Brand, Hanno, ed. *The German Hanse in Past & Present Europe: A Medieval League as a Model for Modern International Cooperation?* Groningen: Castel International Publishers 2008.

———, ed. *Trade, diplomacy and cultural exchange: continuity and change in the North Sea area and the Baltic, c. 1350–1750*. Hilversum: Verloren, 2005.

Brand, Hanno and Leos Müller, eds., *The dynamics of economic culture in the North Sea and Baltic Region: in the late Middle Ages and early modern period*. Hilversum: Verloren, 2007.

Brandt, Ahasver von. "Die Hanse und die nordischen Mächte im Mittelalter." in Klaus Friedland et al., eds. *Lübeck, Hanse, Nordeuropa*. Cologne: Bohlau, 1979.

———. "Die Veckinchusen-Handlungsbücher: Vorgeschichte, Problematik und Verwirklichung einer Quellenedition," *Hansische Geschichtsblätter* 93 (1975): 100–112.

———. *Die deutsche Hanse als Mittler zwischen Ost und West*. Cologne: Westdeutscher Verlag, 1963.

———. "Die Hanse als mittelalterliche Wirtschaftsorganisation," in A. v. Brandt, et al., eds., *Die Hanse als mittelalterliche Wirtschaftsorganisation*. Cologne: VS Verlag für Sozialwissenschaften, 1963.

———. *Die Hanse und die nordischen Mächte im Mittelalter*. Opladen: Westdeutscher Verlag, 1962.

Brandt, Klaus, Michael Müller-Wille, and Christian Radtke, eds. *Haithabu und die frühe Stadtentwicklung im Nördlichen Europa*. Münster: Wachholtz, 2002.

Bruns, Friedrich. *Die Lübecker Bergenfahrer und ihre Chronistik*, Berlin: Quellen und Darstellungen zur hansischen Geschichte, 1900.

Burkhardt, Mike. "The German Hanse and Bergen—New Perspectives on an Old Subject" *Scandinavian Economic History Review* 58 (2010): 60–79.

———. *Der hansische Bergenhandel im Spätmittelalter. Handel—Kaufleute—Netzwerke*, Quellen und Darstellungen zur hansischen Geschichte, vol. 60. Cologne: Bölau, 2009.

———. "One hundred years of thriving commerce at a major English sea port. The Hanseatic Trade at Boston between 1370 and 1470", in Hanno Brand and Leos Müller, eds., *The Dynamics of Economic Culture in the North Sea- and Baltic Region in the Late Middle Ages and Early Modern Period*. Hilversum: Verloren, 2007.

———. "Das Hanse*kontor* in Bergen im Spätmittelalter—Organisation und Struktur." *Hansische Geschichtsblätter* 124 (2006): 21–70.

———. "Die Geschichte des Bergenhandels im Spätmittelalter. Handel, Kaufleute, Netzwerke." Doctoral Dissertation, University of Copenhagen, 2006.

———. "Policy, Business, Privacy—contacts made by the merchants of the Hanse *Kontor* in Bergen in the Late Middle Ages", in Hanno Brand, ed., *Trade, diplomacy and cultural exchange: Continuity and change in the North Sea area and the Baltic c. 1350–1750*. Hilversum: Verloren, 2005. 136–151.

———. "Die Ordnungen der vier Hanse*kontore* Bergen, Brügge, London und Nowgorod" in Antjekathrin Graßmann, ed. *Das hansische Kontor in Bergen und die Lübecker Bergenfahrer*. International Workshop Lübeck 2003. Lübeck: Archiv der Hansestadt, 2005.

Burgard, Friedhelm. *Hochfinanz im Westen des Reiches 1150–1500*. Trier: Verlag Trierer Historische Forschungen, 1996.

Burt, Ronald S. *Toward a Structural Theory of Action: Network Models of Social Structure, Perception, and Action*. New York: Academic Press, 1982.

Bussmann, Klaus, Heinz Schilling, *1648, Krieg und Frieden in Europa*. Munich: Bruckmann, 1998.

Carnevali, Francesca. "'Crooks, Thieves and Receivers,' Transaction Costs in Nineteenth-century Industrial Birmingham." *The Economic History Review* 57 (2004): 533–550.

Carus-Wilson, E.M., N.B. Harte, and Kenneth G. Ponting. *Cloth and Clothing in Medieval Europe: Essays in Memory of Professor E.M. Carus-Wilson*. London: Heinemann Educational Books, 1983.

Child, John. "Trust—the Fundamental Bond in Global Collaboration." *Organizational Dynamics* 29 (2001): 274–88.

Childs, Wendy R. "England's Iron Trade in the Fifteenth Century." *The Economic History Review*, New Series. 34/1 (Feb 1981): 25–47.

Christensen, Aksel E. *Danmark, Norden Og Østersøen, Udvalgte Afhandlinger*. Copenhagen: Dansk historisk forening, 1976.

Christiansen, Tage E., Aksel E. Christensen, Svend Ellehøj, and Erling Ladewig Petersen, eds. *Middelalderstudier*. Copenhagen: Munksgaard, 1966.

Coase, Ronald H. "The New Institutional Economics." *Journal of Institutional and Theoretical Economics* 140 (1984): 229–31.

Clarus, Nicolai. *Bartholomäus Voet und die Freibeuter der Hansezeit. Untersuchungen zum Kaperwesen im Nordeuropa des frühen 15. Jahrhunderts*. (Ph.D. Dissertation. University of Hamburg, 2012).

———. "The Nature of the Firm." *Economica* 4 (1937): 386–405.

Cordes, Albrecht. "Merchant's expectations regarding procedure before foreign courts according to Hanseatic priviledges (12th–16th Centuries)." LOEWE Research Focus "Extrajusdicial and Judicial Conflict Resolution" Working Paper, No. 4. 2013.

———. *Wie Verdiente der Kaufmann Sein Geld? Hansische Handelsgesellschaften im Spätmittelalter*, Handel, Geld und Politik, Vol. 2. Lübeck: Schmidt-Römhild, 2000.

———. *Spätmittelalterlicher Gesellschaftshandel im Hanseraum*, Quellen und Darstellungen zur hansischen Geschichte. Cologne: Böhlau, 1998.

Crumlin-Pedersen, Ole, Christian Hirte, Kenn Jensen and Susan Möller-Wiering, eds. *Viking-Age Ships and Shipbuilding in Hedeby/Haithabu and Schleswig*. Roskilde: Archäologisches Landesmuseum der Christian-Albrechts-Universität, 1997.

Cummings, L.L. and B.M. Staw. *Research in Organisational Behaviour*. Vol. 10. Greenwich: JAI Press, 1990.

Czaja, Roman. *Das Bild und die Wahrnehmung der Stadt und der Städtischen Gesellschaft im Hanseraum im Mittelalter und in der Frühen Neuzeit*. Toruń: Wydawnictwo Uniwersytetu Mikołaja Kopernika, 2004.

Czaja, Roman, et al. *Ziemie Polskie Wobec Zachodu: Studia Nad Rozwojem Sredniowiecznej Europy*. Warszawa: Wydawn. DiG, 2006.

Daenell, Ernst. *Die Blütezeit der deutschen Hanse; Hansische Geschichte von der Zweiten Hälfte des XIV. bis zum Letzten Viertel des XV. Jahrhunderts*. Berlin: Reimer, 1905/1906. Reprint, Berlin: Walter de Gruyter, 1973.

———. *Die Kölner Konföderation vom Jahre 1367 und die Schonischen Pfandschaften. Hansisch-Dänische Geschichte 1367–1385*. Leipziger Studien aus dem Gebiet der Geschichte. Leipzig: Duncker & Humblot, 1884.

Dahl, Gunnar. *Trade, Trust, and Networks: Commercial Culture in Late Medieval Italy*. Lund: Nordic Academic Press, 1998.

Delort, Robert. *Le Commerce ees Fourrures en Occident à la fin du Moyen Ag: (vers 1300–vers 1450)*. Rome: École française de Rome, 1978.

Dessy, Roberta, and Sheilagh Ogilvie. *Social Capital and Collusion: The Case of Merchant Guilds* (CESifo Working Paper Series No. 1037, September 2003). Accessed August 6, 2008. http://ssrn.com/abstract=449263.

Distler, Eva-Marie. *Städtebünde im deutschen Spätmittelalter: Einer rechtshistorische Untersuchung zu Begriff, Verfassung und Funktion*. Studien zur europäischen Rechtsgeschichte. Frankfurt: Klostermann, 2006.

Dobel, Friedrich. "Der Fugger Bergbau Und Handel in Ungarn." *Zeitschrift des Historischen Vereins für Schwaben und Neuburg* 6 (1879): 33–50.

Dollinger, Philippe. *Die Hanse*. Stuttgart: Kröner, 1998.

———. *The German Hansa*. Stanford: Standford University Press, 1970.

Dorpalen, Andreas. *German History in Marxist Perspective: the East German approach*. London: Taurus, 1986.

Dösseler, Emil. *Soests Auswärtige Beziehungen Besonders im hansischen Raum*. Soest: Soester wissenschaftliche Beiträge, 1988.

———, ed. *Toversichtsbriefe für Soest: Schreiben in Nachlassangelegenheiten an die Stadt Soest von 1325 bis 1639*. Münster: Aschendorff, 1969.

Dralle, Lothar. "Der Bernsteinhandel Des Deutschen Ordens in Preußen, Vornehmlich Zu Beginn Des 16. Jahrhunderts." Hansische Geschichsblätter 99 (1981): 61–72.

Duchhardt, Heinz, and Eva Ortlieb. *Der Westfälische Fried: Diplomatie, Politische Zäsur, Kulturelles Umfeld, Rezeptionsgeschichte*. Munich: R. Oldenbourg, 1998.

Dünnebeil, Sonja. "Die Hanse und das europäische Mächtesystem," in Antjekathrin Graßmann, ed. *Niedergang oder Übergang? Zur Spätzeit der Hanse im 16. und 17. Jahrhundert*. Cologne: Bohlau, 1998.

———. *Die Lübecker Zirkel-Gesellschaft: Formen der Selbstdarstellung einer städtischen Oberschicht*. Veröffentlichungen zur Geschichte der Hansestadt Lübeck. Vol. 27. Lübeck: Archiv der Hansestadt Lübeck, 1996.

Düwel, Klaus, and Kommission für die Altertumskunde Mittel- und Nordeuropas. *Untersuchungen Zu Handel Und Verkehr Der Vor- Und Frühgeschichtlichen Zeit in Mittel- Und Nordeuropa*. Göttingen: Vandenhoeck & Ruprecht, 1985.

Ebel, Wilhelm. *Probleme der deutschen Rechtsgeschichte*. Göttinger Rechtswissenschaftliche Studien, Vol. 100. Göttingen: Schwartz, 1978.

———. *Lübisches Kaufmannsrecht Vornehmlich nach Lübecker Ratsurteilen des 15–16. Jahrunderts*. Göttingen: Göttinger Arbeitskreis, 1953.

Ehbrecht, Wilfried. *Störtebeker, 600 Jahre nach seinem Tod*. Hansische Studien, Vol. 15. Trier: Porta Alba, 2005.

———. *Verwaltung und Politik in Städten Mitteleuropas: Beiträge zu Verfassungsnorm und Verfassungswirklichkeit in Altständischer Zeit*. Cologne: Böhlau, 1994.

Ehrenberg, Richard. *Hamburg und England im Zeitalter der Königin Elisabeth*. Jena: G. Fischer, 1896.

Eiden, Herbert. "Die Hanse, die Leipziger Messen und die östmitteleuropäische Wirtschaft." Hansische Geschichsblätter 120 (2002): 73–95.

Elias, Norbert. *The Civilizing Process*. Oxford: Blackwell Publishing, 1994.

Elkar, Rainer S., Cornelius Neutsch, Karl Jürgen Roth, and Jürgen H. Schawacht. "*Vom Rechten Maß der Dinge", Beiträge zur Wirtschafts- und Sozialgeschichte, Festschrift für Harald Witthöft zum 65. Geburtstag. Vol. 1, Sachüberlieferung und Geschichte Vol. 17*. St. Katharinen: Scripta-Marcaturae-Verlag, 1996.

Elkar, R.S., and A. Denzel. *Beiträge der Sektion Beschleunigung und Ausdehnung—Konturen der Bankgeschichte vom 15.–20. Jahrhundert des Historikertages 2004*. Kiel, 2004.

Ellenhard, Gottfried, Godfrey, and Hermann Bloch. *Annales Marbacenses Qui Dicuntur: Accedit Annales Alsatici Breviores*. Hannoverae et Lipsiae: impensis Bibliopolii Hahniani, 1907.

Engel, Karl. "Die Organisation der deutsch-hansischen Kaufleute in England im 14. und 15. Jahrhundert bis zum Utrechter Frieden 1474." *Hansische Geschichtsblätter* XIX (1913): 173–226.

Enghoff, Ingrid Bødker. "Fishing in the Baltic Regions from the 5th Century BC to the Sixteenth Century AD: Evidence from Fish Bones." *Archaeofauna 8* (1999): 41–85.

———. "Denmarks's First Fishing Industry?" *Maritime Newsletter from Roskilde, Denmark 6*, May 1996.

Englert, Anton. *Large Cargo Ships in Danish Waters 1000–1250. Evidence of Professional Merchant Seafaring Prior to the Hanseatic Period, Ships and Boats of the North.* N.p: Roskilde, 2008.

Erstland, Geir Atle. "Was the Kontor in Bergen a Topographically Closed Entity?" in Antjekathrin Graßmann, ed. *Das hansische Kontor zu Bergen und die Lübecker Bergenfahrer—International Workshop Lübeck 2003*. Lübeck: Archiv der Hansestadt Lübeck, 2005.

Esser, Raingard. "Germans in Early Modern Britain." in Panikos Panayi, ed. *Germans in Britain since 1500*, London: Bloomsbury Academic, 1996.

Etting, Vivian. *Queen Margrete I, 1353–1412, and the Founding of the Nordic Union.* Northern World, v. 9. Leiden: Brill, 2004.

Ulf Christian Ewert and Marco Sunder. "Trading Networks, Monopoly, and Economic Development in Medieval Northern Europe: An Agent-based Simulation of Early Hanseatic Trade." in Sunhild Kleingärtner and Gabriel Zeilinger, eds. *Raumbildung durch Netzwerke? Der Ostseeraum zwischen Wikingerzeit und Spätmittelalter aus archäologischer und geschichtswissenschaftlicher Perspektive.* Zeitschrift für Archäologie des Mittelalters. Beiheft 2. Bonn: Habelt, 2012. 131–153.

Ewert, Ulf Christian and Stephan Selzer. "Wirtschaftliche Stärke durch Vernetzung." in Mark Häberlein and Christof Jeggle, eds. *Praktiken des Handels: Geschäfte und soziale Beziehungen europäischer Kaufleute in Mittelalter und früher Neuzeit.* Konstanz: UVK Verlagsgesellschaft, 2010.

Fahlbusch, Friedrich Bernward. "Zwischen Öffentlichem Mandat und Informeller Macht: Die Hansische Führungsgruppe." *Hansische Geschichtsblätter* 123 (2005): 43–60.

———. "Regionale Identität. Eine Beschreibungskategorie Für Den hansischen Teilraum Westfalen Um 1470?" *Hansische Geschichtsblätter* 112 (1994): 139–59.

Fangerau, Heiner and Thorsten Halling, eds. Netzwerke: Allgemeine Theorie oder Universalmetapher in den Wissenschaften? Ein transdisziplinärer Überblick. Bielefeld: Transcript Verlag, 2009.

Fisher, Raymond Henry. "The Russian Fur Trade, 1550–1700." (Ph.D. Dissertation, University of California 1937) University of California Press, 1943.

Fonnesberg-Schmidt, Iben. *The Popes and the Baltic Crusades, 1147–1254.* Northern World, v. 26. Leiden: Brill, 2006.

Fouquet, Gerhard, Mareike Hansen, Carsten Jahnke, and Jan Schlürmann, eds. *Von Menschen, Ländern, Meeren. Festschrift für Thomas Riis zum 65. Geburtstag.* Tönning: Der andere Verlag, 2006.

Fouquet, Gerhard, Matthias steinbrink and Gabriel zeilinger, eds., *Geschlechtergesellschaften, Zunft-Trinkstuben und Bruderschaften in spätmittelalterlichen und frühneuzeitlichen Städten*, Stadt in der Geschichte, vol. 30. Stuttgart: Jan Thorbeke Verlag, 2003.

Fouquet, Gerhard. "Geschäft und Politik, Ehe und Verwandtschaft—Briefe an den Nürnberg-Lübecker Kaufmann Matthias Mulich vom Winter 1522/23." in Helmut Bräuer and Elke Schlenkrich, eds. *Die Stadt als Kommunikationsraum. Beiträge zur Stadtgeschichte vom Mittelalter bis ins 20. Jahrhundert. Festschrift für Karl Czok zum 75. Geburtstag*, Leipzig: Leipziger Universität-Verlag, 2001. 311–346.

———. "Ein Italiener in Lübeck: Der Florentiner Gherardo Bueri (gest. 1449)." *Zeitschrift des Vereins für Lübeckische Geschichte und Altertumskunde* 78 (1998): 187–220.

Friedland, Klaus, ed. *Brügge-Colloquium des hansischen Geschichtsvereins 1988. Referate und Diskussionen*. Cologne: Quellen und Darstellungen zur hansischen Geschichte, 1990.

———. "Hamburger Englandfahrer 1512–1557." *Zeitschrift des Vereins für Hamburgische Geschichte* 46 (1960): 1–44.

———. "Der Plan des Dr. Heinrich Suderman zur Wiederherstellung der Hanse." *Jahrbuch des Kölnischen Geschichtsvereins 31/32* (1956/57): 184–244.

———. *Die Hanse*. Stuttgart: Kohlhammer, 1991.

———. *Frühformen Englisch-Deutscher Handelspartnerschaft: Referate u. Diskussionen d. Hans. Symposions im Jahre d. 500. Wiederkehr d. FriedensvVon Utrecht in London vom 9.–11. September 1974*. Cologne: Böhlau, 1976.

Fritz, Wolfgang D. *Dokumente zur Geschichte des deutschen Reiches und seiner Verfassung: 1354–1356*. Weimar: Böhlau, 1978.

Fritze, Konrad, Eckhard Müller-Mertens, and Johannes Schildhauer. *Der Ost- und Nordseeraum: Politik—Ideologie—Kultur vom 12. bis zum 17. Jahrhundert*. Weimer: Böhlau, 1986.

Fritze, Konrad, Eckhard Müller-Mertens, and Walter Stark. *Autonomie, Wirtschaft und Kultur des Hansestädte*. Weimar: Böhlau, 1984.

Friis-Jensen, Karsten, and Peter Zeeberg. *Saxo Grammaticus. Gesta Danorum. Danmarkshistorien*, Vol. 1–2. Copenhagen: Det Danske Sprog—og Litteraturselskap, 2005.

Frode, Fyllingsnes. "Notow—hanseatane si hamn på Avaldsnes" *Lokalhistorisk Tidsskrift* 41/1 (2004): 3–21.

Frontzek, Wolfgang. *Das städtische Braugewerbe und seine Bauten vom Mittelalter bis zur frühen Neuzeit, Häuser und Höfe in Lübeck*, Vol. 7. Neumünster: Wachholtz, 2005.

Fröschl, Thomas, ed. *Der Reichsdeputationstag zu Worms 1586*. Göttingen: Vandenhoeck und Ruprecht, 1994.

Fryde, Natalie. *Ein mittelalterlicher deutscher Grossunternehmer: Terricus Teutonicus de Colonia in England, 1217–1247*. Stuttgart: F. Steiner, 1997.

———. "Arnold Fitz Thedmar Und Die Entstehung der Großen Deutschen Hanse." *Hansische Geschichtsblätter* 107 (1989): 27–42.

Gehrke, Roland. *Die Hanse Und Polen*. Hamburger Beiträge Zur Geschichte Der Deutschen Im Europäischen Osten. Lüneburg: Institut Nordostdeutsches Kulturwerk, 1996.

Gelderblom, Oscar C. "From Antwerp to Amsterdam: The Contribution of Merchants from the Southern Netherlands to the Commercial Expansion of Amsterdam (c. 1540–1609) *Review* 26 (2003): 247–282.

Gelius, Rolf. "Färbewaren Im Seehandel der Ostseeländer." Hansische Geschichsblätter 121 (2003): 93–122.

———. "Teer und Pech im Seehandel der Ostseeländer im Letzten Jahrhundert der Hanse (1550–1650)." Hansische Geschichsblätter 120 (2002): 181–203.

Goetz, Leopold Karl. *Deutsch-Russische Handelsgeschichte des Mittelalters*. Lübeck: O. Waelde, 1922.

Götze, Jochen. "Von Greifswald nach Stralsund. Die Auseinandersetzungen der Deutschen Seestädte und Ihrer Verbündeten mit König Valdemar von Dänemark 1361–1360." *Hansische Geschichtsblätter* 88 (1970): 83–122.

Gonzáles de Lara, Yadira. "The Secret of Venetian Success: A Public Order, Reputation-Based Institution." *European Review of Economic History* 12 (2008): 247–85.

Grafe, Regina and Oscar Gelderblom. "The Rise and Fall of Merchant Guilds: Re-thinking the Comparative Study of Commercial Institutions in Premodern Europe." *Journal of Interdisciplinary History* XI (2010): 477–511.

Graichen, Gisela and Rolf Hammel-Kiesow, eds. *Die deutsche Hanse: Eine heimliche Supermacht*. Hamburg: Rowohlt Verlag, 2011.

Granovetter, Mark. "Economic Action and Social Structure: The Problem of Embeddedness." *American Journal of Sociology* 91 (1985): 481–510.

Grassby, Richard. "Die Letzten Verhandlungen Zwischen England Und der Hanse (1603–1604)." Hansische Geschichsblätter. 76 (1958): 73–120.

Graßmann, Antjekathrin. *Das hansische Kontor zu Bergen und die lübecker Bergenfahrer: International Workshop Lübeck 2003* Veröffentlichungen Zur Geschichte Der Hansestadt Lübeck. Vol. 41. Lübeck: Schmidt-Römhild, 2005.

———. *Ausklang und Nachklang der Hanse im 19. und 20. Jahrhundert*. Trier: Porta Alba Verlag, 2001.

———. *Niedergang Oder Übergang?: Zur Spätzeit Der Hanse Im 16. Und 17. Jahrhundert*. Köln: Böhlau, 1998.

———. "Einleitung." in Philippe Dollinge., *Die Hanse*. Stuttgart: Kroner, 1998.

———, ed. *Lübeckische Geschichte*. Lübeck: Schmidt-Römhild, 1988.

Graßmann, Antjekathrin and Rolf Hammel-Kiesow. *Lexikon des Mittelalters, vol. 5*. Munich: Artemis, 1991.

Graßmann, Antjekathrin, Michael Hundt, Rolf Hammel-Kiesow. *Das Gedächtnis der Hansestadt Lübeck: Festschrift für Antjekathrin Graßmann zum 65. Geburtstag*. Lübeck: Schmidt-Römhild, 2005.

Greif, Avner. *Institutions and the Path to the Modern Economy: Lessons from Medieval Trade*. New York: Cambridge University Press, 2006.

———. "Institutions and Impersonal Exchange: From Communal to Individual Responsibility." *Journal of Institutional and Theoretical Economics* 158 (2002): 168–204.

———. "The Fundamental Problem of Exchange: A Research Agenda in Historical Institutional Analysis." *European Review of Economic History* 4 (2000): 251–284.

———. "Contract Enforceability and Economic Institutions in Early Trade: The Maghribi Traders' Coalition." *American Economic Review* 83 (1993): 525–548.

———. "Institutions and International Trade: Lessons from the Commercial Revolution." *American Economic Review, Papers and Proceedings* 82 (1992): 128–133.

Greif, Avner, Paul Milgrom, and Barry R. Weingast. "Coordination, Commitment, and Enforcement: The Case of the Merchant Guild." *Journal of Political Economy* 41 (1994): 745–76.

Grey, Chris and Christina Garsten. "Trust, Control and Post-Bureaucracy." *Organization Studies* 22 (2001): 229–250.

Greve, Anke. "Gast und Gastgeber: Hansekaufleute und Hosteliers in Brügge im 14. und 15. Jahrhundert." in Volker Henn and Arnved Nedkvitne, eds. *Norwegen und die Hanse. Wirtschaftliche und kulturelle Aspekte im europäischen Vergleich* (Kieler Werkstücke). Frankfurt: Peter Lang, 1994. 95–107.

Häberlein, Mark and Christof Jeggle. *Praktiken Des Handels in Spätmittelalter Und Früher Neuzeit*. Konstanz: UVK Verlagsgesellschaft, 2010.

Hammel-Kiesow, Rolf. *Die Hanse*. Darmstadt: Primus Verlag, 2009.

———. *Die Hanse*. Munich: Beck, 2008.

———, ed. *Vergleichende Ansätze in der hansischen Geschichtsforschung* Hansische Studien, Vol. 13. Trier: Porta Alba Verlag, 2002.

———. *Seefahrt, Schiff und Schifferbrüder. 600 Jahre Schiffergesellschaft zu Lübeck, 1401–2001*. Lübeck: Schiffergesellschaft, 2001.

———. "Neue Aspekte zur Geschichte Lübecks bis zum Ende des 13. Jahrhunderts: Von der Jahrtausendwende bis zum Ende der Hansezeit. Die Lübecker Stadtgeschichtsforschung der Letzten Zehn Jahre (1988–1997). Teil 1." *Zeitschrift des Vereins für Lübeckische Geschichte und Altertumskunde* 78 (1998): 47–114.

———. "Hauseigentum Im Spätmittelalterlichen Lübeck. Methoden Zur Sozial- Und Wirtschaftsgeschichtlichen Auswertung der Oberstadtbuchregesten." *Lübecker Schriften zur Archäologie und Kulturgeschichte* 10 (1987): 85–300.

Häpke, Rudolf, ed. *Niederländische Akten und Urkunden zur Geschichte der Hanse und zur deutschen Seegeschichte*. Munich: Duncker & Humblot, 1913.

———. *Brügges, Entwicklung zum mittelalterlichen Weltmarkt*. Berlin: Curtius, 1908.

Hartung, Julius. "Die Spiele der Deutschen in Bergen." *Hansische Geschichtsblätter* 7 (1877): 89–114.

Hauschildt, Jürgen. "Entwicklungslinien der Organisationstheorie." *Berichte aus den Sitzungen der Joachim Jungius Gesellschaft der Wissenschaften e.V.* 5/5 (1987): 3–21.

Haussig, Hans Wilhelm. *Die Geschichte Zentralasiens und der Seidenstrasse in Islamischer Zeit*. Darmstadt: Wissenschaftliche Buchgesellschaft, 1988.

Heckscher, Eli F. *Sveriges Ekonomiska Historia Från Gustav Vasa*. Stockholm: Bonnier, 1935.

Heckscher, Eli F., Harald Westergaard, and C.S. Fearenside. *The Continental System*. Oxford: The Clarendon Press, 1922.

Heine, N.G., and Hans Lassen. *Østersøproblemer Omkring 1200*. Humanistiske Studier Vol. 2. Copenhagen: Universitetsforlaget Munksgaard, 1941.

Heineken, Hermann. "Der Salzhandel Luneburgs mit Lubeck bis zum Anfang des 15. Jahrhunderts" (Doctoral Dissertation, Friedrich-Wilhelms-Universitat zu Berlin, 1908).

Heitz, Gerhard, Manfred Unger and Heinrich Sproemberg. *Hansische Studien: Heinrich Sproemberg zum 70. Geburtstag*. Berlin: Akademie-Verlag, 1961.

Helbig, Herbert. *Gesellschaft und Wirtschaft der Mark Brandenburg im Mittelalter*. Berlin: de Gruyter, 1973.

Helbig, Herbert and Knut Schulz. *Beiträge zur Wirtschafts- und Sozialgeschichte des Mittelalters: Festschrift für Herbert Helbig zum 65. Geburtstag*. Cologne: Böhlau, 1976.

Helle, Knut. "Die hanseatischen Kaufleute in Bergen während des Mittelalters" in Ingrid Øye, ed. *Bergen und die deutschen Hanse*. Bergen, 1996.

———. *Kongssete of Kjøpstad: Fra Opphavet Til 1536*. Bergen bys Historie, Vol. 1. Bergan: Univ. Forlag, 1982.

Henn Volker, ed. *Die hansischen Tagfahrten Zwischen Anspruch Und Wirklichkeit*. Hansische Studien. Trier: Porta Alba, 2001.

———. "Was war die Hanse?" in Jörgen Bracker, Volker Henn and Rainer Postel, eds. *Die Hanse. Lebenswirklichkeit und Mythos*. Lübeck: Schmidt-Römhild, 1998.

———. "Innerhansische Kommunikations- und Raumstrukturen: Umrisse einer neueren Forschungsaufgabe?" in Stuart Jenks and Michael North, eds. *Der hansische Sonderweg? Beiträge zur Sozial- und Wirtschaftsgeschichte der Hanse*. Cologne: Böhlau, 1993.

———. "Über die Anfänge des Brügger Hanse *kontors*." *Hansische Geschichtsblätter* 107 (1989): 43–66.

———. "Entfaltung im Westen: 'Hansen' auf den niederländischen Märkten" in Volker Henn, et al., eds. *Die Hanse: Lebenswirklichkeit und Mythos. Ausstellung des Museums für Hamburgische Geschichte*, Vol. 1. Hamburg: Bracker, 1989. 42–45.

Henn, Volker, and Arnved Nedkvitne, eds. *Norwegen und die Hanse. Wirtschaftliche und kulturelle Aspekte im europäischen Vergleich*. Beiträge zur schleswig-holsteinischen und skandinavischen Geschichte, Vol. 11. Frankfurt: Kieler Werkstücke, 1994.

Henricus, Leonid Arbusow and Albert Bauer. *Heinrici Chronicon Livoniae = Heinrichs Livländische Chronik*. Editio altera / ed. Scriptores Rerum Germanicarum in Usum Scholarum Ex Monumentis Germaniae Historicis. Hannoverae: Impensis Bibliopolii Hahniani, 1955.

Herrmann, Rainer. "Lübeck und die Päpste (1201–1267)." *Zeitschrift des Vereins für Lübeckische Geschichte und Altertumskunde* 75 (1995): 9–52.

Higounet, Charles. *Les allemands en Europe centrale et orientale au Moyen âge*. Paris: Aubier, 1989.

———. *Die deutsche Ostsiedlung im Mittelalter*. Berlin: Siedler, 1986.

Hirsch, Theodor. *Danzigs Handels- und Gewerbsgeschichte unter der Herrschaft des deutschen Ordens*. Wiesbaden: M. Sändig, 1969.

Hoffmann, Richard C. *Fishers' Craft and Lettered Art: Tracts on Fishing from the End of the Middle Ages*. Toronto Medieval Texts and Translations, Vol. 12. Toronto: University of Toronto Press, 1997.

Hoffmann, Erich and Frank Lubowitz. *Die Stadt im westlichen Ostseeraum: Vorträge zur Stadtgründung und Stadterweiterung im Hohen Mittelalter*. 2 Vols. Kieler Werkstücke. Frankfurt: P. Lang, 1995.

Hoffman, Erich. "Konflikte und Ausgleich mit den skandinavischen Reichen." in Volker Henn, et al., eds. *Die Hanse: Lebenswirklichkeit und Mythos. Ausstellung des Museums für Hamburgische Geschichte*, Vol. 1. Hamburg: Bracker, 1989. 66–71.

Hoffmann, Gabriele and Uwe Schnall. *Die Kogge: Sternstunde der deutschen Schiffsarchäologie*. Schriften des Deutschen Schiffahrtsmuseums. Vol. 60. Hamburg: Convent, 1991.

Holland, Paul W. and Samuel Leinhardt. *Perspectives on Social Network Research*. New York: Academic Press, 1979.

———. "A Method for Detecting Structure in Sociometric Data." *American Journal of Sociology* 75 (1970): 492–513.

Hollstein, Bettina and Florian Straus, eds. *Qualitative Netzwerkanalyse: Konzepte, Methoden Anwendungen*. Wiesbaden: VS Verlag für Sozialwissenschaften, 2006.

Horby, Kai. "Øresundtolden og den Skånske Skibstold." in *Middelalderstudier, Tilegnede Aksel E. Christensen på Tresårsdagen*. Copenhagen: Munksgård, 1966.

Houtte, J.A. van. *Essays on Medieval and Early Modern Economy and Society*. Symbolae Facultatis Litterarum et Philosophiae Lovaniensis, Vol. 5. Leuven: Leuven University Press, 1977.

———. “The Rise and Decline of the Market of Bruges.” *Economic History Review* 19 (1966): 29–47.

Huang, Angela. *Die Textilien des Hanseraums. Produktion und Distribution einer spätmittelalterlichen Fernhandelsware*. (Doctoral Dissertation, University of Copenhagen, Faculty of Humanities 2013).

Hubel, Achim and Bernd Schneidmüller. *Aufbruch ins zweite Jahrtausend: Innovation und Kontinuität in der Mitte des Mittelalters*. Mittelalter-Forschungen, Vol. 16. Ostfildern: Thorbecke, 2004.

Hucker, Bernd Ulrich. *Kaiser Otto IV*. Hannover: Hahnsche Buchh., 1990.

Hummell, Hans J. and Rolf Ziegler. *Anwendung Mathematischer Verfahren zur Analyse Sozialer Netzwerke*. Duisburg: Sozialwissenschaftl. Kooperative, 1977.

Hundsbichler, Helmut, ed. *Die Vielfalt der Dinge. Neue Wege zur Analyse mittelalterlicher Sachkultur. Gedenkschrift in memoriam Harry Kühnel*. Wien: Verlag der Österreichischen Akademie der Wissenschaften, 1998.

Iacobucci, Dawn. *Networks in Marketing*. Thousand Oaks, Calif.: Sage Publications, 1996.

Igel, Karsten. *Zwischen Bürgerhaus und Frauenhaus. Stadtgestalt, Grundbesitz und Sozialstruktur im spätmittelalterlichen Greifswald*. Städteforschung, vol. A71. Cologne: Böhlau, 2010.

———. “Wohin in der Stadt? Sozialräumliche Studien und innerstädtische Mobilität im spätmittelalterlichen Greifswald.” in Jörg Oberste, ed. *Repräsentationen in der mittelalterlichen Stadt*. Forum Mittelalter-Studien, vol. 4. Regensburg: Schnell and Steiner, 2008. 179–192.

———. “‘... und schal by der Lowen namen blyven’. Identität und Selbstdarstellung städtischer Führungsgruppen im spätmittelalterlichen Hanseraum im Spiegel ihrer Häuser und Höfe.” in Sünje Prühlen, Lucie Kuhse and Jürgen Sarnowsky, eds. *Der Blick auf sich und die Anderen. Selbst- und Fremdbild von Frauen und Männern in Mittelalter und früher Neuzeit. Festschrift für Klaus Arnold*. Nova Mediaevalia. Quellen und Studien zum europäischen Mittelalter, vol. 2. Göttingen: V & R Unipress, 2007. 315–348.

———. “Der Raum als soziale Kategorie. Methoden sozialtopographischer Forschung am Beispiel Greifswalds um 1400.” in Stefan Kroll and Kersten Krüger, eds. *Städtesystem und Urbanisierung im Ostseeraum in der Neuzeit. Urbane Lebensräume und historische Informationssysteme*. Berlin: LIT, 2006, 265–300.

———. “Greifswald um 1400. Zur Stadtgestalt und Sozialtopographie Greifswalds im Spätmittelater.” *Baltische Studien* 88 (2002): 20–42.

Illinitch, Anne. “New Organisational Forms and Strategies For Managing in Hypercompetitive Environment.” *Organization Science* 7 (1996): 211–20.

Irsigler, Franz. “Hansischer Kupferhandel im 15. und in der Ersten Hälfte des 16. Jahrhunderts.” *Hansische Geschichtsblätter* 97 (1979): 15–35.

———. "Der Alltag einer hansischen Kaufmannsfamilie im Spiegel der Veckinchusen-Briefe." *Hansische Geschichtsblätter* 103 (1985): 75–99.

Isenberg, Gabriele. "Soest, ein frühes Wirtschaftszentrum (1.–12. Jahrhundert n. Chr.)", *Bericht der Römisch-Germanischen Kommission* 83 (2002): 265–281.

Jäger, Helmut, ed. *Civitatum communitas. Studien zum europäischen Städtewesen. Festschrift Heinz Stoob zum 65. Geburtstag*. Cologne: Böhlau, 1984.

Jahnke, Carsten. Mit Strukturen von gestern auf Märkte von morgen? Hansische Kaufleute und deren Handelsorganisation an der Wende vom 15. zum 16. Jahrhundert, proceedings from the 130th Hansische Pfingsttagung, 2014, forthcoming.

———. *Die Hanse*. Stuttgart: Reclam 2014.

———. "Die Hanse: Überlegungen zur Entwicklung des Hansebegriffes und der Hanse als Instutition resp. Organisation." *Hansische Geschichtsblätter* 131 (2013): 1–32.

———. "The Influence of the Hanseatic League on the Cities in the North Sea and Baltic Sea Area: Some Reflections on the Triad—cities—Hanseatic League." in Engberg, et al., eds. *Archaeology of Medieval Towns in the Baltic and North Sea Area*. Copenhagen: Syddanks Universitetsforlog, 2009. 51–63.

———. "Der Aufstieg Lübecks und die Neuordnung des südlichen Ostseeraumes im 13. Jahrhundert." in Roman Czaja and Carsten Jahnke, eds. *Städtelandschaften im Ostseeraum im Mittelalter und in der Frühen Neuzeit*. Towarzystwo Naukowe w Toruniu, Wyd. 1. Ark. wyd. 12. Torun: Towarzystwo Naukowe w Toruniu 2009. 29–72.

———. "Zur Interpretation des Ersten Lübecker Schiffssiegels," *Zeitschrift des Vereins für Lübeckische Geschichte und Altertumskunde* 88 (2008): 9–24.

———. "Handelsstrukturen im Ostseeraum im 12. und beginnenden 13. Jahrhundert. Anstäze einer Neubewertung." *Hansische Geschichsblätter* 126 (2008): 145–185.

———. *Geld, Geschäfte, Informationen. Der Aufbau Hansischer Handelsgesellschaften und Ihre Verdienstmöglichkeiten, Handel, Geld und Politik*, Vol 10. Lübeck: Schmidt Römhild, 2007.

———. "Netzwerke in Handel und Kommunikation an der Wende vom 15. zum 16. Jahrhundert am Beispiel Zweier Revaler Kaufleute." (Habilitation, University of Kiel, 2004).

———. *Das Silber des Meeres: Fang und Vertrieb von Ostseehering zwischen Norwegen und Italien (12.–16. Jahrhundert)*. Cologne: Böhlau, 2000.

Jähnig, Bernhart and Peter Letkemann. *Danzig in Acht Jahrhunderten: Beiträge zur Geschichte eines hansischen und Preussischen Mittelpunktes*. Quellen und Darstellungen zur Geschichte Westpreussens, Vol. 23. Münster: Nicolaus-Copernicus-Verlag, 1985.

Jansen, Max. *Jakob Fugger der Reiche*. Lepizig: Duncker & Humblot, 1910.

Jaritz, Gerhard. "Österreichische Bürgertestamente als Quelle zur Erforschung Städtischer Lebensformen des Spätmittelalters." *Jahrbuch für Geschichte des Feudalismus* 8 (1984): 249–64.

Jeannin, Pierre. "Lübecker Handelsunternehmungen um die Mitte des 16. Jahrhunderts." *Zeitschrift des Vereins für Lübeckische Geschichte und Altertumskunde* 43 (1963): 19–67.

———. "Die Hansestädte im europäischen Handel des 18. Jahrhunderts." Hansische Geschichsblätter 89 (1971): 41–73.

———. "Les relations économiques des villes de aa Baltique avec Anvers au XVIe siècle, I." *Vierteljahrsschrift für Sozial- und Wirtschaftsgeschichte* 43 (1956): 193–217.

Jenks, Stuart. "Transaktionskostentheorie und die mittelalterliche Hanse." *Hansische Geschichtsblätter* 123 (2005): 31–42.

———. *The Enrolled Customs Accounts: (Tna: Pro E 356, E 372, E 364) 1279/80–1508/09 (1523/1524)*. Kew: List and Index Society, 2004.

———. "Die Hansen in England: Wirtschaftliche und politische Bedeutung ihres Handels (1380–1474)," in: *Volker Henn et al. (eds.): Norwegen und die Hanse: Wirtschaftliche und kulturelle Aspekte im europäischen Vergleich*, Frankfurt am Main (1994): 109–160.

———. *England, die Hanse und Preussen: Handel und Diplomatie, 1377–1474*. 3 vols. Quellen und Darstellungen zur hansischen Geschichte. Köln: Böhlau, 1992.

———. "A Capital Without a State: Lübeck Caput Tocius Hanze (to 1474)." *Historical Research* 65 (1992): 134–149.

Jenks, Stuart and Michael North, eds. *Der Hansische Sonderweg?: Beiträge zur Sozial- und Wirtschaftsgeschichte der Hanse*. Quellen und Darstellungen zur hansischen Geschichte. vol. 39. Cologne: Böhlau, 1993.

Johanek, Peter, and Heinz Stoob. *Europäische Messen und Märktesysteme mm Mittelalter und Neuzeit*. Cologne: Böhlau, 1996.

Johansen, Paul, and Heinz von zur Mühlen. *Deutsch und Undeutsch im mittelalterlichen und frühneuzeitlichen Reval*. Ostmitteleuropa in Vergangenheit und Gegenwart, 15. Cologne: Böhlau, 1973.

Johansson, Johan. *Om Noraskog. Äldre och nyere Anteckningar*, Part I (Stockholm: Ivar Haegeströms Boktryckeri, 1875), Part II (Stockholm: Ivar Haegeströms Boktryckeri, 1881–1882) here I, III f. See also Eli F. Heckscher, *Sveriges ekonomiska Historia från Gustav Vasa* (Stockholm: Albert Bonnier Förlag, 1935–1949), here I, Bil 1.

Johnsson, K. "Coin Circulation and the Pattern of Hoarding in the Viking Age and Middle Ages." *XII. Internationaler Numismatischer Kongress Berlin* (1997): 911–916.

Jonasson, Gustaf. *Medeltidens Örebro*. Malmö: Liber, 1984.

Jones, Gareth R. "Transaction Costs, Property Rights, and Organizational Culture: An Exchange Perspective." *Administrative Science Quarterly* 28 (1983): 454–67.

Jordan, Karl, ed. *Die Urkunden Heinrichs des Löwen, Herzogs von Sachsen und Bayern*. Stuttgart: Anton Hiersemann, 1957.

Jörn, Nils, Detlef Kattinger, and Horst Wernicke. *"Kopet Uns Werk by Tyden": Beiträge zur hansischen und preussischen Geschichte; Walter Stark zum 75. Geburtstag.* Schwerin: Helms, 1999.

———. *Genossenschaftliche Strukturen in der Hanse.* Quellen Und Darstellungen Zur hansischen Geschichte. Cologne: Böhlau, 1999.

Jörn, Nils, Ralf-Gunnar Werlich, and Horst Wernicke. *Der Stralsunder Frieden von 1370: Prosopographische Studien.* Quellen und Darstellungen zur hansischen Geschichte. Cologne: Böhlau, 1998.

Jörn, Nils, Werner Paravicini, and Horst Wernicke, eds. *Hansekaufleute in Brügge, Teil 4: Beiträge der Internationalen Tagung in Brügge April 1996* (Kieler Werkstücke, Reihe D: Beiträge zur europäischen Geschichte des späten Mittelalters 13). Franfurt: Peter Lang, 2000.

Jörn, Nils. "With Money and Bloode." *Der Londoner Stalhof im Spannungsfeld der englisch-hansischen Beziehungen im 15. und 16. Jahrhundert.* Quellen und Darstellungen zur hansischen Geschichte. Cologne: Böhlau, 2000.

———. "Die Versuche von Kaiser und Reich zur Einbeziehung der Hanse in die Anstrengungen zur Abwehr der Türken im 16. und 17. Jahrhundert." in Nils Jörn and Michael North, eds. *Die Integration des südlichen Ostseeraumes in das Alte Reich.* Quellen und Forschungen zur höchsten Gerichtsbarkeit im Alten Reich, Bd. 35. Cologne: Böhlau 2000, 393–423.

———. "Die Auseinandersetzungen zwischen Hanse und Merchant Adventurers vor den Obersten Reichsgerichten im 16. und 17. Jahrhundert." *Zeitschrift des Vereins für Lübeckische Geschichte und Altertumskunde* 78 (1998): 323–348.

Kattinger, Detlef, Jens E. Olesen, and Horst Wernicke, eds. *Der Ostseeraum und Kontinentaleuropa 1100–1600: Einflussnahme, Rezeption, Wandel.* Schwerin: T. Helms, 2004.

Kattinger, Detlef. *Die Gotländische Genossenschaft: Der Frühhansisch- Gotländische Handel in Nord- Und Westeuropa.* Quellen und Darstellungen zur hansischen Geschichte. Cologne: Böhlau, 1999.

Kattinger, Detlef, Horst Wernicke, and Ralf-Gunnar Werlich. *Akteure und Gegner der Hanse: zur Prosopographie der Hansezeit.* Hansische Studien. Weimar: H. Böhlau, 1998.

Kazakeviécius, Vytautas, Baltijos regiono istorijos ir archeologijos institutas. *Archaeologia Baltica.* Vilnius: Alma littera: Lietuvos Istorijos institutas, 1995.

Kazakevičius, Vytautas, and Vladas Žulkus, ed. *The Balts and their Neighbours in the Viking Age.* Vilnius: Zara, 1997.

Keene, Derek. "Ein Haus in London: Von der Guildhall zum Stalhof." *Hanse* 1 (1989): 46.

Kellenbenz, Hermann. *Schwerpunkte der Kupferproduktion und des Kupferhandels in Europa: 1500–1650.* Kölner Kolloquien zur Internationalen Sozial- und Wirtschaftsgeschichte. Vol. 3. Cologne: Böhlau, 1977.

Kent, D.V., F.W. Kent. *Neighbours and Neighbourhood in Renaissance Florence: The District of the Red Lion in the Fifteenth Century*. Locust Valley [N.Y.]: J.J. Augustin, 1982.

Kikuchi, Yuta. "Hamburgs Handel mit dem Ostseeraum und dem mitteleuropäischen Binnenland vom 17. bis zum Beginn des 19. Jahrhunderts. Warendistribution und Hinterlandsnetzwerke auf See-, Fluss- und Landwegen." (Doctoral Dissertation, Ernst-Moritz-Arndt Universität Greifswald, 2013).

Kleingärtner, Sunhild and Gabriel Zeilinger, eds. *Raumbildung durch Netzwerke? Der Ostseeraum zwischen Wikingerzeit und Spätmittelalter aus archäologischer und geschichtswissenschaftlicher Perspektive*. Zeitschrift für Archäologie des Mittelalters, Beiheft 23. Bonn: Hablet, 2012.

Klosterberg, Brigitte. *Zur Ehre Gottes und zum Wohl der Familie: Kölner Testamente von Laien und Klerikern im Spätmittelalter*. Kölner Schriften zu Geschichte und Kultur. Vol. 22. Cologne: Janus, 1995.

Kohn, Meir. "Merchant Associations in Pre-Industrial Europe." *The Origins of Western Economic Success: Commerce, Finance, and Government in Pre-Industrial Europe* (Hanover: Department of Economics, Dartmouth College 2003), Accessed 1 June 2014. http://ssrn.com/abstract=427763.

Koppe, Wilhelm. "Die Hansen und Frankfurt am Main im 14. Jahrhundert." *Hansische Geschichtsblätter* 71 (1952): 30–49.

———. *Lübeck-Stockholmer Handelsgeschichte im 14. Jahrhundert*. Neumünster: K. Wachholtz, 1933.

Koppmann, Karl, and Friedrich Bruns. *Die Chroniken der Niedersächsischen Städte. Lübeck*. Leipzig: S. Hirzel, 1884.

Kresse, Walter. *Materialien zur Entwicklungsgeschichte der Hamburger Handelsflotte 1765–1823*. Hamburg: Hamburger Museumsverein, 1966.

Kroker, Werner, and Ekkehard Westermann. *Montanwirtschaft Mitteleuropas vom 12. bis 17. Jahrhundert: Stand, Wege und Aufgaben der Forschung*. Bochum: Deutsches Bergbau-Museum Bochum, 1984.

Kroman, Erik, and Peter Jørgensen, eds. *Danmarks Gamle Købstadlovgivning*. 5 vols. Copenhagen: Rosenkilde og Bagger, 1951.

Koren Wiberg, Christian. *Hanseaterne og Bergen. Forholdet mellem de kontorske og det bergenske bysamfund*, Bergen: J. Grieg, 1932.

Kühnel, Harry, Helmut Hundsbichler, Gerhard Jaritz, and Thomas Kühtreiber. *Die Vielfalt der Ding: Neue Wege zur Analyse mittelalterlicher Sachkultu: Internationaler Kongress, Krems an der Donau, 4. bis 7. Oktober 1994: Gedenkschrift in Memoriam Harry Kühnel*. Vienna: Verlag der Österreichischen Akademie der Wissenschaften, 1998.

Kuske, Bruno. "Die Handelsgeschäfte der Brüder Veckinchusen." *Hansische Geschichtsblätter* 47 (1922): 187–195.

Lappenberg, Johan Martin and G.H. Pertz, eds. *Arnoldi Chronica Slavorum*. Hannover: Impensis bibliopolii Hahniani, 1868.

Lappenberg, Johann Martin. *Urkundliche Geschichte des hansischen Stahlhofs zu London*. Hamburg: 1851 (reprint 1967).

Larsson, Gunnar. *Bergsbruket som Kolonisationsfaktor i Bergslagen, speciellt Noraskog och Linde Bergslaget*. Seminar Papers. Umeå: Universitetet, Avd. för arkeologi, 1984.

Laumann, Edward O. and Franz Urban Pappi. *Networks of Collective Action: A Perspective on Community Influence Systems*. New York: Academic Press, 1976.

———. "New Directions in the Study of Community Elites." *American Sociological Review* 38 (1973): 212–30.

Lechner, Georg. *Die hansischen Pfundzollistend des Jahres 1368: (18. März 1368 bis 10. März 1369)*. Quellen und Darstellungen zur hansischen Geschichte. Lübeck: Verlag des hansischen Geschichtsvereins, 1935.

Leciejewicz, Lech. "Sachsen in Den Slawischen Ostseestädten Im 10.–12. Jahrhundert." *Zeitschrift für Archäologie* 21 (1987): 75–81.

Lindberg, Erik. "Club Goods and Inefficient Institutions: Why Danzig and Lübeck Failed in the Early Modern Period." *Economic History Review* 62 (2009): 604–628.

Line, Philip. *Kingship and State Formation in Sweden, 1130–1290*. Northern World, Vol. 27. Leiden: Brill, 2007.

Lloyd, T.H. *England and the German Hanse, 1157–1611: A Study of Their Trade and Commercial Diplomacy*. Cambridge: Cambridge University Press, 1991.

———. "A Re-Consideration of Two Anglo-Hanseatic Treaties of the Fifteenth Century." *English Historical Review* 102 (1987): 916–30.

Loose, Hans-Dieter. "Der Verfall der Reichsordnung in der Wahrnehmung der Bürger der Reichsstädte Lübeck, Hamburg und Bremen 1801–1806." in Michael North and Robert Riemer, eds. *Das Ende des Alten Reiches im Ostseeraum. Wahrnehmung und Transformation*. Cologne: Böhlau, 2008, 144–155.

Lopez, Robert S. *The Commercial Revolution of the Middle Ages, 950–1350*. Englewood Cliffs: Prentice-Hall, 1971.

Lorenzen-Schmidt, Klaus-Joachim. *Geld und Kredit in der Geschichte Norddeutschlands*. Neumünster: Wachholtz Verlag, 2006.

———. *Kleines Lexikon Alter Schleswig-Holsteinischer Gewichte, Maße und Währungseinheiten*. Neumünster: Wachholtz, 1990.

Lucassen, Jan and Rinus Pennix. *Newcomers: Immigrants and Their Descendants in the Netherlands 1550–1995*. Amsterdam: Het Spinhuis, 1998.

Lucassen, Jan and Lucassen, Leo. "Art. Niederlande" in Klaus J. Bade et al., eds. *Enzyklopädie Migration in Europa: vom 17. Jahrhundert bis zur Gegenwart*. Munich: Fink, 2007. 95–109.

Luhmann, Niklas. *Vertrauen: Ein Mechanismus der Reduktion sozialer Komplexität*. Stuttgart: UTB, 2000.

Lunden, Kåre. "Hanseatane og Norsk Økonomi i Seinmellomalderen. Nokre Merknader." *Norsk Historisk Tidsskrift* 46 (1967): 97–129.

Lundkvist, Sven. *Gustav Vasa och Europa: Svensk Handels- och Utrikespolitik, 1534–1557*. Stockholm: Svenska bokförlaget, 1960.

Luntowski, Gustav. "Dortmund und die Hanse." in Norbert Reimann, ed. *Dortmund: 1100 Jahre Stadtgeschichte: Festschrift*, Dortmund: Ruhfus, 1982. 129–149.

Lusiardi, Ralf. *Stiftung und städtische Gesellschaft: Religiöse und Soziale Aspekte des Stiftungsverhaltens im Spätmittelalterlichen Stralsund*. Stiftungsgeschichten, Vol. 2. Berlin: Akademie Verlag, 2000.

Mączak, Antoni, and Henryk Samsonowicz. "La Zone Baltique: L'un de éléments du marché Européen." *Acta Poloniae Historica* 11 (1965): 71–99.

Mager, Friedrich. *Der Wald in Altpreussen als Wirtschaftsraum*. Ostmitteleuropa in Vergangenheit und Gegenwart. v. 1–2. Cologne: Böhlau, 1960.

Magnusson, Lars. *Sveriges Ekonomiska Historia*. Stockholm: Rabén Prisma, 1996.

Maik, Jerzy. *Sukiennictwa Elblaskie w Sredniowieczu*. Łódź: Polska Akademia Nauk, 1997.

Mäkeler, Hendrik. "Wikingerzeitlicher Geldumlauf im Ostseeraum. Neue Perspektiven," *Quaestiones Medii Aevi Novae*. 10 (2005): 121–149.

Mantels, Wilhelm. "Der Hansische Geschichtsverein," *Hanische Geschichtsblätter* 1 (1871): 3.

Markovits, Claude. *The Global World of Indian Merchants, 1750–1947. Traders of Sind from Bukhara to Panama*. Cambridge Studies in Indian History and Society, 6. Cambridge: Cambridge University Press, 2000.

Martin, Janet. *Treasure of the Land of Darkness: The Fur Trade and its Significance for Medieval Russia*. Cambridge: Cambridge University Press, 1986.

McCabe, Ina Baghdiantz, Gelina Harlaftis, and Ioanna Pepelasis Minoglou. *Diaspora Entrepreneurial Networks: Four Centuries of History*. Oxford: Berg, 2005.

Mehl, Heinrich. *Historische Schiffe in Schleswig-Holstein. Vom Nydamboot zur Gorch Fock*. Heide: Westholsteinische Verlagsanstalt Boyens, 2002.

Meinhardt, Matthias and Andreas Ranft. *Die Sozialstruktur und Sozialtopographie Vorindustrieller Städte: Beiträge eines Workshops am Institut für Geschichte der Martin-Luther-Universität Halle-Wittenberg am 27. und 28. Januar 2000*. Berlin: Akademie Verlag, 2005.

Meyer, Gunnar. *'Besitzende Bürger' und 'elende Sieche'. Lübecks Gesellschaft im Spiegel ihrer Testamente 1400–1449*. Rostock: Schmidt-Römhild, 2010.

Mickwitz, Gunnar. "Die Hansakaufleute in Wiborg 1558/1559." *Historiallinen Arkisto, Toimittanut Suomen Historiallinen Seura*. XLV (1939): 107–193.

———. *Aus Revaler Handelsbüchern. Zur Technik Des Ostseehandels in Der Ersten Hälfte Des 16. Jahrhunderts*. Helsingfors: Societas scientiarum Fennica, 1938.

———. "Neues Zur Funktion Hansischer Handelsgesellschaften." *Hansische Geschichtsblätter* 62 (1937): 24–39.

Minchinton, Walter. *The Baltic Grain Trade, Five Essays*. Exeter: Association for the History of the Northern Seas, 1985.

Mohrmann, Wolf-Dieter. *Der Landfriede im Ostseeraum Während des späten Mittelalters* Regensburger Historische Forschungen; Vol. 2. Kallmünz: Lassleben, 1972.

Mollwo, Carl. *Das Handlungsbuch von Hermann und Johann Wittenborg*. Leipzig: Dyksche Buchhandlung, 1901.

Munro, John H. "The 'new Institutional Economics' and the Changing Fortunes of Fairs in Medieval and Early Modern Europe: The Textile Trade, Warfare, and Transaction Costs." *Vierteljahrschrift für Sozial- und Wirtschaftsgeschichte* 88 (2001): 1–47.

Mosler-Christoph, Susanne. "Die Materielle Kultur in den Lüneburger Testamenten 1323 bis 1500." (Doctoral Dissertation, Georg-August-Universität Göttingen, 1998).

Mühle, Eduard. "Zur Frühgeschichte Novgorods. Von den Anfängen bis gegen Ende des 12. Jahrhunderts." in Ferdinand Seibt, Ulrich Borsdorf, and Heinrich Theodor Grütter, eds. *Transit Brügge-Novgorod. Eine Straße durch die europäische Geschichte*. Heidelberg: Vernissage-Verlag, 1997. 159–166.

Müller, Ulrich. "Networks of Towns—Networks of Periphery? Some Relations between the North European Medieval Town and its Hinterland." in Sunhild Kleingärtner and Gabriel Zeilinger, eds. *Raumbildung durch Netzwerke?* Bonn: Habelt, 2012.

———. "Case Study 3: Trading centre—Hanseatic towns on the southern Baltic Coast: Structural continuity or a new start?" in Babette Ludowici, et al., eds. *Trade and Communication Networks of the First Millennium AD in the northern part of Central Europe: Central Places, Beach Markets, Landing Places and Trading Centres*. Stuttgart: Konrad Theiss Verlag, 2010.

Müller-Mertens, Eckhard and Heidelore Böcker. *Konzeptionelle Ansätze der Hanse-Historiographie*. Hansische Studien. Trier: Porta Alba, 2003.

Müller-Wille, Michael ed. *Novgorod. Das mittelalterliche Zentrum und sein Umland im norden Russlands*. Neumünster: Wachholtz-Verlag, 2001.

———. *Rom und Byzanz im Norden: Mission und Glaubenswechsel im Ostseeraum Während des 8.–14. Jahrhunderts*. Abhandlungen der Geistes- und Sozialwissenschaftlichen Klasse, Jahrg. 1997. Stuttgart: F. Steiner, 1997.

Murray, Alan V., ed. *Crusade and Conversion on the Baltic Frontier 1150–1500*. Aldershot: Ashgate, 2001.

Murray, James M. *Bruges, Cradle of Capitalism, 1280–1390*. Cambridge: Cambridge University Press, 2005.

Poul Grinder-Hansen and Kirsten Christiansen. *Margrete I, Regent of the North: The Kalmar Union 600 Years, Essays and Catalogue*. Copenhagen: Danmarks Nationalmuseum, 1997.

Nicholas, David. *Medieval Flanders*. London; New York: Longman, 1992.

Nielssen, Alf Ragnar. "The Importance of Hanseatic Trade for the Norwegian Settlement in Finnmark." in Volker Henn and Arnved Nedkvitne, eds. *Norwegen und die Hanse. Wirtschaftliche und kulturelle Aspekte im europäischen Vergleich*. Frankfurt: Kieler Werkstücke, 1994.

Nirrnheim, Hans. *Das Handlungsbuch des Vicko von Geldersen*. Hamburg: Kessinger Publishing, 1895.

Nitsche, Peter, Ekkehard Klug, and Jan Kusber. *Zwischen Christianisierung und Europäisierung: Beiträge zur Geschichte Osteuropas in Mittelalter und Früher Neuzeit: Festschrift für Peter Nitsche zum 65. Geburtstag*. Quellen und Studien zur Geschichte des Östlichen Europa, Vol. 51. Stuttgart: F. Steiner, 1998.

Nohria, Nitin and Robert G. Eccles. *Networks and Organizations: Structure, Form, and Action*. Boston: Harvard Business School Press, 1992.

Noodt, Birgit. *Religion und Familie in der Hansestadt Lübeck Anhand der Bürgertestamente des 14. Jahrhunderts*. Lübeck: Schmidt Römhild, 2000.

Nordmann, Claus. *Nürnberger Großhändler im spätmittelalterlichen Lübeck*. Nürnberg: Kirsche, 1933.

North, Douglass C. "Institutions and Credible Commitment." *Journal of Institutional and Theoretical Economics* 149 (1993): 11–23.

———. *Institutions, Institutional Change, and Economic Performance* The Political Economy of Institutions and Decisions. Cambridge: Cambridge University Press, 1990.

———. "Transaction Costs in History." *Journal of European Economic History* 14 (1985): 557–76.

———. *Structure and Change in Economic History*. New York: Norton, 1981.

North, Michael. *The Expansion of Europe, 1250–1500*. Manchester: Manchester University Press, 2012.

———. *Geschichte der Ostsee: Handel und Kulturen*. Munich: Beck, 2011.

———. "Die Auswirkungen der Kontinentalsperre auf das nördliche Deutschland und den Ostseeraum," in: Andreas Klinger, Hans-Werner Hahn, and Georg Schmidt, eds., *Das Jahr 1806 im europäischen Kontext. Balance, Hegemonie und politische Kulturen*. Cologne/Weimar/Vienna: Böhlau 2008, 101–122.

———. "Reich und Reichstag im 16. Jahrhundert—der Blick aus der angeblichen Reichsferne." in Maximilian Lanzinner, and Arno Strohmeyer, eds. *Der Reichstag 1486–1613: Kommunikation—Wahrnehmung—Öffentlichkeit*. Göttingen: Vandenhoeck & Ruprecht, 2006. 221–236.

———. *From the North Sea to the Baltic: Essays in Commercial, Monetary and Agrarian History, 1500–1800*. Aldershot: Variorum, 1996.

———. *Geldumlauf und Wirtschaftskonjunktur im südlichen Ostseeraum an der Wende zur Neuzeit (1440–1570): Untersuchungen zur Wirtschaftsgeschichte am Beispiel des*

Grossen Lübecker Münzschatzes, der Norddeutschen Münzfunde und der schriftlichen Überlieferung. Sigmaringen: J. Thorbecke, 1990.

———. "Early Modern Copper Trade and Transport: The Copper Finds of the Elbe", in *5th International Congress of Maritime Museums. Proceedings 1984*. Hamburg: Haarmann, 1985, 63–66.

North, Michael and Robert Riemer, eds. *Das Ende des Alten Reiches im Ostseeraum. Wahrnehmung und Transformation*. Cologne: Böhlau, 2008.

Nowak, Zenon Hubert, Janusz Tandecki, and Henryk Samsonowicz. *Die preussischen Hansestädte und Ihre Stellung im Nord- und Ostseeraum des Mittelalters*. Torun: Uniwersytet Mikoája Kopernika, 1998.

Oesterreich, H. "Die Handelsbeziehungen der Stadt Thorn zu Polen. Von der Gründung der Stadt bis zum Ende des Sechzehnten Jahrhunderts, 1232–1577, Teil I." *Zeitschrift des Westpreussischen Geschichtsvereins*. XXVIII (1890): 1–92.

Ogilvie, Sheilagh. *Institutions and European Trade: Merchant Guilds, 1000–1800*. Cambridge: Cambridge University Press, 2011.

Olsen, Olaf, Jan Skamby Madsen, Flemming Rieck, and Ole Crumlin-Pedersen. *Shipshape: Essays for Ole Crumlin-Pedersen, On the Occasion of His 60th Anniversary, February 24th 1995*. Roskilde: Viking Ship Museum, 1995.

Oppl, Ferdinand, ed. *Stadt und Eisen*. Beiträge zur Geschichte der Städte Mitteleuropas, Vol. 11. Linz: Österreichischer Arbeitskreis für Stadtgeschichtsforschung, 1992.

Osborn, Richard N. and John Hagedoorn. "The Institutionalisation and Evolutionary Dynamics of Inter-Organisational Alliances and Networks." *Academy of Management Journal*. 40 (1997): 261–78.

Øye, Ingvild, ed. *Bergen und die deutsche Hanse*. Bergen: Bryggens Museum, 1996.

Pagel, Karl. *Die Hanse*. Brunswick: Georg Westermann Verlag, 1952.

Pappi, Franz Urban. *Methoden der Netzwerkanalyse*. Techniken Der Empirischen Sozialforschung, Vol. 1. Munich: Oldenbourg, 1987.

Papritz, Johannes. "Das Handelshaus der Loitz zu Stettin, Danzig und Lüneburg." *Baltische Studien*. 44 (1957): 73–94.

———. "Das Stettiner Handelshaus der Loitz im Boisalzhandel des Odergebietes, unter Besonderer Berücksichtigung seiner Beziehungen zum Brandenburgischen Kurhause." (Doctoral Dissertation, Friedrich-Wilhelms-Universität, Berlin, 1932).

Paravicini, Werner. "Hansische Personenforschung: Ziele, Wege, Beispiele." in Rolf Hammel-Kiesow, ed. *Vergleichende Ansätze in der hansischen Geschichtsforschung*. Hansische Studien, Vol. 13. Trier: Porta Alba, 2002. 247–272.

———, ed. *Hansekaufleute in Brügge*. Frankfurt: Peter Land, 1999.

———. "Lübeck und Brügge: Bedeutung und erste Ergebnisse eines Kieler Forschungsprojektes." in Hubertus Menke, ed. *Die Niederlande und der europäische Nordosten*. Neumünster: Wachholtz, 1992. 91–166.

Pelc, Ortwin, Gertrud Pickhan and Norbert Angermann. *Zwischen Lübeck und Novgorod: Wirtschaft, Politik und Kultur im Ostseeraum vom frühen Mittelalter bis ins 20. Jahrhundert: Norbert Angermann zum 60. Geburtstag*. Lüneburg: Institut Nordostdeutsches Kulturwerk, 1996.

Pelus, Marie-Louise. *Wolter von Holsten, Marchand lubeckois dans la seconde moitié du seizième siècle: Contribution à l'étude des relations commerciales entre Lübeck et les villes livoniennes*. Quellen und Darstellungen zur hansischen Geschichte. Cologne: Böhlau, 1981.

Pichierri, Angelo. *Die Hanse—Staat der Städte. Ein Ökonomisches und Politisches Modell der Städtevernetzung, Stadt, Raum und Gesellschaft, Vol. 10*. Opladen: Leske & Budrich, 2000.

Piirimäe, H., Mati Laur, Enn Küng, and Stig Örjan Ohlsson. *Die Baltischen Länder und der Norden: Festschrift für Helmut Piirimäe zum 75. Geburtstag*. Tartu: Akadeemiline Ajalooselts, 2005.

Ping Li, Peter. "Towards a Geocentric Framework of Organizational Form: A Holistic, Dynamic and Paradoxical Approach." *Organization Studies* 19 (1998): 829–61.

Pitz, Ernst. *Bürgereinung und Städteeinung: Studien zur Verfassungsgeschichte der Hansestädte und der deutschen Hanse*. Quellen und Darstellungen zur hansischen Geschichte. Cologne: Böhlau, 2001.

———. *Europäisches Städtewesen und Bürgertum: Von der Spätantike bis zum hohen Mittelalter*. Darmstadt: Wissenschaftliche Buchgesellschaft, 1991.

Põder, Kaire. "Credible Commitment and Cartel: The Case of the Hansa Merchant in the Guild of Late Medieval Tallinn." *Baltic Journal of Economics* 10 (2010): 43–60.

Poeck, Dietrich W. *Die Herren der Hanse. Delegierte und Netzwerke*. Kieler Werkstücke, vol. E8. Frankfurt am Main: Peter Lang, 2010.

Pölnitz, Götz. *Fugger und Hanse*. Studien zur Fuggergeschichte, Vol. 11. Tübingen: J.C.B. Mohr, 1953.

Postel, Rainer. "Hamburg zur Zeit des Westfälischen Friedens." in Klaus Bußmann and Heinz Schilling, eds. *1648: Krieg und Frieden in Europa*. Münster: Westfälisches Landesmuseum für Kunst und Kulturgeschichte, 1999. 337–343.

———. "Der Niedergang der Hanse." in Jörgen Bracker, Volker Henn and Rainer Postel, eds. *Die Hanse: Lebenswirklichkeit und Mythos*. Lübeck: Schmidt-Römhild, 1998. 165–193.

———. "Zur 'erhaltung dern commercien und darüber habende privilegia:' Hansische Politik auf dem Westfälischen Friedenskongreß." in Heinz Duchhardt, ed. *Der Westfälische Friede. Diplomatie, politische Zäsur, kulturelles Umfeld, Rezeptionsgeschichte*. Munich: Oldenbourg, 1998. 522–539.

Powell, Walter W. "Neither Market nor Hierarchy: Network Forms of Organization." in Grahame Thompson et al., eds. *Market, Hierarchy and Networks: The Coordination of Social Life*. London: Sage, 1991. 265–276.

Puhle, Matthias. *Hanse, Städte, Bünde: Die Sächsischen Städte zwischen Elbe und Weser um 1500*. 2 vols. Magdeburg: Magdeburger Museen, 1996.

———. *Die Vitalienbrüder: Klaus Störtebeker und die Seeräuber der Hansezeit*. Frankfurt: Campus Verlag, 1992.

———. "Der Sächsische Städtebund Und Die Hanse Im Späten Mittelalter." *Hansische Geschichtsblätter* 104 (1986): 21–34.

———. *Die Politik der Stadt Braunschweig Innerhalb des Sächsischen Städtebundes und der Hanse im späten Mittelalter*. Braunschweig: Waisenhaus, 1985.

Quack, Sigrid. "Global Markets in Theory and History: Towards a Comparative Analysis." in Jens Beckert and Christoph Deutschmann, eds. *Wirtschaftssoziologie*. Kölner Zeitschrift für Soziologie und Sozialpsyshologie, Vol. 49. Wiesbaden: VS Verlag für Sozialwissenschaften, 2009.

Reed, Michael I. "Organization, Trust, and Control: A Realist Analysis." *Organization Studies* 22 (2001): 201–228.

Reinhard, Wolfgang. *Freunde und Kreaturen: "Verflechtung" als Konzept zur Erforschung Historischer Führungsgruppen: Römische Oligarchie um 1600*. Schriften der Philosophischen Fachbereiche der Universität Augsburg, Vol. 14. Munich: Ernst Vögel, 1979.

Renken, Fritz. *Der Handel der Königsberger Grossschäfferei des deutschen Ordens mit Flandern um 1400*. Weimar: H. Böhlaus, 1937.

Richefort, Isabelle, and Burghart Schmidt. *Les relations entre la France et les villes hanséatiques de Hambourg, Brême et Lubëck: Moyen Âge-XIXe Siècle = Die Beziehungen zwischen Frankreich und den Hansestädten Hamburg, Bremen und Lübeck: Mittelalter-19. Jahrhundert*. Bruxelles: Archives Ministère des Affaires Étrangères, 2006.

Rigby, Steve H. "Boston and Grimsby in die Middle Ages." (Doctoral Dissertation, University of London, 1982).

Riethmüller, Marianne. *To Troste Miner Sele: Aspekte spätmittelalterlicher Frömmigkeit im Spiegel Hamburger Testamente (1310–1400)*. Hamburg: Verlag Verein für Hamburgische Geschichte, 1994.

Ripperger, Tanja. *Ökonomik des Vertrauens. Analyse eines Organisationsprinzips*. Tübingen: Rainer Hampp Verlag, 1998.

Ritter, Thomas and Hans-Georg Gemünden. "Die Netzwerkende Unternehmung: Organisationale Voraussetzungen Netzwerk-Kompetenter Unternehmen." *Zeitschrift für Organisation* 67 (1998): 260–65.

Rohmann, Gregor. "Der Kaperfahrer Johann Stortebeker aus Danzig. Beobachtungen zur Geschichte der Vitalienbrüder." *Hansische Geschichtsblätter* 125 (2007): 77–119.

Rolley, Francine. "Entre économie Ancienne Et économie de Marché: Le Rôle Des Réseaux de Parenté Dans Le Commerce Du Bois Au Xviii[e] Siècle." *Annales de démographie historique* (1995): 75–96.

Rörig, Fritz and Paul Kaegbein. *Wirtschaftskräfte im Mittelalter; Abhandlugen zur Stadt- und Hansegeschichte*. Cologne: Böhlau, 1959.

Rörig, Fritz. *Die Entstehung der Hanse und der Ostseeraum*. Cologne: Hermann Böhlaus, 1971.

———. *Die europäische Stadt und die Kultur des Bürgerturms im Mittelalter*. Göttingen: Vandenhoeck & Ruprecht, 1955.

———. *Der Markt von Lübeck: Topographisch-statistische Untersuchengen zur deutschen Sozial- und Wirtschaftsgeschichte*. Leipzig: Quelle & Meyer, 1922.

Rösch, Gerhard. "Zur Bildung des Kaufmanns und Seefahrers in Nordeuropa. Zwei Texte des 13. Jahrhunderts." *Hansische Geschichtsblätter* 110 (1992): 17–41.

Roslund, Mats. *Guests in the House: Cultural Transmission between Slavs and Scandinavians 900 to 1300 A.D.* Leiden and Boston: Brill, 2007.

Rutkowski, Jan and M. Rakowska. *Histoire économique de la Pologne avant les partages*. Paris: Champion, 1927.

Rybina, Elena Aleksandrovna. "Einige Fragen der Beziehungen zwischen Novgorod und der Hanse." in Horst Wernicke and Nils Jörn, eds. *Beiträge zur hansischen Kultur-, Verfassungs- und Schiffahrtshistorie*. Hansische Studien x. Weimar: Böhlau, 1998. 323–330.

Ryckaert, Marc. "Geographie eines Weltmarktes: Hansel und Stadttopographie im mittelalterlichen und frühneuzeitlichen Brügge." in Klaus Friedland, ed. *Brügge Colloquium des hansischen Geschichtsvereins 1988. Referate und Diskussionen*. Quellen und Darstellungen zur hansischen Geschichte. Cologne: Böhlau. 1990. 3–12.

Sarnowsky, Jürgen and Burghart Schmidt. *Die Kontinuität der hansischen Dimension im baltischen Raum*. Hamburg: DOBU Verlag, 2008.

Sattler, C. *Handelsrechnungen des deutschen Ordens*. Leipzig: Duncker & Humblot, 1887.

Sauer, Hans. *Hansestädte und Landesfürsten: Die wendischen Hansestädte in der Auseinandersetzung mitdDen Fürstenhäusern Oldenburg und Mecklenburg während der zweiten Hälfte des 15. Jahrhunderts*. Quellen und Darstellungen zur hansischen Geschichte. Vienna: Böhlau, 1971.

Schäfer, Dietrich. *Das Buch des Lübeckischen Vogts auf Schonen*. Lübeck,: Hansischer Geschichtsverein, 1927.

———. *Die Deutsche Hanse*. Monographien zur Weltgeschichte. Bielefeld: Velhagen & Klasing, 1914.

———. *Die Hansestädte und König Waldemar von Dänemark*. Jena,: G. Fischer, 1879.

———. "Zur Frage Nach der Einführung Des Sundzolls." *Hansische Geschichtsblätter* 2/5 (1876): 33–43.

Schildhauer, Johannes, Konrad Fritze and Walter Stark. *Die Hanse*. Berlin: Deutscher Verlag der Wissenschaften, 1974.

Schildhauer, Johannes. "Zur Verlagerung des See- und Handelsverkehrs im nordeuropäischen Raum während des 15. und 16. Jahrhunderts." *Jahrbuch für Wirtschaftsgeschichte*. 4 (1968): 192–206.

Schlesinger, Walter. *Die deutsche Ostsiedlung des Mittelalters als Problem der europäischen Geschichte: Reichenau-Vorträge 1970–1972*. Sigmaringen: J. Thorbecke, 1975.

Schlüter, Wolfgang. *Die Novgoroder Schra in Sieben Fassungen vom xiii.bBis xvii. Jahrhundert*. Lübeck: Lübcke und Nöhring, 1916.

Schmandt, Raymond H. "The Gotland Campaign of the Teutonic Knights." *Journal of Baltic Studies* 6 (1975): 247–58.

Schmidt-Rimpler, Walter. *Geschichte Des Kommissionsgeschäfts in Deutschland, Vol. 1: Die Zeit bis zum Ende des 15. Jahrhunderts*. Halle: Waisenhauses, 1915.

Schmidt-Wiegand, Ruth. "Hanse und Gilde. Genossenschaftliche Organisationsformen im Bereich der Hanse und ihre Bezeichnungen." *Hansische Geschichtsblätter* 100 (1982): 21–40.

Schmidt, Burghart. *Hamburg im Zeitalter der Französischen Revolution und Napoleons (1789–1813)*. Hamburg: Verlag Verein für Hamburgische Geschichte, 1998.

Schmidt, Georg. "Städtehanse und Reich im 16. und 17. Jahrhundert." in Antjekathrin Graßmann, ed. *Niedergang oder Übergang? Zur Spätzeit der Hanse im 16. und 17. Jahrhundert*, Cologne: Böhlau, 1998. 25–46.

Schneidmüller, Bernd. *Die Welfen und ihr Braunschweiger Hof im hohen Mittelalter*. Wiesbaden: Harrossowitz, 1995.

Schnurmann, Claudia. *Kommerz und Klüngel: Der Englandhandel der Kölner Kaufleute im 16" Jahrhundert*. Göttingen: Vandenhoeck & Ruprecht, 1991.

Schonewille, Mark. "Risk, Institutions and Trade: New Approaches to Hanse History." Working Paper, Nijmwegen, 1998.

———. *Hanse Theutonicorum*. Groningen: Rijksuniversiteit Groningen, 1997.

Schubert, Ernst. "Novgorod, Brügge, Bergen, London: Die *Kontore* der Hanse." *Concilium Medii Aevi* 5 (2002): 1–50.

Schulte Beerbühl, Margrit, and Jörg Vögele. *Spinning the Commercial Web: International Trade, Merchants, and Commercial Cities, c. 1640–1939*. New York: Peter Lang, 2005.

Schulte Beerbühl, Margrit. *Deutsche Kaufleute in London: Welthandel und Einbürgerung (1660–1818)*. Munich: Oldenbourg, 2007.

Sedov, Valentin. "Skandinavische Elemente im frühmittelalterlichen Pskow." in Aleksander Loit, Evalds Muguerevičs, and Andris Caune, eds. *Die Kontakte zwischen Ostbaltikum und Skandinavien im frühen Mittelalter*. Studia Baltica Stockholmensia 9. Stockholm: Centre for Baltic Studies. 1992.

Seifert, Dieter. *Kompagnons und Konkurrente: Holland und die Hanse im späten Mittelalter*. Quellen und Darstellungen zur hansischen Geschichte. Cologne: Böhlau, 1997.

Selart, Anti. *Livland und die Rus im 13. Jahrhundert*. Quellen und Studien zur Baltischen Geschichte. Cologne: Böhlau, 2007.

Selzer, Stephan. *Die mittelalterliche Hanse*. Geschichte Kompact. Darmstadt: WGB, 2010.

———. "Trinkstuben als Orte der Kommunikation: Das Beispiel der Artushöfe im Preußenland (ca. 1350–1550)." in Gerhard Fouquet, et al., eds. *Geschlechtergesellschaften: Zunft-Trinkstuben und Bruderschaften in spätmittelalterlichen und frühneuzeitlichen Städten*. Stuttgart: Jan Thorbecke Verlag, 2003. 73–98.

———. *Artushöfe im Ostseeraum: Ritterlich-Höfische Kultur in den Städten des Preussenlandes im 14. und 15. Jahrhundert*. Frankfurt am Main: Peter Lang, 1996.

Selzer, Stephan, and Ulf Christian Ewert. "Die Neue Institutionenökonomik als Herausforderung an die Hanseforschung." *Hansische Geschichtsblätter* 123 (2005): 7–29, 28.

———, eds. *Menschenbilder—Menschenbildner: Individuum und Gruppe im Blick des Historikers*. Hallische Beiträge zur Geschichte des Mittelalters und der Frühen Neuzeit, Vol. 2. Berlin: Akademie Verlag, 2002.

———. "Verhandeln und Verkaufen, Vernetzen und Vertrauen: Über die Netzwerkstruktur des hansischen Handels." *Hansische Geschichtsblätter* 119 (2001): 135–61.

Sicking, Louis. "Die Offensive Lösung. Militärische Aspekte des holländischen Ostseehandels im 15. und 16. Jahrhundert." *Hansische Geschichtsblätter* 117 (1999): 39–51.

Sicking, Louis J., and Darlene Abreu-Ferreira. Beyond the Catch: *Fisheries of the North Atlantic, the North Sea, and the Baltic, 900–1850*. Leiden: Brill, 2008.

Simson, Paul. *Danziger Inventar, 1531–1591. Mit einem Akten-Anhang*. Inventare Hansischer Archive des Sechzehnten Jahrhunderts, Vol. 3. Munich: Duncker & Humblot, 1913.

Skyum-Nielsen, Niels. "König Waldemar von Atterdag von Dänemark: Persönlichkeit und Politik." *Hansische Geschichtsblätter 102* (1984): 5–20.

Slaski, Witold von. "Danziger Handel im XV. Jahrhundert auf Grund eines im Danziger Stadtarchiv Befindlichen Handlungsbuches Geschildert." (Doctoral Dissertation, Ruprecht-Karls-Universität Heidelberg, 1905).

Söderberg, Tom. "Stora Kopparberget under Medeltiden och Gustav Vasa." Thesis, Stockholm, 1932.

Sosson, Jean-Pierre. "Das Osterlingenhuis in Brügge." Albert d'Haenens, ed. *Die Welt der Hanse*. Brussels: Mercatorfonds, 1984.

Sprandel, Rolf. "Die strukturellen Merkmale der hansischen Handelsstellung in Brügge." in Klaus Friedland, ed. *Brügge-Colloquium des hansischen Geschichtsvereins 1988. Referate und Diskussionen*. Quellen und Darstellungen zur hansischen Geschichte. Cologne: Böhlau, 1990. 69–81.

———. "Die Konkurrenzfähigkeit der Hanse im Spätmittelalter." *Hansische Geschichtsblätter* 102 (1984): 21–38.

———, ed. *Quellen zur Hanse-Geschichte*. Darmstadt: Wissenschaftliche Buchgesellschaft, 1982.

———. *Das Eisengewerbe im Mittelalter*. Stuttgart: A. Hiersemann, 1968.

Spufford, Peter, Wendy Wilkinson, and Sarah Tolley. *Handbook of Medieval Exchange*. London: Boydell and Brewer, 1986.

Spufford, Peter. *Power and Profit: The Merchant in Medieval Europe*. New York: Thames & Hudson, 2003.

Stark, Walter. "Techniken und Organisationsformen des hansischen Handels im Spätmittelalter," in Stuart Jenks, et al., eds. *Der hansische Sonderweg? Beiträge zur Sozial- und Wirtschaftsgeschichte der Hanse*. Cologne: Böhlau, 1993. 191–201.

———. *Untersuchungen zum Profit beim hansischen Handelskapital in der ersten Hälfte des 15. Jahrhunderts*. Abhandlungen zur Handels- und Sozialgeschichte. Weimar: Verlag H. Böhlaus Nachfolger, 1985.

———. *Lübeck und Danzig in der zweiten Hälfte des 15. Jahrhunderts*. Abhandlungen zur Handels- und Sozialgeschichte, Vol. XI. Weimar: H. Böhlaus Nachfolger, 1973.

———. "Der Utrechter Frieden von 1474 zwischen der Hanse und England." *Zeitschrift für Geschichtswissenschaft*. 19 (1971): 891–903.

Stefke, Gerald. "Der Lübecker Bürgermeister Johann Wittenborg, hingerichtet 1363—Zu Geschäftsmoral und Amtsethos eines hansischen Kaufmanns und Ratsherrn." *Hansische Geschichtsblätter* 126 (2008): 1–144.

Stein, Rostock Wilhelm. "Handelsbriefe aus Riga und Königsberg von 1458 und 1461." *Hansische Geschichtsblätter* 9 (1898): 59–128.

Stieda, Wilhelm, ed. *Hildebrand Veckinghusen: Briefwechsel eines deutschen Kaufmanns im 15. Jahrhundert*. Leipzig: Verlag von S. Hirzel, 1921.

———. "Kabelgarn und Steine, Zwei Revaler Ausfuhrartikel." *Beiträge zur Kunde Est-, Liv- und Kurlands* 7 (1910): 153–208.

———. *Revaler Zollbücher und -Quittungen des 14. Jahrhunderts*. Hansische Geschichtsquellen. Halle: Verlag der Buchhandlung des Waisenhauses, 1887.

Stoob, Heinz. *Die Hanse*. Graz: Styria, 1995.

———. "Lübeck Als 'caput Omnium' in der Hanse." *Blätter für deutsche Landesgeschichte* 121 (1985): 157–68.

———. *Slawenchronik: Helmoldi Presbyteri Bozoviensis Chronica slavorum*. Berlin: Rütten & Loening, 1963.

Stoob, Heinz, Friedrich Bernward Fahlbusch, Helmut Jäger, Franz Petri, and Heinz Quirin, eds. *Civitatum Communitas: Studien zum europäischen Städtewesen: Festschrift Heinz Stoob zum 65. Geburtstag* Städteforschung. Cologne: Böhlau, 1984.

Streb, Jochen. "Die Politische Glaubwürdigkeit von Regierungen im Institutionellen Wandel. warum ausländische Fürsten das Eigentum der Fernhandelskaufleute der Hanse Schützten." *Jahrbuch für Wirtschafts-geschichte*. 1 (2004): 141–56.

Stromer, Wolfgang von. "Der innovatorische Rückstand der hansischen Wirtschaft." in Knut Schulz, ed. *Beiträge zur Wirtschafts- und Sozialgeschichte des Mittelalters: Festschrift für Herbert Helbig zum 65. Geburtstag*. Cologne: Böhlau, 1976): 204–217.

———. "Die ausländischen Kammergrafen der Stephanskrone—Unter den Königen aus den Häusern Anjou, Luxemburg und Habsburg—Exponenten Des Großkapitals." *Hamburger Beiträge zur Numismatik* 27/29 (1973): 85–106.

———. *Oberdeutsche Hochfinanz, 1350–1450* Vierteljahrschrift Fèur Sozial- Und Wirtschaftsgeschichte. Beihefte; 55, 56, 57. Wiesbaden: F. Steiner Verlag, 1970.

Stützel, Peter. "Die Privilegien des deutschen Kaufmanns in Brügge im 13. und 14. Jahrhundert." *Hansische Geschichtsblätter* 116 (1998): 23–63.

Tandecki, Janusz. "Weinbau im mittelalterlichen Preußen." *Beiträge zur Geschichte Westpreußens* 12 (1991): 83–99.

Techen, Friedrich. "Das Brauwerk in Wismar." *Hansische Geschichsblätter*. 41 (1915): 263–352.

Tepp, Peter. "Untersuchungen zur Sozial- und Wirtschaftsgeschichte der Hanse- und Salzstadt Kolberg im spätmittelalter: Strukturwandel und Soziale Mobilität." (Doctoral Dissertation, Universität Hamburg 1980).

Tesdorpf, W. *Gewinnung, Verarbeitung und Handel des Bernsteins in Preussen von der Ordenszeit bis zur Gegenwart. Eine Historisch-Volkswirtschaftliche Studie*. Jena: G. Fischer, 1887.

Thierfelder, Hildegard. *Rostock-Osloer Handelsbeziehungen im 16. Jahrhundert: die Geschäftspapiere der Kaufleute Kron in Rostock und Bene in Oslo*. Weimar: H. Böhlaus Nachfolger, 1958.

Thompson, Grahame. *Between Hierarchies and Markets: The Logic and Limits of Network Forms of Organization*. Oxford: Oxford University Press, 2003.

Tielhof, M. van. *The 'Mother of All Trades': The Baltic Grain Trade in Amsterdam from the Late Sixteenth to the Early Nineteenth Century*. Leiden and Boston: Brill, 2002.

Timmler, Elisabeth. "Die Sprache der Kaufleute im Novgorod des 12. bis 15. Jahrhunderts." (Doctoral Dissertation, Freie Universität Berlin, 1991).

Tits-Dieuaide, Marie-Jeanne. *La formation des prix céréaliers en Brabant et en Flandre au XVe siècle*. Brussels: Éditions de l'Université de Bruxelles, 1975.

Todd, Joan Markley. "Baltic Amber in the Ancient Near East: A Preliminary Investigation." *Journal of Baltic Studies* 16 (1981/1985): 292–301.

Trezzini, Bruno. "Konzepte Und Methoden der Sozialwissenschaftlichen Netzwerkanalyse: Eine Aktuelle Übersicht." *Zeitschrift für Soziologie* 27 (1998): 378–94.

Trzoska, Jerzy. *Strefa Baltycka w XVI–XVIII Wieku, Polityka—Spoleczeństwo—Gospodarka, Ogólnopolska Sesja Naukowa Zorganizowana z Okazji 70-Lecia Urodzin Professora Edmunda Cieslaka*. Gdańsk: Komisja Historyczna, 1993.

Unger, Manfred. "Die leipziger Messe und die Niederlande im 16. und 18. Jahrhundert." *Hansische Geschichsblätter*. 81 (1963): 20–38.

Unger, Richard W. "Feeding the Low Countries Towns: The Grain Trade in the Fifteenth Century." *Revue belge de philologie et d'histoire* 77/2 (1999): 329–358.

Urban, William L. *The Baltic Crusade.* Chicago: Lithuanian Research and Studies Center, 1994.

Urry, John. "Social Networks: Travel and Talk." *Journal of Sociology* 54 (2003): 155–175.

Van der Wee, Herman. *The Growth of the Antwerp Market and the European Economy, Fourteenth–Sixteenth Centuries* (The Hague: Martinus Nijhoff 1963).

Voeltzer, Friedrich. *Lübecks Wirtschaftslage unter dem Druck der Kontinentalsperre.* Lübeck: M. Schmidt-Römhild, 1925.

Vogel, Walther. "Zur Größe der europäischen Handelsflotten im 15., 16. und 17. Jahrhundert: Ein historisch-statistischer Versuch,." A. Hofmeister, ed. *Forschungen und Versuche zur Geschichte des Mittelalters und der Neuzeit: Festschrift Dietrich Schäfer zum siebzigsten Geburtstag dargebracht von seinen Schülern*, Jena: Gustav Fischer, 1915. 268–333.

———. *Geschichte der deutschen Seeschiffahrt.* Berlin: Reimer, 1915.

———. *Die Hansestädte und die Kontinentalsperre.* Munich a.o.: Duncker & Humblot, 1913.

Volckart, Oliver. "Kartelle und Monopole im Ordensland Preußen zu beginn des 16. Jahrhunderts: Bernsteinregal und Münze in der Sicht des Rent-seeking-ansatzes." *Vierteljahrsschrift für Sozial- und Wirtschaftsgeschichte* 84/1 (1997): 1–32.

Vollrath, Hanna, Stefan Weinfurter, and Odilo Engels, eds. *Köl: Stadt und Bistum in Kirche und Reich des Mittelalters: Festschrift für Odilo Engels zum 65. Geburtstag.* Cologne: Böhlau, 1993.

Wachowski, Krzysztof and Jacek Wittkowski. "Wroclaw Wobec Hanzy." *Archaeologia Polski* XLVIII, 1–2 (2003): 201–21.

Warncke, J. "Bernsteinkunst und Paternostermaker in Lübeck." *Nordelbingen* 10 (1934): 428–64.

Wasserman, Stanley and Katherine Faust. *Social Network Analysis: Methods and Applications* Structural Analysis in the Social Sciences, Vol 8. Cambridge: Cambridge University Press, 1994.

Wasserman, Stanley and Joseph Galaskiewicz. *Advances in Social Network Analysis: Research in the Social and Behavioral Sciences.* Thousand Oaks [CA]: Sage Publications, 1994.

Watts, Duncan. "Networks, Dynamics, and the Small-World Phenomenon." *American Journal of Sociology* 105 (1999): 493–52.

Wee, Herman Van der. *The Growth of the Antwerp Market and the European Economy, Fourteenth-Sixteenth Centuries.* The Hague: Martinus Nijhoff 1963.

Weinbaum, M. "Stalhof und deutsche Gildhalle zu London." *Hansische Geschichtsblätter* (1928): 45–65.

Weinrich, Lorenz, ed. *Vitae Sanctorum Episcoporum Adalberti Pragensis et Ottonis Babenbergensis Historiam Germanicam et Slavicam Illustrantes*. Ausgewählte Quellen zur deutschen Geschichte des Mittelalters, Vol. 25. Darmstadt: Wissenschaftliche Buchgesellschaft, 2005.

Wellman, Barry and Stephen D. Berkowitz. *Social Structures: A Network Approach*. Cambridge: Cambridge University Press, 1988.

Wernicke, Herbert and Nils Jörn. *Beiträge zur hansischen Kultur-, Verfassungs- und Schiffahrtsgeschichte*. Abhandlungen zur Handels- und Sozialgeschichte. Weimar: H. Böhlaus Nachfolger, 1998.

Werveke, Hans van. "Das Wesen der Flandrischen Hanse." *Hansische Geschichtsblätter* 75/76 (1957/1958): 7–20.

Westermann, Ekkehard, Christoph Bartels and Markus A. Denzel, eds. *Konjunkturen im europäischen Bergbau in Vorindustrieller Zeit: Festschrift für Ekkehard Westermann zum 60. Geburtstag*. Stuttgart: Franz Steiner, 2000.

Westermann, Ekkehard. *Bergbaureviere als Verbrauchszentren im vorindustriellen Europa: Fallstudien zu Beschaffung und Verbrauch von Lebensmitteln Sowie Roh- und Hilfsstoffen (13.–18. Jahrhundert)*. Stuttgart: Franz Steiner Verlag, 1997.

Westrate, Job. "Abgrenzung durch Aufnahme. zur Eingliederung der süderseeischen Städte in die Hanse, ca. 1360–1450." *Hansische Geschichtsblätter* 121 (2003): 13–40, at 17.

Wheeler, John. *A Treatise of Commerce Wherein Are Shewed the Commodities Arising by a Well Ordered and Ruled Trade, Such as That of the Societie of Merchants Aduenturers Is Proued to Be: Written Principally for the Better Information of Those Who Doubt of the Necessarinesse of the Said Societie in the State of the Realme of England*. London: Iohn Harison, 1601.

Widera, Bruno. "Tucherzeugung und Tucheinfuhr Polens und der Rus vom 10.–13. Jahrhundert im Lichte Technologischer Untersuchungen. Materialien aus Danzig und Novgorod." *Zeitschrift für Geschichtswissenschaft* 9 (1961): 944–48.

Wiechmann, Ralf. *Edelmetalldepots der Wikingerzeit in Schleswig-Holstein: vom "Ringbrecher" zur Münzwirtschaft*. Neumünster: Wachholtz, 1996.

Wiegandt, Jürgen. *Die Plescows: Ein Beitrag zur Auswanderung Wisbyer Kaufmannsfamilien nach Lübeck im 13. und 14. Jahrhundert*. Cologne: Böhlau, 1988.

Wild, John Peter and Frances Pritchard. *Northern Archaeological Textiles: Nesat Vii; Textile Symposium in Edinburgh, 5th–7th May 1999*. Oakville [CT]: Oxbow Books, 2005.

Williamson, Oliver E. "Transaction-Costs Economics: The Governance of Contractual Relations." *Journal of Law and Economics* 22 (1979): 233–61.

———. *Markets and Hierarchies: Analysis and Antitrust Implications*. New York: Free Press, 1975.

Winterfeld, Luise von. *Hildebrand Veckinchusen: Ein hansischer Kaufmann vor 500 Jahren*. Bremen: Friesen Verlag, 1929.

Witthöft, Harald. "Struktur und Kapazität der Lüneburger Saline seit dem 12. Jahrhundert." *Vierteljahrschrift für Sozial- und Wirtschaftsgeschichte* 63 (1976): 1–117.

Wolf, Thomas. *Tragfähigkeiten, Ladungen und Maße im Schiffsverkehr der Hanse vornehmlich im Spiegel Revaler Quellen*. Quellen und Darstellungen zur hansischen Geschichte. Cologne: Böhlau, 1986.

Wubs-Mrozevicz, Justyna and Stuart Jenks, eds. *The Hanse in Medieval and Early Modern Europé*. Leiden: Brill, 2013.

Wubs-Mrozevicz, Justyna. "Rules of Inclusion, Rules of Exculsion: The Hanseatic *Kontor* in Bergan in the Late Middle Ages and its Normative Boundaries." *German History* 29 (2011): 2–4.

———. *Traders, Ties and Tensions: The Interaction of Lübeckers, Overijsslers and Hollanders in Late Medieval Bergen*. Hilversum: Verloren, 2008.

———. "Hinrick van Hasselt, Rebell und Bergenfahrer aus Deventer." *Hansische Geschichtsblätter* 124 (2006), 1–20.

———. " 'Ale goede coepluyden . . .'. Strategies in the Scandinavian trade politics of Amsterdam and Lübeck c. 1440–1560." in Hanno Brand and Leos Müller, eds. *The Dynamics of Economic Culture in the North Sea- and Baltic Region in the Late Middle Ages and Early Modern Period*. Hilversum: Verloren, 2007. 86–101.

Zahnd, Martin. "Spätmittelalterliche Bürgertestamente als Quellen zu Realienkunde und Sozialgeschichte." *Mitteilungen des Instituts für österreichische Geschichtsforschung* 96 (1988): 55–778.

Zenhäusern, Gregor. *Zeitliches Wohl und ewiges Hei: Studie zu mittelalterlichen Testamenten aus der Diözese Sitten*. Sitten: Staatsarchiv, 1992.

Ziegler, B. "Kaufmännischer Unterricht und Muster*kontor* in Brügge." in: *Zeitschrift für das gesamt kaufmännische Unterrichtswesen* 6 (1903): 169–172 and 196–200.

Zöller, Sonja. *Kaiser, Kaufmann und die Macht des Geldes: Gerhard Unmaze von Köln als Finanzier der Reichspolitik und der "Gute Gerhard" des Rudolf von Ems*. Munich: Fink, 1993.

Index

www.ingramcontent.com/pod-product-compliance
Lightning Source LLC
LaVergne TN
LVHW010555300926
849162LV00002B/338